Settlement, Struggle and Success

The Charles and Joy Staples South West Region Publications Fund was established in 1984 on the basis of a generous donation to The University of Western Australia by Charles and Joy Staples.

The purpose of the Fund is to highlight all aspects of the South West region of Western Australia, a geographical area much loved by Charles and Joy Staples, so as to assist the people of the South West region and those in government and private organisations concerned with South West projects to appreciate the needs and possibilities of the region in the widest possible historical perspective. The fund is administered by a committee whose aims are to make possible the publication by UWA Publishing of research and writing in any discipline relevant to the South West region.

Charles and Joy Staples South West Region Publications Fund titles

1987
A Tribute to the Group Settlers
Philip E. M. Blond

1992
For Their Own Good: Aborigines and Government in the Southwest of Western Australia, 1900–1940
Anna Haebich

1993
Portraits of the South West
B. K. de Garis

A Guide to Sources for the History of South Western Australia
Compiled by Ronald Richards

1994
Jardee: The Mill That Cheated Time
Doreen Owens

1995
Dearest Isabella: Life and Letters of Isabella Ferguson, 1819–1910
Prue Joske

Blacklegs: The Scottish Colliery Strike of 1911 Bill Latter

1997
Barefoot in the Creek: A Group Settlement Childhood in Margaret River L. C. Burton

Ritualist on a Tricycle: Frederick Goldsmith, Church, Nationalism and Society in Western Australia
Colin Holden

Western Australia as it is Today, 1906 Leopoldo Zunini, Royal Consul of Italy, edited and translated by Richard Bosworth and Margot Melia

2002
The South West from Dawn till Dusk Rob Olver

2003
Contested Country: A History of the Northcliffe Area, Western Australia
Patricia Crawford and Ian Crawford

2004
Orchard and Mill: The Story of Bill Lee, South-West Pioneer
Lyn Adams

2005
Richard Spencer: Napoleonic War Naval Hero and Australian Pioneer
Gwen Chessell

2006
A Story to Tell (reprinted 2012)
Laurel Nannup

2008
Alexander Collie: Colonial Surgeon, Naturalist and Explorer
Gwen Chessell

The Zealous Conservator: A Life of Charles Lane Poole John Dargavel

2009
"It's Still in My Heart, This is My Country": The Single Noongar Claim History South West Aboriginal Land and Sea Council, John Host with Chris Owen

Shaking Hands on the Fringe: Negotiating the Aboriginal World at King George's Sound
Tiffany Shellam

2011
Noongar Mambara Bakitj and *Mamang*
Kim Scott and Wirlomin Noongar Language and Stories Project

Guy Grey-Smith: Life Force
Andrew Gaynor

2013
Dwoort Baal Kaat and *Yira Boornak Nyininy*
Kim Scott and Wirlomin Noongar Language and Stories Project

2014
A Boy's Short Life: The Story of Warren Braedon/Louis Johnson
Anna Haebich and Steve Mickler

Plant Life on the Sandplains: A Global Biodiversity Hotspot
Hans Lambers

Fire and Hearth (revised facsimile edition) Sylvia Hallam

2015
Running Out? Water in Western Australia Ruth Morgan

A Journey Travelled: Aboriginal–European Relations at Albany and Surrounding Regions from First Colonial Contact to 1926
Murray Arnold

The Southwest: Australia's Biodiversity Hotspot
Victoria Laurie

Invisible Country: South-West Australia: Understanding a Landscape Bill Bunbury

2016
Noongar Bush Medicine: Medicinal Plants of the South-West of Western Australia
Vivienne Hansen and John Horsfall

2017
Never Again: Reflections on Environmental Responsibility After Roe 8
Edited by Andrea Gaynor, Peter Newman and Philip Jennings

Ngaawily Nop and *Noorn*
Kim Scott and Wirlomin Noongar Language and Stories Project

2018
Dancing in Shadows: Histories of Nyungar Performance Anna Haebich

2019
Meeting the Waylo: Aboriginal Encounters in the Archipelago
Tiffany Shellam

Refuge Richard Rossiter

That Was My Home: Voices from the Noongar Camps in Fremantle and the Western Suburbs
Denise Cook

2020
Many Maps: Charting Two Cultures First Nations and Europeans in Western Australia
Bill and Jenny Bunbury

2021
Naturalist on the Bibbulmun: A walking companion
Leigh Simmons

2022
The Alert Grey Twinkling Eyes of C.J. DeGaris: The story of the pioneer who revolutionised publicity, aviation, publishing, and created Kendenup David Nichols

2023
No Longer a Wandering Spirit: Family and kin reclaiming the memory of Minang woman Bessy Flowers Sharon Huebner and Ezzard Flowers

The French Collector: Journal and Letters of Théodore Leschenault, Botanist of the Baudin Expedition
Paul Gibbard

Settlement, Struggle and Success

Margaret River and its Old Hospital, 1924–2024

Jenny and Bill Bunbury

First published in 2024 by
UWA Publishing
Crawley, Western Australia 6009
www.uwap.uwa.edu.au

UWAP is an imprint of UWA Publishing
a division of The University of Western Australia

This book is copyright. Apart from any fair dealing for the purpose of private study, research, criticism or review, as permitted under the *Copyright Act 1968*, no part may be reproduced by any process without written permission. Enquiries should be made to the publisher.

Copyright © Jenny and Bill Bunbury 2024

The moral right of the authors have been asserted.

ISBN: 978-1-76080-276-9

 A catalogue record for this book is available from the National Library of Australia

Cover image by Stephen Blakeney
Typeset in Bembo Book by Lasertype
Printed by Lightning Source

CONTENTS

Introduction	vii
Acknowledgements	xi
Map of Margaret River and District	xv
Map of Margaret River Townsite circa 1950s	xvi
Chapter One: Wooditjup Bilya–Margaret River	1
Chapter Two: Endeavor Expedite!	39
Chapter Three: A Primitive Wooden Structure	65
Chapter Four: Very Little Money	99
Chapter Five: A Proper Standard	149
Chapter Six: A Small, Rather Slow, Hospital and a Rosy Future	205
Chapter Seven: A Perennial Source of Discontent	267
Chapter Eight: An Extension of Life	299
Notes	335
Bibliography	375
Photographic Credits	385
Index	389

INTRODUCTION

From Jenny

Some years ago, Bill and I attended an exhibition of photographs by local photographer Stephen Blakeney. The venue for this show was the Rosa Brook Hall, originally the local schoolroom for the children of group settlers in the 1920s and beyond. As a school, this building would also have been the centre of the district's social activities, including dances, which helped to maintain and raise the spirits of people living through those difficult times. Rosa Brook is a surviving settlement from that era. It remains a small isolated population centre surrounded by forest, and it is a place where it is easy to imagine the challenges of the past.

Stephen's wife, Ros, already a good friend, cornered me in the hall and explained that the old Margaret River hospital – which, like the Rosa Brook school, had been built at the advent of the Group Settlement Scheme – would be celebrating one hundred years of service to the district community in just a few years time: May 2024 to be precise.

Moreover, the Margaret River Community Centre, which had taken over, conserved and preserved these old wooden buildings when the new hospital opened in 1990, would, in 2020, mark thirty years of stewardship. Ros thought it important that both these events be appropriately commemorated. Would I be interested in writing this history?

Well, yes, it did sound like a worthwhile endeavour. Having lived for some years in this district, I was aware of many aspects of Margaret River's group settlement past, but I also knew that many people and even some long-term local residents had very little knowledge of that past. Few knew that the old hospital was the first publicly funded building in the town, built initially at a cost of £1,100 (£100 over budget!) Then there was the very special story of the Margaret Cecil Rest House, built in 1929 for expectant mothers with donations from the 'Margarets of Britain' and the support of members of the English aristocracy: the Cecil family.

From Bill

In 1979 I was making a film in Albany for the then Education section of the ABC on the economy of that region. During that process, I discovered that Denmark (WA) had been, in the 1920s, the centre of an ill-fated government-backed farming venture known as the Group Settlement Scheme. At that time, this seemed to be a little-known story as far as the rest of Australia was concerned. So in 1982 I went back with my audio recorder and made the first of many history documentaries for ABC Radio National, called *They Said You'd Own Your Own Farm*. At that time, I was able to record the memories of some of the original groupies as well as the stories of their children.

Margaret River was also one of the four main areas in WA selected for group settlement and it was this scheme that led to the influx of new settlers to the district and to the building of the government-funded hospital in the town.

Then, in 1996, when we had already bought a home in Margaret River, I made another documentary, *Margaret River: A Changing Landscape*, which looked at both the group settler experience in the 1920s and the advent of a surfing culture, vibrant wine and tourism industries and other recent social and economic changes delivered by a growing and increasingly diverse population.

This book covers some of those developments and expands on themes that I was able to deal with only briefly in that one radio program.

I have always seen the commitment of people in this community helping each other during those years of social isolation, economic hardship and self-help as a legacy handed down to later generations living and working in this now much-appreciated corner of south-west Australia. Interviewing local people for this book has confirmed the traits I sensed and identified over twenty-five years ago. Margaret River is a place in which something of that group settlement determination lives on.

INTRODUCTION

From Jenny and Bill

Initially, for the community centre's thirtieth birthday celebrations in 2020, we made an audio documentary titled *A Place of the Heart*, which chronicles the story of how the old hospital buildings were saved as well as covering the development of the Margaret River Community Centre since the old hospital closed in 1990. We recorded interviews with twenty people who had been involved in some way in saving, or working in, the community centre.

We then considered this much larger task: how to tell the story of the now heritage-listed old hospital. We saw this as an opportunity to write this account within the context of the town and district's development and growth. So, while the old hospital's history takes centre stage, the aim has been to describe some of Margaret River's history and development and thereby to give readers a richer knowledge and understanding of life in this region during much of the twentieth century.

We also thought that it would be essential to provide some background on pre-European history and early European settlement in this region. Chapter One concentrates on how the traditional custodians, the Wadandi, cared for this Country and lived with the land many thousands of years prior to European settlement, and how they kept healthy without what Europeans would regard as essential medical facilities. The first chapter also summarises the interaction between the First Australians and the early European settlers in this region.

Chapter Two briefly explains the Group Settlement Scheme, which brought a large population increase to the Margaret River district and was the impetus for the appointment of a doctor (1923) and the establishment of a small hospital in the town (1924). Chapter Three draws from interviews, contemporary newspaper articles and reports from visiting government officials to paint a picture of conditions in the early years of the hospital. It also documents some of the difficulties and hardships that the newcomers to the district faced.

Chapter Four takes the story to the 1930s and explores the effects of the Great Depression on the hospital and the wider local community, while Chapter Five covers the 1940s and the 1950s, which also saw some more prosperous times for local farmers and businesses following the end of World War II.

Yet, as Chapter Six reveals, Margaret River remained a rural backwater and its hospital was threatened with closure in the 1960s

INTRODUCTION

because no doctor was willing to set up practice in the town. It was not until the 1970s that the district became a mecca for surfers and a popular tourist destination with a worldwide reputation for its fine wines. Dairy farming also became more profitable, while forestry and timber milling declined in importance. Throughout this period, the old hospital remained an essential community service and an important source of employment for nurses and other staff. But by the 1970s its buildings were no longer fit for purpose, leading to a long community campaign for a new hospital, which is covered in Chapter Seven.

The book concludes with a chapter that draws on the interviews recorded for *A Place of the Heart* and summarises the old hospital's role in continuing to serve the district as the Margaret River Community Centre, by providing a range of health and social services including the Margaret River Community Centre for Children, which now occupies the former Margaret Cecil Rest House, originally built to provide accommodation and comfort for expectant and nursing mothers.

ACKNOWLEDGEMENTS

There is a popular saying that it takes a village to raise a child. There is no doubt that it also takes a community of interested and committed individuals to ensure that a book gets completed and published!

The management committee and staff of the Margaret River Community Centre, which now occupies and cares for the old Margaret River hospital, were the instigators of this project and have paid for the transcriptions of some new interviews Bill undertook for this project and for the purchase of some of the photographs. Our friend Janice Bowra, as always, produced excellent and accurate transcripts.

We would like to thank the Community Centre Committee, Chair Jessica Worrall and all members of that committee, as well as Centre Manager Lydell Huntly, Childcare Centre Director Amber Fairbrass and administration staff Alison McKenzie, Leanne Sutton, Pam Murphy and Tam Callaghan, who are all equally passionate about maintaining the history of these heritage buildings in which they work. Former staff member Lyn Moorfoot was an early inspiration. Her work over many years in researching the history of these buildings provided valuable insights into this story. Danielle Haigh, who previously worked for the community centre and also interviewed long-term Margaret River residents for the *Augusta-Margaret River Mail*, provided early advice and encouragement.

We would also especially like to acknowledge former Chair Sally Hays and long-term committee member Anne Shepherdson. Both have been part of a small informal group who have willingly provided guidance and advice when necessary. Without Anne's assistance, we would not have obtained some pivotal interviews, including with

ACKNOWLEDGEMENTS

long-time Margaret River medical practitioner Dr Eithne Sheridan, who came to Margaret River from Ireland with her husband, Dr John Lagan, in 1968 when no local doctors wanted to practise medicine in a backwater like Margaret River!

We are particularly delighted that Ros Blakeney, who, after more than thirty years, is still a member of the Margaret River Community Centre Committee, agreed to research and select pictures for this book. Ros, as always, enlisted her professional photographer husband to take additional photographs. This is particularly fitting since Steve has acted as 'official photographer' for the community centre over the years.

In addition to Sally, Anne and Ros, our informal 'reference group' included John Alferink, who read every word and saved us, as relative newcomers to the area, from (we hope) too many inaccuracies. Thelma Burnett researched and provided additional material on the local St John's Ambulance Sub-Centre. Fran Temby, who not only spent her childhood south of Margaret River, but was also Director of Nursing in both the old and new hospitals, gave us valuable advice. All these people read an earlier draft of the book, as did local bookseller Keith McLeod, whose knowledge of the Margaret River district spans not only his lifetime but also those of his parents and grandparents. We are particularly grateful to Keith and Pauline McLeod for their interest in, and enthusiasm for, this project. Their commitment to ensuring that this book is well-publicised in the district is much appreciated. The maps of the Margaret River district and the town of Margaret River (circa 1950) were drawn and patiently revised by local artist and designer, Emily Jackson. In finalising the maps, we were able to rely again on John Alferink's detailed knowledge of both the town of Margaret River, as it was in earlier times, and the geography and history of the Cape to Cape region.

It will become apparent to readers that in many ways the 'star' of chapters six and seven is Judy Wake, who not only nursed at both the old and new Margaret River hospitals for over forty years, but also led the fight for a new Margaret River hospital for almost a quarter of a century. Judy has also documented the final years of the old hospital and the construction of the new building. She read early drafts of the book, twice. Her contribution to this project has been immense.

The Margaret River and Districts Historical Society, especially President Viv Halsall and volunteer archivist Jenny Redman, have also been strong supporters of this project. They have spent many hours sourcing photographs and other documents for us. Chapter Seven: 'A Perennial Source of Discontent' could not have been written without letters and other documents from the 1970s and 1980s which the society has retained and which were not available through the State Records Office.

The material held by the Western Australian State Records Office (SROWA) underpins much of this story, demonstrating as it does the financial and other difficulties involved in servicing this small but, for Margaret River residents and visitors, important hospital. We are grateful to Gerard Foley and his willing and helpful staff, who must have wondered how many more times we would request the same files! Books such as this could not be written without the resources available through the SROWA and the State Library and their ever-supportive staff. Thanks are also due to our local Margaret River Library, which continues to provide an invaluable service for people living in regional Western Australia and maintains a series of local history folders containing material collected by local historian, the late Mae Wise. The hospital admissions and surgery records back to 1924 are still located at the 'new' Margaret River Hospital. Thanks are due to Kerrie Lenton who made these registers and the Margaret Cecil archive available to us on several occasions.

We have included in the bibliography a list of people interviewed by Bill specifically, for this book or previously for other projects. Many thanks to all the people who have shared their stories and memories with us and in some instances have also provided photographs. We have also been very fortunate to have had access to interviews that the Margaret River and Districts Historical Society conducted in earlier years, with individuals now deceased. Access to these recordings has enabled us to capture memories of people working in the Margaret River Hospital in the first half of the twentieth century. We have also included extracts from several interviews conducted by the Busselton and Districts Oral History Group and thanks are due to Colleen Liston for providing us with copies.

Other Margaret River friends have helped in small but significant ways. Stuart Hicks intervened to secure a further interview with Wadandi Cultural Custodian Zac Webb, while Delys Clancy provided a copy of the very first edition of the *Augusta-Margaret River Mail*. Emma-Clare Bussell helped to fill in some gaps about the life and work of her ancestor, Alfred John (Jack) Bussell, who did more than most early settlers to record the languages and stories of his Aboriginal childhood carers and playmates.

We are, once again, very grateful to UWA Publishing and to publishing manager Kate Pickard, who agreed to support and publish this book well before much of it was written. Our UWAP editor, Kelly Somers, was meticulous in picking up mistakes of all kinds and providing helpful guidance when it was clear that there were options for cutting unnecessary text. We also gratefully acknowledge financial assistance from the Charles and Joy Staples South West Region Publications Fund.

MARGARET RIVER AND DISTRICT

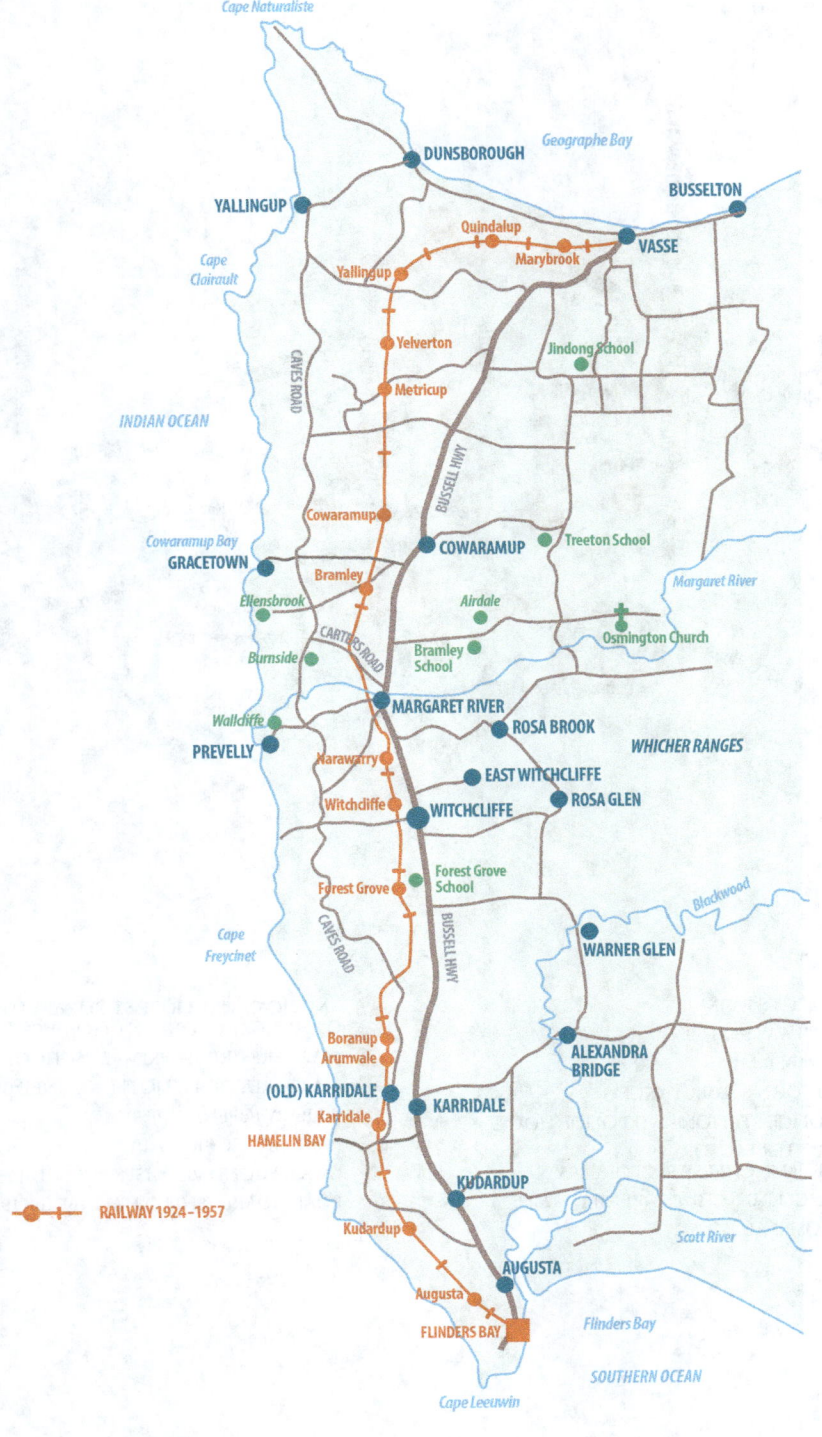

MARGARET RIVER TOWNSITE CIRCA 1950s

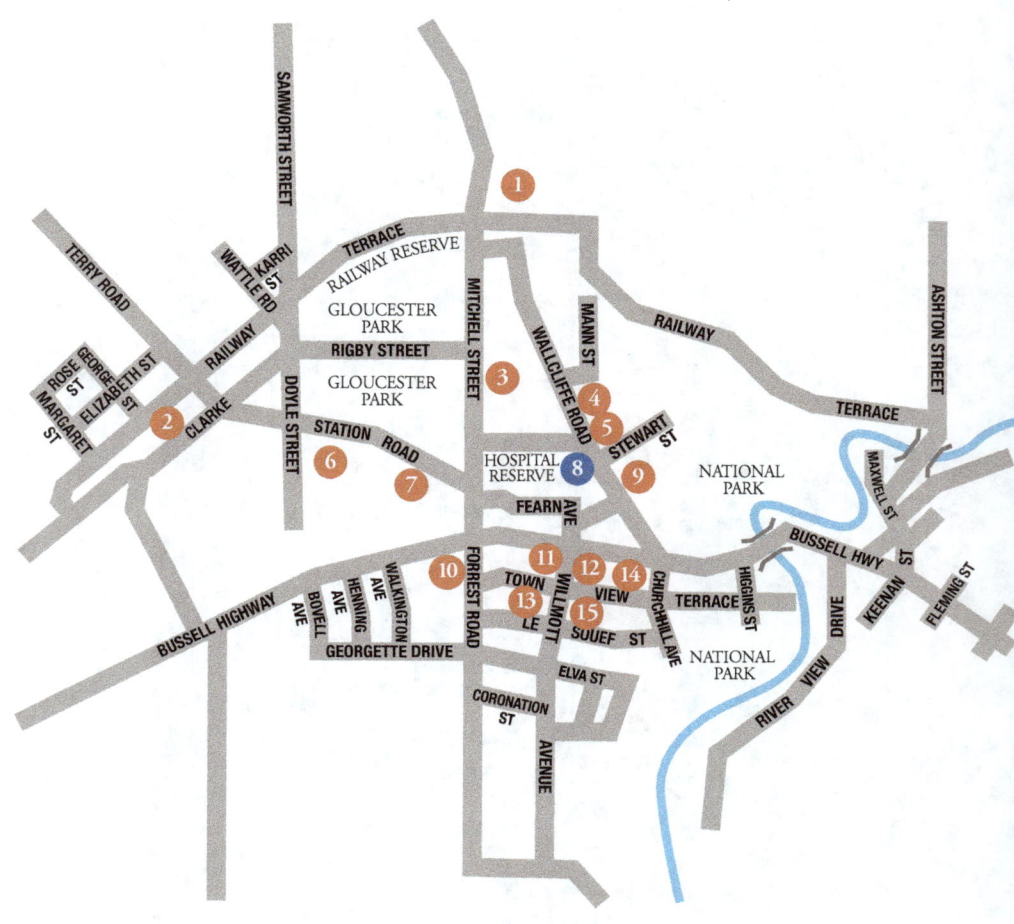

1. SMITH'S FARM
2. RAILWAY STATION
3. TIMBER MILL
4. ST JOHN'S AMBULANCE
5. POLICE STATION AND POLICE HOUSE
6. BUTTER FACTORY 1930 BECAME CHEESE FACTORY 1952
7. ANGLICAN CHURCH (BUILT 1926)
8. HOSPITAL
9. ANGLICAN ORDER OF ST ELIZABETH OF HUNGARY CONVENT (TO 1957)
10. MARGARET RIVER PRIMARY SCHOOL
11. MARGARET RIVER HOTEL (OPENED 1936)
12. LIBRARY (OPENED 1959)
13. POST OFFICE (BUILT 1956)
14. CWA (SECOND PREMISES OPENED 1956)
15. ROAD BOARD (SHIRE) HALL (BUILT 1936)

Chapter One

Wooditjup Bilya–Margaret River

This is the story of the old Margaret River Hospital (1924–1990), now the Margaret River Community Centre. Over one hundred years, these wooden buildings have witnessed many developments within the Margaret River district, such as the 1920s Group Settlement Scheme, which brought more people, including British migrants, to south-west Western Australia. Yet this history did not begin with the hospital's construction, or even with the arrival in the 1850s of European settlers.

The Wadandi, the saltwater people of the Capes region, are the original inhabitants and traditional custodians of this part of south-west WA. They have existed in harmony with, and cared for, this Country from time immemorial.[1] As Iszaac (Zac) Webb, Wadandi Cultural Custodian, explains:

> The managing of the Country (our boodja) was done in conjunction with the seasonal cycle. So there are six major seasons but there are another six micro ones in between, and the old people would use those systems to manage the Country.[2]

During their seasonal migration, the Wadandi travelled between Bunbury (Goomburrup) and Augusta (Talanup). This practice continued for some time after the first European settlers arrived in the south-west. Europeans termed this practice 'walkabout' without understanding its purpose. But as Zac's grandfather, George Webb, explained, it was routinely travelling up and down the coast that enabled the Wadandi to care for, and survive in, this corner of the Australian continent.

> White people used to refer to 'walkabout'. Oh, he's gone on walkabout.' Walkabout was a means of survival. The Bibbulmun (Pibelmen) and Wadandi tribes used to travel up and down the coast. Now they'd walk for a day and set up camp (what they used to call a mia-mia camp), made out of sticks, rushes and paper bark, in a dome shape. And they'd stop there for a month or so, or whatever, they'd hunt and fish there. When they reckoned that was exhausted then they would move on, but before doing so they would set light to the countryside around; put a slow fire through it and burn all the Country; burn it off. So on their return, say in three months time or six months time, all that Country would be green and fresh game would come in. Animals would come to feed on the green grass and that's how they used to stock up on new food.
>
> It might take them about six months or nine months or more to travel from Augusta to Bunbury. On the return trip they would do the same but they would not sleep in the same mia-mias, the buildings that they left there. They would shift off a little bit further, about ten or twenty yards away, and build new ones, because if there was a death in the family, they reckon that the spirit would come and dwell in that place when they left there.[3]

On their travels, the Wadandi would cross what we now know as the Margaret River. As Zac Webb relates, for the First Australians this is the Wooditjup Bilya, which was created by magic when Wooditj, a Wadandi saltwater man, met and fell in love with Milyean, a young Pibelmen woman from the people of plenty,

Wadandi Cultural Custodian, Iszaac (Zac) Webb. Courtesy Nature Conservation Margaret River.

but she was already promised to his older brother. So Wooditj and Milyean ran away together, but her father, Ngarut, followed them to get his daughter back. The Wooditj Bilya (the river) was created when Wooditj, angry with Ngarut, took up his stick and struck it against a rock, causing the spring to gush from the ground. The story, as told by the Wadandi, also describes the river's journey to the ocean, while Ngarut eventually gave Milyean and Wooditj his blessing but asked that they leave and go to new Country. Ngarut's body is buried at the cliffs near the river mouth and his spirit still watches over the river.[4]

Alfred Bussell, the youngest of the Bussell brothers, came to this area when he moved south from the Vasse (now Busselton) in the 1850s. By then the Wooditjup Bilya was already known to Europeans as the Margaret River. Alfred had arrived in the south-west of Western Australia in 1830 as a fourteen-year-old boy, accompanying his older brothers, including John Garrett Bussell, the family patriarch. In migrating to the other side of the world, the Bussells were hoping to achieve the social status and financial security that they could not achieve in England after the early death of John and Alfred's father, William, a clergyman.[5]

There seems little doubt that it was John Garrett Bussell who named the river and that the 'Margaret' in question was Margaret Whicher,[6] an Englishwoman who never lived in Western Australia and probably never knew that she had a river, and later a town, named after her. While on a visit back to England in 1837, Bussell had asked Margaret Whicher's parents for her hand in marriage. He was rejected, on the grounds that their daughter, then not quite sixteen years old, was too young to embark on an arduous adventure so far away from her parents.[7] The naming of the river may have been related more to a desire to acquire land and property than evidence of a romantic attachment. At the time, James Whicher, Margaret's father, and his brother-in-law, Captain Robert Yates, who was also Bussell's cousin, were contemplating a joint sheep-farming venture in the infant colony.[8] That scheme did not eventuate and Yates and Whicher never came to Western Australia. But the three men may have been looking at a newly printed map of the area when Bussell named three geographical features: the Margaret River; its source, the Whicher Ranges; and a nearby hill, Mount Yates,[9] in the Margaret River hinterland.

When, some fifteen years later, Alfred Bussell was looking for a new start, away from the Vasse, his immediate impulse was to look south, to land not yet settled by any Europeans. Alfred had married sixteen-year-old Ellen Heppingstone in 1850. His move to an area not previously settled may also have been partly because other members of his family disapproved of his marriage. John's wife Charlotte, in particular, snubbed Ellen at social gatherings because the Heppingstones had come to Australia as servants.[10] According to family descendant Ian Heppingstone:

> After they had lived at the Broadwater for four or five years and had become the parents of two children, Ellen, a very practical young woman, became very dissatisfied with their prospects at the Vasse and

decided that they must seek fresh pastures. On being asked by Alfred "But where will we go?" she said, "Anywhere, as long as we get out of this place." They decided to go southwards. The exact date is not known but it was probably in 1855. The trip was made by a six-team bullock wagon with canvas awning. The forty-mile trip took several days and the party consisted of Alfred, Ellen and two children, a man named Kelly and a native guide.[11]

Kelly found the thick bush oppressive and left the Bussells at a place that became known as Kelly's Farewell, now Metricup, and returned to the Vasse.[12] But Alfred, Ellen and their two eldest children continued their journey southwards towards the Margaret River. Alfred was subsequently granted a pastoral lease of 20,000 acres (8,094 hectares) of crown land on either side of the mouth of the river and extending two miles inland.[13] Their first house was on the stream north of the Margaret River that Alfred named Ellensbrook and was known to the Wadandi as Mokidup. The Bussell's second home, Wallcliffe, would be built on the south side of the Margaret River itself and near to the river mouth.

Ellensbrook, the Bussell family's first home *circa* 1920. Courtesy David Jenkins.

Alfred and Ellen's unhappiness with life at the Vasse may have been affected by the fact that a few years earlier he had been unsuccessful in obtaining a position as a local police constable, which would have provided a secure income. In his application Alfred had made the following claim:

> I should be obliged also by you informing His Excellency that I have for many years made the habits and language of the natives my study and that I have perfect assurance of my ability to perform satisfactorily the duties of the office.[14]

This knowledge would stand Alfred in good stead when he moved to Mokidup, since he and Ellen were largely dependent on the Wadandi for both local information and practical assistance in everyday life. Greg Bussell, a direct descendant of Alfred and Ellen, points out there was considerable and necessary interaction with the traditional custodians of Country.

> We know that when Alfred and Ellen came to Ellensbrook, the Aboriginal people looked at that site and said, 'This is a good place to build your house because it's got free water running past the door, and it's protected from the ocean'. And the same thing happened when they moved to Wallcliffe, they were shown the site down there on the river, so there was that cooperation. And the Aboriginal people helped in the house with Ellen, because they had a lot of kids. And Alfred had the stockmen to work on the land.[15]

Zac Webb agrees that Alfred and Ellen Bussell took advantage of information provided by the Wadandi.

> Definitely. They were very reliant on the knowledge and on knowledge sharing, and I guess they were open at that time to learning those sorts of things. Whereas sometimes other families weren't so open to listening to Aboriginal people or had that sense of working together with them. Our families worked closely together in establishing areas such as Ellensbrook and Wallcliffe house. Our people became stockmen and nurses and things like that.[16]

When Alfred and Ellen's one-year-old son, Jasper, died in 1864, the Wadandi mourned with the parents as Alfred wrote to his brother John:

> The natives called him Japany kind, from the frank and agreeable expressions which he always carried. I cannot but name that their grief was manifested in a wonderful manner, they sat beside and encircled the bereaved mother as she leant upon the fence. Big tears rolled down their black faces. They sat a while in this way and then passed off in silence with heads cast down. It was very remarkable. Why did they feel or seem to feel for an infant's death in a white man's house?[17]

According to Frances Terry, who had access to some of the Bussell letters, the rapport which Alfred Bussell established was a two-way street: Alfred learned about local medicinal plants from the local people and in turn was trusted by them to help to cure their ills.[18]

Arguably, Alfred and Ellen Bussell could not have succeeded in their agricultural endeavours without a labour force and the only one readily available, apart from occasional deserters from American whaling ships, were the local inhabitants. Later, Alfred's eldest daughter, Fanny Brockman, refers in her diary to Aboriginal stockmen, including Jemmy, who was with the Bussells for many years, and John Williams and Jimmy Long, who were of mixed European and Aboriginal parentage.[19]

For the remainder of the nineteenth century, the Bussells and other settlers relied on the labour provided by the original inhabitants of this land. Importantly, Aboriginal women helped to raise Alfred and Ellen's children. Wadandi cultural custodian Zac Webb has been handed down memories of these interactions:

> (The children) were brought up speaking our language, so speaking *Dwordan*, which is one of our dialects here, and *Doosan*, which is the dialect around Busselton. We were told that Jack was raised by Granny Ngilgee and Granny Nandinong as well. Sometimes they would actually wet nurse him as well, singing songs and stories on

> Country when he was a little baby and growing up through his entire childhood. And this is how he became very well versed in those languages.

'Jack' was Alfred John Bussell, the oldest surviving son of Alfred and Ellen who, as Frances Terry wrote, lived between these two very different worlds.

> So John learned what they wanted him to of the white man's lore and more and more after Ellen's death escaped as soon as he could to the companionship of the natives, hunting kangaroos and quokkas, stealing their wild honey from the bees in the cliff, bringing home his fish to old Chloe in the kitchen who would fling her arms wide and cry in delight. 'Master John, where did you catch that fine fish?'[20]

The Wadandi, in common with other Aboriginal people, initially thought that these white people were their ancestors returning as spirits. They did not realise that the Europeans had come to stay and to take over the land that was their home. As Zac Webb explained:

> When our people first saw non-Indigenous people, European people, we were very welcoming, because the old people saw them as being spirits of some of their children who may have passed away, and by coming back on Country, the old people said that 'they have been on spirit journey, and they forgot their Country', their boodjara. So, our people would take them to ngamma (waterholes) and the Country places, saying 'Remember this is where we used to sit. Remember this.' So when they then saw the fences being put up and getting excluded, they weren't too sure what was going on.[21]

Most of the fencing and importing of cattle in this area was undertaken initially by Alfred Bussell, who can claim to have been the first European-style 'farmer' in the district. The dairy was mainly left to Ellen, while Alfred devoted his time to cattle raising and to market gardening, producing potatoes, for which there was a ready market at the Swan (Perth) as well as from visiting

American whaling ships. Alfred also obtained additional pastoral leases in the south-west, the largest being no less than 65,535 acres, which he obtained in 1871.[22] These leases were issued by a colonial government with no understanding of Aboriginal physical or spiritual connection to Country because, as Zac Webb points out:

> We weren't conventionally farming the land in the practices of Western wet culture of farming in an arid country. We didn't have hooved animals. We didn't have cows; we didn't have these things. So the perception from the settlers was that we were Neanderthal. We were savages. We weren't doing what they were doing. Everyone fears what they don't understand and I think our Aboriginal culture is so complex that it's hard for people to relate to that intricacy and that you don't have to alter Country. You live with it.[23]

Alfred Bussell's leases were on the Country which had provided the Wadandi with the requirements for life. Now the bush was being cleared and waterways fenced off, preventing access by Zac Webb's ancestors.

> Waterways are such critical things for Aboriginal people in general, because water is life and that's the thing as humans that we all have in common, we can none of us last more than three days without water. And water had that vital thing, food sources which sit in the water sources, like mussels and marron and gilgies. And then you've got your ducks and swans, that would have eggs and all sorts of things. So there's a food source, and then there are travel routes, being able to get down to the ocean and to the salt water. And by not having access to these rivers or waterways, it became very hard for Aboriginal people to be able to survive in that situation.[24]

Historian Geoffrey Bolton summed up the essential difference right across this continent between all the newcomers, in this instance the Bussells, and the traditional custodians of this land.

> Unaware of commerce and agriculture, invincibly ignorant it seemed of any sense of economic motivation, the Aborigines in all their centuries of occupation contented themselves with the lives of nomadic hunters, merely scratching the surface of the continent. By contrast the nineteenth Europeans prided themselves on transforming the wilderness into a great pastoral empire, a tempting source of gold and a working man's paradise sustaining the thriving cities of Melbourne and Sydney.[25]

While Alfred Bussell learned the local language and seemed to have been on good terms with the Wadandi, he was, in common with all European settlers, focused on creating the type of agriculture with which he was familiar, and had long been practised in the northern hemisphere by the English. Yet his children, and in particular his son John, did whatever they could to keep the local language and culture alive. They absorbed and wrote down the stories they had learned in the nursery. Frances Terry, writing about the Bussells' early years in the Margaret River area, recorded that Jack Bussell seemed happy only 'when trailing after the natives, learning what they taught him of the bush, and storing in his prodigious memory the legends they told him of their race'.[26] Jack died in 1940 but his interest in Wadandi culture lasted to the end of his life. Robert Breeden, born in Busselton in 1928, remembers Jack Bussell's commitment to recording the local language and culture:

> I was about a twelve-year-old when I became aware of old Jack Bussell because he lived up from us along Fairbairn Road. I wasn't aware earlier that he had handwritten notes, which were later typed up, about the local Aboriginals, stories, and many things in this area. He maintained he was the last of the white fellas to fluently speak the local dialect.[27]

In April 1938, two years before Jack Bussell's death, the *West Australian* printed an article about his work:

Alfred John Bussell, known as John or Jack.
Courtesy Vernon Bussell.

An interesting vocabulary of the South-West Language with a descriptive introduction has been prepared by Mr Alfred John Bussell...There are very few living at the present time who can speak the South-West native language correctly, he said in a letter to the Western Australian Historical Society recently. In this district there are only five half-castes and myself.

Describing his own knowledge of the language, Mr Bussell said that he had been able to speak it from childhood and had learnt a number of the native legends and stories, some of which he had incorporated in the introduction to his book...Mr Bussell is a direct descendant of the well-known pioneering family of the same name.[28]

Jack Bussell recorded much of the information that he had collected over a lifetime in notebooks, including details of the medicines and remedies used by the First Australians living in the south-west of Western Australia.

Drugs and medicines

1. There is one plant in the south-west which they call mulga which they eat to purify the blood when they have skin disorders.

2. No preparation. They just chew it up and swallow it.

3. Just eaten – that is chewed and swallowed.

4. Narcotics are not known amongst them. If so, they are not used. There is one herb or root existing in the south west which they call mena, red in colour, which they roast in the ashes which is hotter if anything than cayenne pepper. This they eat and it gives them energy which I believe because I tried it once.

5. The oil and fat of most of…in fact you may say, all of the animals and reptiles they eat is used medicinally both for inward and outward appliances. They also have mulga stones which they use for healing disease (see magic).

6. The effects are genuine enough re the oils they take inwardly for it goes a long way re the morphine stick. The mulga stones they have. I have one of their mulga stones myself. There is no European equivalent I know of.

A description of 'Magic' follows that of medical remedies:

1. Magic is practised by only certain individuals who have been qualified by their elders who of course have that power.

2. These individuals are supposed to be able to do things which are impossible to any other but those that are in the craft and of course they are supposed to be men of high knowledge.

3. Magic is on rare occasions directed against individuals who have committed some offence and strange to say those individuals invariably die. The ceremony with these things is the doctors and wise men hold a council. They find him guilty of the misdemeanour in question. They chant his sentence and strange to say he invariably dies a lingering death within about six moons.

4. Magic used for healing disease

The procedure is, the person who is to be performed on is laid on his or her back, rubbed all over with a mulga or bulgee stone all the time grunting and hissing and saying a word now and again and to wind up with, presses the sick person prettily heavily on the part of the body most affected with each of his feet which finishes up the performance and strange to say the individual nearly always gets well pretty quickly.

5. Magic is used for rainmaking. All the men in the camp where the rain is wanted, get blackboy rush torches and light them and run up and down shouting and singing. This was done of course when the old men thought that rain was pretty sure to come.

6. I have never known magic to be used to increase the food supply.

7. The detection of…is generally supposed to be done by magic whether it is or not to convince the young of their powers in that way.

8. There are special objects or individuals who have magic directed against them but there are no special times or places associated with the practice of magic.

9. Women are not recognised in any of these affairs of magic.[29]

Jack Bussell wrote further notes about the health of the Wadandi and their medicines.

> They relied greatly in their wild state on animal, fish and reptile oil for medicinal purposes – both internal and external. They had great faith in goanna (iguana) and carpet snake oil and fat for particular diseases,

they used black snake oil. They reckoned it was more effective than goanna or carpet snake oil for cases of rheumatism. Whale oil was quite a speciality for bad cases of rheumatism if they could get it but of course, they could not very often find a dead whale but when they did, they would smell them a good distance off.

There also seemed to be no call for dentistry: 'The teeth are just rinsed with a mouth full of water and in their wild state, their teeth never seem to decay, I have never known any of them to have their teeth extracted.'

Zac Webb describes the connection between health and living with the 'bountifulness of Country'.

> I guess they kept healthy by using these natural resources around us, that being from nature weren't processed and didn't have any refined sugars. They kept healthy by living with Country. For us as Aboriginal people, we would live with Country going with the seasons, utilising the medicines and the bush foods; living with the bountifulness of Country and having clean water and clean rivers and drinking from these streams. It was all about the cultural belief that if you look after the Country, that Country is going to look after you and keep you healthy. It's going to provide everything: shelter, medicine and food.[30]

While 'living with Country' could not always prevent accidents, even here, the traditional ways were sometimes more effective than Western medicine. Zac's grandfather, George Webb, born in 1935, recorded how, as a young boy, he survived an accident when the local hospital had sent him home to die.

> When I was young, they told me that I was with my father and grandfather in the spring cart…I was two at the time. Anyhow I fell off the cart, or I must have been grabbing the wheel, and it pulled me down under the wheel and the wheel went over my head. It squashed all my skull and they rushed me to Bunbury hospital. They operated on me but they couldn't do no more for me, so they more or less sent me home to die. There was nothing else they could do; there was haemorrhage on the brain. So they sent me off to die.

Now, when they took me home my grandparents contacted this doctor-man. His name was Alec Bilbung. He was a great warrior of the sou'west Aboriginal tribe. He was more or less a loner. He had magic powers. He was a pretty strong medicine man. He said to them, when they took me home, to leave me by the window and to leave the window open. They done this and that evening, this bird landed on the window sill. It was in the form of an owl or a little eagle, and this bird hopped into bed with me; got under the blankets in bed with me. It stopped there all that night and the next day it went. Now they said it was the doctor-man, that he'd come with his magic powers to heal me and in doing so he got into bed with me in the form of this bird; that's the way he travelled.

…And that's why I believe in the doctor-man of the Mobarin-man and that's the thing that they said that cured me, this man with his great powers, Alec Bilbung.[31]

In George Webb's lifetime there was overlap between traditional Aboriginal medicine and the home cures introduced by newcomers:

Well, I suppose the main home remedy was, and I suppose a lot of white people used it too. If we had a cold, my grandmother used to give us a couple of drops of eucalyptus in a teaspoon of sugar and we used to suck that or eat that. The other remedy was for boils or carbuncles and my old auntie, she used to put a bluebottle on there that used to suck all the bad stuff out of the carbuncle. But the other one, for sores, we used this soap and sugar poultice. We'd get the soap and make it so it was soft and then mix the sugar in with it to make a poultice out of that.

And the old people used the black snake. They used to get the fat out of the black snake and he was good for rheumatism. And the long-tailed goanna, they used to get the oil out of that. Also emu was good.

Emu oil or kangaroo oil was used in a different way, too, not only remedies but the old people used it when they used to go hunting. They used to smear themselves with emu oil, so if they happened to get on the wrong side of the wind, and the animals smelled them, they just thought it was another emu coming along. The human smell would be gone out of them and they would just smell the emu oil which would enable 'em to get close to 'em.[32]

While Jack Bussell spent much of his later years recording the knowledge gained from a childhood spent with the Wadandi people, later generations of the Bussell family also consider that the knowledge imparted to their grandfather and father by the original inhabitants has shaped some of their everyday practices. Alfred's great-grandson, Greg Bussell, describes some of those influences:

> We used to catch marron quite a lot down the river. But we were always taught by Dad to only catch what you can eat. And I know other people would go there and get a huge bag of them. We did the same with fishing, catching herring. You'd get enough to feed the family for a day or two. And then there was the burning. We used to lease all the coast, north of the Margaret River up to Ellensbrook. There were no fences and as kids, we used to go out on the horses, checking on the cattle. And on the way home, we were given a box of matches. And Dad would say, 'Can you throw a match in that bit of bush'. And that's what we did. Every year, we burnt pieces of the coast. And that was really what Aboriginal burning was about.[33]

Overall, however, it was the culture and the activities of the European newcomers that would prevail. It quickly became apparent that this region was an important source of timber. Mills were established at Quindalup to the north of the Margaret River and at Augusta to the south. These settlements provided a market for the produce grown by Alfred and Ellen Bussell.[34] But for the Wadandi, the coming of the timber industry spelled trouble. In contrast to a business that involved chopping down trees and sawing them into pieces, traditional culture had taught First Nations people that:

> We need the tree but the tree doesn't need us. We need the tree because the tree is going to give us shade. It's going to take our carbon dioxide and give us oxygen, but we don't give anything back to the tree. And especially nowadays, we just go along and chop them all down and

turn them into timbers and turn them into houses, not respecting the parts of the tree. For us, we would still make houses and things but we wouldn't destroy the entire tree. You would utilise parts of the tree but you would sing and talk to that tree and thank that tree for what it's given you, shelter and warmth.[35]

This philosophy of living and working with nature differed strongly from that of timber merchant, building contractor and pastoralist Maurice Coleman Davies, who came west from South Australia in the late 1870s.[36] Coleman Davies soon saw the potential of the local karri trees to create personal wealth. His presence in the district is first mentioned by Fanny Brockman in April 1881: 'Sent Peter to Wallcliffe for some cows. Mr Tomb and Mr Davies stayed for dinner and then went on to Quindalup.'[37] At this time, the two men would have been inspecting the forests they were negotiating to buy.

Coleman Davies was also a major player in the pastoral industry which was developing in the north of the state and he was soon doing business with Alfred Bussell at Wallcliffe:

16 April 1881,

A.P Bussell, Esq.

Dear Sir

I am taking up some land and shall require about thirty head of cattle if you can sell them under the following conditions.

The price to be fifty (50) shillings per head, age and description to be agreed upon and delivery to be taken by me within one month of the date of sale.

The use of your run free of all charges until I require them and the increase born to the same to be my property.

Should you agree to my proposal I would allow you the use of such cattle for dairy purposes free of all charge provided they are properly taken care of by you during the time they are in your possession.

I shall be glad to receive your reply as soon as possible.

I remain dear Sir

Yours truly,

M.C Davies.[38]

Forty-four cattle were duly delivered to Coleman Davies.[39]

As Iszaac Webb relates, from necessity some Wadandi people found work in the new timber industry and formed relationships with the newcomers: 'Samuel Isaacs, he was the stockman for the Bussell family. He used to get all the wood and all the forestry products and bring them up into the Jarrahdene Mill.'[40] Along with Alfred and Ellen's daughter Grace, Sam Isaacs is remembered for saving passengers and sailors from the wreck of the *Georgette* in 1876.

He was the son of an Aboriginal mother and probably of a Native American mariner.[41] Sam was taken in by Alfred and Ellen as a child when he turned up on their doorstep, having apparently lost a herd of pigs he was driving north for Captain Molloy.[42] Sam remained working for the Bussells for much of his life and, according to Keith McLeod's father, Dudley became known in the district as the 'greatest post and rail fencer'. Sam's work was so good that some of his fences still exist.[43]

While the exploitation of the karri and jarrah forests undertaken by Coleman Davies and others would not have been dreamed of by the original inhabitants, in this new European-style economy, timber would become, in the last quarter of the nineteenth century, the main industry in this corner of south-west Western Australia. Coleman Davies set up his main mill and township at Karridale between the Margaret River and Augusta. This soon became the largest settlement south of Busselton and influenced development around the Margaret River. By 1900 the Karridale township consisted of stores, offices, the principal mill and workshops. It was serviced by dirt roads and forty miles of railways extending north of the Margaret River.

Timber mill at Karridale 1912. Courtesy State Library of Western Australia 229171PD.

Herbert Davies' (son of M. C. Davies) house at Karridale. Margaret River and Districts Historical Society (MR&DHS).

The town also boasted a school, public library, hall, sporting field, racecourse, church and rectory with a resident clergyman and also a qualified physician.[44] So for the people living along the Margaret River, the nearest doctor was now in Karridale rather than Busselton.

While a succession of 'qualified physicians' practised at Karridale, a proper hospital did not open there until 1909. It was much needed, as this report of a serious accident at Flinders Bay jetty in 1908 illustrates. A worker named John Prentice was buried under a load of timber and ultimately died, but not before the inadequacy of the hospital arrangements was highlighted.

> He was taken to the Karridale 'hospital' over the Company's line. The 'hospital' is a lodging house where boarders eat their meals to the accompaniment of groans of patients. The sun beats relentlessly on an iron roof and converts each single roomed shanty into a bakers oven. In one of these Prentice died. No room is reserved for hospital purposes and they are shared by patient and lodger indiscriminately.[45]

A year later, in 1909, Coleman Davies' timber company, now known as Millars Karri and Jarrah Company, provided another building to be used as a hospital and employed a nurse: 'Nurse Harrison, who comes highly recommended from the Government Health Officer, has entered upon her duties as nurse at the local hospital.'[46] But the *South-Western News* reported complaints about the lack of government support in establishing the Karridale hospital.

> Those who have worked so hard to make the hospital here an established institution are greatly disappointed at the treatment meted out to them by the Government. The member for the district, as well as the Colonial Secretary, have been written to, to see if a subsidy could not be granted or some assistance given, and in both cases a negative reply was received, merely stating that only in indigent cases could any assistance be looked for.[47]

In August that year, another serious accident occurred and the hospital was the scene of the required surgery.

> A painful accident happened at the Jarrahdene mill a few days ago when Mr J. Purvis lost a portion of his hand through it coming into contact with a circular saw in motion. The mill foreman, Mr Jas. Ross, lost no time in conveying the injured man to Karridale hospital where he was treated. On Tuesday the thumb and first finger were amputated by Drs Kearney of Karridale and Lionel Robertson of Busselton.[48]

The Karridale community continued to support the hospital and the local newspaper reported in October 1912 that:

> The annual hospital ball was held in the Karridale Agricultural hall on Saturday evening, the 26th of September, and was without doubt the most successful that has been held there for a number of years.[49]

However, by this time the timber industry centred on Karridale was in sharp decline. There was no longer sufficient viable wood to cut – a situation which was the antithesis of the Wadandi approach to managing Country. The last mill, Jarrahdene, closed in 1913, the year that Coleman Davies died.[50] As the Karridale population dwindled, the need for a hospital and doctor there also decreased. While a small hospital would be opened there for the group settlers in the 1920s, the town would never again provide a home to a medical practitioner.

The substantial buildings erected at Karridale remained standing for over half a century but the Karridale fire of February 1961 would burn down all the surviving buildings, including Millars Trading Store (also the post office and liquor shop), the fuel depot, six mill houses, the hospital, the Anglican Church, the CWA Hall, the Karridale Hall and two privately owned houses.[51]

For over thirty years, from 1881 to 1913, timber operations in the Karridale district also supported the livelihood of the Bussells and other settlers now living in the Margaret River district.

Newcomers included A. C. R. Loaring and Neil McLeod, who had been attracted to Western Australia by the gold rush, formed a partnership and bought land in the area. In addition to running livestock, mainly beef cattle, the partners also set up a market garden with Karridale being the main outlet for their produce.[52]

Although the timber industry centred on Karridale lasted little more than a quarter of a century, it did create improvements in the district's roads and led to the opening of the area's first 'tourist' accommodation. The Vasse-Karridale Road, which followed a route similar to that of the current Caves Road, was initially the main thoroughfare between Busselton and the Margaret River as well as being the main overland route from Bunbury to Karridale. In 1878, in anticipation of the establishment of the Karridale mills and thus of an increase in traffic, a bridge had been built across the river at Burnside, also known as the Lower Margaret, where previously there had only been a ford.[53] Fanny Brockman, Alfred Bussell's eldest daughter, then established a boarding house at the

Bridge over the Margaret River near Burnside, November 1901. Courtesy State Library of Western Australia 025902PD.

Lower Margaret crossing. Given that it took two days to drive a horse carriage from Busselton to Karridale, a 'half way house' became an overnight stop.[54] This was Bridge House, later known as Old Bridge House.[55] Fanny initially leased this establishment to the Keenans, who had moved south from the Vasse. In 1889 the business was taken over by the Higgins family.[56]

Bridge House lost its importance as an overnight stop when Coleman Davies persuaded the State Government to construct a new, more direct road between Busselton and Karridale/Augusta. In July 1892 the Government Gazette advertised for tenders to build a new bridge across the Margaret River further inland, to service the new direct route.[57] This bridge became known as the Upper Margaret and it would eventually determine the location of the Margaret River townsite.

There was considerable opposition to the proposed new road from Lower Margaret landholders, including Fanny Brockman and Stewart Keenan.[58] But the Higgins family soon realised that the future for their business lay at the new bridge and re-established themselves on ten acres beside the river. They then operated livery stables to cater for Coleman Davies' coach horses as well as a boarding house. Now the main requirement was to provide meals for travellers rather than overnight stays. With an early start and a change of horses at the Higgins establishment, the new route allowed the entire journey between Busselton and Karridale to be completed in one day.[59]

This shorter route between the two settlements crossed the river further inland and determined not only the eventual location of the townsite, but also, more than twenty years later, the preferred site for the Margaret River Hospital. At the same time, the area around the new townsite was still mainly thickly forested, while most of the land cleared for agriculture was nearer to the Lower Margaret.

While the timber mills operated, Karridale had been an important market for the meat and dairy goods produced by settlers around the Margaret River. The timber-exporting ports constructed by Coleman Davies at Hamelin and Flinders Bays were also used to send vegetables and butter from the Margaret River to Bunbury and Perth. But as the timber industry contracted, settlers at the Lower Margaret had to find new sources of income. Perhaps surprisingly, tourism provided some of the answers.

Alfred Bussell died in 1882 and his son John (Jack) took possession of Wallcliffe, as stipulated in his father's will, when he reached the age of twenty-three in 1888. The following year John married Marion Reynolds, daughter of settlers in the Busselton area. In addition to his interest in local languages and culture, John's early enthusiasms included discovering and promoting the district's caves.[60] In the late nineteenth and early twentieth centuries, there was considerable public enthusiasm for cave exploration and young John Bussell was one of the first people to encourage others to admire and explore the spectacular local caverns. He also offered visitor accommodation at Wallcliffe House, as stated in this advertisement in the *West Australian* on 20 February 1893:

TO TOURISTS

Visitors to the Southern District during the summer months will find excellent accommodation at WALLCLIFFE HOUSE and will be afforded every facility for visiting the Magnificent Caves lately discovered on the coast near the Margaret River. The Scenery in the vicinity is grand and Bathing Accommodation excellent. The Mineral Waters recently found are equal to the spa waters of Germany.

For terms apply to the undersigned, giving a fortnight's notice.

A. J. Bussell,

Wallcliffe House, Vasse.[61]

Several of John's house guests later wrote to the newspapers about their wonderful holiday. They described how, after travelling by steamer to Busselton, John Bussell greeted them and drove them south, crossing the Margaret River bridge at sunset. Visitors were then welcomed to Wallcliffe by Marion and, in the following days, escorted by John into a wondrous world below ground, often with only candles to light the way.⁶²

While John Bussell can be credited with helping to initiate south-west tourism,⁶³ by 1895 his personal dreams of a great future for the Margaret River district were over. His pregnant wife, Marion, died in October 1895 after an accident while driving herself to Busselton in a pony and trap. Dr Hungerford was summoned from Busselton but could not save her life. At the same time, John was in severe financial difficulties, as his sister Fanny Brockman wrote:

> 1895 October: I have not written in my journal all this time. I have been away at poor old Wallcliffe having a most heartbreaking time nursing our poor dear Marion but all we could do could not save her. She died on Wednesday last week. Poor young thing, so sad. Poor old John, I do not know what poor old John will do. He has gone to Perth now; His business is in an awful mess.⁶⁴

Wallcliffe House surrounded by bush 1901. Courtesy State Library of Western Australia 02542PD & RWAHS BA 819.

The Bussells' business was indeed in trouble. Problems had begun before Alfred's death. In 1880 he had written to his sister-in-law Charlotte in England:

> There has been disaster with us this year which has driven us all apart (such as are left together at least), the calves began to die, twenty died in a fortnight and as you know Charlotte our milking depends on them.– No calves, no milk and our beef sales depend on them...[65]

All the Bussells' lands were now mortgaged and the bank appointed a manager to oversee affairs until the businesses, including Wallcliffe House, could be sold. John and his younger brother Fred then went to the Eastern Goldfields as prospectors. In his later life John (by now known as Jack) became a stockman and station manager. He also worked in the north-west and as a cattle drover. Later, Jack joined the railways, remarried and had a large family. But he never again lived on the land that his parents had farmed in the Margaret River area,[66] and is now mainly remembered for his work in recording the local Wadandi language and dialects.

While John Bussell's involvement in promoting the Margaret River caves came to an end,[67] public enthusiasm for cave exploration remained. In March 1900 the Chief Inspector of Lands, Mr C.E. May, forwarded a report on the Margaret River caves to the Western Australian Minister for Lands. One section of his report is reminiscent of later tourist brochures.

> The district possesses almost every desideratum for a perfect holiday to please diverse tastes. There is a trip by land or by sea...when a steamer is provided as it would be at once if excursionists knew what they would enjoy in escaping the summer heats in this salubrious latitude. They could go by way of Busselton, see the caves in a leisurely excursion down to Cape Leeuwin, then driving or riding to the banks of the Blackwood River at Augusta to fish and shoot over Hardy's Inlet or steam or sail to Flinders Bay, and follow the caves up to Boodidup *(now known as Boodjidup)* Brook to bask by the

waters of the brook that is fed from a silver spring gushing from the side of Witchcliffe cave.[68]

Even now, this might sound like the gateway to a magical holiday experience. Notwithstanding the flowery language, intending visitors would have been wise to note the paragraph under the heading 'The trip as it is to-day' and to heed Mr May's comment that beyond Busselton (the railhead), the road south was little more than a track.

Despite access difficulties, if, in the early years of the twentieth century, the area around the Margaret River was known beyond the state's boundaries for anything at all, it was for its spectacular caves. One early visitor wrote:

> The beautiful country and the grandeur and magnificence of the caves on the Margaret River constitute one of the most delightful holiday resorts in Australia. The whole of the coast-line from Cape Naturaliste to the Leeuwin, is simply honeycombed with some of the most superb caves to be found, probably in the world.[69]

First car to visit the Margaret River caves and Cape Leeuwin 1907. Courtesy State Library of Western Australia 21350PD RWAHS BA110.

It would be over three-quarters of a century before Margaret River became a national and international tourist destination. In 1900 the area could still be reached only over rough unmade roads, while the railway from Busselton would not arrive for almost another quarter of a century.

At the end of the nineteenth century, there was still no Margaret River townsite. Fanny Brockman makes numerous references in her diary to 'going to town' but, for the Bussells and other settlers at both the Lower and Upper Margaret, this meant a trip to Busselton (or, as it was still often called, 'the Vasse'). After Karridale declined, this was also the location of the nearest doctor and hospital.[70]

Despite the lack of a townsite, residents living along the river established a Margaret River Progress Association in 1908. It was this organisation which would later lobby for the appointment of a medical officer and the establishment of a hospital. The original proponents for this association were settlers living at the Lower Margaret and included A.C.R. Loaring, the then owner of Wallcliffe House.[71] The founding of the Progress Association suggested that the settlers saw a bright future for the district. It also demonstrated the strong sense of community involvement which would continue over the following decades. Without this 'people power' lobbying for local amenities, the district would have had even fewer government-provided services.

While there was no demand for a local medical service in 1908, several of the families living around the Margaret River had young children and were asking the State Government build a school. After much debate about location, the building was sited midway between the 'Upper Margaret' and the 'Lower Margaret'. The district's first educational establishment became known as the Trinders School because it was built close to land owned by local settler John Trinder,[72] whose family boarded some of the school's teachers.[73]

Following success in obtaining a government-funded facility, and in order to argue for other government services, the settlers then decided to establish a more permanent community organisation.

The inaugural meeting of the Progress Association was held at Wallcliffe House in December 1908 and the main resolutions were recorded in the local newspaper, the *South-Western News*:

> After discussion it was decided to form an association to be called the Margaret River Progress Association. Mr F. Bussell J.P. was elected chairman and Mr L.E. de Mole secretary. The gathering was called together by Mr Loaring and satisfaction was expressed on all sides that at last a representative body was brought (into) existence to look after local matters.[74]

The chairman, Fred Bussell, was the younger surviving son of Alfred Bussell and, unlike his brother John (Jack), after returning from the Goldfields he farmed in the district for the rest of his life. While the group's membership varied over the following years, meetings of the association were held regularly at 3.30 pm on the first Sunday of the month at members' homes. Those present dealt with issues of local significance. Some were minor concerns, such as a request to the Colonial Secretary asking to have the cemetery fenced.[75] Whether this was to keep people or animals in or out of the area was not specified.

Many issues involved correspondence with government departments on matters such as the bounty for capture of wild dogs[76] and a request to close local coastal bays to net fishing.[77] Another significant issue raised at the October 1920 monthly meeting of the Progress Association was the lack of adequate telephone communication, particularly because of the potential for accidents in the local caves, then still the major tourist drawcard.

> The only business brought forward was the question of telephonic communications between Mr Connelly's, the cave guide residence and Yallingup. It was decided that the Deputy Postmaster General be written to on the subject. This is very necessary owing to the large amount of traffic to the Caves, and should accidents happen there is no way of getting a

> doctor quickly. This was brought home very forcibly to the meeting, for while it was in progress, one of the cave cars arrived with a lady passenger very badly hurt through the car bumping over a bad part of the road. The accident was so serious that the car had to leave at once to get a doctor out to attend the patient. Had Mr Connelly been connected per phone a great deal of time would have been saved.[78]

More than one hundred years later, the adequacy of telephone communications in this area is still a lively discussion topic.

In 1910, concern that 'the district is likely to be dotted with public buildings several miles apart in the near future if a townsite is not made available shortly' had prompted the Progress Association to write to the State Government's Minister for Lands requesting that a townsite be declared at 'the Upper Margaret Bridge'.[79] Lots on the north side of the Margaret River were surveyed in 1912[80] and the townsite was gazetted in 1913, as reported in the *South-Western News*:

> MARGARET RIVER. New Townsite. The Government has set apart the land within the area described-hereunder, as Town and Suburban, to form a Townsite on the main Busselton-Augusta road, near the Margaret River, to be known and distinguished as 'Margaret River':—Bounded on the north and east by lines extending west 100 chains, and north 100 chains, from a point situated 50 chains east of the 24-mile post on the Karridale-Busselton road; the opposite boundaries being parallel and equal. Area, 1,000 acres.[81]

Despite this declaration, Margaret River remained a small wayside settlement.[82] Yet the decision to create the townsite at this location meant that, in due course, the Margaret River Hospital, the town's first publicly funded, and for many years its most substantial, building, would be built at the Upper Margaret. The Higgins establishment, which included stables to accommodate the mail coach horses, had been built on the south bank of the river and this then became the main business centre. When the railway finally arrived in late 1924, the station would be built to the south of this townsite.

In the preceding decade, the extension of the railway was one of the main issues that concerned the Margaret River Progress Association.[83] Members saw improved communication as the key to further development and to arresting population decline. The European population of the area began to increase only when the Margaret River district was selected to receive English migrants, returned soldiers and some Australian would-be farmers under what became known as the Group Settlement Scheme. It was this influx of newcomers which would lead to the demand for a resident medical officer and for a small hospital to be built in the townsite.

It was perhaps an irony that while the white settler population was decreasing, the timber industry and the land clearing already undertaken were also making the area around the Wooditjup Bilya a less hospitable environment for the Wadandi people. They had been able to keep healthy without doctors or a hospital by living with Country, but this way of life was no longer an option in an environment completely altered by European settlers. While it was often said in later years that Aboriginal people did not live in the Margaret River district because it was 'taboo', Zac Webb refutes this suggestion, pointing out that:

> It got to a point where because the land had been cleared, and deforested, there was no life there. So there's no culture there. The culture exists, but if there's no peppermint tree, then there's no possum. If there's no possum, then there's no cicadas. There are no insects, there are no flowers upon the tree, the pollinators don't come. So it's breaking down a whole environmental process, basically. And so old people would say, 'well, that's bad land. So why would we go there?' Because when you come to an open paddock, there is no medicine, no bush food. You can't sing about a possum or a tree or an insect when they don't exist there anymore.[84]

There are other reasons why, in the twentieth century, the original inhabitants were no longer prominent in this landscape. Politicians and interest groups viewed Indigenous populations as a doomed race, fated to die out in the face of modernisation and dispossession. Traditional boundaries and barriers had been broken down through intermarriage with Europeans, especially in the south-west of WA, where by the end of the nineteenth century most individuals classified as Aboriginal people were also descended from settlers, creating a population with both Aboriginal and European heritage. Many Europeans now thought that the aim should be to 'breed out' that Aboriginality, as historian Anna Haebich suggests:

> At the turn of the century ideas of race-mixing led to assumptions about all sorts of terrible consequences. Particularly it was thought that the offspring would inherit the worst of both sides, that you would be left with an intermediate race of people who fitted with neither the parents, the black mother nor the white father. So the question was: what would be the future of these people in what was to be basically a White Australia?[85]

One of the first pieces of legislation passed by the new Commonwealth Government was the *Immigration Restriction Act 1901*, which aimed to limit non-British migration but also formally ushered in the White Australia Policy with all its connotations of white supremacy.[86] Aboriginal people did not fit into this 'white world'.

For its part, the Western Australian Government saw its duty as one of benign benevolence, which aimed to make the passing of Aboriginal people less painful, relieve the misery of the old and indigent, and either put the able-bodied to work, or leave them to fend for themselves, until the colonisers required their land and labour.[87]

In 1897, the Western Australian Parliament passed legislation which supposedly had as its intent 'the better protection of the Aboriginal race of Western Australia'.[88] This Act was superseded by the now infamous *Aborigines Act 1905*, which sought to regulate the lives of all Indigenous people who were deemed to come within the broad ambit set out in section 3:

> Every person who is—
>
> (a.) an aboriginal inhabitant of Australia ; or
>
> (b.) a half-caste who lives with an aboriginal as wife or husband; or
>
> (c.) a half-caste who, otherwise than as wife or husband, habitually lives or associates with aborigines; or
>
> (d.) a half-caste child whose age apparently does not exceed sixteen years,
>
> shall be deemed an aboriginal within the meaning of this Act, and of every Act passed before or after this Act, unless the contrary is expressed.
>
> In this section the term half-caste includes any person born of an aboriginal parent on either side, and the child of any such person.[89]

This legislation now ruled the lives of anyone deemed to be Aboriginal within this definition. It specified where a person could live, who they could marry and how they could be employed. Furthermore, the employment of every person deemed to be 'Aboriginal' within this definition was to be subject to section 17 of this legislation.

> 17. It shall not be lawful to employ any aboriginal, or a male half-caste under the age of fourteen years, or a female half-caste, except under permit or permit and agreement.[90]

It would become impossible now for settlers like the Bussells to continue to employ anyone subject to this legislation without the involvement and approval of the Chief Protector of Aborigines.

Henry Prinsep was the first occupant of this office. Prinsep had married Josephine, the youngest daughter of Alfred's older brother, John Garrett Bussell. Alfred and Ellen Bussell's second-eldest daughter, Edith, lived at Ellensbrook, and with Prinsep's support, ran a 'farm school' for young 'natives' and 'half-castes.'

> who cannot for some reason be lodged in other recognised institutions. They are taught reading and writing – indoor work for girls, sums and milking, vegetable gardening and all small farm industries so as to become useful farm hands, both male and female, in a practical manner and such as in vogue in country districts. The children are encouraged to bathe frequently. They spend every Sunday on the sea beach and have plenty of milk and vegetables and meat food.[91]

Edith Bussell's 'school' operated between 1899 and 1917 and catered mainly for mixed-race children. Projects such as this were much favoured by Prinsep, and no doubt by Edith, who obtained government funding as well as a free source of labour. Children were sent to the farm school from all over the state – another factor in breaking down traditional connections to Country. Some of the children sent from the north of the state to Ellensbrook never returned to their traditional land.

Edith Bussell at Ellensbrook. Courtesy David Jenkins.

The impact of the *Aborigines Act 1905* on First Nations peoples was summarised by historian Lois Tilbrook as having:

> A singularly negative and embittering effect on relationships between Aboriginal people and others in the south-western part of Western Australia because people classified as Aboriginal were subject to legal and consequent social disabilities and disadvantages. People whose lifestyle was indistinguishable from that of the general society were now brought under this Act and severely limited in their freedom of choice, movement and opportunity. From being regarded as 'ordinary citizens', they were suddenly made to feel different and apart and had to face the fact that they were seen in law as belonging to a rejected section of Australian society.[92]

And, as playwright Jack Davis explained, there was always the fear of being sent away from traditional Country to a government institution, such as that at Moore River, which was designed to separate people of Aboriginal descent from the 'white' population: 'A magistrate only had to sign a piece of paper and say "you are going to Moore River" and people would be sent there accordingly and hundreds of people were uprooted like this and sent there'.[93]

The legislation directly affected south-west Wadandi families who sought to remain on their traditional Country by working for the newcomers. George Webb was mainly employed on potato farms at Marybrook, west of Busselton, and as his grandson Zac explained, the family was able to evade the 'Welfare', the government department tasked with removing children from their families to institutions such as Moore River or, closer to home, Roelands Mission, north of Bunbury.

> We had to work with a lot of the farmers at the time. So my grandmothers and grandfathers and father and everything, they would work with lots of the local farmers. But when the spud picking dried up, and there was no work, down here, grandmother Vilma's father, Jimmy Gillespie, would load them all up on this old horse and cart and they would make their way to places like Toodyay. It was a

way that her father kept them one step ahead of the authorities so that they could never be taken away.[94]

Families such as the Webbs were careful not to advertise their Aboriginal heritage. But Tom Doyle, whose family came to Margaret River as group settlers in 1922, knew Indigenous people who continued to live around Margaret River, including some who had originally been sent to Edith Bussell's farm school.

> They'd come and have a chat with anybody; there was no such thing as drink problems with them; they were citizens just the same as everyone else and mixed with everyone. Some people, of course, didn't bother about them but by and large they were accepted as members of the community and that's how they carried on their living. They did quite a bit in the way of kangaroo hunting and they sold skins. They just made a living and that was it.[95]

Despite the need to keep quiet about his Aboriginal heritage and to earn a living by digging potatoes for 'white' farmers, George Webb kept his Wadandi culture alive for his son Wayne and grandson Zac. Later in life:

> George got into the school systems and the Education Department and started running cultural things, and it's just picked up since then, so we've just carried that torch, really, and kept on carrying it through school.[96]

Tom Doyle was also friendly with Fred Isaacs, a son of Sam Isaacs, who continued to live in Margaret River over a long lifetime.

> I always remember, he came along to our place one time, discussing some of his business which he used to do with my dad. We were very friendly together. And he explained the fact that on any such things as income tax or anything like that he always referred to his nationality as Aboriginal.[97]

Fred performed many essential jobs in the town. In 1926 he was granted permission to place a pump on the Margaret River and for

Sam Isaacs and son Fred 1917. MR&DHS.

many years carted water when rainwater tanks, including those at the hospital, ran dry, as they did in late summer. He was employed by the Augusta-Margaret River Road Board (later Shire), clearing and constructing roads, digging graves at the cemetery (as Keith McLeod remembers), issuing dog licences and managing the dog pound as well as caretaking the Gloucester Park sportsground – all jobs needed for the new economy to function.[98] In 1936 Fred Isaacs sold the land he had inherited from his father, Sam, and built a house in town. In 2002, when that building was in danger of demolition, it was moved to the Old Hospital Heritage Precinct in recognition of the important part that the Isaacs family had played in the early European history of the Margaret River district.

For much of the twentieth century, moving and preserving the house of a Wadandi man, a descendant of the First Australians, would have been unthinkable. When Athole Stewart (1906–1958), a great-grandson of Alfred and Ellen Bussell, wrote a somewhat romanticised account of their story, he characterised 'this green corner' as an empty land.

SETTLEMENT, STRUGGLE AND SUCCESS

> While wars rolled over Europe the green corner languished, Wallcliffe with it. Men saw the land was empty. Hastily they brought others from England to fill the green void, settling strangers in groups, bidding them to build a new life. But the forest treated them harshly, as though resentful of past scars. It wrapped its foliage round them, tripped their feet with its thickets, baffled them with its immensity and sent away all but the most resolute.[99]

But 'this green corner' had never been empty. Alfred and Ellen Bussell had been able to forge their new life along the Margaret River only with help from the long-term inhabitants, and traditional custodians of the land, the Wadandi people. The Bussell children had learned the local language and listened to the traditional stories handed down through generations of First Australians. These are stories which Jack Bussell, his youngest sister Filomena Terry, and his niece Deborah Buller-Murphy, daughter of Grace Bussell (famous for her role in rescuing passengers from the wreck of the *Georgette*), recorded for later generations of European settlers.[100] Yet living in this green corner would still be only 'for the most resolute' of the group settlers, who began to arrive in the early 1920s.

Margaret River: the Rivermouth. Courtesy Scott Baxter, Gralyn winery.

Chapter Two

Endeavor Expedite!

Following the collapse of the timber industry around Karridale, the population of the area covered by the then Augusta Road Board decreased from 446 in 1911 to 200 in 1921.[1] This would have included not only European settlers but also 'those people of Aboriginal descent who were accessible to ordinary enumeration procedures, and included what were termed "half-castes"'.[2] It is likely therefore that some Wadandi people, particularly those such as the Isaacs family, who worked for white settlers in the area, were counted in this assessment. However, little more than a year after this census, Harold Crofts, secretary of the Margaret River Progress Association, wrote to the Premier, the Hon. Sir James Mitchell, to draw attention to the sudden population increase and the resulting need for both a doctor and a hospital in the still small town of Margaret River.

> My association has instructed me to bring the following before your notice. Between Busselton and Augusta, owing to the Group Settlement there has been an increase of about 1000 souls in the

population. There is one doctor in Busselton only. It is impossible for him to attend to this great increase and we think there is room for a doctor to be stationed at the Margaret which is a very central spot.[3]

This population expansion followed the decision to make the area one of four regions in the south-west within which Western Australia's Group Settlement Scheme would operate. The first groups were established in the Margaret River district in 1921 and the scheme deliberately encouraged young men with wives of child-bearing age to apply.

Group settlement was one of several ultimately unsuccessful Australian migration and land settlement plans developed in the 1920s. It was supported by Australian state and federal governments as well as by the British Government. All these schemes assumed that sturdy and loyal citizens of the British Empire would create prosperous farming communities within this seemingly empty virgin land.[4] As historian Geoffrey Bolton commented:

> It looked like a likely coming together of two different needs, Britain had been at war with Germany in the First World War and politicians like Lloyd George had promised the servicemen a land fit for heroes to live in.[5]

Britain itself, with high levels of postwar unemployment, was unable to make good on that promise but Australia seemed to be in a good position to do so.

> Western Australia felt itself to need more people and more migrants, and had plenty of land. And Western Australian politicians like Sir James Mitchell and Sir Hal Colebatch saw the two as fitting together beautifully. They had already had the experience of opening the State's wheatlands and they saw the south-west as the place where dairy produce could come from. Western Australia, at that time, was still importing dairy produce from Victoria and everyone thought that this was scandalous in a place with such potential.
>
> There was also a common belief that because the south-west supported very tall timber that it would also grow long grass and cattle

would all get fat. So, after the war, the West Australian Government stepped forward with great enthusiasm to offer itself as a place where the Empire's settlement schemes could take place. Mitchell made his one and only trip overseas in 1922 to finalise the details of the scheme and he was received with great enthusiasm by British politicians and newspaper editors. Western Australia seemed like the promised land.[6]

While one of the areas selected for group settlement was around Busselton and southwards to just north of Augusta, the others were the district known as the Peel Estate, inland from Rockingham, land between Manjimup and Northcliffe, and country west of Denmark.[7]

The first ship bringing 823 British migrants arrived in Fremantle in January 1921 and in 1923, 10,000 new group settlers disembarked.[8] New arrivals were often conveyed straight to the south-west and put to work clearing the dense bush. But some newcomers were left to find their own way to their assigned group. Tom Doyle, son of a group settler, recalled meeting a stranger on the road.

> One Friday afternoon we were coming down the road and we got to the Rosa Brook turn-off and there was a chap sitting down on a log. He was eating a bit of a snack, probably a tin of bully beef and done up very flashily, Charlie Chaplin moustache, one thing and another, and anyhow, my dad pulled up and asked him what he was doing there and he said, 'I'm going out Group Twenty-two'.

This was at Rosa Brook, about thirteen kilometres or nine miles from the 'turn-off'.

> It was in June and it was pretty wet weather. And dad said, 'How did you get here?' Oh, the truck had just dumped him off there and told him he could make his way out to his group. My dad said, 'Have you had any experience in the bush?'
>
> He was from London and he'd got off the ship from England the day before, spent one night in the immigrants' home, got on the train, was sent to Busselton, got on the truck, and there they left him to make his own way, about ten miles through a rough bush track.

My dad was horrified at this and he gave him a bit of advice…He said…get on your way along that bush track, and if you get off the track and don't know where you are, you get alongside of a jarrah tree, get bark off the lee side, and roll it up. And he explained how to get some dry wood. 'Have you got some matches?' Yes, he smoked cigarettes, so he had some matches and so dad explained how to light a fire and said, 'Whatever you do, don't start wandering around in the bush'. There was nothing there for miles and miles around.[9]

Tom thinks the man must have reached his destination safely as there was no word of a new arrival being lost in the bush.

In 1923, Tom Cleave, a young government surveyor, was sent from Perth to map out roads that would service the new settlements. He had plenty of opportunity to observe the newcomers and their situation.

The Doyle family (young Tom at left of picture) at Bassendean just prior to going on Group 12. Courtesy State Library of Western Australia 3847B/2.

ENDEAVOR EXPEDITE!

We saw a lot of the group settlers. They were all pommies from the cities of England. Terrible! They were dumped down there in their bell tents to start with and subsequently in tin huts which were erected in settlements around a well.

Oh, I was sorry for them, particularly the women who had to live under these primitive conditions. The idea was to fully clear five acres and to partly clear, I think, fifteen or twenty acres on each of the farms and then to allocate the farms to the various settlers with probably some allowance sufficient to buy sheets of iron and so on so they could erect their home.

As Cleave observed, many of the newcomers were city dwellers.

They were quite unused to bush life. In summertime down there, when the bush was tinder dry, it would catch alight without any provocation at all. These people would use a lot of kerosene to light

A group settler's tin hut. Courtesy State Library of Western Australia 005130D.

the fire in their stove. They'd put the dried bramble and stuff in them but they still used kerosene. And they were doing clearing with gelignite. They'd bore holes in a tree perhaps six inches, a sapling six inches which could be knocked over with about two or three hits of a sharp axe. They'd drill a hole in it and put a charge of gelignite into it. They were quite unrealistic and stupid. Still they were here.[10]

Later observers such as Agda Wyatt, wife of Margaret River's first policeman, were surprised that so many new arrivals had no farming experience and little knowledge of country life: 'You must remember that some of the groupies had probably never seen a cow and some of the 'overseers' (foremen) had no idea how to use an axe, let alone milk a cow'.[11] And as a Denmark observer recalled, one new settler told her that the only time she had seen a cow was cut up in a butcher's shop.[12]

Nevertheless, in the next ten years, a total of thirty groups were established within what is now the Shire of Augusta Margaret River before the scheme was effectively discontinued in 1930.[13]

Gelignite was used to blast timber. MR and DHS.

Initially, the government paid group settlers three pounds a week 'sustenance'. During this time, they had to work together to clear some of the land of trees and shrubs. Each group was overseen by a foreman.

> The foreman had to have expert knowledge of the country, methods of clearing, sinking of wells, preparation of pastures, cultivation of vegetable crops, fencing, drainage and a whole host of other day to day requirements of the pioneering group. For this he was paid £6 a week, double the pay of a settler on sustenance and slightly more than a man could earn on piecework if he had a good contract.[14]

The men appointed as foremen were often, like Harold Crofts and Bill Blain, other British migrants but with little farming experience. Blain had taken up land around Witchcliffe, but to make a living he had had to work 'off farm' sleeper cutting and clearing the new railway line from Busselton to Margaret River. When the Group Settlement Scheme was established, he became foreman of Group 22 at Rosa Brook.[15]

While foremen did not always possess the knowledge and skills required, they had a great deal of power as well as influence over activities. Each group was initially issued with one horse and cart and the foreman could decide how and for what purpose this conveyance could be used. In November 1923, a meeting of the Margaret River Progress Association was poorly attended and the *South-Western News* reported that:

> The reason for such a decrease in numbers was attributed to Group foremen refusing the use of group conveyances.
>
> The meeting not being representative of all groups, some important business had to be held over, and it was decided to make the December gathering one which will deal exclusively with medical and hospital affairs. Group foremen are to be asked to make conveyances available for this occasion, and it is hoped that there will be a big attendance.[16]

Settler's home near Karridale 1924. Courtesy State Library of Western Australia 005145D.

As the name implies, the group was the basic functional unit of the scheme, as Stan Dilkes, the son of a group settler, explained:

> They built a tin shack on each location which was about 200 acres and they worked as a group. They had this main camp where the men used to go out every day. They would each work without nominating which block they were going to get. They would all work together on each block and cleared what they call the 25 acres, and to this day you go onto some of these old group settlement properties and the farmer will say, 'that's the old 25 acres over there', now beautifully cleared of course.[17]

Many men had wounds or disabilities from their service in World War I. But as Philip Blond, a boy on Group 51 near Cowaramup, noted, all the would-be farmers had to do was to pass a fitness test, sign their name and board a boat.[18] The risk of sickness or death far from medical help had to be accepted. Ailments were treated with home remedies and grandma's cures. Sloan's Liniment, Zam-Buk ointment, eucalyptus oil and oil of cloves were common helpers in the medicine chest.[19] Tom Doyle, who as a teenager living with his family on Group 12 was involved in clearing work for a short time, recalled the treatment of illnesses and accidents in that environment:

> My dad was recognised a little bit as being handy in the fact that he was an ex-AMC (Australian Medical Corps) man. In his time as a medical corps chap, so he knew a little bit of first aid and he used to do a little bit of bandaging. The other great help in this respect was one of the settlers' wives, Mrs Jenkins. Mrs Jenkins was a trained nurse. And of course, if anyone was sick, (they) would generally get the help of either or both of these to look after things... Billy Chambers drank some kerosene. He was only a little nipper about three years old, so Nurse Jenkins...made up an emetic...to try to get this out. Years afterwards I found out that was the wrong thing to do but that was her idea to get it out of Billy as quickly as possible. He recovered all right.

Skin diseases were another problem:

> One of our settlers, Jack Nelligan, he got some form of erysipelas, as they diagnosed it. It was a sort of reddening of the skin, a very itchy and painful business and Arthur Chapman (the group foreman) being an old bushman he had a few very definite little things such as Bates' Salve, Elliman's Embrocation and a few things. One of his remedies was a chilli ointment...He looked at this business of Jack's and he reckoned a bit of this chilli ointment would do the trick and my old dad was just in time to stop him putting this on old Jack. He said, 'No you don't do that, you dab it with flour'. So we got a bit of calico bag and we got some flour and dabbed Jack's face up till he got over this. But these were our medical arrangements on the groups in those days.[20]

It was cases like these which led the Margaret River Progress Association to seek government support for the appointment of a doctor.

> Many incidents are happening, although not serious, but need medical attention and it means that patients have to travel many miles to get attention. We should be glad to know that some arrangements could be made to meet any emergencies that should arise.[21]

On receipt of this letter, Premier Mitchell sought advice from the government's Principal Medical Officer, Dr Everitt Atkinson, noting, perhaps with some surprise, that there appeared to be a need for a doctor in the Margaret River area. Apparently, Mitchell's enthusiasm for this scheme had not extended to planning medical services for the increased population. The reply sent to the Progress Association some two months later was not, initially, encouraging. Effectively, the message was 'help yourselves' and that the government was not prepared to assist or act unless the local community guaranteed financial support for the engagement of a doctor. Official advice was that:

> There is certainly a big increase in population in the Margaret River district consequent to group settlement but the contention of the government all along has been that these group settlers must be treated no differently from other settlers. When dealing with any proposal for assisting the settlement in a district of a medical officer we want to know what the district itself is prepared to do and generally by combining together the settlers raise a guarantee of £300 or £400 per annum.[22]

The Colonial Secretary replied to the Progress Association suggesting that, in addition to requiring the settlers to raise an annual sum for both doctor and hospital, a medical fund should be established with the requirement that each family contribute one shilling per week. Of that shilling, the doctor would receive seven pence, the hospital four pence for treatment and medicine, while the twelfth penny would be provided to the doctor for transport costs. All subscribers to the scheme would then be entitled to medical treatment for themselves and their families.[23]

On Sunday 10 December 1922, the Margaret River Progress Association held a 'meeting of considerable importance' at which the Colonial Secretary's letter was discussed and it was agreed that a copy should be sent to all groups in the district for discussion, and that each should report to the next meeting.[24] It was also decided that the various group associations should affiliate with the existing Progress Association, which would henceforth be known as the Margaret River and Districts Progress Association.[25] The inclusion of the term 'districts' recognised that new arrivals were placed in small communities, each housing about 20 families, and often creating new localities such as Rosa Brook and Forest Grove. These settlements, and particularly schools, were known initially by their group number. For example, Group 85 was in the area later known as Osmington.[26]

The Progress Association replied to the Colonial Secretary's proposal with some confidence. They thought that the formation of a medical fund might be possible.[27] Most groupies were still reliant on the State Government's weekly three pounds 'sustenance pay'. The Colonial Secretary, who was obviously aware that it might be difficult to persuade these new arrivals to pay their one shilling a week, then suggested that this sum could be deducted from their weekly sustenance money, the inference being that payment would not be optional.[28]

The secretary of the newly branded Progress Association was now M.L. Hugall, on Group 17 at Bramley, another new locality a few kilometres north-east of the Margaret River townsite. On 5 April 1923, Hugall wrote to the Colonial Secretary noting that his association had been informed officially of a proposal to erect three hospitals in group settlement areas and thus hastened to request that one of these be erected in Margaret River. Hugall also advised that the association, presumably after consultation with the groups, could offer £500 per annum for a medical practitioner to be obtained from subscribers to the proposed medical scheme and thus the Progress Association 'would like to know if anything more is required before a doctor is sent along'.[29]

This correspondence clearly caused some surprise when it reached the Principal Medical Officer. Dr Atkinson noted that this was the first he had heard of plans to erect hospitals in group settlement districts.[30] The state's Public Health Department had not planned for this influx of new settlers. In his reply to the Progress Association, Dr Atkinson confirmed that the government would provide a subsidy of £100 per annum, given that the Margaret River district had offered to collect £500 per annum locally. At the same time, he asked for more details on the area to be covered, the groups affected and the possibilities for the doctor to undertake private practice outside the proposed medical scheme.[31]

It is not clear how the Progress Association heard about the proposal for new hospitals in group settlement areas, but one of the people now working on the new settlers' behalf was W.G. Pickering, MLA, local member of State Parliament from 1917 to 1924 for what was then known as the Sussex electoral district (later Vasse) and which included the towns of Busselton and Margaret River. When Pickering visited Margaret River to open the new District Hall on Saturday 14 April 1923, he was asked about the provision of a doctor and hospital for the area. Pickering quickly took up this cause and met the Colonial Secretary on 9 May 1923. Correspondence between the department and Pickering then confirmed that the government would subsidise a medical officer's salary and that the town would get its hospital. The hospital proposal, as outlined to Pickering, was modest in scale:

> In the first place it is not considered that a large institution is necessary, but a small building with minimum accommodation for a nurse and maid. One small male ward and one small female ward plus a small maternity ward, should meet requirements and this accommodation protected by verandahs, could no doubt be put up at a reasonable figure.[32]

This proposal established a pattern which would continue throughout the sixty-six years of the hospital's operation: accommodation insufficient to meet local requirements and additions and extensions delayed or inadequate for community need.

The Colonial Secretary also noted that it would be essential for the appointment of a doctor to be guaranteed before 'any attempt is made to build a hospital'.[33] In any event, it seems that the Progress Association was preparing to recruit a doctor. The local newspaper reported on a meeting of the association in August:

> Vile roads, mud, and water did not stop delegates from almost every group in the district attending a meeting of the District Progress Association on Sunday last. One of the most important matters down for discussion was that of medical officer and hospital, and by invitation Dr Rigby and Mr Geo. Cross, of Busselton, were present.
>
> A proposal to secure the services of a resident medical man was discussed from all angles, and it was ultimately resolved to ask Dr Rigby to accept the position. This Dr Rigby agreed to do under certain conditions.[34]

It would seem likely that Dr Rigby's appointment had been decided before the meeting and that he was 'waiting in the wings' since only three days later secretary Hugall advised the Colonial Secretary that arrangements had been made 'for a Doctor Rigby to transfer his practice to Margaret River'.[35] In further correspondence Hugall officially advised the Public Health Department that Rigby had commenced practice at Margaret River on Tuesday 14 August and that the doctor would be made aware that he needed to apply to the department for appointment as the local medical officer. This would enable the government to pay the agreed subsidy.

When Dr Rigby took up this appointment, he was already very experienced, having practised in the coal-mining town of Collie since the turn of the century. Rigby had been the local doctor there during the 1919 Spanish flu pandemic and had been commended by the state's Principal Medical Officer for his work. He had left Collie in October 1920 and moved to Perth after, it would seem, a disagreement with the locally powerful Miners Union.[36] So by 1923

Rigby was clearly looking for another position in the state's southwest. He was to practise in Margaret River for almost ten years.³⁷

The local community found that Dr Rigby was more than just a doctor. He entered fully into the life of the district. In Collie he had also been the town's mayor for some years.³⁸ In Margaret River he became a member of the Augusta-Margaret River Road Board and a justice of the peace. He played chess and involved himself in the sporting life of the town, including cricket matches.

BIG CRICKET
MATCH AT MARGARET
DR RIGBY VANQUISHED

> A match, reminiscent of the days when Dr Grace faced all comers, was played at Margaret River on Wednesday, when a controversy as to the respective merits of Dr W.H. Rigby and Mr T. Moloney as cricketers resulted in a private match being held between these two gentlemen for £5 a side…Mr Moloney was many years ago prominent in New South Wales cricket, while Dr Rigby, in his younger days, was no mean exponent of the national pastime.³⁹

Such pleasant events were well into the future when Rigby arrived in Margaret River in August 1923. At that time there was no surgery, no house and, of course, no hospital. Tom Doyle recalls that the doctor initially set up his surgery in a little room at the front of the local hall. This served the purpose until his house and surgery were built near the corner of what is now Bussell Highway and Wallcliffe Road.⁴⁰ These premises remained the residence and surgery for successive doctors for many years.

The doctor also had to create his own medicines. As one settler observed:

> Old Dr Rigby used to mix his own potions up in a little surgery-cum-chemist shop he had on part of the verandah of the old hall on

Dr William Rigby – first doctor in Margaret River.
Courtesy Coalfields Museum Collie.

certain days of the week. On the other days of the week, he'd see you in the passage of his house.[41]

As Tom Doyle recalled, there was no dentist so the doctor also had to pull teeth.

Jack Nilsson, the groupie foreman of Group 63, was telling me how he had a chap on the group and they were grubbing away on one block and this chap he was in horrible pain with toothache. He said, 'We'll fix that. I know it's Dr Rigby's day down at Karridale today.' So, they were working fairly close to the road and as soon as they heard this car coming, they ran out onto the road and pulled the old doctor up and he said, 'Look,' he said, 'I've got a chap with a toothache'. 'Righto,' he said. So he sat him down on the mudguard of his car and there and then he took the tooth out and that was it.[42]

Myra Willmott (then Myra Stuchbury) was one of the first Margaret River nurses to work with Dr Rigby. She recalled that his main antiseptics were kerosene and methylated spirits and she found his methods less than hygienic in many ways.[43] Enid Garstone came to Margaret River in 1928 and recalled seeing Dr Rigby, who then owned one of the few cars in the district:

> I remember he used to drive up to the hospital in this car, and he always had his two Pomeranian dogs with him. The dogs used to jump out of the car and rush into the hospital, wherever they pleased and he'd follow them in, never bothering about washing his hands, and just come along and have a look at people. He really was quite a character.[44]

And according to Tom Doyle:

> It was understood on the side that he (Dr Rigby) came to Margaret River because there was no pub there and so he could handle things a little bit easier that way. He was quite a whisky addict. Some of the girls that worked at the hospital told me that he was very difficult to work with on account of this weakness, if one could call it such. But at the same time, he could be recognised also on the other hand as a mighty one of what we call the GP of which there are very few today... He'd think nothing of getting on his horse and riding twenty miles to go and see someone in that way.[45]

Margaret River could have fared worse. In a district where communities were linked only by 'vile roads', Rigby was always willing to go south to Kudardup and Karridale. Valerie Everett, in her account of her parents' experience on the group settlements, recounts the story of George Wall, the nine-year-old son of a group settler. When George became sick with abdominal pains, the Busselton doctor refused to come out unless he was paid sixty pounds on arrival. Obviously, no group settler had that kind of money. In contrast Dr Rigby went out to the settler's home and performed an appendectomy on Wall's kitchen table and it was a case of 'you pay me when you can'.[46] Tom Doyle also remembered

Dr Rigby as 'a clever old-time doctor who would tackle any job without asking for prior payment'. While living on Group 12, the Doyles had witnessed an episode where a Busselton doctor had refused to visit a settler with silicosis until he was guaranteed a fee of five pounds to attend. This was at a time when the groupies were receiving three pounds a week in sustenance money.[47]

So, by the end of 1923 Margaret River had a resident doctor, but there was still no hospital, while roads in the 1920s were little more than muddy tracks.

A newspaper report in October 1923 described some of the challenges faced by Dr Rigby.

> The urgency for repairs to our roads and the establishment of a hospital at Margaret River was instanced a day or two ago by the experience of Dr Rigby. To attend a serious case, the Doctor travelled three times to Group 4 [at Karridale], and on each occasion the motor car got 'bogged'. On one trip he was held up for an hour and a half in the middle of the night. Such occurrences are annoying enough to the casual traveller, but when it happens to a doctor on a life or death errand, it becomes a very serious matter...The absence of hospital accommodation and a trained nurse necessitated an operation in a Group hut, with a settler and a settler's wife as assistants.[48]

Finally, the Public Health Department began to take seriously the government's responsibility for providing hospitals in group settlement areas and Dr Atkinson, the Principal Medical Officer, seemingly realised that the newcomers were unable to provide funding for a hospital as well as for a doctor. On 26 September 1923 he advised the Minister for Public Health that:

> With reference to an interview that Mr Pickering had with you in regard to a hospital at Margaret River, you will remember that the question was raised of the £ for £ subsidy being provided. Most of the people of this area are group settlers and I fear it is out of the question

> to evolve any scheme whereby such an amount of money as would be necessary could be provided locally, while a joint and several guarantee for the payment of any such money would be impossible to obtain.
>
> I would recommend therefore, that the Government erect the hospital and if necessary, subsidise the nurse to the extent of £50 per annum, provided the local people by subscription equip the hospital and maintain it.
>
> I think a suitable building can be constructed for about £800 to £1000, and I am at present conferring with the Principal Architect in regard for it. One plan has been prepared but certain alterations, with a reduction of cost in view, has necessitated preparation of another plan.[49]

This memorandum represented a significant departure from the previous self-help policy and as a result the Margaret River Hospital became the first publicly funded building in the town. By 31 October 1923 final plans had been prepared for what the government referred to as the 'Cottage Hospital for Margaret River', but clerical staff in Perth were unclear as to whether a site had been selected. On 8 November, the Principal Medical Officer telegraphed Dr Rigby: 'GLAD IF YOU WILL ASSIST PUBLIC WORKS OFFICER IN SELECTION SITE FOR HOSPITAL'.[50] Rigby immediately replied by telegram: 'HOSPITAL SITE QUITE SATISFACTORY USE ALL ENDEAVOR EXPEDITE BUILDING URGENTLY WANTED RIGBY'.[51]

Confusion and disputes between government departments in Perth were already alive and well. On 23 November, the Surveyor General wrote to the Under Secretary for Lands stating that the matter of selecting a suitable site had been dealt with and while not confirming that the location had been finalised, complained about interference in what the Surveyor General saw as his domain.

> The matter was already being dealt with by this Department. As you will see by this file, instructions were issued to Mr Senior Staff Surveyor Hicks to select a suitable site after consultation with the interested parties and also instructions if necessary for a block to be marked. It is wrong for another branch of this Department to

write separately to the Public Works Department suggesting the Department should send an officer to report on this site for it naturally causes complications and interferes with action that has already been taken. I think some steps should be taken to put a stop to this practice.[52]

A few days later, on 29 November, despite his displeasure and indignation, the Surveyor General was able to advise the Under Secretary for Lands that the site had been selected and that it was on the main road and close to the proposed railway siding.[53] In fact, it was neither. Then, on 3 June 1924, a week after the hospital opened, the Under Secretary for Lands issued a minute stating that Lot 33 in the Margaret River township had been approved by the Governor in Executive Council as reserved as the hospital site.[54]

The hospital itself was built at the northern end of a ten-acre hospital reserve. Most of this land remained undeveloped bushland for some sixty years, when the reserve was also able to accommodate a new hospital, aged-persons accommodation (Mirrambeena) and premises for Silver Chain.

Correspondence in November 1923 between the various parties, including the Department of Public Works, the principal architect and the principal medical officer in Perth, about progress towards completing the building, suggests that someone, probably W.G. Pickering, MLA, was making waves behind the scenes as the completion of the hospital was described as a matter of extreme urgency 'due to the number of maternity cases coming up'.[55]

All the usual reasons for delays in construction were soon apparent: shortage of materials, lack of transport, site not finalised and, of course, an expected cost overrun – in this case £100, which was 10 per cent of the overall cost. The additional expenditure was duly approved by the Premier, Sir James Mitchell.[56]

While it is not apparent that the Premier inspected the hospital site himself, he did visit Margaret River in December 1923, with the *South-Western News* reporting on the visit in an article headed: 'The Father of the Groups * Sir James Mitchell *Amongst the Settlers* Enthusiastic Reception'. Dr Rigby moved a vote of thanks to the

Premier.[57] No doubt he would have spoken to Sir James about the new hospital. But there would have been little to view because when the department secretary, F.J. Huelin, visited the location the following month, he reported that:

> Yesterday, when visiting the site, which is in a fine position, central and on high ground, we found that all the scantling had been delivered but no clearing had been commenced. The heap of scantling was the only sign of the intended hospital…The hospital is urgently needed, Dr Rigby stating that he knows of quite 100 maternity cases due in the next three months, among the settlers around Margaret and southwards thereof.[58]

Rigby also advised Huelin that the medical scheme had about 260 members and that this number was likely to increase to at least 300 by the time the hospital opened.[59] Huelin's memorandum indicated that this was all the local support that the hospital would be likely to receive and that it would be economical for his department to take direct responsibility for administration, 'as we

Sir James Mitchell and settlers, 1925. Courtesy State Library of Western Australia 005129D.

can carry on with less expense in various ways'.[60] Hospital staff and the wider Margaret River community were to become very familiar with the efforts of the authorities in Perth to minimise expenditure on their hospital.

Initially, the Progress Association was given the option of control by a local committee or by the department. The correspondence explained that if a local committee controlled the hospital there would be no government help except for an agreed subsidy. With departmental control the government would accept financial and administrative responsibility, collecting all fees that can 'reasonably be secured from patients who have been treated'.[61] Not surprisingly, the Progress Association replied that Dr Rigby thought that departmental management would be advisable and this became the agreed funding and management model. Local secretary Hugall then asked a personal question:

> Could you let me know what clerical duties are necessary in a hospital such as the one being built at Margaret River. Could they be performed during evenings and weekends? I hold first class references and if there is anything doing, I would put in an application.[62]

Hugall evidently realised that life as a group settler was not going to reap the financial rewards touted by the scheme's promoters.

Work on the hospital must have then progressed quickly because, by 1 March 1924, the department was predicting that the building would be finished within a fortnight. There was still a question as to whether a morgue was needed and, if one was built, whether it could also be used to house an orderly. The morgue was constructed but it was later moved from its original position behind the main hospital building when the Margaret Cecil Rest House was built in 1929.[63] The morgue remained in use, as constructed, until 1990. It was then known by hospital staff as the 'cream shed' as its structure was identical to the small buildings erected at farm gates to house cans for pick-up by the cream carrier.[64] When the hospital became the Community Centre, the old morgue became the gardener's shed.

Hospital morgue built 1924, before restoration. MRCC.

Original Hospital Admissions Book and record of surgeries performed. Courtesy Margaret River Hospital.

On 24 May 1924, newly appointed Matron Margaret Ward advised secretary Huelin that she expected the opening to be imminent: 'It was my intention to have the hospital open at the beginning of the week but owing to the carpenters and painters not yet finished, work has been delayed. Hope to be open by Wednesday 28inst.'[65]

The hospital opened one day earlier, on Tuesday 27 May 1924. The first patient, described as a butcher, was admitted for a poisoned hand. He spent fourteen days in the hospital and was not discharged until 10 June.[66] Meanwhile, the first baby was born in the hospital on Saturday 31 May. The mother was the wife of a settler on Group 63, Rapid Landing. She was discharged in mid-June.[67]

Many aspects of the hospital were unsatisfactory. When the Minister for Lands and Migration, W.C. Angwin, visited the hospital on 8 June 1924, he listed a variety of problems:

1. There is no doubt that the hospital is too small.

2. The Centre Room should have the doors opening on verandahs placed in the corner of the room instead of centre as at present as beds are now across such doors ...

3. There is an uncovered well about 14 or 15 Feet from hospital. If same was on a Group area in similar conditions there would be hell to pay by health officials. The matron uses disinfectants but I must admit it is disgraceful.

4. There is necessity to erect nurses' quarters and for the matron. Then the room now used by the matron could be used for hospital purposes.

5. I note that the tank stand was built too high and to get over the difficulty between the eaves of the roof and tank stand there was cut out a portion of the top of the tank. The tanks are also badly leaking in almost every joint.

W.C. Angwin, Minister for Lands.

I am also of the opinion that the dog box used as an office by matron on the verandah might be lined.[68]

Both Matron Ward and Dr Rigby followed up with complaints to the department in Perth. The matron advised that the promised extra room was unfinished, that the hospital would have no water for summer if the leaking tanks were not fixed, and that, overall, a lot of the building work was unsatisfactory.[69]

In 1924, new mothers generally spent several weeks in hospital before they could return to their primitive homes in the bush. Moreover, injuries such as the first patient's poisoned hand took some time to treat in this pre-antibiotic age. So for Dr Rigby the most serious problem was the new hospital's almost immediate overcrowding. He reported that the population was still increasing with new groups being established. Three timber mills were in operation and the imminent opening of the Margaret River railway was likely to result in an influx of railway employees.[70] As Dr Rigby pointed out, overall, the total population of the area could soon increase to two thousand.[71]

By August, Rigby had resorted to telegraphing the Principal Medical Officer: 'Hospital over-crowded kindly hurry building or could you send large goldfield tent relieve temporary'.[72] When the department replied that the tent option was not practical,[73] the frustrated doctor wrote directly to the Hon. Philip Collier MLA, who had replaced Sir James Mitchell as Premier in April 1924.[74] In that correspondence Rigby asked the new Premier: 'How can we expect competent nurses to come when they have one bedroom between them and their only sitting room is the kitchen?'[75]

The department in Perth was beginning to realise that mistakes had been made in planning the Margaret River Hospital. Dr Rigby wrote to the Principal Medical Officer again on 25 August 1924 stating that he had three serious accident cases requiring surgery and that 'the want of an operating room has been felt seriously'.[76] There was also a recognition that the hospital was indeed too small and 'not fit for purpose'. Secretary Huelin admitted that the decision to build the hospital had been made 'rather hurriedly' and that 'development in the area had been greater than anticipated'. Additional groups had been established and there were new timber mills. As a result there was serious overcrowding in the hospital.[77]

On 18 September 1924, Dr Rigby was advised that the government had approved building extensions including quarters for matron and nurses. There was also provision for a surgery and an operating theatre.[78] The approval was for expenditure of £925, only marginally less than the original cost of building the hospital. Secretary Huelin noted that the principal architect had explained that the building costs were high 'because conditions of work in a relatively remote place like this are very uncertain'.[79] The reality of life in the state's south-west was now becoming apparent to the bureaucrats in Perth, including Huelin.

> At a place like Margaret River, it must be remembered that there is no sanitary service, and no milk supply. We must attend to our own pans, and may have to consider keeping our own cow. These issues affect that of whether a full time orderly is to be maintained.[80]

No sanitary service and no milk supply — an irony given the aims of the Group Settlement Scheme. But now Margaret River did have a doctor and a publicly funded hospital.

Margaret River District Hospital *circa* 1924. MR&DHS.

Chapter Three

A Primitive Wooden Structure

Overcrowding at the new hospital would continue at least until the required and hastily approved extensions were completed. In October 1924, Matron Ward advised the Secretary of the Public Health Department that:

> At present there are 15 pts in hospital and 3 more expected tomorrow making 8 maternity cases and with the 3 coming tomorrow will make 11. Then there are 7 general cases. I do not know how I am going to accommodate them all as there is not even verandah space now. I will continue to be busy as there are 8 maternity cases booked for November.[1]

Myra Willmott, then Sister Stuchbury, experienced this situation firsthand:

> When I came to Margaret River in 1924, the hospital was just a skeleton hospital really; there were no linings, no nurse's quarters, just a kitchen and dining room for the hospital and where the nurses had their meals.

> The hospital was built to accommodate six women, six males and midwifery. But we exceeded that number by far. When they came, they were put on the verandahs, inside the wards and outside, wherever there was a space; we couldn't worry if there was a man next to a woman or a mother and son in the one bed. We used to push the beds up closer until sometimes we'd reach up to 27.[2]

Facilities of all kinds were severely limited. There was no electricity. Ted Ashton recalled that kerosene lamps were the only form of lighting: 'And it was the orderly's job to keep them filled and light them. The orderly had boots with iron heels and you could always hear him coming.'[3] Myra Willmott had to cope with these conditions every day:

> All the wards had a stove in the centre of each and we boiled the water on these for washing the patients, and all cleaning purposes. These stoves smoked like mad, too.
>
> There was one room attached to that building for the matron. She wouldn't share it with her nurses so we slept where we could. We had hurricane (kerosene) lamps for light, a part-time orderly cleaned the

The hospital in the 1920s. MR&DHS.

lanterns and chopped the wood. Every bed patient was washed in bed and they were fed in bed as there was no dining room or anywhere else to feed them. Our bathroom was a very small room, no bath just an enamel jug and basin and that was where we washed.[4]

The water supply remained problematic. The rainwater tanks leaked and their capacity was insufficient for the hospital's needs. As Ted Ashton explained, it was a case of carting water:

Old Freddie Isaacs was the only one in the area to cart water then so I think the hospital would have had to buy it from him, I remember him charging ten shillings for carting one hundred gallons of water, so that was probably what the hospital paid.[5]

But as fast as Fred Isaacs carted water from the river, the hospital used it up.[6] And for heating the water?

There was a No. 3 Metters Stove in the kitchen with a big black urn always sitting on it, heating the water. We sterilised the instruments by boiling the water on the stove, wrapping them in a towel and

First matron and nurses quarters – a group-type house, built 1924. MR&DHS.

then we put them in the oven just to sterilise the towel...As for hours worked — as long as we could keep awake. We didn't have days off. There was nowhere to go anyway. We spent most of our time off washing floors.[7]

Some inadequacies, such as the hospital's lack of a water supply, would take many years to resolve. In December 1924 Secretary Huelin of the Public Health Department wrote that because of the remoteness of Margaret River, 'we must keep our own cow to provide the milk supply, and we must sink a well to give us a water supply'.[8]

More trees had to be removed and the area fenced to enable a cow to be kept. In January 1925 the Department of Works and Trading Concerns advised the Colonial Secretary that a sum of fifteen pounds needed to be provided for the necessary trees to be 'pulled'.[9] In many cases trees which had been 'ring-barked' in order to eventually kill them were still standing.

In addition to tree removal, Matron Ward asked for two hundred cypress plants to create a hedge at the front of the hospital, because patients sleeping on the verandah had no privacy from the street in front of the building.[10] At the same time, Secretary Huelin sent rose cuttings from his own garden in Perth.[11] This rare personal and unofficial act would have been much appreciated. These would have been the very first roses planted at the hospital, a building which one hundred years later has a well-tended rose garden. No group settler would have been in a position to grow roses in 1924.

In July of that year, the local Progress Association had encountered another problem: lack of money in the medical fund which had been set up to support the doctor and the hospital: 'The unfortunate position which the Committee finds itself placed in is chiefly caused through some of the groups not paying for their membership cards'.[12] The groupies were not unwilling to pay, but they had no spare cash. In 1924 most newcomers were on the sustenance allowance from which they had to pay for every item needed for themselves and their often growing families. Not surprisingly, therefore, the parlous state of the local Medical Fund remained a problem. At the association's August meeting, it was decided to hold a series of fundraising dances, with the first to be arranged for August 16 and others to follow in September and October.[13] The *South-Western News* reported on the October dance as follows:

> The dance held at Margaret River on Saturday night in aid of the local Medical Fund was well supported, and a most enjoyable evening was spent by the large number who attended. Miss Cotton and Messrs Edwards and Morrison provided excellent music, and the thanks of the committee is extended to them for their services. Secretary Hugall advises that arrangements are already in hand for a grand dance to raise funds for the hospital comforts, the date fixed being November 22nd.[14]

While the government had left it to the groups to agitate for, and then support, both a hospital and other medical services, it paid much more attention to educational facilities. The provision of schools had the highest priority, even above housing. Education was a must, partly because there was often a leeway of several years between children leaving the United Kingdom and attending school in Australia. They needed to finish their schooling with a basic education in the three Rs: writing, arithmetic and reading.[15] The settlers were keen for their children to be able to attend school and, in some places, the land was donated by a family. Bill Blain, who had come to the district from Scotland, where education was much prized, provided the site on his homestead block for the Group 57 (Witchcliffe) school. When the school closed in 1945, his son, Edward, was not best pleased that he had to buy back this portion of his homestead block from the Education Department.[16]

Group schoolrooms were frequently the venue for dances, which provided a welcome relief from the everyday privations of life on the land. The Education Department stated that schoolrooms were to be made available to the settlers at reasonable intervals, never

North Jindong group school. Courtesy Ros Craig.

less than monthly, for dances or other recognised forms of group entertainment.[17] Ern Smith was a teacher at Bramley (Group 17) and his sister described a dance in the school there:

> Harry Lonsdale, a sleeper truck driver could play the piano and Mr Beer, a 'groupie' played the drums...Kerosene lanterns were hung around the school for lights, candles in the candlesticks on the piano, children and dogs slept on the floor and a great night's dancing was enjoyed by all. The ladies brought plates of supper and tea was made from water boiled in the copper on a stand.[18]

Groups 6 and 7 were at Nuralingup, renamed Forest Grove in 1925.[19] This school opened for business at the beginning of 1923 and eighty pupils enrolled. The head teacher was twenty-one year old John Tonkin, destined to become Premier of Western Australia almost fifty years later. His political views were largely formed by what he saw as government incompetence and indifference to conditions in the group settlements. Among his pupils, one family of four children rode on one horse nearly ten kilometres to school each

Group 6 school at Nuralingup (Forest Grove) with John Tonkin (teacher). Courtesy State Library of Western Australia 000884D.

day.[20] Young and inexperienced as he was, Tonkin gained respect from parents as he advocated for the settlers. When he headed a deputation to government, W.C. Angwin, Minister for Lands and Migration in the state's Labor government, was impressed: 'This young man knows what he is talking about. It's my first real insight into their district's problems. I'm learning more from him than I have in the first four months.'[21]

John Tonkin's skills extended to dealing with unexpected events. One afternoon as school ended, he asked two boys to clear up some litter they'd left in the school yard. 'Please Sir, Dad wants us back home. We'll be in trouble if we're late.' John told them, 'It'll take you two minutes'. They complied and then raced home. John started marking lessons on the verandah. But not for long. An angry parent arrived. 'What's all this about keeping my kids in when I need them at home?' at the same time rolling up his sleeves for a scrap. John pointed out that the verandah wasn't a good site for a fight, but just up the hill there was a clear space. As they walked up in the spring sunshine, John drew attention to the wildflowers bursting into life. They reached the top of the hill, shook hands and both went home.

A year later, when John Tonkin was due to be moved to a school in the Wheatbelt, that groupie headed a petition for the teacher to be retained in the district.[22] Tonkin was then appointed to the new Rapid Landing school just to the south of the Margaret River townsite.[23]

While Tonkin's campaigning on behalf of the group settlers was much appreciated by people in the district, the best morale boost was the official arrival in Margaret River of the railway on 7 November 1924. In practice, the railway was running south of Busselton by late 1923.[24] Philip Blond, then a six-year-old child on Group 20, remembers that on 14 December a special train gave families from Witchcliffe northwards a free ride to the Busselton Show.[25]

When the hospital had opened earlier that year, the railway connecting Margaret River with Busselton was not yet fully operational, making transport for serious medical cases to a better-equipped hospital difficult, if not impossible, as Myra Willmott described:

> I've gone out with him (Dr Rigby) to a group child very ill and he'd give them a couple of aspirin and leave them there. No room in the hospital. They should have gone to Busselton really, but no railway, just no transport.[26]

At this time, only four settlers in the area had motor vehicles.[27]

When the long-anticipated day arrived (the *South-Western News* had taken up the cause for the railway to be extended as early as 1909), a bevy of politicians made their way to Margaret River to be present when the new line would be formally opened by the Minister for Works, Alex McCallum. The *Group Settlement Chronicle* reported the official opening:

> At a signal from Mr McCallum, the engine (which someone had forgotten to decorate for the occasion) advanced slowly, and the silken bonds were broken to the accompaniment of prolonged cheering.[28]

Minister McCallum's speech covered the usual expectations of the time, namely that the Group Settlement Scheme would provide Western Australia with the dairy industry it lacked. His theme was that:

> The people of the State looked to them [the south-west] to eventually put a stop to the sending out of the State about £2,000,000 annually for food products that should be produced here. We should be a self-reliant community...The two millions being sent away should go into the settlers' pockets.[29]

Cows need grass to produce milk, but the country on which this dairy industry was to be established was not the fertile land of the politicians' expectations, even when cleared of its native vegetation. Stan Dilkes, who later worked for the Western Australian Department of Agriculture, summed up the reality of the situation:

> It was a very hard way to open up the country...Whilst these areas grew tremendous trees, from the point of view of pasture, the soils were absolutely dead poor and they would hardly support grass at all. Certainly, it had no nitrogen in the soil whatsoever which you need for grass.[30]

In an environment dominated by large trees and dense undergrowth it was generally impossible, at first, to rear and graze animals or to plant vegetable gardens.

Yet this situation opened up opportunities for some of the older, established families like the Bussells and the Willmotts, who had eked out a living by raising cattle and selling meat, butter and vegetables wherever they could. Now, as group settlers arrived, Fred Bussell and his young son Desmond started a butchering business, as Desmond's wife, Jean, later recalled:

There was nothing like that here then. Desmond and his father used to kill the beasts on the farm and take the meat around the settlements in a horse and cart. After a while they opened a shop in Margaret River, opposite where the hotel is now.[31]

Other long-term settlers saw the potential for starting new businesses. Dudley McLeod also became a butcher,[32] while Fred and Kittie Bussell grew fruit which they sold to the newcomers, a business later taken over by the Doyle family when George Doyle realised there was more money to be made from market gardening than dairying on a partly cleared group settlement block.[33] The Doyles soon moved to Margaret River and bought land along the Yalgardup Brook from Fred Bussell. Few of the new settlers had transport so delivery to their blocks was important. Tom Doyle described their vegetable and fruit delivery round, which included the Margaret River Hospital.

Harold and Tom Doyle cultivating in market garden. Courtesy State Library of Western Australia 3847B16.

> We did local trade round the townships. Went out to the group settlement areas, which were still in the camp stage, and also we went out to Pilgrim's Mill and around and about with the horse and cart. And it was the general thing, about two or three days a week to go into these various parts and that was for the sale of vegetables and of course this was quite a part of our income.[34]

In the early days of group settlement, the government called tenders for a local sawmill. One of the successful joint tenderers, J.T. Pilgrim, became the manager and thus the business was always known locally as Pilgrim's Mill. In addition to cutting sleepers for the South African and South Australian railways, the new company gained contracts to supply 248 group houses for the Busselton area and a further 97 for Denmark.[35] Many of the mill workers were young married men and their wives kept the maternity beds full. In addition, much of the work carried out at the mill involved dangerous activities. Accidents were not uncommon and mill employees provided a regular source of patients for the new hospital. The admission register for the 1920s showed accidents to be the most common reason for people being hospitalised. Most patients were injured group settlers or timber workers, including sleeper cutters, who had damaged or even chopped off a toe or a finger in their efforts to clear the thick bush.[36]

In October 1925 several mill workers were admitted with gastroenteritis. Hygiene was clearly an issue. At the same time, there were very few hospital admissions for communicable diseases, apart from the occasional case of influenza.[37]

In August 1924, Dr Rigby told Premier Philip Collier that 'we are now housing 3 accident cases from the mills, really serious surgical cases', and one of the doctor's arguments for increasing the number of hospital beds was the establishment of even more mills in the district.[38] In 1925 there were 85 mill employees plus up to one hundred sleeper cutters. By February 1928 the number of mill workers had risen to 119, while the East Witchcliffe settlement eventually included 20 family houses, quarters for single men, boarding houses, a meeting hall and a general store.[39] The vegetables supplied by the Doyles would have been in great demand!

The Doyle family also grew and sold kikuyu grass to farmers. Another local resident – and founder of the Perth Zoo, Colonel Le Souef – had introduced this grass from Africa and it proved to be useful cattle fodder and a staple grass in the area. Later group settlers were advised to purchase kikuyu plants when their ship docked in South Africa en route to Western Australia.[40]

Initially there were few cattle on the new settlements and cows were mostly kept for milk and butter. Many new arrivals could not afford to buy meat regularly from the town's new butchers and the more enterprising families supplemented their protein intake with local wildlife. Tom Doyle's family were grateful for the expertise of their foreman on Group 12.

> We were fairly well off as far as meat was concerned because Arthur Chapman being a great bushman and kangaroos being very plentiful

Colonel Ernest Le Souef at his home in Glen Ellie. Courtesy State Library of Western Australia BA1101/1/10/382.

around there at the time, Arthur would very often go and get one. And we'd get a lump of kangaroo which helped very much as far as our meat supply was concerned.

In addition to kangaroos, quokkas were an excellent source of protein.

> One of our staple diets as far as meat was concerned was the quokka. And they were just there in thousands…If we walked from our humpy and (went) down towards the creek, there'd be a shuffling and a scuffling in the bush. It was very much bracken fern country around, particularly when we crossed over the creek to get up onto the hill on the other side and there were quokkas everywhere.[41]

But not for much longer. The last quokka was seen in the Augusta-Margaret River area in the 1930s.[42]

When Tom and Enid Garstone came to Margaret River in 1928, they were better prepared than most new settlers to take on the challenge of creating productive agricultural land, having previously farmed in the Great Southern region of WA. After arriving in Margaret River, Tom initially cleared a ten-acre block and within twelve months they had grown a potato crop, and acquired four cows, two horses and a sulky. Tom also took on clearing contracts to keep them going.[43] That same year, Tom and Enid's second child was born in Margaret River Hospital. While there, and later as a nurse, Enid Garstone observed casualties among some of the non-maternity patients.

> There were lots of people coming into the hospital with toes chopped off – people from England who had never been in forests before. The casualty and operating (areas) were very crude, but it was amazing the things they did in there and the casualties they treated.

Enid also described the still very basic building that was the Margaret River Hospital in 1928.

> There was no electric light. It was a primitive wooden structure with outdoor toilets with pans. The bathroom was at the end of a corridor. The poor nurses had to walk up and down this awful verandah in

wind and rain...There were so many babies born at this time that sometimes you'd have to get off the bed because there was only one bed in the labour ward.

Enid found that the hospital's facilities were still almost as limited as they had been when the hospital first opened in 1924.

The nurses' dining room/office was very small; the kitchen was a separate building and there was a little sort of shack on the end of it where they stored things. Sometimes they'd put the babies in there of a night, which wasn't a good idea as it was terribly draughty.

The big black urn with the brass tap still stood on the wood stove and hospital food left much to be desired:

When they made porridge of a night for next morning's breakfast, they used to put it in a basin and put it down into the top of this urn – the fire was kept going all night. You could cut the porridge with a knife when it came around in the morning. Breakfast was a 'hunk' of porridge with milk and sugar and a piece of bread and butter they'd spread the night before. It was hardly edible, but if you didn't eat it you got into trouble.

Enid also observed that the hospital had to deal with a range of emergencies, many of which resulted from the new settlers' failure to understand their new and unfamiliar environment.

In those days clearing with gelignite, there were so many people badly injured and some blown to pieces. They'd put gelignite in logs and blast them up or into the trees to bring the trees down. One chap put a gelignite in a log which didn't go off, so the next day he went down with an auger and of course he put it down too far – his wife picked up what was left of him in a bucket!

In June 1926 there was a horrific accident at Forest Grove involving gelignite. The Hoult family were leaving the district and had sold the stove they had only recently purchased for heating and cooking. While farewelling her neighbour Mrs Atkins, Mrs Hoult lit the old stove not knowing that her husband had stored a bag containing two plugs of gelignite in it. The *Western Mail* reported on the incident as follows:

TRAGEDY ON GROUP 6

EXPLOSION OF GELIGNITE

THREE WOMEN KILLED

A terrible tragedy occurred at Forrest (sic) Grove, in the past known as Nuralingup. In intensity it overshadows anything that has hitherto been known in connection with group settlement, and its magnitude and sad features cast quite a gloom over the 50 contemporary groups in the Busselton-Margaret-Augusta area.

In the midst of a farewell visit of one neighbour to another, and following immediately upon the utterances of words of sincere regret at the parting and ending of almost daily meetings and companionship, three women, close friends, were suddenly hurled into eternity. A trio of broken-hearted husbands could tell little of the actual occurrence, but it is clear that the explosion which caused the deaths was caused by gelignite that had been placed in an old oven for safe keeping. The dead women are: Mrs Edith Hoult (26), wife of Arthur Hoult, group settler; Mrs Emma Hoult (60), her mother-in-law; and Mrs Ros Eleanor Atkins (37), wife of Leonard V. Atkins, group settler. Mr Hoult, sen., aged 60 years, and his infant grandson of 14 months, who were standing at the kitchen door, had miraculous escapes, being blown out into the yard where they lay unconscious for some time...

Dr W.H. Rigby was at the scene of the accident shortly after it occurred, and with the nurses of the Margaret River Hospital rendered every assistance.[44]

Even when they did not cause death, accidents with gelignite frequently resulted in a callout for Dr Rigby and victims requiring hospitalisation. On 29 November 1927, the *South-Western Times* reported the following incident.

PREMATURE EXPLOSION

GROUP SETTLER INJURED

> The already lengthy list of accidents with gelignite on the groups was added to on Tuesday, when a group settler on Group 86, named A. Harrison, was seriously injured as the result of a premature explosion of gelignite.
>
> The unfortunate man...was engaged in blasting a root which was in the line of some fencing posts. Exact details of what caused the explosion are not ascertainable, but from the report of an eye witness to the occurrence, there appears little doubt that the gelignite exploded prematurely, splitting open the lower portion of Harrison's face and throat, and laying the flesh bare.
>
> Dr Rigby, of Margaret River, was immediately informed, and Dr S.C. Joel, of Bunbury, was summoned to perform an operation.
>
> Harrison, who is a married man, with one child, is in the Margaret Hospital in a critical condition.[45]

The local hospital also had to deal with mental health problems, particularly among women who had been transported to a different world, as Enid Garstone remembered.

> One person came into hospital quite delirious because she felt the trees were walking in on her. Unfortunately, she had to be sent away to an asylum because she just couldn't take it. She had worked in a lace factory before she came to Australia from England. Her mother had looked after her babies as they came along while she went back to the factory to work. She had had a corner shop by her all her life and

A PRIMITIVE WOODEN STRUCTURE

Group settlement houses were often surrounded by ring-barked and dead trees. MR& DHS.

she came out here where you had to rely on stores coming out – when they could get through because of the bog and all that sort of thing.[46]

Some men also found it impossible to deal with the situation that confronted them. Elwyn Franklin's grandfather Cecil Streatfield came to Australia in 1923, having previously fought in World War I, where he had suffered from shell shock. He had also been gassed in the trenches and taken prisoner in Belgium. Unsurprisingly, he was unable to cope with some of the events that he later witnessed as a group settler:

> There was a tree-felling accident which killed Cecil's friend and neighbour. Another neighbour shot himself and was virtually decapitated. My guess is that with the scars of war, the trials and tragedies of group settlement, looking after his wife, Beatrice and young family, grandfather's mental health deteriorated. These events caused him to snap, retreating into some sort of shocked state where he wasn't

his normal self. He woke up one morning and realised that he didn't know who or where he was and attacked his wife.[47]

Beatrice was understandably very frightened and Cecil was taken to Lemnos Hospital in Perth where he was to remain for the rest of his life. His wife and their eleven-year-old son, Eric, were left to take care of the farm and two younger children. Both remained undefeated by the challenges they faced. Eric became a hardworking farmer, a transport business owner and, despite his lack of schooling, a skilled mechanic.[48]

Beatrice Streatfield also remained strong and adapted to these reduced living conditions. But, as Enid Garstone observed, some migrant women were terrified by the endless tall trees.

> Women came in with nerves shattered because they had never been in forests before and they were just put out there with no idea how bad it would be. Some of them used to have a reel of cotton and put it from tree to tree, when going out to get the mail so that they'd be able to find their way back to their shack![49]

While reels of cotton might not have been practical or available, it was very common for settlers to mark trails with blazes on trees. Joyce Payne describes her family's arrival at their new home on Group 76, east of Alexandra Bridge, in 1927:

> After following a track (by the way, there were no roads as such in those days, they were all tracks, some worse than others), they went through the bush following a blazed trail, winding in and out between giant-size trees. As we travelled then, it was almost three miles with all the turns. Mum was quite convinced we were totally lost, but Dad was shown how to observe blazed marks; all on one side of the trees for going in, while all on the other side for coming out. An important thing for any 'new chum' to remember when first finding himself in the unknown bush as it was then. No 'self-respecting Aussie' or 'old timer' would venture into any unknown part of the bush without an axe to blaze their trail. Dad's first lesson in bushcraft.

With the departure of carrier and truck, we were left to take in the fact that we had arrived at our home in the middle of nowhere, with nothing to see but trees and the Australian bush. Then was not the time to see its beauty, only to feel its awesomeness under the leafy canopy above, so tall were the trees that pressed closely around.[50]

For Joyce Payne's family, the Smiths, Karridale was the nearest settlement. When her parents boarded their train in Busselton, they had been told that Karridale was a thriving timber town, as indeed it had been some years earlier.[51] But none of this was apparent in 1927 when the Smiths' train drew into Karridale station:

> The train moved slowly forward – ah, we were going on then! But no; clear of large stacks of timber, my parents with heads out of the window read KARRIDALE in big letters on a board…All there was for Mum and Dad to see, when they alighted from the train in a dazed, bewildered manner, was a tiny tin shed, a raised area of earth and gravel extending for some yards and a boarded sign proclaiming Karridale. The huge trees crowded close on all sides and there were piles of timber stacked high, back from the railway line to a considerable depth. The tin shed was not even meant for a shelter but was locked for Railway use only and windowless.[52]

When the Smiths arrived in 1927, Karridale did have its own hospital, mainly for maternity cases, where again the people in need were the group settlers. In November 1923, the chairman of the Karridale Medical Association had written to the Minister for Health asking for a nurse to be sent to Karridale:

> During the past few months, no fewer than three children have been born on the Groups, with no nurse of medical assistance near but who can say that the next one will not be a serious one and instead of an increase in our district, a death of perhaps two.[53]

The State Government agreed that a small hospital should be established at Karridale in a building owned by the Millars timber company.⁵⁴ On 27 December 1923, the *Daily News* published in Perth reported that:

> The Colonial Secretary (MR R. S. Sampson) said this morning that the government had been offered by Messrs Millars' Timber and Trading Company, the use of a cottage at Karridale for the purpose of establishing a maternity hospital for the residents of that Group Settlement area. This offer the government has accepted with pleasure and equipment is now being supplied to make it capable of holding six beds. The Minister for Education (Mr John Ewing) had recently visited Karridale and had telegraphed saying that the residents were most enthusiastic in regard to the government's decision.⁵⁵

Since a new building was not required, the Karridale hospital opened three months before Margaret River, on 2 February 1924, as the *Group Settlement Chronicle* reported:

> On Saturday the 2nd February at 4 o'clock Miss Elphick, Matron of the Karridale Hospital at the request of the Advisory Committee, publicly opened the hospital amidst many of the group settlers and inhabitants of Karridale, Augusta and Margaret River...Great satisfaction was loudly expressed by all present. This certainly reflects credit on the Matron, who has been busy since the day she arrived. The general inspection over, everybody partook of tea. A vote of thanks was passed to the Matron for her energy and pluck in making the hospital what it really is.⁵⁶

While the government provided a subsidy of fifty pounds per year for Matron Elphick's employment,⁵⁷ resources to equip and run the hospital were limited, with the newspaper article concluding: 'The Matron of the Karridale Hospital appeals for any old linen that can be spared. Should your hens lay twice a day, the hospital will be glad of the second one.'⁵⁸

In a letter to the Reverend J.W. Foley-Whaling, the Public Health Department stated that patients would have to make their own arrangements for medical attention and that payment would need to be resolved between the patient and Dr Rigby.[59] However, Matron Elphick was told that, in the case of 'indigent' patients, Dr Rigby would be entitled to mileage and sustenance if sent for by the matron,[60] and the doctor did visit Karridale on a regular basis.[61]

Myra Willmott, then Sister Stuchbury, accompanied Dr Rigby on some of these 'surgery visits', which often involved dentistry as well as other medical treatments. She was horrified by his lack of attention to cleanliness and his use of kerosene and methylated spirits as antiseptics.

> Dr Rigby used to have 'roadside surgery' when he went to Augusta, for the groupies. It was too far for them to walk to town. The nurses with him tried to do their work like they were trained to do in their training days. But Dr Rigby wouldn't have any of that. When I first came here, I always took clean towels with us. They weren't always that clean, these groupies; I suppose they never had much chance to wash. I've known him take a lad's teeth out, and when the mouth bled, he'd just get hold of their singlet and put it up to their mouth. Strange to say we didn't see these patients in hospital very often. They must have survived somehow. If they had an infected arm or anything Rigby would just open it, sitting on a log in the bush.[62]

Karridale operated mainly as a maternity hospital and while patients might initially be treated there, accident victims and cases of serious illness were transported to Margaret River. There was a fatal accident in August 1925 when Ronald Pearce, a worker on the Karridale dump, was knocked down by a motor lorry and one wheel passed over his body. The local newspaper reported that Pearce:

> was immediately conveyed by Mr Jack Wholley, the driver of the lorry, to the Karridale Hospital close by and was later taken to the Margaret River Hospital for attention by Dr W.H. Rigby. Pearce gradually sank and expired on Tuesday last from a ruptured liver. It appears that the deceased had

> arranged to accompany a picnic party on the lorry to a football match at Deepdene and, when the vehicle approached him, he crossed in front.[63]

The football match in question would have been a soccer match. Australian Rules football had been played at Karridale in the days of Coleman Davies' timber operations. However, when the last mill closed in 1913 and the workforce left the district, 'the sound of the barrackers at Karridale went with them and was not to be heard again for twenty years'.[64]

Given that most group settlers were from Britain, soccer became the first ball game to gain popularity in the district.[65] Smiler Gale, born in 1935, recalls that his father, an English migrant, had played soccer when he first arrived in the south-west.

> In those days, of course, he played soccer. I can't remember him playing soccer. That was in his early days. But when the real game came along, as it says in footy, he got involved in that. He was made a life member as a matter of fact, from the Margaret River Football Club Association.[66]

When many of the British settlers moved to Perth or the Goldfields, enthusiasm for soccer waned and Australian Rules began to take a hold. The *South-Western News* reported on a game between Augusta and Margaret River held on 28 August 1932 as 'the first game of Australian Rules played in the region for many years'.[67] From then on it seemed inevitable that this football code would predominate in the Augusta-Margaret River region.

As people left the district and properties were deserted, the government in Perth questioned the level of public services required in the region. By 1927, the Department of Works and Labour, which was responsible for hospital maintenance, was asking about the need for hospitals in both Margaret River and Karridale. Secretary Huelin agreed that Karridale:

> was not much used mainly due to the fact that the only doctor in the area is located at Margaret River and therefore it is only right and

proper that all serious cases go into the hospital nearest the doctor. In years to come, as things develop there will probably also be a doctor at Karridale.[68]

It would be almost half a century before another hospital was built south of Margaret River and the location would be Augusta, not Karridale. In the late 1920s the need for two hospitals south of Busselton became an issue to be debated because the number of patients being admitted at Margaret River was declining.

Officially this situation was attributed to the fact that local roadworks had now been completed and that it was easier for cases to travel to Busselton.[69] But Acting Matron Haidee Rae told Department Secretary Huelin that she thought the number of admissions would continue to decline.[70] Records show that admissions to Margaret River Hospital did decrease in 1927. For example, only twenty-six patients were admitted in June of that year, whereas in the previous year, there had been thirty-three admissions in June. The reasons for hospitalisation in both years included appendicitis, nephritis, abscesses, influenza and the usual crop of accidents, some of which required amputation of fingers or toes.[71]

It seemed that patients preferred to go to Busselton rather than be treated by Dr Rigby at Margaret River. While the matron did not put her concerns in writing, Dr Rigby was frequently drunk. Enid Garstone recalled that 'He had a car and he also had a man called William to do the garden and drive the car when the doctor was too drunk to drive it — which was quite often!'[72] The doctor's fondness for whisky was perhaps not surprising given the situations he had to contend with but his presence, while essential at times, was also clearly a trial to hospital staff. In July 1927 Kittie Bussell wrote to her sister-in-law after taking morning tea at the hospital with the matron (McWhinney).

> Matron says she takes her holidays next week and will not return. She cannot keep a nurse for the Doctor. In fact, things seem to be anyhow: There are three frightfully ill men in the hospital, that poor

young Dunkley, the linesman who fell from the ladder is mental from head injuries.[73]

The next year, 1928, did not begin auspiciously for the hospital and Enid Garstone was lucky that the building was still standing when she went there to have her second child. In February the townsite experienced a serious bush fire which destroyed buildings, including a garage. The hospital was saved by a small group of local men. Acting Matron Rae wrote to Secretary Huelin commending the efforts of 'Samworth, Crofts, Dunbars (2) and McQueen otherwise we should have been burned out'.[74] The principal architect in Perth wanted to know why the fire came close 'when the grounds were kept clear'. It was left to the department secretary to explain that: 'the bush comes up close to the hospital and that, although our orderly is gradually utilising the timber for firewood, there is a lot of timber still lying around'.[75]

The maternity cases that constituted a large portion of the hospital's patients were mostly women married to group settlers who lived hours away, sometimes a day's travel by horse and buggy from the Margaret River townsite and thus from the hospital. They needed to avoid a last-minute journey that might accelerate labour. The issue became: where to stay? Boarding-house costs were generally out of the question while the hospital was already overcrowded and had no spare beds for those not immediately classified as patients.

This problem was first raised by Matron May McWhinney with the Augusta-Margaret River Road Board in July 1926.[76] She advised that women-in-waiting were sleeping on the hospital verandah and that she was charging them three shillings a day for meals, a sum which, she said, they grumbled at having to pay. Alternative accommodation was urgently required but no boarding house could make a profit from such a venture and the government had neither the money nor the inclination to build a hostel for these women.[77]

By 1927, the Bush Nursing Trust, a joint creation of the Silver Chain Nursing Association and the Red Cross, had opened maternity hostels for pregnant women at Wyalkatchem in the Wheatbelt and in Busselton, while in the following year it would establish a rest home in Denmark, another group settlement area.[78] There were no plans to build a similar facility in Margaret River. However, as new nurses quarters were to be built at Margaret River, the department offered to sell to the Bush Nursing Trust the group-type house in the hospital grounds that had been erected in late 1924 as accommodation for the matron and nurses. The department also offered to provide meals and collect charges from the women-in-waiting making use of the hospital's facilities.[79] The inducements were seemingly insufficient, or possibly the trust considered that with a hostel in Busselton there was no need for a maternity rest home in Margaret River. In any event the Bush Nursing Trust rejected this proposal.[80] This may have been because the trust secretary was aware that help for Margaret River's mothers-in-waiting was already on offer.

In September 1926 Australia had received a visit from an Empire parliamentary delegation. This association (later the Commonwealth Parliamentary Association) had been set up by the British Parliament in 1911 to promote links with, and democracy within, the various countries within the then British Empire.[81] Members of the delegation visited all states of Australia and found time to donate a replica of the British House of Commons Speaker's Chair to the newly built Parliament building in Canberra.[82]

This Empire parliamentary delegation was headed by James Gascoyne-Cecil, fourth Marquis of Salisbury, son of a former British prime minister. The Cecil family traced its importance in British public affairs back to the sixteenth century, when a direct ancestor of the Marquis, Robert Cecil, the first Earl of Salisbury, had been Secretary of State to the first Queen Elizabeth and then to James I. The Marquis was accompanied by his nephew, Lord Evelyn Cecil, and by delegates from South Africa and Canada, India and Southern Rhodesia. It was an all-male delegation apart

Empire Delegation 1926 meeting with group settlers. Courtesy State Library of Western Australia 005132D.

from Mrs Tawse Jolie from Southern Rhodesia, but a number of family members accompanied the men, including Lord Evelyn's wife and daughter.

When visiting Western Australia, Mrs Jolie commented that in other states she had heard little about the situation of migrant women. The Marquis of Salisbury agreed, saying that he was surprised before arriving in Western Australia that they had not been told about how these British women were faring.[83]

It was possibly Sir Evelyn Cecil's wife, Alicia, Lady Cecil, and their daughter Margaret who alerted the delegation to the plight of women on the group settlements.[84] Lady Cecil was herself Vice-Chairman of the Society for the Overseas Settlement of British Women.[85] As the *Daily Mail* (Brisbane) reported on 7 October 1926, 'she was firmly resolved to have her knowledge of Australian conditions first hand. Her first visit will be to the group settlements in Western Australia.'[86]

A fortnight later Lady Cecil and her daughter Margaret spent two days visiting the groups around Margaret River. On Saturday 23 October 1926, Lady Cecil was interviewed on the train at Busselton Station. She stated she was agreeably surprised at the amount of development that had taken place but thought that migrants were given inadequate information about conditions before leaving England. Her visit to Margaret River Hospital had shown her that every care and consideration was given to patients but that the provision of a rest home for expectant mothers was urgently needed.[87]

October would have been the perfect month for Lady Cecil's visit. She was known mainly for her expertise as a gardener and amateur botanist. Lady Cecil's biographer, Sue Minter, stated that:

> In Western Australia she was aware of the extent of the indigenous flora resulting from the isolation of the region: 'There are plants with pedigrees stretching back into geological periods which have survived in this corner of the globe, cut off by sea and desert from outside influences.'[88]

Minter also noted that Lady Cecil was aware that much of the indigenous flora was threatened by the spread of agriculture during the previous half-century.

One might have expected Lady Cecil's interest in flowers and gardens to have soon superseded her interest in the plight of Margaret River's group settlers. But this did not happen. Perhaps it was helpful that W.C. Angwin, who, as the Minister for Lands and Migration had accompanied members of the Empire delegation, became Western Australia's Agent General in London in March 1927.[89] Thus, in June that year, Department Secretary F.J. Huelin advised his minister:

> Before the Honorable Mr Angwin left here, we happened to be chatting together and he mentioned that Lady Cecil, who interested herself in group settlers here, had her attention drawn to this need at Margaret River and promised to set about raising funds. My attention

was drawn recently to an English paper which indicated that Lady Cecil is taking action along these lines, but of course, how long this will take to reach maturity I have no idea. We certainly need the addition.⁹⁰

By November there was more positive news and it was Margaret Cecil, Lady Alicia's daughter, who became patron of the new rest house as the Perth *Daily News* reported:

> Towards the end of last year Miss Margaret Cecil, daughter of Lady [Alicia] Cecil, the wife of one of the visiting Empire Parliamentary delegates, visited Group Settlements at Margaret River, and was impressed with the necessity that existed there for a rest home for waiting mothers. On her return to London an appeal was made to the 'Margarets' of Great Britain for funds for this purpose. Already £480 has been raised, with an extra £100 from Lady Apsley, for furnishing. The cost of the building is estimated at £600, and the cost of furnishing at £150. It is hoped to collect the full amount before the end of the year.⁹¹

This hope was duly realised. In November 1928 a contract for £1,225 for erection of the rest home and the new nurses quarters was let. The buildings were to cost £1,400 and eight shillings and the contract was let to Messrs Falkingham and Newman, Busselton.⁹²

Margaret Cecil, now married as Mrs Herbert Lane,⁹³ remained closely involved with the project, writing on 1 April 1929 to local parliamentarian Mr G.W. Barnard, MLA, who would become one of the first trustees of the Margaret Cecil Rest House Association:

> Dear Mr Barnard
>
> You will have heard from Mrs Bussell that I have cabled out £80 for the furnishing of the Rest House and in my letter to her last mail, I told her that I still have £500 invested here. I am hoping that £80 will cover or very nearly cover the cost of completing the furnishings

A PRIMITIVE WOODEN STRUCTURE

and that the remainder of the sum I have collected will be treated as capital in the hands of the trustees namely yourself as MLA for the district and Mr W. J. Mann MLC and the chairman of the Roads Board. The income from this will help towards the upkeep and repairs of the house.

If you find it is necessary to use more than the £80 on furnishing you must use your discretion, but I hope to retain as much as possible as capital as I cannot raise any more. As soon as I hear from you that you agree to these arrangements. I will ask Mr Angwin to cable out the £500 ...

I am so very glad to hear that the building is nearly completed.

Yours sincerely

Margaret Lane.[94]

Margaret Lane recorded the names of all the women in England and Scotland who had contributed to the rest house appeal. The list, which included a number of titled ladies, was documented for posterity in a book now held at the new Margaret River Hospital.[95]

Margaret Cecil raised funds from the Margarets of England and Scotland for a rest house for pregnant women. Margaret Cecil Rest Home Memorial Cabinet, courtesy Margaret River Hospital.

After the rest house was furnished and opened, four hundred pounds remained for investment, and stock for this amount to mature in 1934 was purchased by the Rest House Trustees in December 1929.[96]

The Margaret Cecil Rest House was opened on Sunday 26 May 1929 by Lady Campion, the wife of the governor of Western Australia.[97] The heading in the *South-Western News* was:

REST HOME AT MARGARET RIVER

Donated by the Margarets of Britain.[98]

The building was occupied before its official opening and the two first babies were named after Margaret Cecil.[99] The girl was Margaret and the boy Cecil. The *South-Western News* reported the opening as follows:

> In bright sunshine on Sunday afternoon at Margaret River, Lady Campion performed the opening ceremony for a building of unusual interest. It is a charmingly designed jarrah villa brightly and comfortably furnished, which is to serve as a rest house for expectant mothers and convalescing women, and which was presented to the Margaret district by the Margarets of Britain. The house is sufficiently large to accommodate six persons and is complete in every way with sitting rooms, kitchen, bathrooms and other conveniences. It has been artistically furnished, separate colour schemes being admirably worked out for each room.

Dr Everitt Atkinson, the state's Principal Medical Officer, and Mr F.J. Huelin of the Public Health Department attended the rest house opening and were thanked for their assistance and it was noted that a committee of ladies together with the matron, Lena Unbehaun, had rendered local support. Margaret Lane had asked that the rest house be managed separately from the hospital and that trustees be appointed to manage the finances. W.J. Mann, MLC, G.W. Barnard, MLA, and Edward Willmott, President of the Augusta-Margaret

River Road Board, had accepted these appointments. The State Government, for its part, had agreed that the building could be erected on a portion of the land reserved for the hospital.

The *South-Western News* then reported on Lady Campion's speech:

> Lady Campion in a happy little speech, spoke first of the pleasure and privilege felt in being associated with such a ceremony...Many hundreds of Margarets scattered over Britain had shown practical interest in the women who, with their husbands and families, were engaged in making homes for themselves in this comparatively new and previously unsettled country.[100]

While Lady Campion's references to south-west Western Australia as a 'comparatively new and previously unsettled country' might sound inappropriate and inaccurate in the twenty-first century, they reflect the way in which people in both countries viewed Australia at the time: an imperial outpost should be made as much like the mother country as possible.

The Margaret Cecil Rest House and the hospital's nurses quarters were not the only buildings erected in 1929 along what was then Wallcliffe Road (now Tunbridge Street). When F.J. Huelin visited Margaret River in July 1929, he noticed that a new police station and quarters had been built on the opposite side of the road.[101] Huelin followed up his internal memorandum on his inspection of Margaret River Hospital with this request to the government's principal architect:

> Some weeks ago, I was at the Margaret River Hospital and noted that a fine new Police Station and quarters had been erected on the opposite side of the road and that the premises had been very nicely finished with an excellent fence along the whole of the street frontage.
>
> The fence of the hospital reserve on all sides is the usual bush post and five wires which when I was there stood out in its pristine dilapidation. The contrast between appearances of the two frontages,

both owned by His Majesty was most striking – even straying stock appreciated the difference because unfortunately our fence was not sufficient to deny them access to our garden.

Would you kindly look into the matter and give us some idea of what a respectable fence, not an elaborate one, would cost?[102]

The principal architect estimated the cost of such a fence as sixty-nine pounds, plus ten pounds for clearing debris along the fence line. His reply was not encouraging:

While a cyclone fence would materially improve the appearance of the hospital property it cannot in any way be regarded as essential, as apart from appearances the existing fence is in good order and is quite satisfactory.[103]

On this occasion the secretary was not deterred and obviously his minister, the Hon. Selby Munsie, was 'on side' as he endorsed the proposal for the new fence.[104]

No doubt a few months later, once the effects of the Wall Street crash of October 1929 and the consequent Great Depression were felt in Western Australia, such 'unnecessary expenditure' would not have been approved and there are no photographs showing that a 'fine fence' was ever built around the hospital.

Opening of the Margaret Cecil Rest House, May 1929. MR&DHS.

Chapter Four

Very Little Money

Jean McDonald, a nurse from Tambellup in the southern wheatbelt, arrived in Margaret River in 1934. Jobs were few and far between in the Depression, even for nurses. She had been told there was a position at the Busselton Hospital but she was sent on to Margaret River.

> I knew nothing of Margaret River so I had no idea of where or to what place I was going. Finally, when it was getting dark the train stopped at this place and suddenly, the carriage doors opened and this young man said 'Excuse me. Are you the nurse for Margaret River?' And that was Desmond Bussell.[1]

Desmond was a grandson of Alfred and Ellen Bussell. His father, Frederick Aloysius Weld Bussell (named for Alfred's friend, Governor Weld), had stayed living and working on the remaining Bussell properties and, as Desmond's son Greg Bussell recalled, young farmers were pleased to have women of their own age come to town.

When the hospital came, there were nurses and of course school teachers. And in those days, always women, so the farmers were happy. My father was one of the few people with a truck so he had the job of meeting the nurses who came to Margaret River off the train. So he got first pick if you like. And my mother, Jean. She was the one he chose.[2]

When Jean reached the hospital, she was:

met by Matron Dawson. At that time there were only four or five nurses on the trained staff at the hospital, and one probationer. It was only a twelve-bed hospital. Things became hectic when there was an upsurge of babies and surgery, so they used to send to Busselton for another nurse to come down.[3]

There had been some positive changes since the hospital opened:

The hospital had improved when I arrived as it did have nurses quarters, which they didn't have when Myra Willmott was here in 1924. There was a men's ward at one end, a ladies ward on the other side of the passage and a maternity ward the other end, all under one roof. Over the back verandah, which was not enclosed, there used

The hospital still had only basic facilities. MR&DHS.

to be a little alleyway; one side of it was a linen cupboard and on the other side was the matron's office. You walked through a little passageway to the kitchen.[4]

Despite new nurses quarters and the establishment of the Margaret Cecil Rest House, this small country hospital remained, when Jean McDonald arrived in 1934, a very basic building with cramped wards, no electricity or reliable water supply, and a very inadequate operating theatre. In response to a request from the matron asking for improvements, Department Secretary F.J. Huelin advised that 'Just now there is very little money available for building purposes and what there is available can only be expended in very urgent and necessary works'.[5]

There was indeed little money for any public works. The Great Depression had hit the state hard. Most groupies had few resources and during the 1930s many 'walked off' their properties. Tom Doyle's family stayed but he was very aware of the deteriorating financial situation in the district:

> The township went into the doldrums. It was just a matter of those who had any form of living at all stayed there; others went on their ways. Quite a few went to the Goldfields to see if there was anything there, but there was not much of course, because the Depression was statewide.[6]

Long before the Great Depression that began with the Wall Street crash of 1929 and deepened during the early 1930s, it was clear that this much-lauded Group Settlement Scheme, which had led directly to the establishment of the Margaret River Hospital, was essentially a failure.

In August 1926 the newly elected member of the state's Legislative Council, W.J. Mann, at the time also the proprietor of the local newspaper, the *South-Western News*, discussed the scheme in his maiden speech.[7] Mann drew attention to the fact that many settlers had been drawn from backgrounds far removed from farming and thus needed more support and assistance than they had received.

> For many years I have lived in the South-West and in that portion of the State where there are now 50 groups. I have had the opportunity of coming closely in touch with many of these new settlers. Amongst them I have met men from all callings in life. Some of them are middle-aged and are endeavouring for the first time to take up a new industry...
>
> I have met amongst them a master of modern languages, a master of arts of Edinburgh, an ex-manager of a Bradford textile mill, ex-bank managers, bank clerks and in one case a man who had been a dress designer...I do not suggest that all these men are unsuitable for the work. Many have got grit and determination. In the aftermath of war, they have been squeezed out of employment or suffered adversity. Because they have a little pluck, they have come to Australia to go on the land.[8]

By 1930 remaining groupies required much more than a little pluck to succeed. But while many left the district, they were often replaced by other hopefuls, keeping the population stable and ensuring that a local hospital remained viable.

Eventually, even some of the more determined and experienced settlers who had managed to establish a small dairy herd could not keep going. The price of cream declined and continued to fall, even as acres under pasture and the number of cows in the area grew.[9] Many families had no choice but to walk off their property, leaving everything but their personal possessions behind. In 1927 the Burton family from the English Midlands had been allocated a block on Group 85 at Osmington, ten miles (17 kilometres) east of Margaret River townsite. Len Burton, a child at the time, later wrote about his family's experience:

> The outcome of the Group Settlement experiment was apparent long before the Depression, the full force of which was not felt by the settlers until 1931. But that year the price of butterfat had plummeted to less than half the value on which the economics of the scheme were based. The State treasury had no funds. State assistance had ceased when the blocks were valued and declared self-sufficient, which, in

many cases, was done prematurely. From that time forward, instead of the settler receiving assistance from the State, interest on the assessed capital value was deducted from cream cheques every three months and supervising foremen were withdrawn. I recall that one month, after deduction of interest, my father received a cheque for $2 to keep the family of five until the next monthly cheque was received.[10]

Despite the Burton family's determination, they could no longer cope with the economic conditions and primitive living arrangements when Len's mother became critically ill.

The situation wore down my mother's health and she developed a duodenal ulcer. She suffered for months, the ulcer finally reaching life-threatening proportions. After diagnosis and palliative care at the Margaret River hospital she was evacuated to Perth for surgery and she was carried off the train on a stretcher.[11]

And so, in October 1932, in the midst of the Depression, we walked off the block on which so much effort had been expended. My father knew he faced a daunting future but he left with his head held high, knowing that he had done his best.[12]

Group house at Warner Glen 1930s. Courtesy Ros Craig.

Two years after the Burtons departed, butterfat prices fell to their lowest price ever: seven pence three farthings, and stayed that way for several months.[13] Joyce Payne's father, James Smith, felt that he could no longer afford to keep the model T Ford that he had bought in 1927 when there had still been optimism among the groupies.[14] But after much consideration the Smith family decided to stay put.

> Dad himself began to wonder if we would be better off elsewhere? So many of our different friends had left. More than ever, those who stayed on felt a strengthening bond between them, enabling each other to keep going. They would debate the pros and cons of going – against staying. Somehow for that bunch of stalwarts, the scales tipped always for staying. It was argued that while those that left unburdened themselves of a great and growing debt, those who stayed would always have something to eat – with milk, butter meat and whatever they could grow for themselves. They also had a roof over their heads, an abundance of wood for their fires and a strong faith in themselves.[15]

Even before the Depression hit, the scheme had become such a drain on state finances that politicians wanted to abandon it. No more groups were established after 1930 when the government transferred the scheme's management to the state's Agricultural Bank. The bank reassessed the settlers' indebtedness and, in so doing, added to the amount that each settler owed the bank. In many cases this proved to be the last straw for the struggling groupies.

There was little that people could do, whether out on farms or running businesses in the town, to improve their financial circumstances. Resentment and frustration boiled over. On Saturday 6 August 1932 a mass meeting sponsored by the Margaret River and Districts Progress Association was held to discuss the situation. The local newspaper reported that between two and three hundred people were present and that there was, not surprisingly, strong criticism of the Agricultural Bank, together with a demand to return control of the scheme to the government.[16]

This meeting was chaired by Dr F.S. Taylor Thomas, who that year purchased the Margaret River medical practice from Dr William Rigby, the latter having returned to Collie, where he lived and worked until his death in December 1942. In a short obituary in the *South-Western News*, Rigby was described as a clever practitioner and a man who always had the courage of his convictions.[17] No doubt local views of the good doctor continued to be mixed depending on their experience of being treated by or working with him. But Rigby had given the Margaret River district many years of service and on 7 July 1932 he was farewelled by the road board where he had previously been an elected member.[18] Filomena Terry also recorded in her diary, 'We all went to a Social and Dance given as a send-off to Doctor and Mrs Rigby'.[19]

Dr Taylor Thomas stayed in Margaret River for only two years but, in that time, he had much to say about the state of the local hospital. He had previously worked in Denmark on the south coast, also a group settlement area, and he had a clear idea of how he wished his medical practice to operate.

> I think the most satisfactory arrangement for all concerned is to let me take a three-years lease of this at a fair subsidy. I cannot suggest the amount until I went into figures (sic): but if this were done it would save money to your department, it would give me control of the nursing which is important to me, and it would enable me to deal with the public on the basis of a composite fee for medical and hospital attendance, an arrangement that worked eminently satisfactorily elsewhere. I hope you will give the suggestion favourable consideration.[20]

But favourable consideration was not forthcoming. The Public Health Department was not prepared to lease the hospital to the doctor, stating that: 'We quite appreciate your position but at the moment, we are unable to do anything in the direction desired by you'.[21] The next issue was the need for hospital improvements. Here doctor and department were on the same side while the 'enemy' was the Department of Works and Labour, which was responsible for the design and implementation of all work in government buildings.

Dr Taylor Thomas was far more active than Dr Rigby had been for some years in undertaking surgery at the hospital. In the first six months of 1932, Dr Rigby performed only fifteen surgical operations; Dr Taylor Thomas then performed forty-five operations between July and December of the same year.[22] Soon after his arrival, he telephoned F.J. Huelin at the Public Health Department. The doctor had found that there was no sink in the operating theatre and that there were insufficient beds in the women's ward, while the men's ward had spare capacity. He asked that building works be undertaken to subdivide the latter to allow for more space for women. He was told to obtain quotations for making the necessary changes.[23] But in July the doctor informed the department:

> With reference to your request for local tenders to be called for certain work at Margaret River hospital. I desire to inform you that while these are being obtained, the hospital received the honour of a visit from the Inspector of Works, Mr Hall, who condemned the proposal, giving me to understand that his chief would not sanction the carrying out of the work.
>
> Meanwhile perhaps his chief will sanction the nursing of women surgical cases in the men's ward as we are now doing. It bids fair to make a local scandal.
>
> Yours F.S Taylor Thomas.[24]

In follow-up correspondence, Dr Taylor Thomas told the Perth bureaucrats that 'this hospital is the *most uncomfortable and badly arranged that I have ever worked in*'.[25]

The fight over the proposed changes continued, while at the same time, Matron Helen Doyle was repeatedly asking the department in Perth to arrange for gutters to be repaired, for a drying room to be built and for changes to the staff dining room. It was in response to these requests that Huelin advised that there was money only 'for urgent and necessary works.'²⁶ Dr Taylor Thomas became increasingly annoyed by the lack of action on the part of public servants in Perth. In February 1933, he was still awaiting 'a very necessary instrument table and laparoscopic lamp. I think it is fair that you should recognise the increased usefulness of this hospital by giving us the few things we ask for'.²⁷

On 20 June 1933 the department finally gave the doctor better news:

> I have to advise you that we have accepted the quote for £85/11/6 by Mr A.E. Mann to carry out various alterations at the hospital including the installation of basins in the operating theatre, a labour ward on the end of the verandah and alterations to lavatories.²⁸

In accepting this quotation, the government's principal architect commented that it seemed to be 'a little on the full side' but that in the circumstances it would be acceptable and accepted.²⁹ Two weeks later in July, after many months of argument about the need for, and the specifications of, a drying shed, a decision was made and the same builder's quotation was also accepted: 'All new structures, as per the existing hospital, to be built in wood.'³⁰

The risk of the timber buildings being destroyed by bushfires was always a serious problem. In the 1930s Margaret River had no piped water supply or town fire service. Summer bushfires were then, as now, a major threat throughout the region, and in its earliest days the hospital buildings had some lucky escapes. In January 1931 a serious fire could easily have destroyed the hospital. Police Constable Wyatt advised his superiors and the Public Health Department that disaster had only been narrowly averted.

> I immediately rode to the fire and saw that the fire was rapidly approaching the Govt Hospital from the rear and as the scrub has grown up within a few yards of the hospital buildings they were in grave danger...I desire to point out that owing to the bush being very close to the hospital and the scrub allowed to grow almost to the buildings themselves, that should the bush at the rear of the

> hospital catch fire it is quite probable that some of the buildings (if not all) would be destroyed and as we have had some very hot days lately and numerous fires about I think the matter should be brought under notice of the Medical Department [sic] with a view of having the scrub cut and cleared back so that the hospital would not be endangered should the bush at the rear catch fire... there is still danger of sparks...and a fire would only have to travel a few chains to be in the hospital reserve.[31]

While, once more, the buildings had been saved, it still took many months of correspondence between the various government agencies in Perth and the Forests Department office in Busselton to arrange for the bush and scrub behind the hospital to be cleared.

In August 1931, a £25 contract was finally let to a Mr Elmers for clearing a fire break around the hospital on the understanding 'that any labour employed will be drawn from the ranks of the local unemployed on sustenance'.[32] This provision can be seen as a 'sign of the times', as was a later request from Fred Collins, the supervising forester in Busselton, that the money to pay Mr Elmers be forwarded to the hospital matron when the job was finished, so that the contractor could be paid quickly: 'as he owes some wages, also his store accounts and horse feed as I know that he has no money to pay same as he has not made much more than his food out of the job as same was worth nearer £60 than £25'.[33] Officials in Perth also agreed that an additional three pounds could be spent on ploughing the area around the hospital to decrease further the fire risk. This contract was let to A.E. Ashton and his subsequent request to the Public Health Department also illustrates the economic situation in the district.

> Dear Sir
>
> About six weeks ago I forwarded to the Department an account for three pounds for Ploughing and Harrowing the Margaret River Hospital grounds.

> Having received no reply, may I ask you if you would be good enough to forward the amount along as I am Hard Pressed [sic] and have a job to keep going not being lucky enough to get any sustenance because again I am unlucky in having a small farm that is not yet sufficiently developed to get my living from it. I have got to manage on little jobs that I can pick up. So, hoping you will understand the position I am in and send cheque.[34]

The department advised that the invoice had already been forwarded to the Treasury for payment, so hopefully Mr Ashton soon received his money.

During the Depression years, the government was always looking for ways to reduce expenditure, including on the small Karridale Hospital only 29 kilometres to the south of Margaret River. On 30 June 1930 Matron Murray was informed that her services would be terminated because the hospital was to be leased to a qualified nurse.[35] By this means the government aimed to save some of the money that it was spending on that institution. Leasing was seen as preferable to complete closure because the department recognised that there would be strong objections to such a move given the rough roads and lack of motor vehicles. Travel from Alexandra Bridge, or even from Karridale, to Margaret River was not an easy or quick journey.

Karridale Hospital was then leased to a Nurse Laffer, who provided in-patient statistics to the department on a monthly basis. The return for October 1932 showed that only six patients had been admitted, while ten had been discharged. These were not unusual numbers for Karridale and Nurse Laffer advised that the population of the area had decreased because group settlers had left their holdings.[36]

In 1933 the department considered complete closure of Karridale Hospital and sought the views of the Agricultural Bank, now in charge of the Group Settlement Scheme.[37] The bank, which was not paying the bills for the hospital's operations, replied that it should remain open on the basis that 're-occupation of the holdings with an improved type of settler should, in the future, make the institution self-supporting'.³⁸ These hopeful words were a long way from the true situation. The settlers were not the problem. The Depression and the resulting low price of butterfat were still large causes of their poverty. Government resources were also stretched and although the Margaret River Hospital was not threatened, in 1935 the local newspaper reported that the government was again intending to close Karridale Hospital. Inevitably there was strong local objection to this proposal from people living around Karridale, Kudardup and Alexandra Bridge.

> Much resentment is expressed at the secrecy in connexion with this matter...The proposal to remove the equipment to Margaret is also resented as much of it was purchased by local subscription for the use of local residents.³⁹

Again, the local residents won the battle and once more the hospital was leased out, this time to Sister Rosina Kenny. But within a year she received the following communication from F.J. Huelin at the Public Health Department:

> Further to my memo of the 12th instant, we have now completed arrangements with the Margaret River Ambulance Committee for the conveyance of patients from your District to the Margaret River Hospital, so that on receipt of this letter you definitely close the hospital and receive no further patients, all of whom must now go to Margaret River Hospital.⁴⁰

The advent of a local volunteer ambulance service in 1936 was a significant milestone. Previously the St John's Ambulance Association had been active in the town, promoting the teaching of first aid. The first classes were held in 1928 with Mr A. Orchard coming from Bunbury to instruct the class. Local resident George Stewart, a group settler who had had ambulance experience in England, was a long-term supporter of St John's and after Orchard's sessions he started first aid classes with Dr Rigby.⁴¹ In October 1931 all students passed their first aid examination.⁴² Dr Taylor Thomas also gave first aid lessons and examined students. In November 1932 eleven individuals received awards and from then classes were held each year.[43] In later years classes were also held at East Witchcliffe, the site of the district's largest timber mill.[44] In the absence of an ambulance service, it had been particularly important for local residents to receive first aid training and in 1933 a Margaret River Ambulance Club was formed to increase local knowledge. The President, Tom Doyle, and the club's patron, Colonel Le Souef, asked that the community support 'these public-spirited men'. The fee to join the club was two shillings while attendance at the course cost seven shillings and sixpence.[45]

The first moves to obtain an ambulance for Margaret River were made by the United Friendly Societies of the District, which organised a meeting on Sunday 1 September 1935, 'With the object of discussing the possibilities of procuring an ambulance for the district, Mr Stewart presided'.[46] The president of the United Friendly Societies said that in some instances it had taken sixteen or seventeen hours to get a patient to hospital and he considered that

Tom Doyle. Commander of the Order of St John (for services to St John Ambulance). MR&DHS.

an ambulance or some form of subsidised scheme was required to afford quick and easy transport of such cases. The meeting decided that a sub-centre of the St John's Ambulance should be established in the district while the United Friendly Societies would fundraise for the purchase of an ambulance. Dr M. Mandelstam, who had succeeded Dr Taylor Thomas as District Medical Officer, became the sub-centre's patron.[47]

When the first committee meeting of the new association was held later that month, the president and secretary of the United Friendly Societies reported on their fundraising activities. Dr Mandelstam advised that Karridale residents had expressed interest in the ambulance proposal as Karridale Hospital was now only a dressing station. The meeting confirmed that the ambulance service would cover the area from Metricup in the north to Cape Leeuwin in the south. Most significantly, the meeting resolved to write to Mr E.V. Brockman, MLA for the Sussex electorate, asking him to endeavour to obtain for the branch about a quarter-acre of government land near the police station to build an ambulance garage and a classroom.[48]

A 'successful and well-supported dance' raised four pounds, ten shillings for the ambulance fund, while other fundraising efforts included a collection box at the local caves and a Popular Girl competition.[49]

Finally, in January 1936 the local newspaper reported that the establishment of the Margaret River Ambulance Sub-Centre was going ahead and that the Lotteries Commission had agreed to provide 350 pounds towards the cost of the ambulance, leaving 100 pounds to be raised locally.[50] Six months later, in July, Margaret River received its first ambulance: 'The members have something of which to be proud, as the van is the most up to date in the State and is equipped with three rubber beds and all first aid appliances.'[51] In handing over the vehicle to the Margaret River sub-centre on 18 July 1936, Captain J.J. Airey, Vice-president of St John's Ambulance Head Centre, congratulated Margaret River on being the first sub-centre in the south-west to procure an ambulance.

The ambulance's first call-out was on 23 July. About half of the requests resulted from accidents.[52] In its first year, forty-nine patients had been transported; twenty-eight were medical cases while there were twenty-one accident victims.[53]

The arrival of the St John's Ambulance Service in Margaret River was a game-changer and this time Karridale Hospital did close, with dressings and drugs transferred to Margaret River.[54] Sister Kenny stayed on as a caretaker and the building remained a government-owned facility, albeit not operational.[55] With the doctor located at Margaret River, Karridale could not compete.

In earlier times, Karridale, not Margaret River, had been 'first cab off the rank' in establishing another important local institution, the annual agricultural show. The first show was held there in 1926 whereas Margaret River did not hold its first event until 1929. For young Leonard Burton, then still living on Group 85 at Osmington, those first annual shows stayed in his memory.

> The annual agricultural show was a feature of most districts. We attended the first of the Margaret River district shows which was held in a paddock on the hill just to the left of the road beyond the bridge at the northern end of town. We also attended the first Show

St John's Ambulance in Margaret River 1937. MR& DHS.

held in the new permanent showgrounds on the other side of the town, near the railway station. It was opened by the then Premier, James Mitchell (later lieutenant Governor, Sir James Mitchell) from the back of a truck.[56]

In 1934, settlers attended the show for the first time at Gloucester Park, the new sportsground.

While agricultural shows, dances and sport provided welcome distractions from the hardships of the 1930s, picture shows were also much appreciated. Bert McLean, then a teenager, helped to bring the latest movies to local halls between Margaret River and Augusta.

> Owen Terry and I used to bring pictures to Cowaramup, Karridale, Witchcliffe, Augusta and the Margaret River Hall about 1929–30 when they were putting the roads in. At Cowaramup we used to show them in the old exhibition hall on the Showground as that was before they had the hall there. At Witchcliffe it was in Fearn's store [later Darnell's store]…and at Augusta there was only a little hall opposite the pub.[57]

The establishment of the South-West Farmers Butter factory in 1930 provided hope for the future of dairy farming, as well as employment for some. A report in the *Manjimup and Warren Times* clearly quoted from a media statement:

> The factory is designed on the very latest principles and to a large extent is a replica on a smaller scale of the Manjimup factory which is the last word on up-to-datedness in butter making. A flash pasteuriser has been installed and every known modern convenience in the Australian and New Zealand world of butter making.[58]

It was seemingly easier to obtain private enterprise to build a butter factory than it was to find public money to upgrade the hospital.

Members of settlers' families often found work at the butter factory but, just as the farmers received little money for their cream,

Butter factory, Opening Day, 1930. Courtesy Kevin Coate.

workers' wages were low. The Communist Party newspaper, the *Workers Star*, ran a campaign for the improvement of conditions in all the south-west butter and cheese factories:

> One factor which plays into the hands of these butter-fat shylocks is the poverty found in these Group Settlements where Group lads, sharing the direst poverty with their parents are only too glad to accept work at almost any price to earn a few shillings.[59]

Cedar (George) Armstrong grew up on Mouquet Farm near Margaret River. His father had taken up this land after returning from World War I. The Armstrongs had lived in the district for many years but times were still:

> hard. Mum and Dad grew spuds and had a garden, milked cows, grew a few pigs, which were made into bacon and sold around the mills and Group Settlements. We lived on spuds, pumpkin, some fish, kangaroo and carrots plus any vegetables that grew. Even though the Depression was hard we never starved, but I remember Dad saying his entire income for the year was 90 pounds. Butter and milk were

made on the farm. Spuds, bacon, and a steer killed and sold around the timber mills and Group Settlements to bring a cash return.[60]

Poverty was the norm and could not be avoided by most people living in the region during the 1930s. However, one small group of Englishwomen, living opposite the hospital, had chosen a life of poverty as well as one of chastity and obedience. The Anglican Sisters of the Order of St Elizabeth of Hungary had been founded earlier in the twentieth century by Mabel Hodge from Torquay in England. She became Mother Elizabeth, and inspired her followers to respond to calls for social support and help.[61]

Mother Elizabeth first visited Western Australia in March 1927, having been invited by the Anglican Bishop of Bunbury 'to work among the women of the Group Settlements'.[62] After establishing a mission in South Bunbury,[63] she travelled to Margaret River, describing the 32-mile journey in her journal: 'The road was so rough that we had to hold on to the framework of the car to save one from bruises. It costs £2 a week on average to keep the unfortunate car in repair.'[64] The 'unfortunate car' belonged to the Anglican priests already living in the town. They were Brother Jim Moore and Brother Charles Smith of the Bush Brotherhood of St Boniface, which had been established in the Bunbury Anglican diocese to bring young priests from England. Mother Elizabeth had been somewhat horrified to find out that her accommodation in Margaret River was to be in the small house occupied by the brothers. Eventually the two men arranged to sleep on someone's verandah and a local woman moved into the priests' house to take care of the nuns.

During her first visit to Margaret River, Mother Elizabeth travelled sixty-five miles with 'never a break in the trees' visiting a school and group settlers.[65] She also selected a site for a Margaret River convent. The block was located just across the road from the hospital. On the other hand, it was some way from the new Anglican church, which had been dedicated on 30 January 1927.[66] Once settled in Margaret River, the sisters would have worn a path between convent and church, taking services at the latter when no priest was available and providing spiritual comfort to hospital patients. In selecting this location, Mother Elizabeth must have considered that it was more important for the nuns to be close to the hospital than to the Anglican church.

The convent, which was to become the home of the sisters based in Margaret River between 1929 and 1957, was constructed by local builder A.E. Mann. Mother Elizabeth did not come to Margaret River again until 1930, when she was able to thank Mr Mann personally: 'The first thing I did on Monday morning was to see Mann, the builder, to tell him how immensely I appreciated the beautiful work he had put into it.'[67]

Sisters Marion and Barbara were already installed in their new home. Both from England, they soon adapted to the conditions associated with their new lifestyle, including dealing with temperamental wood stoves and wearing wellington boots for most of Margaret River's wet winters.[68] The sisters soon gained the respect of the local settlers and their practical help was much appreciated, especially by women giving birth to new babies, when the sisters would often look after the older children. Agda Wyatt, wife of Margaret River's first police constable, lived next door to the convent and was a close observer of their life and activities.

> What wonderful women they were...I can see them now, trudging up a dusty road on their way to help a sick mother and her children, bringing comfort where they could. When the Reverend Mother came out to visit them, she gave them a huge whistle to blow if they ever needed help from my husband. They were often without food. But in answer to their prayers, good folk often left a basket of food for them, even the humble potato.[69]

Mother Elizabeth made several later visits to Margaret River and in 1931 wrote to the Minister for Health offering to set up a medical mission in the district while taking over management of the hospital:

Convent of St Elizabeth

South Bunbury, Feb. 24th 1931

Dear Sir,

I have consulted the Premier's Secretary and he has advised me to lay before you a proposal I made as to the possibilities of us working in the Margaret River district as a Medical Mission. We are at work in that district under the Bishop of Bunbury (we are an Anglican Order) and the scheme I have in mind comprises the control of the Hospital and working with our own doctors and nurses, with a car or caravan for visiting local centres and lecturing on health conditions. We should ask the Government to continue its present grants, or a fair proportion of them, but should work for a fuller service, and an increasing development of local possibilities concerning financial support. The Mission would be aided from England also.

I am desirous of keeping the whole matter entirely private at present as it could not mature for fully two years as I should have to work up interest in it in England.

There would be no denomination bias in our work whatever. We have the good of the people as our sole motive.

I am coming to Perth next Monday and if you could very kindly see me if you are in Perth, I should be very glad to have your opinion about it.

Yours very faithfully

Elizabeth Rev. mother OSEH

Anglican Order of St Elizabeth[70]

Mother Elizabeth had made it clear that she would only take over the hospital if her Order could install its own doctor and if there was sufficient financial support from government. In return, she would offer a comprehensive outreach health and medical service which would meet the needs of the Margaret River district at a level which the government could not provide.

This initiative was first proposed before Dr Rigby had left the town and Mother Elizabeth would have been aware of the difficulties that existed at that time between doctor and hospital. A month before she contacted the Minister for Health, Mother Elizabeth wrote in her diary that she had walked over one day and had:

> a long natter with the Matron of the hospital on medical conditions in this area. Surgical cases have to go to Busselton or Bunbury under present conditions so the work here is mostly midwifery. She has done much to get the Government to improve the former primitive conditions.[71]

No doubt this knowledge would have influenced Mother Elizabeth to propose working with *our own doctors and nurses.*

Unlike Dr Taylor Thomas's subsequent offer to lease the hospital, Mother Elizabeth's proposal was not immediately rejected by the State Government, partly perhaps because the sisters were already well established in Margaret River. An enhanced medical and social support service would have been welcomed by the community, and the minister did meet with Mother Elizabeth.[72] However, eventually her proposal foundered, probably mainly due to the tough economic times but also to the failure of the State Government to underwrite this endeavour. The correspondence appears to have ended when the Minister for Health offered a government subsidy of 'say £700 or £750 per annum'. Hospital expenditure for the 1931 year had been £1,306 and receipts £324.[73] Mother Elizabeth presumably thought that the financial cost to the Order would be too great.

Margaret River remained a district hospital managed and funded by the Western Australian Government while the Anglican Sisters continued to support the local people and to remain an integral part of the local community. Normellie Carpenter (now

Ellie Metcalfe), grew up living next to the hospital and opposite the Anglican convent.

> Yes, my second name is Marion. I was named after Sister Marion. But yes, I more or less grew up in their garden because they were directly across the road from my home. And I spent a lot of time with the sisters. They taught me to sew and to knit.[74]

And while the sisters were not employed by the hospital:

> They would always visit and I've seen Sister Marion, who was a very quietly spoken very religious lady and she would sit with anyone that was really ill. Or if someone was in hospital, they would take the children sometimes so that other family members could get there. But I've seen Sister Marion sit with a patient who was unconscious and I remember the doctor saying, 'You can go home Sister because she doesn't know you are there.' And Sister held up her hand with the lady's hand in hers and she said, 'But she's squeezing my hand,

The Anglican nuns: Sister Marion second from left back & Ellie Metcalfe (Carpenter) girl at front. Courtesy Ellie Metcalfe.

doctor.' So, she did know that Sister Marion was there although she was unconscious.[75]

In the days before the advent of social workers and mental health services, the nuns played an important counselling and support role in the district.

> Yes, and it didn't matter what religion you were, I remember one family of three little girls, they were there for weeks and weeks because their mother had to go into an institution in Perth. She had a mental breakdown and they were very, very Catholic, but there was no Catholic convent here that they could go to. It was just to protect them, nothing to do with religion.[76]

The Anglican church, with its strong connections to the British Empire, provided a much sought after connection to the mother country. Mother Elizabeth was never idle during her visits to Margaret River or indeed when home in England. She arranged for the lay organisation which she had also established, the Confraternity of Divine Love, to support the building of small Anglican churches in group settlement areas around Margaret River.[77] Persuasive woman that she must have been, Mother Elizabeth obtained money from English followers of the confraternity to fund what are now known as the 'hundred pound churches' because each donor was asked to give one hundred pounds towards the cost of a wooden church, which was then built by local carpenters. Cowaramup's church in the park was a hundred-pound church, as was the now isolated church of St John the Evangelist at Osmington, which was paid for by a Mrs Rivington of East Sussex and consecrated on 2 February 1934.[78] Local parishioners provided all the fittings for the church, including the carpets, hangings, curtains and altar cloths.[79] At a time when money was scarce among the remaining group settlers, this willingness to donate to a new church gives some indication of their priorities.

Mother Elizabeth did not see the completed Osmington church until 1936, when she visited to discuss extensions to the convent.[80]

Osmington Church: one of the 'hundred pound churches' paid for by English benefactors. Stephen Blakeney.

On this visit she was surprised to find that a hotel had been built in the main street of the Margaret River townsite: 'A new hotel has been built – very up to date, as they hope to make it a tourist centre. I wonder? Nine miles from the nearest sea.'[81] Up to that time, the hospital had been the most prominent building in town, as this account written by a group settler from Busselton suggests:

> At that time Margaret River town consisted of a bush track winding up the side of the hill from the bridge across the river. Scattered at intervals along each side were about a dozen buildings mostly with hessian walls and a corrugated iron roof. There were three shops and a boarding house and the pride of the town was the hospital.[82]

Unlike Mother Elizabeth, Bernard McKeown, the proprietor and licensee of the new hotel, had no doubt that his enterprise would succeed, as his son Kim recalled:

Dad ventured into the country and decided that Margaret River had a great future and he therefore decided that Margaret River was the place to build a hotel. He initially bought two quarter-acre blocks where the hotel now stands as well as the two lots immediately behind the hotel. The blocks cost 30 pounds each on the main road and 20 pounds for the two behind the hotel.[83]

Until the hotel was built, Margaret River had been virtually a dry town. The only easily available alcohol was sold by the Terry brothers at a liquor camp down by the river bridge and later at their garage.[84] So Saturday 11 April 1936, which saw the official opening of the Margaret River Hotel, was a very big day for this small settlement, as the *South-Western News* reported:

> The newly completed hotel at Margaret River was opened on Saturday last. Mr E.V. Brockman, MLA performed the ceremony. The building which is of pleasing design is one of the most up to date in the South-West and should prove a decided acquisition to the district.[85]

This was also a significant occasion for the hotel owner's daughter, Bernice McKeown. She worked in the hotel bar that evening and when that closed she went up the hill to the ball, which was held in the 'new and commodious Town Hall'. It was there that Bernice met her future husband, Dudley McLeod.[86] And as the newspaper reported:

> The visitors staying at the new hotel helped largely to swell the crowd at the dance, there being over 200 people present. The electric light was available for the first time and greatly enhanced the ballroom...

The electric light at the hall came from the hotel's new generator. The hotel itself fronted Bussell Highway and was the most substantial building to be erected in the town since the hospital was built in 1924. Unlike the hospital, it was built in brick and for

Margaret River Hotel opened in 1936. MR&DHS.

the next half-century remained the largest and most eye-catching edifice in the main street.

Until the hotel was built there was no clearly identified town centre. The railway and the butter factory were at the southern extremity of the townsite, while the hospital was at the northern end near the river crossing. Tom Doyle recalled that shops were built in different areas within the townsite.

> And there were different traders deciding well this is the place and so they put their store, or they put their little bit of a restaurant and one thing and another along the roadway for the road traffic...And it was a little bit undecided until Bernard McKeown built the Margaret River Hotel...and of course, as is usual, the pub was the focal point... It was the establishment of the hotel that made the focus of things.[87]

The land which McKeown had purchased at the back of the hotel was also put to good use, as Kim McKeown explained:

> The two blocks behind the hotel were taken up with fruit trees, chook and duck pens and a very large vegetable garden. We had a fairly large number of Muscovy ducks and on one occasion a dog somehow got into the pens and scared the ducks and they took off and some of

them finished up down on the river near the bridge. We always had a cow to provide milk and cream for the dining room and our cow was kept on a block that dad had bought where Town View Terrace is now. We always had an abundance of milk and cream.[88]

Later the hotel owned blocks on the other side of the highway to accommodate the cow. This was next to the doctor's surgery and Ellie Metcalfe remembers that in the 1950s when the doctor was called to the hospital, he would take a short cut through the hotel's paddocks.

> That was where they had their cows and originally all the butter and cream; everything for the hotel was on the premises or within walking distance of the premises. And so, there were paddocks with cattle grids. So, the doctor could leave the back of his house and quite often Dr Barrett would run through the back to the maternity ward which was the first one you came to, and he would arrive at the hospital out of breath.[89]

When the hotel was built, forestry, including sleeper cutting, remained an important industry. Bernice McLeod recalled that the sleeper cutters, many of whom were on government sustenance, would cash their cheques and spend much of the money at the hotel bar.[90] Most were single men living in one of the town's boarding houses. Don McKenzie remembers about half a dozen sleeper cutters living around Margaret River. His father was a ganger on the railways and one of his jobs was to count the sleepers that came in to the railway siding.

> At times they would have a full sleeper train (as they used to call it) pull out of Margaret River with nothing else but sleepers and when there was a ship at Bunbury or Busselton, they would transport them to there on the Sleeper Special.[91]

While the hotel catered for the locals, including sleeper cutters, Bernice McLeod recalled that it was very much aimed at the tourist trade.

Sleepers were sent by rail to Busselton and Bunbury ports. MR&DHS.

In the early days of the hotel, people booked to stay a week or a fortnight, often arriving by train. This would sometimes arrive at the station a mile away during the late hours of the night. The hotel truck would meet the guests, bringing them back to the warmth of a log fire with coffee and supper. Marron parties to the river and wildflower and cave sightseeing tours were arranged by the family of the licensee. Sometimes fishing at Kilcarnup in the small hotel boat was the choice of some folk. This was part of the hospitality given where the needs of the guests were the hotel's main concern.[92]

Electric lighting was another comfort that the hotel provided for guests, although it was also something of a novelty for townsfolk, as Kim McKeown recalled: 'When we came to Margaret River in 1936 there was no electric power so we had to provide our own. This was provided by a 12-horsepower semi-diesel engine with a 250-volt generator.'[93]

The Margaret River District Hospital had been able to switch on the lights a year earlier, thanks to a 32-volt generator purchased with funds provided by the newly established Western Australian Lotteries Commission. Set up by Act of Parliament in 1932, the Lotteries Commission was to prove an invaluable source of funding for hospital improvements in Margaret River.[94] This was the height of the Depression and with government finances sorely stretched, lotteries money was initially used to provide essential equipment such as X-ray machines and refrigerators as well as nurses quarters extensions and other building works to hospitals across the state.[95] Lotterywest continued to support renovations in the 1990s when the old hospital became the Margaret River Community Centre, making this building one of the longest-term beneficiaries of lotteries funding.

The commission commenced giving grants in 1933.[96] On 14 May 1934, Matron May Wilson advised Secretary Huelin that the local member for the Sussex electorate, Mr E.V. Brockman, had visited Margaret River Hospital:

> He said he felt sure he could secure a sum of money from the Lotteries for us as this is a Group Settlement area and the present increased number of admissions and discharges in and out of Hospital will all help in securing a sum for us. With your approval, this is what I suggest writing and telling him we need two more bedrooms for nurses; ever since I came down here the Nurses' sitting room has been turned into a bedroom for two and three nurses all the time...At present we have seventeen patients *not* counting two middy babies.[97]

The Public Health Department quickly approved the proposal to obtain funds from Lotteries for additions to the staff quarters:

> presuming that the whole of the money needed will be provided. At the moment we cannot make any promise that there would be funds available from this Department towards the cost of the work.[98]

Thus, in March 1935, after an allocation from the Lotteries Commission, the Department of Works and Labour let a contract for two additional nurses' bedrooms, a new dining room and extension of the hospital's outbuildings to 'provide for an electric generator and rotary converter'.[99] The *South-Western News* reported on the installation:

> The electrical lighting plant now being installed in the Margaret River Hospital will undoubtedly be appreciated and be of great benefit both to patients and staff. The installation is a bigger job than might be thought by a casual observer. Over one mile of wire will be necessary and there will be thirty-four lights in the main building and six in the sisters' quarters and seven in the Rest House making a total of fifty-six lights. There will also be six power points. The plant will be run by a 3 h.p Lister petrol engine with 32 volts DC generator. It will have a 32 Vista battery for the night load...[100]

Lotteries had also agreed to provide an X-ray machine to be powered by the generator, but there was no provision for a dark room as the principal architect considered that 'the amount of X-ray work which will have to be carried out at this hospital would hardly be such as to warrant the provision of a dark room being made at the present juncture'.[101] Not surprisingly, this situation soon caused problems, as Dr Mandelstam, then the district medical officer, complained: 'The X-ray plant is now working and as we have no dark room we have to wait until dark to do the developing, this is naturally rather inconvenient.'[102] Eventually, the doctor was informed that the principal architect had been asked to provide both a dark room and a dispensary which Dr Mandelstam had also requested.[103] As there was no pharmacist in the town, the doctor needed to dispense from the hospital any drugs required.

In any event, a pharmacist would probably have received a limited patronage as most people lived outside the townsite and came to Margaret River only when transport was available. This was generally by horse and cart as few people owned a motor vehicle and there were no bus services. So people travelling to attend sporting or community events, such as CWA meetings, often travelled in the back of trucks, as Enid Garstone recalled:

Trucks were used to convey Members and families to picnics etc. O.C. Clarke, R. Swarbrick, West and W. Auger all hired trucks. On 9 March 1928 West's truck for a blackberry picnic to Burnside cost twelve shillings and sixpence and on 21 January 1939 W. Auger conveyed Members and families to a picnic at Redgate and the cost of hire of the truck was one pound and ten shillings.[104]

Roads were unsealed and accidents requiring hospital treatment and admission were not uncommon. If a truck rolled over, the number of casualties could be quite high. The hospital's X-ray plant might well have been needed in late September 1935 when a vehicle heading for Busselton carrying the Margaret River hockey team overturned on Bussell Highway:

20 HURT IN SMASH
Overturning of Truck
ONE CRITICAL

Twenty persons were injured, one seriously when a motor truck carrying a hockey team and its supporters overturned at Margaret River on Sunday morning, stated a report which reached Perth today... Members of the party were hurled from the truck and the injured lay about the roadway for yards on either side of the upturned vehicle.[105]

The newspaper reported that within a few minutes Dr Mandelstam was at the scene rendering first aid and that twenty persons were transported to the hospital where:

> the small staff and the doctor worked on broken limbs and lacerated bodies.... Today there were still five victims in the hospital ward but it was expected that three of these would be sufficiently recovered for discharge this evening. The condition of (Arthur) Wilkinson, however, was said to be critical and his name has been entered on the danger list.

Hospital admissions for that day state that Wilkinson had a fractured skull, while the other passengers sustained injuries including concussion and a broken collarbone. Some were given anti-tetanus vaccinations while, for the first time, the records show that X-rays were used to identify some of the injuries.[106]

Arthur Wilkinson's injuries were so serious that he was transferred to Perth. The account of his transfer illustrates the difficulties (and the cost to families) involved in transporting patients in an era before reliable transport and the arrival of a local ambulance service.

> The condition of Arthur Wilkinson who was badly injured in a motor smash near Margaret River last Sunday week showed little improvement during the week-end and it was decided to convey the injured man to Perth. The services of an ambulance was obtained and on Saturday, Wilkinson was transferred to the Perth Public Hospital where he is at present under observation. Unfortunately the ambulance broke down before reaching Bunbury and the remainder of the journey had to be completed by car. The cost of transferring the injured man to the city was about £20 and a public subscription has been opened at Margaret River in order to raise the money. Already £10 has been contributed, and anyone wishing to help is requested to forward donations to Mr L.F. Gibson who is the principal mover in the appeal.[107]

Almost a year later, in July 1936, another truck carrying 12 passengers overturned on the road between Margaret River and Witchcliffe. The occupants were returning to Kudardup after attending an event in Margaret River. The local newspaper reported that the Margaret River ambulance, which had come into service only two weeks earlier, was quickly on the scene and that the injured were conveyed to the hospital, where they were attended to by Dr Salvi, the relieving doctor, as Dr Mandelstam had left the district.[108] When everyone had been taken to the hospital, it became apparent that a baby, Herbert (Smiler) Gale, who had been on the truck was still missing.

> I can't remember anything about that but my mum tells the story that I was involved with an accident with about nine other people, and they all went to hospital but they left me on the side of the road. They couldn't find me, but mum realised that I was missing so they went back and got me.[109]

The story was picked up in the *South-Western News*: 'Following the accident, Herbert Gale, an infant of eleven months, could not at first be found but was finally located underneath the truck'.[110] Baby Smiler's injuries cannot have been too serious as he is recorded as spending only one day in hospital.[111]

Improvements at the hospital, particularly the installation of electric lighting, had made dealing with large-scale accidents much easier. They were much appreciated by the matron and staff.

> The Under Secretary (Medical) 1 August 1935
>
> Dear Sir
>
> Now that the new two new nurses' bedrooms and the new dining room is in use and the Electric light installed, I would like to thank you on behalf of the staff and myself for having secured comfortable rooms for us, as for the Electric Light, I can't speak too highly of it, as it is just wonderful. A number of people have been up and inspected the improvements, which have caused much added interest, and I think that the new improvements will tend to make the general public take more interest in their District Hospital.
>
> Yours faithfully,
>
> May Wilson
>
> Matron.[112]

This 32-volt machine provided all electrical services to the hospital until the whole town was provided with 24-hour power in 1938.

Electric Light Service

Margaret River now enjoys electric light for 24 hours daily. After much worry and anxiety, the engineer (Mr Nixon) has the plant in effective working condition to carry the extra load. Electric points and radio are being put into use. The Margaret hospital comes under the power station and has the full supply of current.[113]

The nurses were now more comfortable. They had a new dining room and, best of all, the hospital was no longer reliant on kerosene lamps.

At the same time, the effects of years of neglect in maintaining both hospital and grounds were emerging. A year before he officially resigned as district medical officer in July 1936,[114] Dr Mandelstam had written to the department in Perth about these problems: 'For your information, the Margaret River Hospital is in need of re-decoration. I have been told that decay will set in if the buildings are not attended to in the near future.'[115] Possibly as a result of this complaint, the government's Department of Works and Labour prepared a long report listing the repairs needed and an estimated cost of £645. Again, money was provided by the Lotteries Commission, which immediately wrote a cheque for almost half the expected cost – £317.10 shillings – making these renovations possible.[116]

In March 1937 there was another serious bushfire. Once again, this put the spotlight on the hospital grounds, which, like the buildings themselves, had been neglected for several years. Efforts were made to obtain assistance from the road board, though that body seemed reluctant to take action. The Public Health Department, however, which lacked both the people and the equipment to undertake the work, was keen to see the main fire hazard – the undergrowth – removed while retaining the trees, which provided shade.[117]

Both Dr Mandelstam and his predecessor, Dr Taylor Thomas, would have spent a considerable amount of time at the hospital undertaking minor surgery, including tonsillectomies and dental extractions.[118] As district medical officers, both doctors would have treated many diverse accidents which occurred on farms and among timber workers, including sleeper cutters. The list of hospital admissions for 1934 includes the following: septic wounds, back sprains (several), chopped foot, kicked by a horse (the main means of transport and farm power), injury to big toe, injury to right arm, chopped right leg, thrown from horse, infected wound, burnt feet.[119]

Infectious diseases, which in the 1920s were rarely listed in the hospital admissions register, now became a much greater concern. In 1931 there was a single admission of a child with whooping cough, and in the two following years several cases of typhoid fever and meningitis were admitted to the hospital with some cases causing death. The years 1934 and 1935 saw outbreaks of diphtheria and scarlet fever, resulting in hospital admissions.[120] As a consequence, there was demand from the local community for a dedicated isolation ward. The prime mover in this campaign was the Country Women's Association, which now had branches in Margaret River as well as the outlying settlements of Rosa Brook, Rosa Glen, Witchcliffe and Cowaramup.[121]

The Margaret River CWA had been established in July 1931. Mrs Rigby, the doctor's wife, was the inaugural president while Matron Doyle was among the women who attended the first meeting. Many early members were group settlers, including Mrs Les Hugall, wife of the secretary of the Margaret River and Districts Progress Association.[122] Agda Wyatt, the police officer's wife, described that first meeting:

> The inaugural meeting was held in the Parish Hall, Railway Road, through the kind courtesy of Father Clissold of the Bush Brotherhood. Mrs Augur kindly kept the "Urn" going and ladies were requested to bring their own "mugs" and "eats". Meetings were to be held on cream cheque days, so the influx of ladies became a boon to storekeepers – West, Samworth, Smiths, West's (vegies), Rodgers the Butcher, Mansfield the baker, Lucas's store down by the bridge.

> The meeting hall was packed out; what a wonderful turn-out. After singing the National Anthem the meeting was opened and with full acclamation a Branch was formed.[123]

The CWA soon began lobbying for improved local facilities and services. In July 1934 the president of the Margaret River branch, Mrs K.F.M. (Kittie) Bussell, wrote directly to the Hon. Selby Munsie, Minister for Mines and Health in the Collier Labor government. She asked for improvements and additions to the local hospital, including a new nursery ward which would allow the existing nursery to be turned into an isolation ward. Mrs Bussell was also keen to advise the minister that the staff at the hospital was doing very good work under rather trying conditions owing to the lack of accommodation.[124]

The road board also wrote to the minister supporting this proposal:

> Quite recently a number of cases of infectious diseases have had to be treated at the Margaret Hospital. As there was no proper accommodation for infectious cases, makeshift arrangements have had to be made. In the past few months, cases of diphtheria and typhoid fever have had to be treated and it is fortunate that the outbreaks to date have been small.[125]

Matron Wilson confirmed the veracity of this statement.

> During the past twelve months we have admitted five diphtheria cases which were accommodated on the verandah (at the) left end of the hospital. It is not a suitable place and we do need some place for infectious cases.[126]

In response to the matron, the department secretary pointed out that very few country hospitals had isolation wards, while Mrs Bussell was advised, in a time-honoured phrase favoured by governments, that 'the matter was under consideration'.[127]

The following year, both the road board and the CWA tried again to persuade the State Government to fund an isolation ward.

This time they cited support from 'a rally of local CWA branches' (Margaret River, Witchcliffe, Rosa Brook and Cowaramup).[128] Again, the department's response was swift and negative: such a facility was not needed but if it was, the local road board was responsible for the management of infectious diseases. They should provide the facility and fund half the cost.[129] The road board showed no interest in this proposal, although the matter was raised again at a meeting in 1938 when the board received the following letter from a local resident after another outbreak of diphtheria and a case of scarlet fever. The letter was published in the *South-Western News*.

> I wish to draw the attention of your board to the very unsatisfactory housing of patients suffering from infectious diseases. A short while ago two children were taken to the hospital with scarlet fever. Having no infectious ward, a shed that was used as a lamp and tool room was cleared out and the walls whitewashed. There was just room for two beds and that is where the children stayed for just five weeks. The room was just a weatherboard shed unlined, and was a room that I wouldn't think of putting one of my children in even when well. Alongside the shed was the wash house, and all the waste water from the washing ran along an open drain right touching the step leading into the room where the patients were. A number of other children were then brought to the hospital suffering from diphtheria. They were placed on the men's verandah and now at the present time, when I believe there are now about twelve diphtheria patients. I don't know how they are managing. It is not fair on the matron and staff and it is certainly not fair on the patients. Will your board make the position clear to the Minister for Health and see if something cannot be done to better the present conditions?[130]

Despite this writer's graphic descriptions, no action was taken. The road board was still reluctant to pay for an isolation ward, while the Public Health Department had other priorities.

Importantly, although there was no vaccine for scarlet fever, there was an increased emphasis on immunisation against diphtheria when, in early 1937, Dr E.B. Tunbridge purchased the Margaret River medical practice from Dr Mandelstam and commenced a vaccination program. In June 1938 Dr Tunbridge submitted a report to the road board stating that, while eleven cases of diphtheria

Nurses 1936. Sister Cross at front with magpie. Courtesy Judy Wake (provided by Sister Cross for 60th anniversary 1984).

had been reported from different localities in the previous month, he had visited the whole district and over five hundred children were in the process of being immunised. The doctor specifically thanked 'the Margaret River Hospital matron for her splendid assistance'.[131]

Before Tunbridge's arrival, Dr Salvi was one of several temporary medical officers, who, during his short stay, was brigade surgeon and a popular patron of the ambulance sub-centre. The ambulance sub-centre next to the police station was by then nearing completion and in January 1937, the first monthly meeting of the Ambulance Association was held in the new quarters. It was recorded that Dr Mandelstam, who now lived in London, had sent his best wishes and enclosed ten guineas for the building fund.[132] This donation would have been well received as there was still a focus on fundraising. The meeting decided to ask local branches of the CWA to assist in organising an Ambulance Queen competition to raise funds.[133]

Nurses with Dr Salvi, one of several 'locum' doctors in the 1930s.
Courtesy Judy Wake (provided by Sister Cross for 60th anniversary 1984).

In addition to accidents, toothache was a reason for visiting the doctor. Dr John Saunders was another short-term relieving doctor in Margaret River just before World War II. His son Rob remembers him talking about one unfortunate aspect of his job.

> On Saturday afternoon he used to come up to Cowaramup and pull teeth in the back of this church which was the Congregational Church because there were no dentists around the area. And not being a dentist, if people had a toothache, it was easier just to rip them out. And I remember his saying one time that not being a dentist he had all sorts of trouble trying to pull teeth out and he found it a lot easier just to cut them out and not actually pull them out.[134]

After a succession of locum doctors, which included Dr Saunders, Margaret River gained one of its longest-serving district medical officers when Dr Ewen Tunbridge arrived. His tenure lasted officially from 1937 until December 1948.[135] The new doctor was popular in town and the eastern end of Wallcliffe Road would later be renamed Tunbridge Street in recognition of his contribution to the district and to the hospital which fronts that street.

Cowaramup main street. MR&DHS.

Ellie Metcalfe remembers that Dr Tunbridge often sought out her father as a blood donor.

> Well, my first connection in thinking of Dad and the hospital was that Dr Tunbridge was always knocking on the door as they gave blood person-to-person and he had the blood type that could be used for practically everybody and he lived right next door to the hospital so he was very convenient. And Dr Tunbridge was always dragging him off to the hospital and that was my first connection with him and the hospital.[136]

Ellie's father would never talk about the 'bloodletting', but she does recall one memorable event when a man fell off a train travelling from Busselton to Augusta and required a blood transfusion:

> I don't know what injuries he had except that he had lost an arm and a leg. But I know Dad came home and I heard him tell Mum, 'Thanks mate, I'll do the same for you one day' and Dad said, 'I hope to Christ you never have to!' So obviously it was person-to-person blood.

Ellie's father was also the hospital orderly for many years.

> One of the orderlies got the sack because he was drunk and unable to get out of bed. And at the time, Sister Peirce was in charge because Matron Flynn was on holiday and she tried to get him out of bed and he wouldn't open the door. So I got the job of getting in the window and opening the door. Sister Peirce sacked him on the spot. And I went flying home as soon as I could and told Dad and he applied for the job! In those days, it was basically keeping the furnace going for the hot water and a bit of gardening. It was chopping the wood because the stove in the kitchen was all wood-fired. And there was not much contact with the patients. If there was a man that needed a bath, Dad would see him in and out and help him shave or whatever. But nothing medical at all.[137]

After Dr Tunbridge's largely successful diphtheria immunisation campaign, demand for an isolation ward decreased. But the new doctor was less than impressed by the state of the hospital buildings, in particular facilities for maternity patients. In an address to the Augusta-Margaret River Road Board he proposed that the Margaret Cecil Rest House be repurposed as the hospital maternity wing and the existing maternity ward turned into a children's ward. The entire hospital building was, he said:

> In a deplorable condition insofar as the layout was concerned and it was necessary to go through the maternity ward on all occasions when it was desired to reach the operating theatre; no other exit was provided...
>
> Continuing, Dr Tunbridge said that on account of the increasing number of maternity cases, handled at the hospital it had been found necessary to utilise the Margaret Cecil Rest House for the overflow of cases from the hospital. A further suggestion had been made to utilise the whole of the Rest House as a maternity block and with this end in view, the authorities controlling that institution in England had been written to but so far, no reply had been received.[138]

Margaret Cecil Rest House 1936 before conversion to Maternity Ward.
Courtesy Judy Wake (provided by Sister Cross for 60th anniversary 1984).

Since the Rest House was constructed with funds provided by the 'Margarets of Britain', the 'authority in Britain' was Mrs Margaret Lane, formerly the Hon. Margaret Cecil, and the rest house had been administered separately from the hospital.

By the late 1930s, with improvements in roads and communications, there was less need for a rest house and the road board agreed to ask shire residents whether some funds could be raised locally to support the necessary alterations and additions.[139] This proposal was supported by local Member of Parliament W.H.F. Willmott, who wrote to the Minister for Health endorsing the move and suggesting that Lotteries Commission funding could also be sought.

> I have been approached by the people of Margaret River, through Dr Tunbridge, for an extension to the Margaret River Hospital which will make more provision for a maternity ward, which is badly needed at the hospital.
>
> I have approached the Lotteries Commission with regard to the matter and they are agreeable to assist if your department will do the same. I understand they have plans drawn up, with an estimated cost of £1200. The local authorities are prepared to collect £400; I am told they have at present approximately £335 with the balance in view.
>
> The Lotteries Commission will donate £400 if the Health Department will donate a similar amount.
>
> I trust you will give this request your serious consideration, and when the local authorities have collected their quota, the necessary work could be put in hand.
>
> Yours faithfully
>
> W.H.F. Willmott.[140]

Department Secretary Huelin advised his minister to support this proposal, noting that:

> This is the first time that the Margaret River people have done anything for their hospital and the addition of a Maternity Wing is certainly needed at Margaret River.
>
> Now that the local people have made an effort, I recommend that you approve a £ for £ subsidy not exceeding £400 being made towards this work, and I attach draft letter which you may think suitable to send to Mr Willmott.[141]

Dr Tunbridge asked local organisations to send a representative to a meeting at the road board to discuss ways of raising the necessary finance for this project.[142] A Hospital Building Extension Fund was established and collectors were appointed for Margaret River and the coastal areas.[143] On 12 April 1940 the *South-Western News* reported that Margaret River, Rosa Glen, Rosa Brook, Karridale, Warner Glen and Augusta had all paid the maximum sums requested while other localities had contributed a percentage. Agreement from Mrs Lane to repurpose the Margaret Cecil Rest House had also been received in advice sent to W.J. Mann, MLC, a trustee.

> Dear Sir
>
> The following cable message has been received from the Agent General for Western Australia in London on your behalf:
>
> Please communicate following to W. J. Mann MLC. Margaret Lane agrees proposal for Margaret Cecil Rest House letter follows: The cost of this message is 4/9d which amount I shall be pleased to receive at your early convenience.
>
> Yours faithfully
>
> A.G. Reid
>
> Under Treasurer [144]

The rest house trustees also provided £100 towards the building extensions.[145]

The new maternity wing was officially opened by the then Minister for Health, Mr A.H. Panton, MLA, on Saturday 13 July 1940.[146]

> The structure forms an extension to the Margaret Cecil Rest House and comprises a four-bed ward, private rooms, a modern nursery, sterilising room and modern conveniences.
>
> Speaking from twelve years' experience in country hospitals, the district Medical Officer, Dr E.B. Tunbridge expressed his intense pride and gratitude at the completion of the new wing. He considered that with the money available the District Architect, Mr C. Hall, had designed a good building of which the doctor felt sure there was no equal outside of the metropolitan area.[147]

In his speech, Rest House trustee W.J. Mann, MLC:

> desired it to be clearly understood, however, that the Margaret Cecil Rest House as such, remained now and for all time dedicated to the purpose for which it was constructed. It must never be merged into the public hospital...This proviso had been laid down by the Margarets of Great Britain before sanctioning the additions and alterations.[148]

The cost of establishing the new maternity wing was approximately £1,300. Government and the Lotteries Commission had each pledged £400. Along with the trustees' contribution, this had left the people of the Margaret River to contribute at least another £400 towards the building fund.[149] In 1939 this was a 'big ask' and it was testament to the spirit of the district, as well as the obviously identified need, that this sum was raised.

Almost two decades after the commencement of the Group Settlement Scheme, families in this largely farming community had little money to spare. Stan Dilkes, the son of a group settler, described the situation around Margaret River in the late 1930s:

> Many farms were just purely abandoned especially coming up to the Second World War and hundreds and hundreds of acres were covered with bracken and the rabbits started to come and that was another big blow. And with the rabbits, the bracken and the standing dead trees and abandoned blocks and poor abandoned houses, that would have been what the areas looked like in the late 1930s just before the second war.[150]

This was the landscape of Stan Dilkes' boyhood: dead trees and abandoned farms. Slowly some of these properties were taken up by others. John Brennan's father was one man who decided to try his hand on the land.

> We came down here when I was eleven years old. My father was a schoolteacher and down there almost every farm was abandoned. The cow yards were broken, you had to repair them and the fences were down because the paddocks were covered in dead trees (which) were always dropping limbs and of course they often fell on the fences. I know in our particular case the hay shed had blown over and the toilet had blown over. That was one of my early memories. We had no toilet, the wooden dunnies as they were called were about fifty metres from the house.[151]

Other new arrivals came from the West Australian Wheatbelt, where prices for grain had fallen so low that cropping had become uneconomic. These more experienced farmers who were offered old group settlement properties were attracted by the promise of higher and more regular rainfall. They, too, were often shocked at the state of the farms they took over. In 1941 Betty Earl's family, the Clews, moved from an established farm near Merredin to Cowaramup.

> What a shock it was when the house we left had been a well-built house. It was a groupie house and was well built, but derelict, no lining, tin ceiling. Animals had been sheltering in it. No windows, and four rooms, a verandah out the front, dunny down the back, a room out

the side for the dairy. The dairy was in a reasonable condition but it had to be cleaned out before we could get any cows.[152]

Encouragement for families like the Clews and the Brennans to take up these abandoned farms came from the Agricultural Bank, which:

> kept dangling financial carrots to would-be buyers. The terms on offer when we came to Rosa Brook, thirty kilometres east of Margaret River, in 1937 were fifty pounds sterling deposit on a farm with a debt of five hundred pounds sterling. There was interest payable on the balance immediately and after three years principal payments on the total amount owed, paid annually.[153]

No one was going to make a fortune from farming an old groupie block but the main occupations in the district were still dairying and forestry. Apart from the butter factory, the hotel, a few shops and, of course, the hospital, there were few sources of employment, especially for women. Jessie Sharp (nee Campbell) was born in 1921 and grew up on Group 7 at Forest Grove. She left home aged eighteen in 1939 to go nursing.

> The boys stayed on because they had the (timber) mills. There was nothing for the girls. We didn't get enough money to pay for board. We all went into nursing as it was a job that had accommodation.[154]

For girls like Jessie, leaving home and training as a nurse provided a welcome escape from life on the farm.

> Girls were bad news in those days. We used to work like slaves on the farm like the blokes did – carting hay, making fences. There was plenty of work for us to do. When we came home from school, we did the milking and before we went to school. We had about fifteen cows.

As far as possible, everyone, especially farming families, made do with what they had. Clothes were homemade and often repurposed. Smiler Gale, the baby left under an overturned truck in 1936, was five years old in 1940. He remembers a childhood at Kudardup spent in hand-me-down clothes.

> I was second in line with the four eldest boys, and I only got George's clothes and I wore them second-hand. But Brian, who is number four, he was in the fourth round when these clothes got pretty old and ragged. I can remember again when it rained and going to school, we had a super (fertiliser) bag with corners turned inside and the super bag then created a hat and also a raincoat...That's the way it was. Parents couldn't afford clothes.[155]

Some years earlier, one mother on Group 17 at Bramley had been unable to send her children to school:

> Owing to them having no warm clothing. I am endeavouring to get them clothes & will send them as soon as possible. The School Master here is aware of this fact.[156]

Shops in the smaller settlements, including Rosa Brook, Witchcliffe, Cowaramup and Kudardup, supplied essential foodstuffs that could not be grown locally, as well as kerosene for lighting and heating. By 1940 Margaret River, in addition to general stores, boasted a newsagency, a pharmacy and a post office as well as a petrol station with a garage.

While services in town were at last growing and there was a continuous electricity supply, there was no reticulated water supply. Since its opening in 1924, the hospital had relied on rainwater tanks and a well. When these failed, water had to be carted from the river. The lack of a reliable water supply also had implications for sewerage. In December 1937 Matron McLeod reported that members of the Lotteries Commission who had viewed the hospital's sanitary arrangements were less than impressed. The visitors stated that the commission would look favourably on any request for funding and that substantial assistance would be available should such a proposal be put before it.[157] Unfortunately, tests in 1938 showed that the hospital well could not provide enough water to support a sewerage system. The local road board was then asked about the possibility of installing a townsite water supply.¹⁵⁸ While initial promises were made, it appeared that the matter would not be progressed 'in the near future'.¹⁵⁹

Meanwhile, the district architect came up with an innovative solution to the hospital's water problem. The Railway Department pumped the water needed for its steam engines from the river and also already supplied water for the butter factory's operations. Since the hospital was on lower ground than the factory, a pipeline installed between the two buildings could deliver water to the hospital through gravity feed. All that was required was half a mile of piping and, once a secure water supply was available, the sewerage system could be addressed.¹⁶⁰

However, World War II intervened and it was not until 1946 that this pipe was laid and the hospital's water supply problem resolved. The town and outlying areas of the district would wait even longer for piped water, which would eventuate only in more prosperous times, after World War II.

Wheatbelt farmers were shocked at the state of the farms. Courtesy Thelma Burnett.

Chapter Five

A Proper Standard

When the Minister for Health, Mr A.H. Panton MLA, opened the new maternity wing at the Margaret River District Hospital on Saturday 13 July 1940, he stated that his department was anxious to bring country hospitals, including Margaret River, 'up to a proper standard of efficiency'.[1] Over the next two decades, there would be many attempts, mostly spearheaded by the local community to achieve this aim. Success in meeting it would be hard-won. The establishment, in 1947, of a Hospital Visiting and Advisory Committee[2] (sometimes later known as the Margaret River Hospital Amenities Committee) would prove to be important not only in funding additional comforts, but also in advocating directly to the minister of the day for improvements in the facilities.

Since its opening in 1929, the Margaret Cecil Rest House had been administered separately from the hospital by the Rest House Association. After the maternity ward moved into that building, the association retained the sitting room as a place for waiting and nursing mothers to rest while in town.[3] The *Margaret River News* reported on a committee meeting held on 20 July 1941:

> Since the opening of the new maternity annex to the Margaret River Hospital in July 1940, the Rest House has been greatly appreciated by mothers and utilised to a much greater degree than previously. Over the winter months it was regarded with outstanding favour by reason of its cosiness and home-like atmosphere.[4]

The meeting report continued:

> Contact...had been maintained with England as far as possible through Mrs Margaret Lane and newspapers received. While from Western Australia, illustrated Christmas periodicals were forwarded and acknowledged with thanks. Mention was made of the painful and ever dangerous period through which the Margarets of Britain, in common with others, were passing and fervent wishes for the nation's speedy victory and admiration for the courage, determination and cheerfulness of the people of Britain was expressed.[5]

There was a sense that the war now raging in Europe was far from Margaret River. This is probably how many Western Australians saw the situation five months before Japan entered World War II. On the other hand, by July 1941, thousands of Australian troops, including Tom Doyle and Duncan McLeod from Margaret River, had been evacuated from Crete[6] and Germany had attacked the Soviet Union.[7]

When the association held its next meeting, just six months later, it was still business as usual.

> Mrs H. West, honorary secretary, submitted the annual report which showed that as an auxiliary to the hospital, the Rest House was providing a very acceptable service. The number of patients accommodated showed a slight increase over that of the past year...The thanks of the subscribers was tendered to Dr Tunbridge and Matron Dunbar for the kindly interest shown to Rest House patients.[8]

Matron Dunbar was an ex-officio member of the Margaret Cecil Rest House Association committee, which was still responsible for the maintenance and purchase of amenities for the sitting room in the rest house. Formerly Agnes Livingstone, Matron Dunbar had been a nurse at the hospital in the 1930s when her courtship had been recorded in the local newspaper.

MARGARET RIVER NOTES

(From Our Correspondent)

PERSONAL

Sister A Livingstone of the Margaret River Hospital is spending her annual leave with her brother at Quairading.

Mr A Dunbar is enjoying a holiday somewhere in the wheat country.[9]

Agnes Livingstone and Alec Dunbar were married on 1 September 1934.[10] Their son Robert (Bob) was born the following year, but Mrs Dunbar's good fortune did not last.

> They had a couple of probably very happy years and then unfortunately my father died of a heart attack in 1938 in March, and she of course had had to give up her job in the hospital because she was married.[11]

While married women were not permitted to work in a government hospital, this prohibition did not apply to widows. The hospital required a matron and Mrs Dunbar needed financial stability. Thus,

> At a road board meeting, Mr Key, who was the representative of Alexander Bridge, moved at the meeting that the widow Dunbar should be approached to see if she would become the hospital matron.[12]

The Public Health Department was prepared to accept the road board's recommendation and offer the position to a widow, but it would have been beyond consideration for her young son to be housed at the hospital. Bob went to live with the Samworth family,

Sister Agnes Livingstone marries Alec Dunbar, Sept 1934. Courtesy Bob and Judy Dunbar.

who ran a shop in town, but he was often taken to the hospital to see his mother on a Sunday.

> She had a complete house beside the hospital. It's been moved back into the grounds a bit now, but it used to be right beside one of the entrances to the hospital. And I would be dropped off on a Sunday morning sometimes to spend the day with mum, because she might have had the day off. And I remember walking out to the cemetery. We would walk from the hospital out to the cemetery and back again for the day.[13]

The 'complete house' Bob referred to was the small group-type wooden structure built for the matron and nurses in 1924 and which, in the 1930s, also housed live-in domestic staff. When plans were being drawn up in early 1940 to turn the rest house into the hospital's maternity ward, Agnes Dunbar asked the medical undersecretary whether separate accommodation could be provided for the matron.

The main hospital before renovation. MR&DHS.

> I would recommend for your consideration that new accommodation be provided for myself, pointing out that at the present time, the domestic staff and I are in the same building. If this is given me, my bedroom and sitting room would be available for the domestics and I certainly would be able to enjoy more privacy than I do at present.[14]

This request received some support from District Architect Charles Hall, who advised:

> that we might consider the provision of two rooms for the Matron (bedroom and sitting room) to be built adjacent to the present nurses' quarters, and that if we do anything in the matter it would be advisable to have the work carried out whilst the other work is in progress.[15]

Given the exigencies of wartime and the usual lack of funds, officials in Perth were not enthusiastic about extending the scope of works and a matron's flat was not built until a decade later, long after Matron Dunbar had left the position to marry a local shopkeeper. As Mrs Jack Thomas, she remained a member of the Rest House Association committee.

The Rest House Association committee met on the very day (3 February 1942) that the Japanese first bombed Port Moresby, capital of Papua and home to a small Australian garrison. The fall of Singapore was imminent.[16] Not surprisingly there was now some suggestion that times were not 'normal'.

> The question of utilisation of the Rest House in the event of evacuation from congested centres was referred to and it was resolved to allow the matter to remain in the hands of the committee and Matron Dunbar, always providing that accommodation was available for women eligible and who desired admission.[17]

'Congested centres' was presumably a euphemism for territory that might fall into Japanese hands in the event of the war spreading to Western Australia.

World War II was now influencing the lives of many local people. Shopkeeper Bill Darnell had gone into business in 1937 with his tennis partner, English migrant George Shervington,[18] and although they owned general stores in Witchcliffe and Rosa Brook, both men were prepared to serve their country:

> We tossed up to see who went first. He got away and I didn't. We managed to run it while he was away with everyone else helping. When I went into full-time VDC (Volunteer Defence Corps) in Busselton when the Japs were knocking at the door, I said to Mum, 'Well I have to go'. We had a company of men in the district and we all promised that we could go at an hour's notice if we were called up.[19]

Farming, unlike shopkeeping, was a reserved occupation. The nation had to be fed. After the evacuation from Crete, Tom Doyle continued his army service overseas, but in 1944 he was discharged to help his father and brother. On his return Tom became aware that conditions on the land had changed for the better. It was:

> becoming a bit more mechanised even in those days. The small tractors and this sort of thing. And there was also, one could see,

quite an influx of people who wanted to get on the land and of those who had picked out Margaret River and its area as a very congenial place. And this was I think the incentive for quite a few and there was quite a boost in farming in those days.[20]

Some farmers took advantage of this 'boost in farming' by taking over abandoned group settlement blocks. Cedar (George) Armstrong's father did well out of leasing, buying and selling this land,[21] while the *South-Western News* reported that:

> There are only three vacant group blocks north of the Margaret River in this district. South of the Margaret River there are 10 in the Margaret Ward and 5 in the East Ward, 33 in the Karridale Ward and 5 in the Blackwood Ward. This indicates a very definite faith in the potentialities of our district, and in the future of land settlement...[22]

Yet much of the land was still uncleared and hard work was required to make progress. Kevin Coate, growing up in the town, observed that:

> It was pretty tough for anyone trying to live off the land. In those days it was a seven day a week job. Except during summer, there was a brief respite for people as they used to dry cattle off in summertime. But then again as a by-product of milking, most families had some pigs and they had to keep milking a few cows because milk was the main thing to keep the pigs going.[23]

Cedar (George) Armstrong had taken over his family's farm, Mouquet Farm on Caves Road, in 1942.

> When I took it over I was 18. I had about 50 acres or so cleared, little bits of swamp land and patches for spuds all over the auction...
>
> There were 14 cows, two horses, a spring cart, a couple of pigs and a couple of calves. And from then on, we worked like hell and cleared this country. Eventually...we had five hundred acres cleared and I had a Guernsey stud there for 16 years...We also had Poll Dorset sheep.[24]

SETTLEMENT, STRUGGLE AND SUCCESS

Some farmers took over abandoned group settlement blocks. Courtesy Thelma Burnett.

The hard work involved in farming did not end with the dropping of two atomic bombs on Japan and the cessation of hostilities in August 1945. But all those who had served in the armed forces could now return home. Branches of the Returned and Services League had been formed in the district after World War I, with the Margaret River RSL being established in 1928. In 1935 branches were also set up in Rosa Brook/Rosa Glen, Cowaramup and Witchcliffe.[25] In January 1945, the annual meeting of the Margaret River sub-branch of the RSL was held with President Mr R.G. Forrester presiding 'over a large attendance among whom were an appreciable number of younger returned men'.[26]

Some returning soldiers required medical treatment at the local hospital. One benefit from the war had been the speedy development of penicillin as an effective drug for treating infections, particularly in war wounds. This new 'wonder drug' had now reached Margaret River Hospital.

> It is worthy of note that the wonder drug Penicillin was used during the week-end in our hospital for the first time

on record. A young soldier who developed a rare condition following a complicated operation had a visit on Sunday from Lieutenant Colonel Moss O.C. of Medical Wards at Hollywood Hospital. As the soldier's condition warranted the use of Penicillin, Col. Moss had brought a supply. This was used as from Sunday night and has caused a considerable improvement in the patient, who may now be considered out of danger. Col. Moss considers that the drug would be available in any particular civilian case if required, from now on, as supplies are in every way quite adequate.[27]

The end of the war also allowed for improvements to the Margaret River townsite, as the *South-Western News* informed its readers in December 1945:

Post war reconstruction works have begun at Margaret River. However, to the passer-by it looks more like destruction for the forlorn looking footpaths are being torn up to place underground the telephone cable. Gone shortly will be the telegraph poles and wires and with them, 'tis said most of the static now heard in town on the radios.[28]

Kevin Coate, aged ten when the war ended, paints a picture of the town at that time:

Margaret River at that time was a very small town; gravel road going through the main street, horse trough outside the hotel. A lot of people were still travelling by horse and cart. Vehicle travel was restricted in lots of ways during wartime because of shortage of fuel.[29]

On the first day of 1946, the *Hospital Benefits Act 1945* came into effect. This legislation represented the Australian Government's first involvement in the provision of health services and included local as well as national implications. The federal government needed to occupy this space because small public hospitals, like Margaret River, struggled to raise enough revenue to cover their costs, especially since the demand for medical services was increasing.³⁰ The new legislation specified that everyone must have access to the public wards of Australian hospitals free of charge.³¹ This had implications for the local hospital fund; families could pay an annual subscription that would cover them for any hospitalisation costs, but this arrangement became redundant with the proclamation of the new legislation as patient fees would now be covered by the Commonwealth Government. Accordingly, the Public Health Department advised Acting Matron Wright that:

> The government now assumes liability for treatment of patients in public wards and allows a rebate of six shillings per day for patients in intermediate or private wards. The fund conditions will have to be revised – I think that it would be as well to let the Fund lapse.³²

The fund was discontinued and householders who had paid subscriptions in advance received a refund. The amount reimbursed to eligible contributors ranged from thirty shillings paid to R.H. Earl and W.A. Miller to £2.2.0 refunded to F.V. Castle.³³

The end of the war brought other changes that affected demand for medical services. Previously the population of the area covered by the Augusta-Margaret River Road Board had fallen slightly from almost 3,000 when the Group Settlement Scheme closed in the 1930s to 2,790 in 1947. There was then a slow but steady increase in the settler population to a peak of 3,625 in 1954.³⁴

The War Service Land Settlement Scheme instituted by the Commonwealth Government contributed to that population growth. Margaret River was one of the districts selected for participation in this scheme, which encouraged returned servicemen to take up abandoned group settlement blocks. In May 1946 the *West Australian* reported that:

> here there is ample evidence of the work which has been, and is being done in linking and reconditioning of blocks to bring them up to the new 50 cow standard set by the Commonwealth Government. This involves the establishment of approximately 160 acres of pasture, with a proportion

which can be cut for meadow hay or sown with other crops. In most cases there are a few acres of summer land which will be cleared for potato or maize crops.

In their abandoned state, overgrown with bracken and suckers and scrub with fallen timber all over the paddocks, fences down and cottages and sheds derelict, the holdings are far from attractive. But already enough work has been done to show the possibilities that exist in them.[35]

Frank Watterson was one returned soldier who benefitted from the War Service Land Settlement Scheme, taking up 278 acres at Kudardup in 1947. Frank and his wife Beryl could see at once that turning the land, mostly still tree-covered, into a dairy farm was a challenge. Their daughter Fran Temby (then Francine Watterson) remembers 'watching him push down trees, burn up logs, pick up rocks, slash bracken fern and fencing to make it a proper farm. Hard work'.[36] Eventually the Watterson family purchased more land and turned their block into a productive dairy farm.

Compared with the group settlers' formidable task of clearing thickly forested land, many war service land settlement farmers had a slightly easier task removing 'suckers and bracken' thanks to the availability of bulldozers and other equipment no longer

Bulldozers at work. Courtesy Ros Craig.

required by the army.[37] Kevin Coate remembers the first time he saw a bulldozer at work.

> I remember opposite the school or just going down the hill from the school from where the doctor's surgery was (top of town and west side of Bussell Highway), that was all bush and I saw my first bulldozer, pushing down and clearing that land.[38]

As the *West Australian* had suggested, most war service blocks in the Margaret River region were intended to become dairy farms. However, south of the town, around Warner Glen and Karridale, tobacco was initially considered as a possible profitable crop. John Allan from the Department of Agriculture was responsible for selecting blocks: 'I well remember the arduous task of picking out suitable blocks, many of which had been abandoned for many years and were considerably overgrown'.[39] While these newcomers, unlike the earlier group settlers, did not walk off their farms, the tobacco-growing venture was ultimately unsuccessful.[40] Children of tobacco farmers recalled their experience as 'a hard life and a very dirty one'.[41]

Families who took up these war service blocks were sometimes allocated old group settlement cottages. Others were luckier and got a new improved version:

> A compact cottage of 1200 squares, consisting of two bedrooms, lounge room, and kitchen, having front and back verandahs with bathroom and laundry on the back verandah. No. 2 insulheat stove in the kitchen with a Wonderheat unit in the lounge room. Bathroom has a porcelain bath and wash basin.[42]

Most people still relied mainly on rainwater tanks to fill their baths and wash basins, and the hospital always ran short of water in the summer. On 26 January 1944, the then matron advised her superiors in Perth that:

> All tanks have been emptied into the supply well for the use of the hospital and this is almost empty. The carrier Mr G.R. Burton who was engaged to cart water about three weeks ago has not done so

Some war service farmers were given old group houses. MRCC.

> beyond one lot of 200 gallons. I rang Mr Hall of the Public Works at Bunbury today and he is making arrangements with someone more reliable to have 1200 gallons carted immediately.[43]

When the Minister for Works and Water Resources, Albert Hawke, met with a delegation from the road board in April 1945, a member (Mr Oldfield) suggested that the town should be provided with a water supply, pointing out that: 'Margaret River had already gained an excellent reputation as a health centre and was steadily growing in importance'.[44] The minister was not persuaded and replied that while he recognised the position at Margaret River, many other centres required attention. There were towns which were in a deplorable condition and to which water was being carted long distances for many months on end.[45]

The hospital's situation was particularly unsatisfactory but engineers had already suggested a relatively easy solution: water could be delivered to the hospital from the butter factory by gravity feed. After many delays, the *South-Western News* was able to advise its readers that:

> We hear that at last, that word has been given (to) the contractor whose contract was accepted some 6 to 8 months ago to proceed with the installation of the water supply

to the Margaret River Hospital. The delay occurred after tenders were called and accepted when a sample of the river water was found to be contaminated. This will be news to a numbers of locals who have been using this water for years. The supply which will be drawn from the butter factory's overhead tanks, will either be connected to baths, garden and washhouse only – with the present tanks reserved for drinking and theatre purposes – or a chlorination plant will be installed to make the water suitable for all purposes.[46]

Finally, in February 1946, Acting Matron Wright was able to report that, 'The storage tanks have been installed and the new water supply connected to the hospital since Saturday 2.2.46. The tanks were almost empty so this water has been in use since installation.'[47]

The *South-Western News* reported on the opening of the pipeline with a touch of humour:

> Much amusement was caused when it was decided to turn on the water for the first time. To the butter factory went one of the men who carried out the work to turn on the water from the reservoir tank; upon the tank-stand, peering into the tank stood the other men to watch the first trickle of water, and below were assembled the matron and hospital staff. Great was the amazement of those on the tank-stand when through the inlet pipe emerged a Bob Tailed Goanna, when a hurried move was made to turn off the water, the ground audience's exclamations of 'What's wrong?" were quickly answered but not believed until the reptile was captured and exhibited.[48]

In her advice to the department, Sister Wright notes that it would now be important to install septic tank and hot-water systems, which she hoped would not be long following.[49] The lack of a sewerage system meant that all the hospital's lavatories were still earth closets.

The butter factory's tank provided water for the hospital. Courtesy Kevin Coate.

Acting Matron Wright with Nurse Belcher 1947.
Courtesy Judy Oxenbould.

No immediate progress was made, and two months later the then Minister for Education (later premier), John Tonkin, MLA, wrote to his colleague the Minister for Justice and Health, Emil Nulsen, MLA, in the following terms:

> During my visit to Margaret River last week complaints were made about the primitive sanitary conveniences and lack of bathing facilities at Margaret River Hospital. It was stated that as the water is now laid on to the hospital, the installation of a septic system and provision of a hot water system should be possible. I promised to bring the matter under your notice.[50]

However, the minister was advised by the new Medical Undersecretary, Mr Stifold, that he was not prepared to 'recommend that any further money be spent on Margaret River Hospital at present, as this hospital has received a very good share of the limited money available'.[51]

During the war there had been some expenditure on the buildings. Repairs and renovations had been completed in 1943 after the district architect had listed the problems to be addressed at an estimated cost of £150. His summary gives some idea of the state of the building at that time.

> Margaret River Hospital: Repairs and Renovations
>
> The wards themselves are all lined and ceiled (sic) with asbestos, with wooden cover battens, they were calcomined some years ago, and the battens painted, with the exception of the Sterilising Room and Casualty Ward which still has the plain asbestos. Some of the wards, particularly the Women's Ward No. 1, are dreadfully dirty. The walls have been marked by children, and they have attempted to clean off these marks, with the result that the calcimine has been washed off, and the whole presents a very depressing appearance. The bathrooms and E. Cs [earth closets] have never been renovated internally, and two walls of the E. Cs have simply still got studs and weatherboards, which allows for the dust to remain on same. The seats in both are too high, and should be lowered.

> The kitchen has an enamel dado, but the room is very dirty, and the other rooms in this building are showing signs of wear and tear and require renovating.
>
> The Sitting Room in the Nurses' Quarters has not been renovated since its erection. The plaster work is broken on the chimney breast, and this room I think should be done out.[52]

Hospital staff would have been pleased to have received this assessment from an outside authority as it generally fell to the matron to raise problems with the Perth bureaucracy.

After Matron Dunbar left, it proved difficult to find a replacement.[53] Sister Wright was acting matron during and after World War II and as the end of the conflict approached, the hospital was becoming busier. As the *South-Western News* reported, the birth rate was increasing.

> **Who said the stork was shot? He has hovered so persistently over the Margaret River Hospital this week that a record must surely be broken. Seven babies with mammas well and pappas happy.**[54]

Hospital front 1950s. MR&DHS.

By November 1945, the acting matron was reporting an acute staff shortage:

> Sister A King has finished here from 28.11.45. This leaves one trained sister – double and four assistant nurses, including one whose mother has poor health, so she wishes to leave soon...
>
> We have been very busy nearly all this month, we have had 25–30 patients including a case of meningitis and a very severe burning case – 3rd degree who was transferred to Perth Hospital last week end.[55]

To make matters more difficult for hospital nurses and domestic staff alike, the winter of 1946 would prove to be the wettest on record, with rain falling on all but one of the 31 days in July.[56] One can only imagine the difficulty for staff trying to dry sheets and towels. A proposal to build a new drying shed and a covered way between the main hospital and the maternity wing (the Margaret Cecil Rest House) was very welcome. Plans for these additions were sent for approval to the acting matron in January 1946. Sister Wright's reply to the department suggests the pressure under which the nurses were operating.

> I am sorry I could not return them (the plans) earlier, but we have been very busy, and I have only one trained Sister here, so it has been almost impossible to do anything but the nursing side of the position. I hope we will be able to have some trained staff very soon or we ourselves will be patients.[57]

Again, on 17 January, when Sister Wright returned the revised plans, there was clearly still a staff shortage: 'I am sorry I was so long replying, but all my time was taken up with the nursing side of the position as you must now realise'.[58]

In May 1946 Sister Wright reported that staff were catching colds from having to brave the wet weather when walking in the open air between the two buildings.[59] Two months later she advised that the workman commencing building the covered walkway and drying shed was 'a pleasing sight'.[60]

These welcome new buildings were finally completed in September 1947, coinciding with the arrival of a new matron, as reported in the *South-Western News*: 'Matron Catherine Flynn who has been matron at Derby took over the position at Margaret River Hospital during the weekend'.[61] The same article mentioned 'planned building works', including the sewerage and a hot-water system.

> The new improvements to the Hospital which we all hope will not be long forthcoming, are designed to meet the needs of the district for the next 10 years when it is hoped that an entirely new hospital will be built further back from the road and on the hill overlooking the town...

Covered way between the main hospital and the maternity wing in the Margaret Cecil Rest House built 1946–1947. Stephen Blakeney.

> A hot water service and sewerage have first priority, with two new single wards for isolation and especially sick cases. There will also be an alteration to the staff quarters, the most likely arrangement being a matron's flat.[62]

A new hospital would not be built for another 40 years and the contract for these improvements, including the matron's flat, was not let until July 1949.

The Hospital Visiting and Advisory Committee proved useful in lobbying for these building works.[63] The committee included the road board chairman, Mr Willmott, while Dr Tunbridge and Matron Flynn were ex-officio members and Mr C.D. (Doug) Shepherdson was the secretary. A priority list of 'amenities' for possible purchase was compiled by Dr Tunbridge:

> wireless, night-ease mattresses for the comfort of the patients, and trays with crockery and coloured sets, mats, etc, lights over the back of the beds for patients, amenities for the nurses' rooms and head-lights over their beds and such other facilities as seen desirable as time proceeds and money is available.[64]

In the previous two decades, particularly before the establishment of the Lotteries Commission in the mid-1930s, the limited funds available from government and from local sources meant that the hospital boasted few non-essential amenities. But by the 1940s there was a greater emphasis on patient comfort. In 1941, a former patient had suggested that the community might raise funds for the purchase of a radio set 'which would be the means of keeping the patients in good heart, especially the men'[65] although it was not until 1946 that a radio system for the hospital was seriously considered.[66] Money was raised through a community concert and dance at Margaret River Hall under the auspices of the East Witchcliffe Parents and Citizens Association Concert Committee. The event raised £24 with the *South-Western News* reporting that credit of £17/15/6 was being held by Mr C.S. West of Margaret

River as acting trustee pending appointment of an authorised body to proceed with the scheme'.[67] The 'authorised body' would be the Hospital Visiting and Advisory Committee and a radio system with bedside equipment was the first major purchase. The committee paid one-third of the cost from funds raised locally while the Public Health Department and the Lotteries Commission each paid a further third of the total cost.[68] The list of local subscribers to the radio equipment fund gives some idea of the lengths to which local social and sporting organisations were prepared to go in supporting their hospital.[69]

The Margaret River Football Association was a major generator of the funds raised for the hospital radio system. Australian Rules football had now become the major sport for schools and the community. For Smiler Gale, who for many years ran a hairdressing business in town, sport was an important part of a lifetime spent in Margaret River.

> In fact, I've been president of the golf club, the cricket, the tennis, bowling club, basketball, indoor cricket. I wasn't much good at sport. I just classed me as the average mug, but I enjoyed it all. In those days the town district was very small and because I was in the shop, I knew so many people. I found it was very, very good for communicating and friendship.[70]

Dances in town and in the outlying localities provided another regular opportunity for young men like Kevin Coate to socialise.

> A fortnightly dance was held in the Road Board Hall where young and old danced to music from Frank Wake's band. The program usually included old time favourites such as Gipsy Tap, Gay Gordons, Veleta, Two Step Barn Dance, Destiny Waltz and to end the evening a Modern Waltz.[71]

Thanks to proceeds from all these sources, particularly the New Year's Eve Ball, Matron Flynn was able to inform the hospital advisory committee in March 1948 that the full radio equipment, ordered through the Public Health Department, had 'come to hand': 'Comprising 1 dual channel radio, 23 pillow phones for all hospital beds, 1 loudspeaker for sitting room of nurses' quarters'.[72]

By the end of 1948, the committee reported on a successful first year of operations during which, in addition to the radio installation, it had been able to establish a hospital library, provide four rubber mattresses for the comfort of seriously ill patients and two safe cots for infants. Importantly, too, as its annual report stated, the committee had 'not failed to bring to the notice of the Public Health Department, its responsibility for providing many other improvements and facilities to the hospital'.[73]

The committee's major fundraiser was the Hospital Ball held on New Year's Eve. At the event on 31 December 1948, over 500 people were present and this was also the occasion on which the community officially farewelled Dr and Mrs Tunbridge. The doctor had sold his practice to Dr Paddy Barrett. In his leave-taking speech Dr Tunbridge noted that the hospital still had neither a proper sewerage system nor a hot-water service. He hoped that the hospital committee would be able to obtain these and other necessary improvements.[74]

The advisory committee was already submitting these recommendations to the department. In March 1948, secretary C.D. Shepherdson had written to the undersecretary at the Public Health Department stating a hot-water system was essential for the hospital to function efficiently.[75] A few months later when no action had been taken, Shepherdson wrote again, this time to the Minister for Health, pointing out that there had still been no progress on either the sewerage or the hot-water system, and that the cost of sanitary removal for the year ending 30 June 1948 had been £90/17/4.[76] The road board also wrote to the Public Health Department to complain about the sewerage and sanitary arrangements.[77] The department's response was predictably vague. The plans for these works, and also for additions to the hospital, had been received but there was 'a large program of works for Western Australian public hospitals and relative urgency had to be assessed'.[78]

The following year, and after further complaints, including one from the South West Council of the Labour Party to the Minister for Public Health, the department undersecretary was able to advise that a contract had been let for the Margaret River Hospital improvements and that this would include sewerage and hot water.[79] The contract let in July 1949 to Busselton builder R. Falkingham and sons was for a large suite of works, including a new staff dining room, an outpatients area and a sterilising room. The contract was for £9,700, of which the Lotteries Commission agreed to pay half.[80] The scope of the contract was later extended when Dr Barrett asked for the inclusion of a new X-ray and dark room to be built close to the new casualty section and for the current facility to be made into one room as a duty office.[81] The doctor later also requested the construction of a children's ward because there had been 'an appreciable increase in the number of children being treated at the hospital'.[82]

In the 1940s and 1950s, more children were being admitted to the hospital suffering from infectious diseases, including measles, meningitis and diphtheria, despite the availability of a diphtheria vaccine.[83] The hospital also saw cases of poliomyelitis. One case of polio was admitted to the hospital in 1948, the first year of polio epidemics in Western Australia.[84] Yet most cases would have been treated at Busselton, which was a designated country hospital for polio patients.[85] In the early 1950s the incidence of polio in Western Australia continued to rise. The state recorded 59 cases in 1950 and this trend continued until 1954.[86] In that year the Margaret River Hospital provided five notifications of poliomyelitis to the Public Health Department as well as three cases of scarlet fever and 10 of meningitis.[87]

Plans for providing the hospital with new buildings and improved services had not materialised by the end of 1950. There were serious problems with the contractor, as a letter from the secretary of the Hospital Visiting and Advisory Committee to Mrs Florence Cardell-Oliver, the then Minister for Health, made clear:

> At the meeting of the undersigned committee held on 23 Nov. last, I was instructed to write calling your attention to deplorable conditions existing at Margaret River Hospital due to the very evident dilatoriness of the contractor...
>
> In due course portions of the extensions reached a semi-constructed stage and a series of excavations were dug throughout the hospital grounds but for several months past no activity whatever has been in evidence. The sewerage contractor and the electrician declare that they can do nothing further until the builders proceed with their work. Officials of the hospital and of my committee have on various occasions been in communication with the contractor regarding the delay but his seemingly disinterested explanation is that supplies of materials, particularly joinery are not available. Further enquiries from the joinery firm that he mentioned seem to indicate that the contractor has not been at all definite in placing any specific order.
>
> In the meantime, conditions at the hospital are decidedly non-hygienic, unpleasant, very unsightly and dangerous for persons moving around the premises. It is reported to the committee that under present conditions, fifteen members of the staff are compelled to use the one and only bathroom available to them.
>
> The difficulties associated with building programs are fully realised but we are convinced that there is little genuine excuse for the long delay in resumption of work at the Margaret River Hospital. Any action that you may be able to take towards ensuring that the contractor completes his work with a minimum of further procrastination will be appreciated.[88]

The undersecretary replied on behalf of the minister that the 'slow progress is giving both the principal architect and myself a good deal of concern'. Despite this unsatisfactory situation, the same builder, R. Falkingham and sons, was awarded another contract (total £3,875) for the construction of the children's ward requested by Dr Barrett and also for completion of the renovations.[89] This contract was not finalised until July 1954, partly, it would seem, due to the death of the business owner.⁹⁰

In addition to problems caused by the delays in completing the building works, the new sewerage system, which provided for the hospital's effluent to be discharged in filter beds on the opposite side of the road and near to the rear of the police station house, proved to be totally unsatisfactory. The Public Health Department soon received complaints from the police as well as from the road board,⁹¹ but the department, which was also responsible for all works associated with the hospital, was reluctant to act with the medical undersecretary commenting that:

> Approval for these works was given only in May 1950. I do not know when the work was completed but the total cost was approximately £2,500. I am now asked to find another £1,500 to install another new system of foul water disposal. It will be extremely difficult to persuade the Treasury to find another £1,500 at this stage and I would like to have further advice as to why the system so recently installed has been found unsatisfactory in so short a time.⁹²

No action was taken and in March 1953 Dr Barrett wrote to the road board about the same matter.

> May I draw the attention of the Board to the disgusting cesspool within 40 yards to the rear of the Police Station caused by the improper disposal of the Hospital sewerage and drainage system. Not only is the quagmire a breeding ground for disease and flies but the foul odour from the same can often be noticed by the whole neighbourhood. From the Public Health point of view, I would be pleased if the Board would approach the responsible department in order to have this deplorable state of affairs put right.⁹³

The road board was only too pleased to pass on this correspondence to the commissioner of public health, head of the government department that had responsibility not only for all matters relating to the hospital, but also for environmental health.

Various solutions to the sewerage problems were suggested. One was to divert the effluent into the nearby national park alongside the Margaret River. Another proposed pumping the material back up the hill to the undeveloped southern part of the hospital reserve. While neither solution seemed ideal, a departmental officer advised the commissioner of public health that:

> It would seem we risk a swamp in the hospital grounds or in the national park for a saving of £250...If there is any doubt, I think the extra £250 would be well-spent on having the nuisance away from habitation in general and the hospital in particular.[94]

It appeared to be permissible to pollute a national park and most probably the Margaret River itself. In any event, the deputy inspector of public works advised that the success of any solution depended on regular maintenance and that perhaps the Public Health Department should arrange for the road board to undertake this work rather than relying on 'the mediocre service given by a changing (hospital) orderly staff'.[95]

Again, neither the Public Health Department nor the Augusta-Margaret River Road Board took action, with the latter advising the commissioner in March 1954 that: 'We have experienced an epidemic during the last few months of meningitis, and four cases have come from houses immediately adjacent to the present site on which the sewerage from the hospital is discharged'.[96] Hospital records for 1954 confirm that in that year, 'as well as the ten cases of meningitis', there were outbreaks of scarlet fever and polio. It is likely that the hospital's sewerage system was at least partly responsible for these occurrences of communicable diseases.[97]

The following month, the department advised the road board that a new contract had been let for the hospital drainage system and this work was completed in May.[98] Complaints from the road board and the police seem to have dissipated, at least temporarily. However, in March 1957 it was reported that one of the three sewerage disposal beds was not working and that further action was required.[99] Problems with the hospital's septic system were never fully resolved until the building was connected to the town's deep sewerage system in 1990.[100] Local residents can remember that in the 1960s and 1970s there was still often a cesspool across the road from the hospital.[101]

In the immediate postwar period, a new preventative health service reached the south-west of WA. The Infant Health Association of Western Australia had been formed in 1923 to work in conjunction with the Public Health Department to establish infant health centres in metropolitan and rural areas.[102] The aim was to address relatively high levels of maternal and infant mortality and more clinics were established in the south-west of Western Australia.

At a meeting of representatives of interested communities in Donnybrook in early 1946, Dr Eleanor (Rita) Stang, Medical Officer for Schools and Supervisor of Infant Health, told attendees that statistics showed the highest death rate of children under one year was occurring in country districts. She attributed this largely, if not wholly, to the lack of infant health centres in the country compared with the city.[103] This meeting then accepted a proposal to establish centres at Margaret River, Cowaramup, Busselton and Capel. Under this plan, a travelling nurse, paid by the Public Health Department, would visit each location on one day a fortnight and local committees would be responsible for providing a consulting room. The aim of the scheme was to train and educate women to 'keep a well-baby well'.[104] A committee was quickly established in Margaret River and members decided to ask the CWA for use of its rest rooms for the clinic to be held on Fridays. Local branches of the CWA also became active in raising funds for an infant health centre.[105]

The Margaret River Infant Health Centre was not built until 1954, a delay that may have been due partly to the fact that the travelling health service, which operated out of Busselton, worked well for many years, as this account by an infant health nurse suggests:

> Friday is Margaret River's Day. Alternately we do Cowaramup on Thursday afternoon after a quick early morning visit to Jarrahwood and that same week we visit Witchcliffe on the Friday morning (a very young and enthusiastic young centre) and in the afternoon do Margaret River as usual.
>
> Margaret River Hospital is visited early on Friday morning to welcome the new mothers and prospective mothers to the Clinic. It is always encouraging to feel the co-operation offered by the married trained nurses in the district who, although they have been matrons of hospital and perhaps handled hundreds of babies, bring their own willingly and courteously, appreciating another opinion on their child, and knowing how often delicate babies have been sent home from hospital in the past, to anxious parents, wishing for just such a service as the Infant Health of the State is now offering and hoping by their very co-operation to bring this service to every country mother.
>
> By half past four we are on our way homeward to Busselton and the mud-splashed Clinic car gets it bi-monthly wash and polish ready for the trip to Donnybrook on the Monday morning.[106]

The continuing lack of a clinic building in Margaret River must have concerned Dr Stang because in January 1950 she again visited the town and encouraged the formation of another local committee to lobby and raise funds for a building, as one member recalled:

> It was agreed at this meeting that we endeavour to raise enough money to build our own Clinic. This was started by Don (John) Juan coming down and holding an amateur concert. Popular Baby Competition and a Debutante ball. After nearly three years we were at last able to discuss plans with the Public Health Architects, Allen and Bennett and Associates. Dr Stang had been a great help to us during this time. The road board had given us a block of land and £500.[107]

The Lotteries Commission provided another £500 and the new clinic was finally opened on Saturday 2 October 1954.

> Last Saturday afternoon was a red-letter day for the committee of the Margaret River Infant Health Centre, as it marked the successful conclusion to nine years of effort – the official opening of its new clinic by the Hon Minister for Health, Mr E. Nulsen MLA.[108]

The provision of infant health (later child health) centres provided the district with an important service. Yet there was still no dental clinic in Margaret River in the 1940s and 1950s. Dental decay was prevalent. As Kevin Coate recalled:

> Most kids had cavities in their teeth at some time. The only dentist available to families at Margaret River without travelling to Bunbury was Mabel Taylor-Thomas…She visited Margaret River about once a month and set up in a room in Dr Tunbridge's (later Dr Barrett's) house or consulting room. A visit to her was a terrifying ordeal, the stuff of nightmares, and to be avoided at all costs until the offending tooth became too painful. She operated a foot powered treadle drill to gouge out cavities. It was probably the whirring of the instrument as it gathered speed and the way the drill bounced around in the cavity I feared most.[109]

Some children had teeth removed at the local hospital. This was not a pleasant experience as Marion Lilly, growing up at Rosa Brook, recalled:

> There was no dentist in Margaret River so we had to go to the hospital to get some of our teeth pulled out , and be put under chloroform, so that was horrible. I recall that event vividly, because when dad picked me up to take me home, we had only just got home and I opened the car door and I spewed everywhere. It tasted revolting and I never forgot that.
>
> My older sister, Heather, she had to get some of her teeth pulled at the same time and they didn't tell her what was going to happen to

her, so she was terrified of the big light that they use in surgery. They had to pin her down and she was absolutely mortified. She has never forgotten it. She was quite traumatised because they didn't warn her what was going to happen, not having been to a dentist before.[110]

In the 1950s, children also often went to the local hospital to have their tonsils removed. Marion's friend Elwyn Franklin remembers this as being a terrifying occasion.

> Yes, I had my tonsils out there. I remember the children's ward. There were about four beds and I think two iron cots in there. I had to go in twice for my tonsils because they left a little bit behind the first time. And the second time, I was terrified because they didn't give me any anaesthetic. They sprayed something down my throat and this man's coming towards me and I thought he's going to pull something out of my throat. They just came at me with some tongs and I had to open my mouth. They gave me some ice-cream afterwards, which of course, made everything better![111]

Fran Temby, then Francine Watterson, recalls much happier times:

> Looking back on it now, life on the farm as children was idyllic. We had so much outdoor play: climbing trees, playing in the haystacks, in the wheat bins and on the tractor in the paddock. Catching tadpoles, frogs, making daisy chains, feeding the calves, getting the cows in for milking. We had such fun playing with the cats and kittens, about 20 of them, all outdoor cats to catch mice. We would go to our grandparents' home in Bunbury for holidays, and when we returned home, half the cats were missing. Dad reassuringly said they had gone on holidays![112]

Lloyd Shepherdson's playground was the East Witchcliffe timber mill.

> Building cubbies within, and chucking planks across from timber stacks to timber stacks – daring one another to walk the plank – getting narrower and narrower planks etc – good risky fun and not too many accidents.[113]

Regular jobs were also part of Lloyd Shepherdson's life at East Witchcliffe:

> The daily chores of collecting milk from the neighbouring dairy farm, at 4.30am precisely, all the kids would gather with their billy cans and line up to get the fresh warm milk, then 'swan' on home via the old sawdust heap, covered in lucerne trees (tagasaste) next to the tennis courts. We'd set up play areas, play chasey, cops and robbers and cowboys or ambush the girls. So the milk could come home late, often with sawdust in it. We would get scolded again. But the milk would always be scalded anyway and scalded cream is to die for. The other painful daily chores were getting a barrow of wood to the house, two bottles of kero for the fridge, empty the grey water from the sink onto the fruit trees, feed the chooks, collect the eggs, feed the cats and dog.[114]

However, children could not always meet demand for labour. After World War II, workers were needed in all areas of the economy and in every state and territory, including the south-west of WA. Australia's population in 1945 was seven million.[115] In Europe there were an estimated eleven million displaced or stateless persons, many of them from countries such as Poland and the Baltic republics, where national boundaries had been redrawn and/or where one dictator, Hitler, had been replaced by another, Stalin.[116] In 1947, the Federal Minister for Immigration, Arthur Calwell, initiated a migrant program to bring to this country people who met the requirements of the White Australia policy. Many migrants came from Latvia, Lithuania or Estonia (the three Baltic republics) as well as from Poland and Germany, and were often known collectively as 'Balts'.

In the late 1940s a displaced persons' camp was established over the road from Kevin Coate's house:

> This was for people fleeing from war torn Europe. As a condition of their entry into Australia they agreed to work for about two years as fettlers or navvies for the Western Australian Government

SETTLEMENT, STRUGGLE AND SUCCESS

> Railways…They were usually referred to as New Australians or in Margaret River as Balts. Six families lived over the road from us and each was provided with two tents for sleeping the family and a three-sided attachment to cook in and use as a living room. It looked like a tent city.[117]

Ellie Metcalfe, who lived next door to the hospital, remembers that:

> Many of them got jobs with either the railway or the forestry. And a lot of the wives got jobs as domestics in hotels. We had quite a few working at the hospital and some of them even brought their children with them and they played in the grounds while the mothers did their four or five hours of cleaning. They were all lovely people once you got to know them.[118]

Ellie remembers one particular 'Balt', Bolis Kasparis, known in Margaret River as 'Bob'.[119] He was thought to be Russian or possibly Polish. When 'Bob' died in the late 1970s, a number of letters with Polish stamps were found among his effects.[120] The lives of many

European refugees living in Margaret River in the 1950s. Courtesy Kevin Coate.

of the new arrivals had been strongly affected by their wartime experiences.[121] Bolis Kasparis's situation certainly highlights those complications, as Ellie Metcalfe recalled.

> Bob (Bolis) had married in Russia and had had eight children but had left Europe unaware of what had happened to them. So, he married again in Margaret River a nurse at the hospital. However, the Red Cross then found his first wife and eldest son still in Russia. So, she came and the second wife went back to Perth.
>
> Bob stayed in Margaret River with his first wife and lived opposite the hospital, where he became the orderly. They had lots of gatherings with others who had come from Russia, including Margaret River's first vet. There was plenty of vodka at those parties.[122]

Nick Kovalevs, the district's first qualified veterinary surgeon, was a Latvian refugee. He came to Margaret River in 1951 after completing the required two years of 'indentured labour' at the Northam Military Camp Power House.[123]

Postwar migrants less qualified than Kovalevs, often found work in forestry or at the timber mills, which, together with dairying, remained Margaret River's main source of employment. East Witchcliffe was the largest mill, where the company was owned and managed by the Shepherdson family. As Lloyd Shepherdson recalled:

> East Witchcliffe was a small town on its own. The population was about 40 houses. West Witchcliffe, what is now Witchcliffe was probably smaller, but it was on the main railway line so probably had a few more services and shops. Darnell and Shervington had the post office. There'd be regular movies and dances and things at the East Witchcliffe Hall which I think was bigger and probably more used than either of the halls in Witchcliffe which were the CWA or Druids.[124]

In the daytime East Witchcliffe was steam-powered, running both the mill and a large electric generator. At night a diesel generator provided lighting until 10pm.

When a simple pulley system with a fish hook on the end, hooked over an ordinary alarm winder of the clock strapped to a bench. Quite a few times pictures or a dance was on in the mill hall and somebody hadn't altered the alarm so darkness would befall at 10pm until somebody went and cranked the diesel up again.[125]

Many farmers also worked in one of the timber mills because there was still so little money in dairying.[126]

In 1949 the Forests Department needed more workers and it was decided to run a school for tree fallers particularly aimed at 'New Australians'.[127] Kevin Coate, who had already worked for the forestry for three years, joined that group and on one occasion found himself in the Margaret River Hospital. He had been pedalling back for lunch on his push bike, trying to beat his mates on motorcycles, when:

> a stick flew up and wedged in the front fork of the bike propelling me head first over the handle bars...My head was covered with blood and one ear was virtually torn off hanging by a thread...On awakening in hospital, I was told my ear had been successfully re-attached with twenty-three stitches.[128]

Dr Barrett performed the necessary surgery at the Margaret River Hospital and then drove Kevin to recuperate at his parents' house in Bunbury.

According to Coate, 'Dr Barrett had a fondness for fast cars, particularly Mark V Jaguars, two of which he crashed, luckily without injury to himself or others'.[129] Nurse Joyce Challis became very familiar with rapid journeys between Margaret River and Augusta in Paddy Barrett's Jaguar.

> Paddy Barrett went about two hundred miles an hour. He used to bring me to do a surgery down here and I often got a lift down on my days off work to come and see my boyfriend, Harold, at that time.[130]

She experienced one particularly memorable trip: 'We were passing Bill Darnell's store in Witchcliffe. It was a stony gravel road, no bitumen and ouch! A stone hit the window of his Jaguar. That was very frightening.'[131]

Ellie Metcalfe remembers Dr Barrett as an interesting character:

> Paddy Barrett was about six foot six, a very impressive, a very nice-looking man. He drove a Jaguar and when Paddy was on the wards, it was, 'He's here!' Do the right thing you know. He was always very nice, and very nice to me. He was very laid back. Somebody was pretty low and he would say, 'I think they might cash their chips before morning'.[132]

Growing up in Margaret River, Greg Bussell also remembers Paddy Barrett, mainly for giving needles.

Dr Paddy Barrett – Margaret River's doctor in the 1950s.
Courtesy Ellie Metcalfe.

> Certainly Paddy Barrett, he was an imposing figure. But in those days, when we had all our injections at their house it was at the top of the main street, and we actually filed through a room, in one door and out the other side and got a needle as you went through. So I don't know that we liked Paddy Barrett's house all that much.[133]

Lloyd Shepherdson, living at East Witchcliffe, confessed to a childhood prank.

> Paddy Barrett was a very tall man with a Jaguar. And I know I was part of a group of kids down at the mill that chucked rocks at his car and he chased but he didn't get us. But it wasn't the right thing to do.[134]

East Witchcliffe remained the district's largest timber mill. But there were others, including one on the edge of town which was so close to the hospital that there were repeated complaints by the matron about the dust being blown towards the buildings.

Cowaramup had Ryan's Mill, while the Osmington Mill on Bramley Road (now Osmington Road) was one of the largest timber mills in the area. Elwyn Franklin (nee Streatfield) grew up nearby in the group settlement area known as Airdale.

> And of course, the big thing on our road was the Osmington Mill, which was like a little town on its own with around twenty homes and fifteen single men's quarters and the office building there. There is very little to be seen there now, just the remains of the stone and brick sawdust kilns. Sawdust was used to fuel the steam boilers that drove the mill machinery.[135]

Jarrah remained the most important timber and the Shepherdsons' Adelaide Timber Company at East Witchcliffe serviced the Perth market.

> And sleepers were a big thing both in Western Australia and in South Africa and London, and so there's a pretty big sleeper trade for small sawmills around the place. And then of course, everything went by train up to Busselton jetty or Bunbury wharf. But in my era, it was

Jarrah remained the most important timber. Courtesy Thelma Burnett.

probably more the housing market in Perth. We used to 'train and ship' a fair bit of stuff for the housing market.[136]

The continuing importance of timber to the economy of the south-west meant that the conservator of forests held considerable power and influence when it came to local land use. Not surprisingly, he reacted strongly to a move that threatened a small portion of his empire.

In 1955 the road board contracted town planning consultant Margaret Feilman to prepare a plan for the town of Margaret River. Her draft recommended an entirely new site for a future hospital. She suggested that this should be built across the river, north of the townsite, on land controlled by the Forests Department.[137] Feilman probably suggested this site because she was aware that the existing extensive hospital reserve within the Margaret River townsite could then be released and subdivided for residential or commercial purposes. The road board, soon to become the Shire of

Augusta-Margaret River, would then have been able to take over that land and create a lucrative subdivision.[138]

The Public Health Department had no objection to Feilman's proposal and stated that the site was 'completely favourable and could be reserved for the purpose'.[139] Yet the suggestion that a future hospital could be located on land managed by the Forests Department did not sit well with the conservator. He conveyed his displeasure to the undersecretary for lands who, in turn, informed the road board that:

> The Conservator of Forests sees no unsurmountable reason why the (hospital) reserve should not be wholly situated within the Margaret River townsite. This proposal would mean the closure and remaking of a new road and the destruction of ten to twelve acres of fine karri forest. You should confer with the Town Planning Consultant so that the site does not encroach on State Forest.[140]

The matter was still ongoing in April 1959 when local member of Parliament and also Minister for Lands and Forests, Hon. W.S. Bovell, met a deputation from the road board and explained that release of any land from the state forest reserve needed a resolution from both houses of Parliament.[141] At that meeting it became apparent that neither the chairman (Mr Shervington) nor other board members had seen the contoured plan of the proposed hospital site.[142] There was no more discussion about building a hospital to the north of the town and Superintendent Stewart of the Forests Department summarised this controversy as a 'storm in a teacup'.[143]

Irrespective of the site, a new hospital for Margaret River was still a long way off in the 1950s. When Dr Tunbridge made his farewell speech on 31 December 1948, he foreshadowed the building of a future hospital on the existing reserve. His prophecy was recorded by the *South-Western News*.

> He visualised visiting the town some years hence and seeing a new hospital on the hill facing the town with just the

maternity ward (considerably enlarged) and Margaret Cecil Rest Home as links with the past and early efforts of himself and others.[144]

It was to be another forty years before Dr Tunbridge's vision would be realised. But in the end the new hospital would be built 'on the hill' and on the existing reserve.

By the time Dr Tunbridge left town, there had been some improvements in the hospital's facilities. There was now 24-hour electricity and a secure water supply, thanks to the pipeline from the butter factory. Then, in 1951, the townsite was finally provided with a reticulated water supply and the hospital was able to obtain its water from this source. The scheme was opened by the then Minister for Works and Water Resources (later premier), the Hon. David Brand, MLA. Local Member of Parliament Mr C.H. Henning referred to the 'tremendous development' that had taken place in the district since group settlement,[145] while the *South-Western News* lauded the benefits of the new installation.

> The new scheme is of very modern type. Water is drawn from the river and pumped to overhead tanks from where it is reticulated throughout the town. At the pumping site, an automatic chlorinating system has been installed to ensure purification of the supply and the electrically driven pumps will also be automatically controlled.[146]

The Public Works Department had previously advised that with the advent of a piped water supply there would be adequate water pressure for fire hydrants to be installed within the hospital.[147] The department provided an estimate of £441 for installation. As usual, money was the issue. Nevertheless, the undersecretary, with an eye on public opinion, asked Treasury to approve this expenditure, noting that, 'I admit that it is a large expenditure for a fire service, but if a fire did occur and some of the patients were injured, it would be very difficult to justify the non-provision of such a service'.[148]

The new town volunteer fire brigade was just one of many organisations which took part in the local celebrations for Queen Elizabeth II's coronation on 2 June 1953. The local newspaper's report on this event gives some idea of the industries and organisations active in the district at that time.

> The festivities commenced at 10.15 with a procession which started from Gloucester Park and proceeded via Mitchell Street [*now Wallcliffe Road*], Farrelly Street, Wallcliffe Road [*now Tunbridge Street*], Bussell Highway and Station Road back to Gloucester Park. The procession was headed by the Busselton Brass Band and cars conveying a number of pioneer residents of the district were followed by floats entered by the RSL, branches of the Farmers Union which depicted various aspects of dairying and agriculture, different phases of the timber industry, roadmaking plant, both ancient and modern, the Cowaramup Congregational Mission, St John Ambulance Brigade and Fire Brigade.[149]

Hospital coronation float – Medical Queen. Courtesy Ellie Metcalfe.

To mark the occasion, an oak tree was planted in the park opposite the road board office by board chairman Bill Darnell, who later admitted that a hitch in proceedings had been narrowly avoided.

> I thought to myself, well everything was worked out to the minute but I wonder who is going to produce the tree for me to plant? Unbeknown to the wife – she had five or six oak trees growing around the back of the dunny at Rosa Brook…I took the best one out…Sure enough no one had thought of producing the tree to plant…So I opened the boot and produced the tree.[150]

The Darnell's oak tree flourished!

Stewart Bovell's speech highlighted the district's still strong connection to Britain and Empire, pointing out that:

> 'The monarchy, with only a short break had been continuous since the days of King Alfred, and now we have a Queen who this day is being crowned in the heart of her Empire'.[151]

Nostalgia for the 'mother country' and its empire aside, in the 1950s change and growth was taking place in the district, as Bill Darnell also recalled:

> Well, there was progress in Margaret River to the extent that we never had a bank in Margaret River, a proper bank, and they built the Bank of New South Wales on the corner opposite the hotel. The draper's shop, where Jack Thomas is, that was a new building. It was built on the other side of the highway. The post office was built…Another thing was a fire brigade station…It had to be a brick building…Then of course the police station came on the opposite side of the road, which we had never had before and they had a courthouse adjoining the police station.[152]

The brick post office was opened on 19 March 1956.[153] The booklet issued to commemorate the opening of the new building stated that:

> From an isolated rural settlement, the district has developed into a large community and there is every indication that its progress

Margaret River post office, 1956. Courtesy State Library of Western Australia BA1289/99.

Opening of the Augusta-Margaret River District Library, Margaret River, 1959.
Courtesy State Library of Western Australia 231763PD.

will be maintained and possibly accelerated in the years ahead... Recognition of the growth of the district has been made by the Postmaster General's Dept in providing a modern Post Office, sufficiently large to cope with the existing and future business for many years to come.[154]

Three years later on the opposite side of the street, another brick building, the town's first purpose-built library, was opened.

Joyce Challis arrived in Margaret River from Victoria in 1955:

> The hotel was there on the corner and they were just building the high school and the new post office. All that area grew. But down on the other side of the road there were some old houses and one of those was where you could go and have a meal in this little old house – fish and chips, steak and chips, egg and chips and that was about the menu.[155]

Joyce was the first enrolled nurse to come to Margaret River: 'They hadn't gone through any schooling here. They had just started that for enrolled nurses in Western Australia but I had trained in Victoria.' Joyce came west on a working holiday, initially to break free from nursing because she had been working in that field since she was fifteen, but the prospect of folding and selling handkerchiefs and scarves in David Jones seemed less than exciting. So Joyce applied for nursing jobs:

> I had three choices of nursing jobs and Margaret River was the one I chose because I came from Gippsland in Victoria, which was similar country. But it was October when I came to Margaret River and it was very hot! I arrived on the Friday and the girl whose place I had taken was getting married on the Saturday and I was invited. So I was off and running. The nurses quarters were great and we had parties in that little room.

Like many other nurses, Joyce soon found a husband and she moved to Augusta. Later, when that hospital opened in 1965, she nursed there.

Mary Arthur (then Coulter) also came from Melbourne in the 1950s to nurse at Margaret River. She, too, soon met her future husband, farmer Don Arthur. Mary had trained at the Royal Women's Hospital in Melbourne and was a fully qualified nurse and midwife. She and her friend Joan Harris travelled by train from Melbourne. Mary's daughter Lynda Williams still has the Vespa scooter which they rode to Margaret River.

> There's a Vespa scooter in my garage. Mum and Joan rode that scooter down to Margaret River and it took them eight hours. Some of the roads were gravel. They had to keep stopping and changing who rode in front because it was so cold and on a Vespa scooter it would have been horrendous.[156]

While Joyce Challis and Mary Arthur came to Margaret River to work as nurses, the number of visitors to the district was increasing, leading to the establishment of the Augusta-Margaret River Tourist Bureau Association in 1956.[157] Apart from the hotel, there was little short-term accommodation so most visitors camped on the coast, at places like Hamelin Bay. Local people went fishing at popular spots such as Gnarabup, close to the area known as Rifle Butts, because the Volunteer Defence Force had trained there during World War II.[158] But there were no permanent habitations on the coastal heath.

This situation began to change in 1953 when Geoffrey Edwards, a returned soldier who, like Dudley McLeod and Tom Doyle, had fought in Crete during World War II, bought thirty acres of coastal land for £450. He named the area Prevelly as a thank you to the monks of Preveli monastery who had sheltered him and many colleagues during their wartime retreat from Greece.[159]

The acreage fronted the ocean but had no power, water or telephone connection, was partly a swamp and could be accessed only by a rough track. Initially it was a local joke that the owner of the Rifle Butts, Brian Terry, had sold it to some 'mug from the city. He's supposed to be going to build a caravan park there. Must be mad, that barren windswept place. Nobody will go out there'.[160]

The locals were proved wrong when this remote spot became Prevelly Park. Moreover, following Geoff's clever roadside advertising, by the late 1950s it was a holiday location 'known from one end of the State to the other'.[161] Eventually this 'barren windswept site' would become a gazetted townsite within the Shire of Augusta-Margaret River.[162]

Apart from Prevelly, there were few tourism developments in the area, but the population increase in the postwar decade was reflected in the opening of the Margaret River Junior District High School in February 1955. Initially the existing primary school, with an enrolment of 265 students, was combined with a high school enrolment of 92, while in the following year the high school began to operate as a farm school. In 1962 the primary and secondary schools separated as numbers increased with the closure of small one-teacher schools, such as Forest Grove.[163] The new school building was constructed at the southern end of the townsite, opposite the existing primary school.

When Kevin Coate attended the primary school in the 1940s, this had been bushland but still useful for children who came to school on horseback.

> In bush opposite to the entrance to the school there was an area where those who rode horses to school could tie them up during the day, usually with a bag of chaff to munch on. Several of the older kids constructed yards from jarrah saplings to put their horses in. I remember several occasions on which news would come from someone in town that a horse had freed itself and was wandering down the main street heading towards home. This would be the cause of much excitement and kids with horses would scatter out of the classroom in an effort to catch it.[164]

From the 1930s onwards, children like Cedar (George) Armstrong had travelled to school with horsepower.

> Mother used to drive us in a horse and sulky into town and then we'd start walking home...As we got older we rode a pony for quite some

years. And it was a long time before we got off the horse and onto a pushbike.[165]

In the 1940s and early 1950s, Judy Dunbar (then Judy Leiper) thought that she was lucky because she and her brothers went to school on horses.[166] But, increasingly, bicycles became the preferred transport. Carolyn Scott found this was the best way to get to Cowaramup school.

> So we were bought, my brother and I, a Malvern Star bike each and we started travelling from Bramley Research Station to school every day. It took about 30 minutes to get up to Cowaramup. My brother and I used to have competitions. I could do 'no hands' all the way up.[167]

For children further from town, the school bus was now an option. When wartime petrol rationing ended, it became feasible to transport children from outlying areas by bus. Accordingly, many one-teacher schools in the area closed in the 1950s and while the number of school bus routes increased, designated routes sometimes meant that children had to change schools.[168] Communities were generally given the option to buy the old school building and Bill Darnell organised for the Rosa Brook school to be purchased for £400.[169]

Before 1950, children wanting to progress beyond primary level at a public school had to board in Bunbury. This was Kevin Coate's experience:

> The closest high school to Margaret River for parents wishing for their children to receive a higher education was Bunbury. For country kids, providing their parents could afford to send them to high school, they would be either boarded at the school hostel or at one of 30 private houses in town.[170]

Later, travel to Busselton for secondary education became an option for boys like Don Miller, born in 1940. However, he soon returned to the family farm: 'Yes, I went to Busselton for two years before this one was built in 1954, I think, and then I did one year there.

Anyway, my dad had a very bad sickness and I went home and milked the cows.'[171]

When the Margaret River Junior High School opened, schooldays could mean long bus trips, as Fran Temby recalled:

> The school bus arrived at our farm gate at seven thirty in the morning. It then drove around the farms and picked up children in Kudardup and Karridale. At the crossroads of Brockman Highway and Bussell Highway, we were transferred to the high school bus. We arrived at high school just before nine o'clock. It was a long trip there and a long trip home, arriving home at 5pm. So it was three hours on the bus every day. There was no senior high school in Margaret River and we had to go away to school for our leaving examinations.[172]

Farming, along with forestry, was still the mainstay of the district's economy and the high school farm played an important role in preparing students for life on the land. Earlier the government had also established an agricultural research station in the district.[173] The Bramley Research Station, situated south of Cowaramup, opened in 1950 with a mandate to undertake research into local livestock and pasture problems.[174] Norm Scott was appointed manager and his family, including young daughter Carolyn, moved into an old group settlement house on the property.

> Yes, I came to live at the research station when I was four and a half years old; on the second of July 1951. The house was a derelict group house, drafty and lousy with fleas. We occupied this house for four years. Over the sink was just like a bucket. And for two years, we showered in the dairy after the cows were milked. Then a bathroom was renovated to a reasonable standard.[175]

The initial research program concentrated on addressing problems associated with dairy farming and animal husbandry. There was a particular emphasis on improving pastures using fertilisers and trace elements. Annual field days were held to allow farmers to view the many experiments and note the progress made.[176]

While the Margaret River Hospital, and indeed the whole townsite, now had an electricity supply, this did not extend to outlying farms. Many families had 'Tilley' lamps which ran on kerosene.[177] Refrigerators, if they existed at all, were also kerosene-fuelled. Don Miller had a 32-volt generator to turn on the lights at home and another to run his milking machines.[178]

Dairy farms also needed a reliable water supply. The Smiths, Yvonne Coate's family, were fortunate that their land extended to the banks of the Margaret River.

> And, because we didn't have the town water supply in those days, Dad had to put a pipeline from the river to a tank on the hill. And he could pump it up to our milking shed and pig yards and things like that.[179]

The Smiths' farm was so close to town that they could almost see the hospital. It was also near the railway line:

> When the train went through in summertime, we had to watch the railway line…I can remember sitting out there with my teddy bear, having to watch if there was a fire started, so I could let Dad know.[180]

The railway was a vitally important transport link for both freight and passengers. As Yvonne's husband Kevin recalled:

> Yes, just about everything came down by rail to be offloaded. The railway made the difference to the district because the roads were terrible in those days. There was a lot of timber, a lot of sleepers and it was quick and easy to get them through to Busselton or Bunbury. And most importantly for us kids, ice-cream used to come down in big containers to Mrs Wright's shop in the main street.[181]

Kevin recalled several train trips from Margaret River to Bunbury during World War II:

> My main impressions on these journeys were drinking water from a water bag, hung on a hook outside the window of the carriage to keep it cool and long waits at Metricup for a goods train to pass. On one occasion I remember the engine driver, who lived opposite us,

walking back from the loco with a large billy of freshly brewed tea for us. Another trip was not so cheerful, when I collected a cinder in my eye after sticking my head out the window of the carriage while the train was in motion. It was a rather painful experience at the time.[182]

Rob Saunders remembers his father telling him about similar train trips:

> He said one time they came down, the train got halfway down and then the train stopped and he couldn't believe it. Everybody got off the train with their picnic baskets, and their blankets. The drivers got out of the train and they sat down and had morning or afternoon tea at the side of the railway track. And he said the kids rushed off into the bush and came back with armfuls of boronia.[183]

Smiler Gale, growing up at Kudardup, south of Margaret River, during the war, also remembers a very slow trip to Perth:

> I can remember going to Perth in the train with a couple of my other siblings, and Mum. We travelled on the train – this was about 1943 – and you can imagine how slow that trip was. In fact, it took about 22 hours but that was the only way we could get to Perth.[184]

The locomotives were steam powered so there was always a danger of fire. While working at the pine plantation in Margaret River, Kevin Coate found out how far sparks could fly.

> From the top of a timber stack, I heard an engine's heavy chugging, indicating it was making hard work of the gradient. As it came into view sparks could be seen in the smoke belching from the smokestack and I spotted several grass fires starting along the railway line.[185]

In no time, Kevin was pumping water into the fire, from a pack spray kept handy for this purpose, and this saved the situation.

The reasons for the line's eventual closure were economic rather than safety related. Road transport was improving while the government-owned railways had always run at a loss. In 1957, the axe fell on unprofitable railway lines, including Busselton to Flinders

Bay. John Alferink, then a ten-year-old schoolboy, remembers the last train leaving Margaret River.

> I was in Standard 4 (Grade 5) at Margaret River Primary School but our class was located in the Anglican Parish Hall on Station Road. So we walked down to the railway station to see the last train leave Margaret River station. I can remember a lot of people being there and local road board people making speeches about how bad things were going to be in the future. The mood wasn't too happy. Anyway, the train left with lots of paper streamers flowing in the wind.[186]

Among the many objections from the road board and others to the railway closure were claims that:

> **The Busselton-Margaret River-Flinders Bay district has in one decade since the end of the war doubled its productivity. The district is expanding so rapidly that heavy rail transport must shortly become an economic necessity.**[187]

Farm productivity increased as pastures improved and the shire population did grow for a time. However, after 1954, numbers decreased at each census until 1981. The future of the district and thus that of the local hospital would depend on the emergence of a very different mixed economy in the last two decades of the twentieth century.

The year 1957 also saw the departure of the Anglican nuns of the Order of St Elizabeth of Hungary, who had worked in the community for thirty years. Their withdrawal from Western Australia was announced in *The Messenger*, newsletter of the Bunbury diocese:

> This decision has been reached, partly because the original work which the sisters came to do, namely to care for the English settlers of the Group Schemes, has been accomplished and partly because of the difficulty of maintaining a sufficient number of young Sisters necessary for the very arduous parish work of the present age.[188]

Margaret River parish said its official farewell to the sisters after a church service in February 1957. Some of the nuns had lived in Australia for thirty years and now regarded Western Australia as home. But they were bound by their vow of obedience to follow orders and return to the country of their birth.

The convent, sited opposite the hospital, was first offered for sale to the State Government for possible use as nurses' accommodation. The Perth bureaucracy appears to have rejected this suggestion without considering any possible merits of the proposal.[189] The Bunbury diocese then sold the building, which, as tourism expanded, was eventually repurposed as the Margaret River Guest House.[190]

The Sisters had left town but the Margaret Cecil Rest House, originally built for pregnant women awaiting the births of their babies, remained as a link with the group settlement past. Although the rest house was now in practical, if not legal, terms part of the hospital, the Rest House Association had continued to meet regularly throughout the 1940s and 1950s. Correspondence was maintained with Mrs Margaret Lane in London and at a meeting on 10 August 1946, the committee resolved to send a food parcel to their benefactor every three months 'while the food position in England is so acute'.[191] Rest House Association meetings seem to have become shorter and less frequent. There was little for the committee to do except provide amenities for the rest house sitting room.

In 1949 the committee decided to hold a ball the following year to celebrate the twenty-first birthday of the rest house.[192] It was agreed that the dance would not be a 'Debs' Ball 'as there were very few debs available'.[193] After this event, the *South-Western News* reported that, 'A most successful ball was held at Margaret River last Saturday evening, the occasion being the celebration of the twenty-first anniversary of the opening of the Margaret Cecil Rest House at Margaret River.'[194] Mrs Margaret Lane also sent her congratulations and best wishes for the twenty-first birthday party.[195]

The committee also received an unexpected letter from a Mrs D. Young.

I felt I would like to write to you on this big occasion of the Rest House 21st birthday on 26 May. My baby was the first born from the house and she was 21 yesterday 22nd May. She is now married and is Mrs Basil Hunt of 22 Keightley Rd, Subiaco. I was wondering if you would like a photo of Margaret to hang in the Rest Home lounge room. We have been away from the South-West for twenty years but I do intend visiting the home the first time I can get down that way. A good friend of mine wrote and told me about the celebration they were going to have for the Home. I enjoyed every minute I was there it being so lovely and comfortable. I had a letter from Mrs Herbert Lane in England not long ago and Margaret often hears from her as she is Margaret's god mother. I must close now and wishing you all the best for the Rest Home's big day.[196]

Margaret Lane in later life. Margaret Cecil Rest House Memorial Cabinet, courtesy Margaret River Hospital.

Most people now had access to motor vehicles and roads had improved so there was little need for the rest house. Yet the committee continued to provide library books and new furnishings for the sitting room which could be used by waiting and nursing mothers. This situation would continue until the late 1970s when the rest house became the hospital's permanent care wing and thus the final curtain would fall on a unique aspect of Margaret River's history.

Meanwhile, in August 1952, Ellie Metcalfe, who had grown up next door to the hospital, began work at the hospital. Matron Flynn was still in charge and was:

> Very unapproachable. But then she had to be above everybody else so I think that was all right. In those days there were five sisters and matron and six nurses. But we were only what I think they call a nursing assistant. We didn't have any qualifications. We learned on the job.[197]

While the hospital now had electricity and a reliable water supply, Ellie's account suggests that conditions for nursing staff had not improved significantly and that the hot-water system, requested over many years, had not yet been installed.

> I started nursing on August 15 1952, 7am. Learning to make a bed! I nursed there for three and a half years. It was very different to what it is these days. All the hot water for washing the patients came from a little tank by the kitchen fire, while all the cooking was done with wood. Breakfast was digestive meal with cold milk and sugar, a slice of bread and butter and a cup of tea. That was it. Occasionally if the fires in the laundry were right, we could make some toast on a long spike, for matron and staff. But that didn't happen very often.

> You wore a raincoat in the winter on night duty to go between the wards because they were all open on both sides and you got wet. There was no connection to the sleeping staff so in an emergency you had to leave the hospital and run to the staff quarters to wake someone up.[198]

Matron Catherine Flynn – longest serving matron at Margaret River Hospital. MR&DHS.

Margaret River Hospital nurses with Matron Flynn (back centre) 1950s. Courtesy Judy Wake. Photo originally provided by Pat Acheson.

Despite some improvements, in 1952 the hospital was still some way from the 'proper standard of efficiency' envisaged by Minister Panton in 1940. But it would need to serve the community for many more years.

Margaret River main street 1950s. Stephen Blakeney.

Chapter Six

A Small, Rather Slow, Hospital and a Rosy Future

In the late 1950s, the principal architect at the Public Works Department was asked to arrange the erection of a notice at the front of the building bearing the name of the Margaret River Hospital and the particulars of visiting hours.[1] Presumably, it had previously been assumed that everyone knew where the hospital was located and when they could visit!

This was a minor matter compared with the requests for renovations to the ageing buildings made repeatedly by both the matron and hospital advisory committee. From 1947, the year of her arrival in Margaret River, Matron Flynn had been requesting a long list of improvements, including repairs to the hospital's guttering. Writing to the Medical Department in 1959, matron advised that, 'One good shower of rain, and the whole back verandah is awash to a depth of at least three or four inches. The girls have to strip off their shoes and stockings to go to the toilet or bathroom.'[2] The following detail recorded by a visiting Medical Department official in that same year gives some idea of the state of the hospital at that time.

> In the dark room, the developing tank was minus a leg, and Matron expressed the opinion that this had been missing during the whole of her term as Matron of the hospital. This seems difficult to believe as Matron has been there for many years.[3]

In any event, a long list of other, more significant items still warranted attention. Requirements included replacing flywire on the hospital windows and doors, and installing a ramp for wheelchairs at the ambulance entrance.[4] The grounds between the hospital buildings needed bitumenising to address flooding experienced during the wet winters.[5] When Francine Watterson was born there, in May 1949, there had been heavy rain and Dr Barrett wore gumboots to walk across the muddy gravel between the main hospital and the maternity ward located in the Margaret Cecil Rest House.[6] It would still be several more years before the pathways between buildings were bitumenised.

While the Public Works Department let contracts for these requirements, it seemed that no one followed up on work not completed. Moreover, items which had been 'overlooked' were regularly added to the list of works, a practice that increased the confusion and gave the principal architect and his department excuses for lack of action. The Hospital Visiting and Advisory Committee was clearly frustrated, writing to the Medical Department in June 1961, and again in September, that the courtyard had still not been bitumenised and the verandah ramp for wheelchair cases had not yet been installed.[7]

However, in September 1961, Matron Catherine Flynn received correspondence acknowledging the lack of support for 'this small hospital, 300 kilometres from Perth'. The letter apologised for delays in completing renovations and improvements to the hospital buildings, admitting that:

> Margaret River has, unfortunately, been one of the most unsatisfactory that the Department has had to handle for many years and it is regretted that your Hospital has been put to so much inconvenience

over such a long period. It is hoped that the situation will be remedied in the near future.[8]

Even after the Medical Department's apology, the Public Works Department failed to ensure that all necessary and contracted work was completed'. In August 1962, Matron Flynn sent the undersecretary a list of repairs, alterations and renovations that had not been carried out as requested. The ramp for the front verandah near the ambulance bay was still non-existent; air-coolers had been approved but not delivered; and the doctors continued to complain about the poor lighting in the operating theatre.[9] Matron's letter concluded:

> I could list still more complaints, but this should be enough. Each Hospital Visiting and Advisory Committee Meeting that I attend, I have to answer that works asked for have still not been attended to. It seems to me, each time, that it puts the Department in a very bad light.[10]

In response, the matron was advised that the 'Public Works has been issued authority to proceed and you will be advised when a tender has been let'.[11] It is probable that Matron Flynn showed this response to the hospital advisory committee, as the secretary, B.E. Nicholl, also wrote to the department, complaining about its lack of action and noting that all thirty-three committee members had signed the correspondence.

> In view of the substantial sums of money raised by this Committee and spent in providing amenities at the Margaret River District Hospital, we strongly urge the Medical Department to carry out all the work which for they have promised to undertake for the Hospital without further delay. In this connection, a proposed ramp was particularly mentioned as being a most urgent necessity for the safety and welfare of patients, particularly casualties being admitted to this hospital.[12]

When this letter produced no action, the committee secretary wrote again on 22 December 1962, making the same request.[13]

Over the years, the Hospital Visiting and Advisory Committee would write many letters to the Medical Department complaining about the lack of government action on building and renovation matters. On the other hand, the department seemed to show a level of efficiency in ratifying the appointment of members to the committee. Each year the undersecretary would write asking for a list of members for the following twelve months and, not infrequently, the department queried some minor point, for example the spelling of a name: was the matron A. Peirce or G. Pierce? What was the Mr Edmeades' initial and what was the correct spelling for Nielson?[14] All nomenclature had to be correct for publication in the Government Gazette but such small-scale questions must have frustrated committee members when there was still no wheelchair access for the ambulance or functioning flywire on ward windows.

In later years, in addition to writing letters to the administrators and politicians in Perth, this committee, also known as the Hospital Amenities Committee, purchased many items which the department could not or would not provide. Carolyn Scott nursed at the hospital for many years and valued equipment provided by the committee: 'They were very good. They bought us an incubator, a blanket warmer for the labour ward, lots of nice chairs, a lot of little extra comforts to help the nurses and the patients.'[15] Coming from working in city hospitals, Fran Temby, as Director of Nursing, appreciated the community spirit which existed in Margaret River and the commitment to providing medical equipment that would not otherwise have been available in this small hospital.

> The friends of the hospital were a group of volunteers who fundraised and helped us with the equipment. They were an amazing group. I was in the Rotary Club and we organised a fun run, and people donated the proceeds of that to the hospital to buy an incubator. Yes, the community was always willing and helpful in making sure we were well equipped.[16]

Despite its official status, the Hospital Visiting and Advisory Committee was not involved in the hospital's management. In the

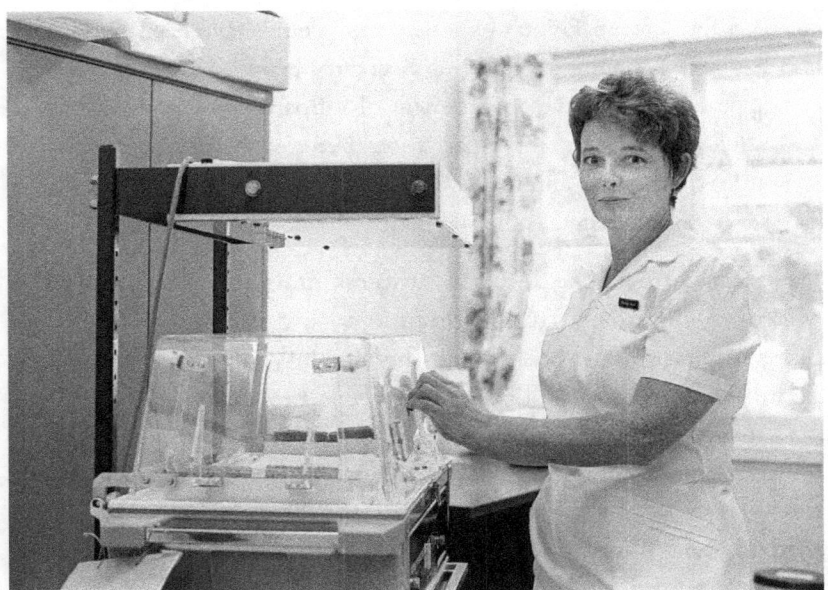

Carolyn Scott with incubator. Stephen Blakeney

early 1960s, the matron was still, in effect, the administrator as well as the person in charge of the nursing side. In the former role she was assisted by Barbara Peirce, sister of nurse and later matron Gay Peirce. Keith McLeod, waiting for the school bus at the Wallcliffe and Caves crossroads in the late 1950s, remembers the Peirce sisters riding their bicycles to work at the hospital. Motor vehicles were sometimes still a luxury item.[17]

In 1960, while Matron Flynn was still in charge, a local resident, Mr A.W. (Scotty) Wilson of Kudardup, spearheaded a move to establish a management committee for Margaret River Hospital. Such a regime already existed in other south-west country locations, such as Bridgetown. However, as usual, money triumphed, with the medical assistant undersecretary writing to the undersecretary that:

> At present Matron is responsible for the admin side as well – assisted by a good female clerk who would not be able to handle the position of Board Secretary as well.

> But for Matron Flynn's experience we could have been faced with having to appoint a Managing Secretary before. However it would appear that with the appointment of a Board we would have either a *full-time* secretary or a part-time (but costly) secretary involving at least £800 per annum. I would not like to see the present clerk's services terminated as she and matron work well together.[18]

It obviously suited the department to maintain the status quo. After Matron Flynn's departure in the mid-1960s, the clerk-in-charge at Busselton Hospital also became the administrator and the person mainly responsible for liaising between the Medical Department (and its departmental successors) and the hospital.

The undersecretary's endorsement of Matron Flynn's capabilities was not always supported by the department's principal matron, who visited the hospital each year. Her 1958 report was relatively uncritical and mainly recorded the staffing levels which, in addition to matron, included one double-certificated sister and three (appointed for short periods) single-certificated sisters, three nursing aides and three nursing assistants, one cook, six maids and three orderlies.[19] The principal matron reported that the appearance of the hospital had improved in comparison with previous years and that it was also better organised. But twelve months later, there were no plaudits for Matron Flynn.

> General appearance of hospital
>
> Very disappointing. Not at all well-kept, in fact the entire premises present a very unattractive appearance. The hospital is well-staffed by domestics and orderlies and there is no excuse for the dirty appearance as the hospital is not busy.[20]

No allowance was made for matters beyond the matron's control, such as the poor physical state of the hospital and other deficiencies that resulted largely from lack of action by the responsible government bodies.

When the principal matron visited the hospital again in 1963, she commented that it was over-staffed and that she was still unhappy with Matron Flynn's administration:

> Miss Flynn has been told on previous visits that her standard of administration is poor and she has from time to time improved. However, on this occasion, having regard to slackness of work, there is no excuse for the general lack of attention to cleanliness and order, particularly the work of the domestics. I voiced my displeasure and she has promised to effect improvement.
>
> Miss Flynn has, we must admit, her limitations but should be given an opportunity to improve. I recommend that Miss Morrissey be sent to Margaret River to evaluate the workload and advise the Matron on method and staffing. This should be done as soon as possible.[21]

Matron Flynn might have sometimes been judged poorly by the principal matron, but she did have one notable success in improving hospital facilities. On a visit to Perth in 1963, she asked whether the existing hospital laundry could be replaced as it was small and unsatisfactory.[22] This original laundry certainly belonged to another era. Beatrice Streatfield, a friend of Matron Flynn, was the laundress there in the 1950s. She told her granddaughter Elwyn that the old laundry was outdoors with covered washing line and coppers for hot water.[23]

The matron's request was well received and she was advised in July that the Public Works Department had been requested to prepare a sketch and estimate for a new laundry, which would be fitted with a washer-hydro extractor and gas-operated drying tumbler.[24] By November, the plans were ready for approval,[25] with construction of this new brick building progressing the following year. In May 1965, when the assistant undersecretary at the Medical Department visited the hospital, he was able to inspect the new laundry 'and other work proceeding. But the new washing machine had not arrived'.[26]

The Brick Laundry built in 1960s and trellis drying shed. Stephen Blakeney

In 1964, the year that the principal matron considered that the hospital was over-staffed, Matron Flynn appointed Judy Wake to a nursing position. Judy had trained as a nurse in England, landing in Western Australia as a 'ten pound Pom' in 1962. After initially being sent to nurse at Derby in the West Kimberley, Judy came south, at first to nurse at the Pemberton Hospital, but then Margaret River seemed an attractive option:

> I had a friend that I was nursing with in Pemberton and she married somebody in Margaret River. And I used to come over on a Saturday quite often, get the cows in and light the coppers while they were at football and they would come back, cook tea and I would spend the weekend with them and that would be nice. I thought it would be nice to be closer, working in Margaret River. And they advertised for someone with midwifery and I thought well, I have Part One. And the matron said, 'As long as you are prepared to cover me on a Sunday afternoon so I can go out'. And I said, 'That will be fine by me too'. I came over then. That was 1964. And I lived in the quarters and that was good there, cosy. It was a friendly sort of hospital.[27]

Judy soon discovered that Matron Flynn

Judy Wake at work. Stephen Blakeney

was a bit of a funny woman. We got on all right. But she didn't like bodies. When there was a body, she tended to disappear into the ether which was a bit hard because you couldn't lay a body out by yourself![28]

Overall, Judy found Margaret River to be a laid-back sort of hospital with its own culture.

It wasn't as regimented as in other places. When something came in, the jobs were automatically dispersed as needed. And you had a laugh and a joke. It was just much more friendly. Our job was making beds, washing and making them up. But if you were busy, the domestics would come and do that for you. You didn't have to ask. And if they were busy, we would help with the meals. I don't ever remember a sister saying, 'Nurse, get a bedpan'. If somebody asked for a bedpan, you went and got it, unless you were doing something sterile. It was much more of a level. You didn't treat people in a hierarchical way.

In the latter half of the 1960s, there was no doctor in Margaret River. Dr Barrett resigned in 1965 while Dr John Wilson who had practised in the district since 1954[29] also closed his surgery in December of that year,[30] and within eighteen months he had also finally left town.[31] Matron Gay Peirce, who had taken over from Matron Flynn, also reported that the local population was concerned about the lack of a permanent medical practitioner: 'There is much concern felt by local residents due to the fact that Dr Wilson is leaving on the 23rd of this month owing to ill-health and that we have no doctor in this area to take over.'[32] At a public meeting held to discuss the situation on 23 February 1966, speakers stated that hospital staff had been reduced and closure could occur because no medical practitioner was prepared to come to the town.[33] For a time in 1966, Dr Clark Stephenson provided a locum service. As Judy Wake recalled:

Matron Gay Peirce. MR and DHS

> Dr Stephenson was a little Pom and he was a man of small stature and he was lovely. He would come in at night time and come along the walkway, and of course he didn't want to disturb the patients, so he used to take his shoes off and so he would appear as from nowhere, make you jump. He was old-fashioned, but he was good and he had some lovely ideas. I did like him.[34]

Dr Stephenson was one of the first of several Margaret River doctors who made a formal case for constructing a brand-new hospital. His report, in 1966, which was commissioned by the Hospital Visiting and Advisory Committee and endorsed by the shire council, suggested that a new building should be constructed and that the existing hospital should be retained as a C-class hospital to house the elderly and infirm because: 'As a hospital the entire building leaves a lot to be desired; to lay out more money on an old building – to adapt the said building to modern conditions is not logical'.[35] Stephenson's report was forwarded to the Minister for Health by Stewart Bovell, MLA for Vasse, together with the comment that this hospital, built to serve the Group Settlement Scheme, had outlived its usefulness and should be replaced by 'a modern structure to serve the district'.[36] This recommendation was endorsed by the Augusta-Margaret River Shire Council, as the local newspaper reported.

> The shire council will notify Land Minister, Bovell that it strongly supports representations being made for a new hospital at Margaret River. This was decided at last week's shire council meeting after members had heard a report by Dr Clark-Stevenson (sic) on the condition of the present hospital. After hearing the report, Cr. G. Kniveton commented that the present building should not be retained.[37]

As a result of Dr Stephenson's advice, the *Busselton-Margaret Times* of 4 August 1966 had also reported, optimistically:

BID FOR NEW HOSPITAL

> **Immediate representations are being made to the Public Health Department for the building of a new 30 bed hospital at Margaret River.**[38]

This newspaper cutting was placed on a Medical Department file with a note attached to it: 'We have no prospect of building a new hospital at Margaret River in view of our loan fund situation, even if it were considered necessary.'[39] Dr Stephenson's departure in October 1966 provided yet another reason not to spend money on renovations and certainly not on a new hospital.

> Advice has been received that Dr Clark Stephenson is leaving Margaret River to go to Maitland NSW. This will leave Margaret River without a doctor and in these circumstances the hospital will be used even less than it has been.[40]

This memorandum to the Medical Department's assistant under-secretary stated that while the hospital had 37 beds, the average occupancy was well below this level of availability.[41] The decision not to build a new hospital was then enshrined in the minutes of a departmental planning meeting on 10 April 1967: 'As Dr Wilson has left the area and the possibility of a replacement is remote, the building of a new hospital at Margaret River should not proceed.'[42]

The lack of a locally based doctor inevitably had a significant impact on the hospital, as Sister Judy Wake recalled:

> During this period, after Dr Wilson left, Dr Williams from Augusta and Dr Cullen from Busselton conducted some patient care and outpatient services but we were left without closely available medical cover and were soon threatened with complete closure.[43]

For the local population, the lack of a resident doctor, who could attend at the hospital when required, presented a particular problem for pregnant women. In the absence of medical practitioner, most babies born to Margaret River women between 1966 and 1968 came into the world in Busselton. Very little surgery was undertaken at the hospital between April 1967 and March 1968.⁴⁴ Long term, a hospital without a doctor was not a viable option. Barry Blaikie, later the local Member of Parliament for Vasse, was then a member of the Augusta-Margaret River Shire Council.⁴⁵ He later recalled the effect that lack of medical services at the hospital had had on the district at that time.

> In 1966, the town's last doctor left and the town went into a serious decline. People started moving away to other towns because there was no longer security of medical treatment here. The shire council decided to advertise worldwide and even built a house at the then considerable expense of $95,000.
>
> An Irish doctor indicated that he wanted to come here and the shire decided to give him a go because he threw in his wife, who also happened to be a doctor.⁴⁶

The doctor in question was Dr John Lagan and his wife was Dr Eithne Sheridan. The latter recalled that they had decided to leave Ireland because:

> There was going to be a lot of trouble there and it had been bubbling on and off and I was doing locums. My husband was a country doctor in his father's practice, which was a problem in its own way, and as well as that, travelling at night time through the country was quite dangerous because there was a civilian military outfit called the B Men (the Ulster Special Constabulary) who could pop out of a ditch at night time and stop you and demand your identification. They were nasty, rude and frightening, and so we decided that it was time to get out and migrate.⁴⁷

But where to go?

> We had thought about the United States and met a lady recruiting for a Chicago hospital and got measured for our uniforms. We came home and looked at our three children and decided we couldn't do that to them. So then we saw an advertisement for multiple practices throughout Australia. I wrote to most of them and picked

Margaret River, and they sent a request for us to travel to London and be interviewed.

The Australia House interviewer could not understand why the doctors wanted to go to such a hot and remote place:

'Oh, what would you want to go there for?' I said, 'Why?' He said, 'It's up north.' And I said, 'It isn't. I bought an atlas, and it's down south.' So anyway, he had another look, because he said there was a station up north called Margaret River. He had a look and I said, 'It's down there.' And he said, 'Oh, right, cold, wet and green. It'll suit you fine!'

It did suit the doctors fine and they were to practise in the town for over 30 years. But initially there were culture shocks:

I didn't know really anything about country places in Australia. I thought it might be a bit like America, where people would come in, on their horses and tie them to the post. But anyway, it wasn't like that, but it was nearly. And it was such a small little place.

And, of course, the first shock was that the house that they told us was built and ready for us wasn't ready. So we had to stay for a night in the hotel, where there was number two shock. There was an apparatus in the hotel room and I said, 'What's that?' And they said, 'That's a Flit gun for the flies and the mosquitoes.'[48]

An even bigger shock for the Irish doctors was the lack of patients:

It had been advertised as a thriving practice and a pleasant place to live, but not much else. But there was no practice as the previous doctor had not been there for three years. The patients would go to the doctor in Augusta, which was a bit of a shock and we had to battle that for a long time.

Before long, the doctors decided that one of them would have to work elsewhere in order to earn a sufficient income to support their family.

A SMALL, RATHER SLOW, HOSPITAL AND A ROSY FUTURE

John said, 'One of us can't stay here. One of us will have to go,' and I couldn't bring the three children with me, so he said, 'I'll go.' We again looked up and found a place in Kwinana and he said, 'You ring up and find out about it.' And I rang up and this lovely Irish Dublin voice said, 'Hello.' And I said, 'What's your name?' And he said, 'Gerry Searson.' And if you've been in Dublin, the Searsons had a big pub, very well known, but anyway, Gerry sat next to me for five years in the university at the lectures to get ticked off the roll. There was Sheridan and Searson beside each other. I told John that I knew this guy and he said, 'Right, I'll go up and see him.' And he went, and he practised there from 1970 until 1997, and I stayed in Margaret River.

Judy Wake worked alongside the doctors for several decades:

They were lovely and they were so good, because for years they never had a holiday together and it didn't matter when you called them, they would come. Dr Sheridan would be here very quickly in a nightie and dressing gown, and Dr Lagan would be a little bit slower, all done up in his suit and tie and everything. I'm not sure he didn't even shave. They were wonderful doctors.[49]

Volunteer ambulance driver Rex Dyer coined an apt phrase for Dr Sheridan: 'I used to call her "the lady in the nighting-gown". Because of the number of times we would get called out and she would arrive in her dressing gown to work on a patient.'[50] Carolyn Scott returned to Margaret River to nurse in 1979. She, too, remembers Dr Sheridan's night-time visits to the hospital to deal with a patient in emergency.

Dr Sheridan was wonderful. She'd turn up in the middle of the night in her dressing gown, her pearls and slippers. She was 'it' for many years and she was terrific. Early days she would do surgery. She was a surgeon and delivered babies. She was also a psychiatrist, too – very good at psychiatry. She was pleasant and good to work with here. She was a good golfer and golfing was her outlet and today she still donates a trophy every year to golf.[51]

For Dr Sheridan, golf was her escape and she often played with hospital matron Gay Peirce:

> Golf was my release when I was annoyed or upset. I would go out and wallop a ball. Released a lot of problems. And Gay used to do that, too. You couldn't talk to us on Wednesdays because we always played golf. We'd come back in time for a cup of tea at three o'clock.[52]

For nursing staff there were also other social activities in the district, not always directly associated with the hospital, that provided relief from everyday work, as Judy Wake recalled:

> There would be weddings and birthday parties and that sort of thing. At Christmas they would put the piano on the back of a flatbed truck. They would chuck lollies out for the kids. Frank would play the piano. That sort of thing went on. It was good.[53]

Dr Eithne Sheridan. Courtesy of Patricia Lagan.

And in due course, Judy married the man who played the piano.

> When I arrived in Margaret River, I spent time with Mary Marsh and her husband. They had a farm and they did cream and milk. And the bloke that drove the tanker was a Pom and he said to me one day, I am going to a party at the weekend, and they are Poms, too, would you like to come? So I went to the party and I met Frank.
>
> And remembering I could be covering Sundays, I would go out with him on Saturdays and he would be playing somewhere every Saturday night and so we'd get back to the hospital about 2 or 3 am and we would sit outside and when the cook came, she would come in the front door and start the breakfast and I would come in behind her so she would have one half of the stove and I would have the other half, cook myself breakfast and then I would go off to bed and get up and do the afternoon shift. That worked well for years.

Just as Judy became a wife as well as a nurse, many other women in the district performed both roles. The hospital was one of the district's major employers and for many families it provided another source of much-needed income. Dairy farmers, dependent as they were on selling cream for butter, found prices sliding even further when Britain joined the European Common Market in January 1973 and butter could be imported cheaply from nearby Denmark. To make ends meet, both of Tim Crimp's parents had to work away from their Rosa Glen farm. His father, John, took a job as a relieving orderly at the hospital. This involved:

> Starting work at the hospital, either Margaret River or Augusta, at 7.30 am. So Dad had to get up at 4 am and milk the cows before driving half an hour to get to town. Then in the afternoon when he finished work about 3.30 pm, he had to come home and help his wife with the milking and the dairy. So they wouldn't get home until about 7.30 or eight o'clock in the evening.[54]

When permanent orderly Ron Metcalfe died in 1976, John Crimp took over his job. The tasks were many and varied. There were two orderlies, one for outside work, gardening and doing maintenance, and the other to help inside the hospital.

> They would swap around a bit but Dad preferred being out in the garden. There was everything from repairing roofs, fixing gutters and plumbing, all sorts of outside work that now would have to be handled by a maintenance man and an orderly wouldn't be allowed to touch those jobs these days. If he was inside, this involved helping with patients, lifting them, and washing them and wheeling them around as well as dealing with ones that became violent because they were alcoholics. You did what you had to do.[55]

Ron Metcalfe's wife, Ellie, who had initially worked at the hospital in the early 1950s, also later nursed there on night duty:

> Because I had four children, one going to school, I would do the night shifts from eleven to seven and I would come home and cook a meal for lunch. Then I would go to bed. My husband was working at the hospital so he'd get tea and I would get up about 7 pm and have a bath or a shower. And be ready to go back to work. I only did two or three nights a week. It wasn't full time.[56]

But it was a busy life. Judy Dunbar (formerly Judy Leiper) grew up on a Cowaramup farm. She returned to the district with her husband Bob after travelling overseas. They needed money:

> And yes, the hospital was the focal point. It probably had more jobs than available anywhere else. But that's how I got the job, necessity, not because I had any specific skills.
>
> A lot of those well-trained nurses were going home and feeding pigs or calves. The husband of a very dear friend of ours worked in the timber mill. She worked in the hospital and they both ran their dairy farm, came home, milked cows. We didn't think it was extra brilliant because everyone was doing things like that.[57]

Don Miller was one dairy farmer who managed to fit the Saturday dances into his busy schedule.

> The old school was out at Bramley and we used to have a dance out there about every two weeks, Marion and I used to dance ourselves silly. She loved it. And we'd go to Cowaramup or Karridale or somewhere every week. It was good.[58]

Dances at the old Bramley School also hold fond memories for a young Elwyn Franklin.

> That was a great time when the school was still there. My mother was a pianist as well. We had dances there every second Friday night, and we'd walk up there with a lantern. We had Frank Wake who would take turns with Mum playing the piano and the kids would scoot around the floor and do the Mexican shuffle. We danced the barn dance, the Boston two step, hokey pokey, Pride of Erin, to name a few. And, you know, it was a wonderful time really, and the ladies brought lovely things to eat for supper.[59]

For the women in particular, dances were a welcome chance to get together socially.

> So, at the dances, the women and the kids would be there conversing, swapping recipes and talking about sewing and probably helping each other out with dress patterns and things like that; talking about how things were going at school for the kids. The men, when not dancing, would congregate around the door or outside on the verandah and talk about farming and the weather.[60]

Francine Watterson (later Temby) and her brother David helped with preparations for dances at Augusta.

> In those days, we would often go with Mum and the other volunteers as they prepared for fundraising balls and dances for the St John Ambulance. We would decorate the hall with balloons and streamers and help prepare the supper. To prepare the floor for dancing the men used to spread a mixture of sawdust and kerosene on the timber floor and then sweep it up.

But in the evening,

> My brother and I had to sleep in the FJ Holden at the front of the hall and we used to wind the windows down and call out to people and we'd get into trouble. But we used to sleep in the car and I think we were the only children who did that.[61]

Social events were important because farming, especially dairying, in the 1960s and 1970s was never an easy life. Pat Gray had never wanted to leave the city and become a farmer's wife but in 1960, when her husband decided to buy land in the district, she had no choice.

> Let's say you don't do anything else much. There is always something to do on the farm. You've got to be there morning and night to feed the calves, put out the hay. Then you have hay time and calving. We were up half the night sometimes pulling a calf away from a cow, the pair of us. Mostly we were successful at that. If we knew a cow was starting to calve as we finished milking, she was kept an eye on until she had the calf. That was the right thing to do. You had to be there for them.[62]

As a newcomer, Dr Eithne Sheridan observed that life was often challenging, both work-wise and financially, for the district's farming community.

> Well, when we came, at the end of summer in 1968, and it was mainly a dairy farming district. The farmers used to get paid on the butter content of their milk, and during the summer there was no content much, and farmers were owing money all round the place and Bill Darnell from the Rosa Brook general store practically used to run his own bank. He'd let them buy and when the milk cheques came in, then he would get his money. And that was for quite a while.
>
> Then in the early '70s, there was a crash or something financial and I know they used to kill the calves because there was no market for them, and you could buy a whole calf or take it for nothing. It was terrible. But then gradually things started to get better.[63]

Earning a living in the Margaret River during the 1960s often required taking on a multitude of jobs. John Alferink's family had arrived from the Netherlands in the 1950s. In the 1960s, John gave up an apprenticeship at the Midland Railway Workshops in Perth and came home to help his ailing father.

> Dad was, at that time, milking three cows by hand, had several pigs, operated the sanitary contract, delivered parcels to various businesses from railway freight services and dug the occasional grave for the shire when it was necessary. Dad and I, as well as operating all the above, started to build a new dairy and increase the cow numbers to 30, which were still milked by hand twice a day. We developed very strong wrists. The dairy was completed in 1966 but with still no milking machine and then Dad died in his sleep aged 52 on 11 September 1966.[64]

Dairying in the 1960s was not particularly lucrative. The State Government maintained a system of milk quotas which was the amount of milk that could be sold as 'whole milk' but until the late 1970s no quotas were allocated to farmers in the south-west. This meant that their only option was to separate milk into cream and whey and to sell the former as 'manufactured milk' for cheese or butter. The low price that the dairy companies paid for cream, or 'butterfat' as it was known, had long been a source of complaint.

However, in the late 1970s, after considerable political lobbying, some Margaret River dairy farmers were issued with market milk quotas. The price for whole milk was much higher than that for manufactured milk and, once issued, these quotas could be bought and sold on the open market.[65] Don Miller was one farmer who lobbied for quotas to be issued to farmers in the Margaret River district.

> Yes, I was involved in getting the quotas. I went to Tommy Duggan's, a whole mob of us went down there to a meeting and old Charlie Court (the Premier) came down. He didn't know what we were talking about but he was the best man I have seen for effecting things.

And about two days later, he was back to us. He said, 'You have got it (milk quotas)!' He said, 'I can see what you are talking about.' And away we went.[66]

For Don, milk quotas 'made a huge difference. We built a new dairy with cement and bricks. It was good. I bought more farms and I ended up with 800 acres.' Greg Bussell has spent a lifetime living and farming in Margaret River. For his family, milk quotas were also:

> huge. I'd say I believe it's one of the biggest changes in the district because it brought a level of wealth which we'd never seen before. I mean, when I grew up in Margaret River, it was a bankrupt society. Nobody had any spare cash. When the quotas came in, suddenly farmers were building new homes, whereas before they were living in old shacks half the time. So yes, a lot of things changed in the town because people could afford to go in and buy their groceries and not book them like they had in the past.[67]

Now that dairy farmers had greater financial security, they were able to get credit from the bank to pay for farm improvements. Bill Darnell, well known as a shopkeeper who himself offered credit in hard times, noted that most of the bush was not actually cleared for farmland until the late 1970s and early 1980s, because then landowners could borrow the money to pay for the equipment and labour needed. And with more country cleared, dairy herds could increase in size.[68]

Greg Bussell recalled that, at the same time, 'We also brought in New Zealand farm advisers. Those people made a massive amount of difference to our farming practices.'[69] The New Zealand farm advisers, paid for by farmers banding together to raise funds included John Chadwick, who was responsible for some of these new ideas:

> Particularly in cattle stock management, he introduced electric fencing, which is a much cheaper form of fencing, because you don't

need so much timber, when before it was all split jarrah fenceposts with thousands of posts in the ground. So, once you put up an electric fence, you only needed a post every chain or half chain across the paddock, and the electricity kept the cattle under control.[70]

For John Chadwick's wife, Margaret, arriving in Margaret River from New Zealand in 1968, the same year that doctors Lagan and Sheridan came from Ireland, was not a pleasant experience:

> I walked into this little wooden house in Le Souef Street. And there was a Metters No. 2 Improved stove. I don't know what the improvement was, because I couldn't find it. And there was a Braemar in the laundry that you had to light a fire under to get hot water. I had two small sons, aged three and fourteen months. And every cupboard in the kitchen was painted a different colour and there was bright red lino on the floor. We got to Margaret River on the first of July. And it rained for five days. And out the back was a big load of wood, wet, green jarrah for the fires and the open fire. So I wasn't happy.[71]

Very soon, however, Margaret realised that she and John had 'picked a beauty'. The district's economic fortunes were slowly changing. In the late 1970s, the price of land and other real estate began to increase.

Over a decade earlier, Smiler Gale and his wife Pat had bought a shop in Margaret River's main street. They sold a variety of items, including toys and bicycles. It was a good business because:

> We knew everybody in town of course, in the main street, and I probably knew most people throughout the district but in any case, that's the way our tradesmen worked, and I wouldn't sell whatever somebody else was selling up the street. We all made a dollar. We weren't really competing against each other.[72]

But in 1977 Smiler and Pat decided on a change of business and lifestyle. They received an offer from another local businessman, Ray Shepherdson, to lease their building for a hardware shop.

> We were trying to sell it at that point and we wanted $28,000. We had bought it for $16,000. So we thought we had done pretty well over 12 years when it came up to that. So, in any case, Shepherdson came up with a deal. He wanted to lease it for two years and said 'I will then pay $30,000 for the building'. So we thought that's a good deal and he did pay us $45 a week for renting it. So we didn't miss out there. But in that two years the whole area sky-rocketed in real estate business and we were committed to sell for $30,000 whereas in actual fact it would have been worth $50,000 to $55,000. So we didn't do too well on that deal.[73]

This increase in property prices between 1977 and 1979 signalled the beginning of a turnaround in the local economy.

While the shire population did not increase in the 1960s and 1970s, Margaret River was becoming a vibrant and lively community where, as Smiler Gale said, everyone still knew everyone else. For Rosa Glen dairy farmer Tim Crimp:

> The district had a different feel then. This was a good time, a happy time. Nobody had much but what they had, they shared. If you didn't help your neighbour, nothing happened. So if there was a tragedy, everyone helped out.[74]

When dairy farmer Don Miller broke his ankle while his dad was also in Margaret River Hospital, Brian Yates, a neighbour two farms down, jumped in his car and milked his cows, and then with another neighbour Brian continued to do the same for several weeks.[75] Such actions were typical of community and individual responses to a medical crisis or other adversity and it seemed that something of the 'caring and sharing' group settlement spirit remained. For Tim Crimp, 'This district has a very long history of hard work and I think that this was the best period for Margaret River'.[76]

Groups were also banding together to form new clubs and associations. Road board members George Shervington, Bill Darnell, Stewart Smith and Charles West had spearheaded the founding of a local rotary club, which received its charter on

17 February 1960. Three years later the Margaret River Apex Club was formed, while a branch of the Business and Professional Women's Club and the Moondyne Arts and Crafts Group were both established in 1973.[77] The following year saw the founding of the Augusta-Margaret River Arts Council (later Arts Margaret River) as an umbrella group, which provided support and advocacy for other community organisations, such as the Margaret River Choral Group, the Spinners and Weavers Group, the Margaret River Art Group, and individual arts practitioners.[78]

There was now a significant number of older long-term residents in the district and they often needed medical and welfare services that the hospital could not offer. In 1972 a branch of Silver Chain, the state's main provider of in-home medical and nursing support, was set up by local farmer's wife Dot Wickham,[79] who Dr Eithne Sheridan remembers as a mover in the community.[80] Before organising and operating this service in Margaret River, Dot had worked as a Silver Chain nurse in Busselton and when she began taking on patients in her home town, the country supervisor asked Dot to start a branch in Margaret River. She later wrote her recollections of setting up this organisation in Margaret River:

> For the first year, I worked at Margaret River alone. My first patient was from Cowaramup. I liaised with Doctors Sheridan and Lagan in Margaret River and Dr Williams in Augusta. For the first seven years, I shared the job with Jean Bussell. Jean and I both came from farming backgrounds in Margaret River…Our respective farming backgrounds proved to be very useful. As the farming community in Margaret River can attest, farming demands a great deal of flexibility and tenacity. The farmers' work schedule is driven by the demands of the farm and in many ways, our work schedule is driven by the needs of the patients. This meant working long and odd hours (we were always on call) and travelling long distances over some rough terrain. Some days we travelled up to 200 kilometres, as our district stretched from the Scott River (east of Augusta) to Wilyabrup.[81]

Dorothy Wickham worked from home, her lounge room becoming the Silver Chain office. She was also instrumental in providing home help to those who needed it in the town and surrounding areas.[82]

> A number of our patients were elderly and lonely, and we felt that this additional care, often a call lasting just a few minutes, gave them a sense of security, of being looked after and of being in a community.[83]

Pat Gray was one home help provider who found working for Silver Chain a very rewarding experience: 'The Silver Chain provided assistance so that ladies could stay in their home. I helped them by doing their shopping, cleaning their house, or anything in general.'[84] Pat also enjoyed talking with some of the district's older identities, some of whom had contributed to the development of the area since group settlement times. Registered nurse and later hospital matron Mary Arthur also worked with Dot Wickham in establishing Silver Chain in the district. Her children sometimes travelled with her to Augusta and Kudardup. Mary's daughter Lynda Williams recalls that:

> We did love it when she was working for Silver Chain. We used to go in the car with her when she was working for them, ride around with her and visit all the oldies. There was a lovely old chap who lived on the hill at Augusta and he had a beautiful big house looking out over the river, Mr Christiansen. And we would sit on the verandah and have a cup of tea with him. And a Mrs Poole out at Kudardup. She used to give us milk in the old sherry bottles and sell us eggs.[85]

In the mid-1980s registered nurse Fran Temby returned from Perth to live in Margaret River. She too worked for Silver Chain and appreciated the social side of this work.

> I loved meeting the clients and visiting them in their homes was very special. And I did enjoy the conversations; a lot of the people were out on farms and I often came back with a dozen eggs and cakes and fruit, so generous of the clients. I felt so privileged to care for those people.[86]

A SMALL, RATHER SLOW, HOSPITAL AND A ROSY FUTURE

In addition to setting up Silver Chain in Margaret River, Dot Wickham was also one of the main instigators of the local Meals on Wheels service. This involved volunteer drivers delivering hot meals to elderly people within a three-kilometre radius of the town. The idea was first raised with the Hospital Visiting and Advisory Committee by Dr Sheridan in October 1971 and the service started in Margaret River in June 1972.[87] It was subsidised by the WA Health Department and meals were prepared in the hospital's kitchen.[88] The hospital committee provided equipment and a local committee of management was established to run yet another voluntary organisation.[89]

As the number of elderly and infirm people in the community increased, the need for permanent hospital care for some older citizens grew. The Hospital Visiting and Advisory Committee first suggested in 1970 that the existing maternity ward in the Margaret Cecil building could be turned into a permanent care wing for elderly patients and then a new maternity wing could be built onto the main hospital because: 'A new maternity ward attached to the main building would be so much easier for staff to manage'.[90] It was obviously not ideal for the maternity wing to be separate from the main hospital and this inconvenient arrangement had been a source of complaint for many years. Senior management in Perth were reluctant to spend money on a new wing and sought the opinion of the department's principal matron on whether the construction of a new maternity ward could be justified. Her report showed little sympathy for this proposal:

> These circumstances have always existed at Margaret River...It would seem to me a very costly undertaking to have to erect a new labour ward and clean-up room, and move the children...Therefore, I do not see the necessity in spending money at this small, rather slow, hospital.[91]

The suggestion that the hospital's maternity wing, in the Margaret Cecil Rest House, should be converted into a permanent care facility rang alarm bells with the Rest House Association. Longtime secretary, Mrs Hilda West, wrote to the Minister for Health, Ron Davies, MLA:

> It is advised that while my Association applauds and supports the proposal, it does not desire that the historical and physical links between the Margaret Cecil Rest House and the hospital should be severed. The original building, since converted to maternity ward, of which the lounge maintained by my Association, in part, was built from funds supported by the 'Margarets of Britain' and not from Government finance...My association trusts that the desire of its members will be considered when the possible siting of a geriatric ward is being made.[92]

The minister's response simply stated that no funds were available for this conversion but that, 'You may rest assured that your Association's views will be considered when dealing with a proposal affecting the maternity ward'.[93]

The bid to once again repurpose the Margaret Cecil Rest House did not go away and eventually the State Government agreed to build a new birth suite at the rear of the main hospital building. The Margaret Cecil building was then converted into a permanent care facility for elderly patients. At least one of the new inhabitants told Sister Judy Wake that she had previously spent time in that same building awaiting the birth of her baby.[94]

Times had changed and the Public Works Department, which no longer managed (or mismanaged) all government building contracts, commissioned Bunbury-based architects Parry and Rosenthal to design the new birth suite and undertake modifications to the Margaret Cecil building. By the end of September 1976, the architects were able to advise the Minister for Works, in a 'completion of contract' letter, that there had been excellent progress and that the standard of work was very good.[95] Despite delays due to shortage of materials and contract variations, the final certificate for completion of contract was issued in May 1977.[96] This was to be the last major building project undertaken at this hospital.

The 1975 contract documents also specified that the work should include 'conversion of the old separate cottage, now referred to as the "Doctors' Suite"'. One bedroom was to become a pathology laboratory, while bedrooms two and three were to be converted to the doctors' consulting rooms.[97] This group settlement-type house, built in 1924, had been the original staff quarters. It then housed the matron and domestic staff but, after a new flat was built for the matron in 1949, the old house had been unused for many years. At various times conversion for other purposes, such as a day room for patients or an outpatients' waiting room, had been suggested. On each occasion, the cottage had been deemed unsuitable for these purposes. It now gained a new lease of life as a surgery and pathology laboratory for doctors Sheridan and Lagan.

When these doctors arrived in Margaret River in 1968, they had been unable to afford to take over the previous doctor's surgery. Thus, they were allowed to use the hospital's treatment and X-ray room for an initial period of six months to 'assess the economics of practice'. This arrangement was continued for a further six

Old Domestic Quarters and Doctors Surgery, 1970s to 1990s. Stephen Blakeney.

months. In April 1969, when the doctors had occupied this area for one year, the hospital's managing secretary advised the Medical Department that:

> Since commencing practice in Margaret River in March 1968, the Doctors have been utilising rooms at the hospital. This tenancy was approved until December 1968. Dr Lagan has requested that the Department consider building an annex to the hospital for use as a consulting room and for his Secretary.
>
> I have suggested to him that he should approach the local shire with a request that the shire provide these facilities for him or to assist him by subsidy.[98]

The shire was unwilling to assist, given that it had already built a house for the doctors. It was then that the hospital's managing secretary suggested that the old domestic quarters could be used as a surgery. While the Medical Department initially rejected this proposal on grounds of expense and unsuitability, once converted, this 1924 cottage met the doctors' requirements.[99]

Matron Peirce had long been asking for a day room for ambulant patients and a waiting room for outpatients. The Medical Department had shown a reluctance to provide either of these facilities or to guarantee the hospital's future, with an official noting:

> With regard to the recreation room (and day room), PWD can be asked for an estimate but whether or not these proceed would depend on cost. If an existing area can be converted, then the costs can be kept to a minimum.
>
> Would you also reply to Matron in the most tactful manner so that the Department's thoughts on the future of the hospital are not conveyed to her at this stage.[100]

The day room was finally created, rather than built, in 1969 by enclosing the east end of the hospital's front verandah.[101]

From 1975 until the old hospital closed in 1990, the rest house remained the permanent care wing, housing elderly patients

Verandah enclosed as Day Room. Courtesy Judy Wake

requiring nursing care on a long-term basis. Judy Wake, who was in charge of this ward during the 1980s, made efforts to create special occasions and outings for the residents, some of whom had few visitors.

> We had a few social events that included the doctors. We'd have barbeques. We'd try and get the relatives and families of the people in permanent care to come in and socialise, and make a bit of a party of it. And I remember Dr Shaun O'Rourke would run the barbeque and Dr Clarke would come, too.[102]

Fran Temby also enjoyed the company of permanent care residents in a manner that was only possible in such a small, local hospital.

> If the hospital was quiet and the weather was nice, we were allowed to take one or two of our permanent care residents out in wheelchairs. They loved the excursions. And I do recall one lady asked us to stop at Red Rooster. And we bought her a small box of hot chips. And another gentleman loved having a small glass of beer at the tavern.

And I think a nurse may have had the odd one on occasion! There were four men and four women residents in permanent care and I remember an old Italian gentleman called each of us by his Italian version of our names. I was sister Francesca, Margaret was Sister Margarita, and Carolyn was Sister Carolina.[103]

Dr Shaun O'Rourke at hospital barbeque. Courtesy Judy Wake

Permanent care: Mrs Busetti with nurse Jenny Slapp. Stephen Blakeney

When the Margaret Cecil Rest House became the hospital's permanent care wing, Margaret Lane had died and her insistence that this building should never be part of the hospital was no longer front of mind. The Margaret Cecil Rest House Association accepted the inevitable. Sir Stewart Bovell, MLA, now one of the trustees, held a special combined meeting of trustees and the ladies committee, at his house, on 11 June 1977. The meeting unanimously resolved to wind up the association and, after providing for a Margaret Cecil memorial cabinet and plaque at the hospital building, to donate funds remaining to the Margaret River Homes for Senior Citizens, then aiming to build homes for older residents. A full attendance of trustees and committee were present. 'This concluded business and a very pleasant social time was spent with our host Sir Stewart who provided a delicious afternoon tea.'[104]

Soon after that meeting, Rest House Association secretary Hilda West forwarded a cheque to councillor Alan Hillier representing the Margaret River Homes for Senior Citizens.

> I refer to discussions at the Augusta-Margaret River Shire Council Building, Margaret River on Saturday 2nd July 1977 between representatives of the Margaret River Homes for Senior Citizens and the Trustees and Committee of the Margaret Cecil Rest House Association.
>
> On behalf of the President (Mrs A.E. Thomas), Vice President (Mrs M.B. Willmott), Committee members Mesdames M. Boulter, E. Smith, M. Todhunter, B. Watterson, and H. West and the Trustees Mrs D.J. Bussell and Sir Stewart Bovell, I have much pleasure in forwarding herewith cheque for $1,300…the proceeds thereof to assist in the establishment of Homes for Senior Citizens at Margaret River.
>
> As my Association requested at the meeting referred to herein, it would be much appreciated if a permanent memento of the Margaret Cecil Rest House could be incorporated in the Margaret River Homes for Senior Citizens.

> The amount of $1,300 is comprised of funds held by the Trustees and Committee of the Margaret Rest House Association on termination of half a century of existence. The Rest House Building has been made available to Margaret River District Hospital for use by geriatric patients.[105]

Shire clerk J.D. Reidy-Crofts replied:

> You may be assured that a permanent memento to the Margaret Cecil Rest House will be incorporated in the Aged Person Homes Project. It is sad to see, after half a century in existence, your committee is 'winding up', however I am sure the spirit of the Margaret Cecil Homes [sic] will live on.
>
> With our best wishes and appreciation of your committee services to our community.[106]

Previously, in October 1976, when it had become evident that the rest house would become part of the hospital, the committee had decided that photographs and records of the Margaret Cecil story would be preserved in a display cabinet in the rest house sitting room and a record of contents would be listed in the minutes. Thus, the minutes of the final meeting of the Rest House Association on 2 February 1979 stated that display cabinet would include:

> the Trustees and Committee Minute books, a book sent by Margaret Cecil listing information and names of the Margarets of Britain who had subscribed to Building Funds, furnishing of Rest House. Photos of Margaret Cecil and her mother Lady Cecil, also pictures, paintings, pieces of monogrammed crockery.
>
> The above items to be held in (perpetuity) till such time as a Western Australian Margaret River Branch of History be formed.[107]

The Margaret Cecil memorial cabinet was transferred to the new hospital when this opened in 1990 and placed on a wall in the main corridor. The full names and offices of the trustees and committee members were also listed in the association's final minutes:

Trustees: Dorothy Jean Bussell, The Hon Sir Stewart Bovell, President: Mrs Agnes Elizabeth Thomas, Vice President: Mrs Myra Stewart Willmott, Members: Mrs Mabel Beatrice Boulter, Mrs Mary Todhunter, Mrs Edna Beryl Watterson, Mrs Eva Smith, Ex officio: Dr Eithne Sheridan, Matron Agatha Lorraine (Gay) Peirce, Hon Secretary/Treasurer Mrs Hilda May West.[108]

Margaret Cecil Rest House memorial plaque. Courtesy Judy Wake

All association funds had now been dispersed and the bank account closed. The Margaret Cecil Rest House Association ceased to exist.

Margaret River Homes for Senior Citizens had also applied for land within the extensive hospital reserve to be made available for the proposed aged accommodation:

> The area of land most suitable for the project is, as inspected, three acres of the southern end of Margaret River Town Lot 33, fronting Mitchell St (now Wallcliffe Road) which is vested in the Medical Department and we hereby make formal application for the above-mentioned land.[109]

The State Government duly granted the land requested and it became the site of the first stage of Mirrambeena Residential Care, which opened in 1979.[110]

While elderly patients could now be cared for in Margaret River and the local hospital could cope with most emergencies, sometimes patients still had to be transferred to other hospitals, mainly to Perth. Carolyn Scott and Judy Wake were two of the nurses who had to accompany patients.

> The only trouble we had was transferring patients because there was only one ambulance and we virtually had to deal with everything. And it had to be very major before we could transfer any very sick patient to another hospital in those days. You'd be in a big Dodge ambulance getting someone to Perth.[111]

The nurses and the ambulance driver also had to cope with any medical problems during the transfer, as Judy recalled.

> In those days there was no radio contact. You were on your own. There was no contact with anybody. But the doctors were very good, they would give us all the instructions and send us off, and we had good drivers.[112]

Rex Dyer was one of those 'good drivers'. A few years after migrating from England, Rex became a dedicated volunteer ambulance driver for the Margaret River St John's Volunteer Ambulance Service. He was also responsible for women being accepted as ambulance drivers, including his wife Betty: 'I said to the committee, which was all male, "Just think about it, if we got the ladies, we would get better lunches".'[113]

For Rex and other drivers, a typical day in the ambulance could start at three o'clock in the afternoon, finish at six o'clock the next morning and include a drive to Perth and back.

> But you have to realise that when you are out on the road, you had no communications, you didn't have radios, didn't have mobile phones.

> You were out there by yourself and you certainly had to use a lot of your initiative. I certainly put a lot into it, but I got a lot out of it.[114]

It was not until 1980 that a radio base station and tower were installed at the hospital.[115] Even for experienced nurses like Judy Wake, 'It was a bit fraught, four hours on your own in the back. We didn't even have a seat or a seat belt. We sat on a box half the time, especially if we had two patients, which we often had.'[116]

Carolyn Scott remembers one trip where Rex Dyer was the driver. A State Electricity Commission employee had been electrocuted.

> So Judy Wake and I had to escort him to Perth in the Dodge ambulance. I think Rex was the driver. Two nurses were sent because we were told he wouldn't make it. Anyhow, he did. But on the way back I do remember Judy and I lying in the back of the ambulances on the stretchers while she told the most amazing jokes, but those Dodge ambulance trips were gross, horrible.[117]

Rosa Glen dairy farmer and hospital orderly John Crimp was also a volunteer ambulance driver. For many years ambulance call-outs came straight to the hospital and because John was often working there, he was frequently asked by the matron to go out to accidents and other emergencies.

> The matron or one of the senior sisters would grab him and off they would go and be the first responders. One of these [emergencies] was in the Brides Cave, where somebody fell about ten metres down and fractured their pelvis and they were in a lot of pain. And Matron Peirce was a fairly large lady so she couldn't be lowered down, whereas Dad was fairly thin so he got the job of being lowered down to inject the person with morphine to calm him down.[118]

John attended some horrific car and other accidents.

> Often, he didn't talk about these experiences for several days. He would be quiet when he came home and he wouldn't say anything. It would be a few days before it would come out and they were usually

fairly gruesome details, such as going into the bush to pick up limbs that had come off in accidents.[119]

For hospital staff, too, as Judy Wake recalled, there were often tough times:

> We used to get together. There was no counselling if something terrible happened and there were some horrible things that happened. We'd have a bad day and we'd just say 'Pub or what?' And on the way home, we'd just stop and have a couple of drinks and a chat and then we'd feel fine and off we'd go home. And that was the way it worked, which was much more sensible.[120]

For many people in the district, sport of all kinds remained their distraction from work. In addition to football, hockey and tennis, by the mid-1960s Augusta, Cowaramup and Margaret River had all formed bowling clubs, and a karate club was established a few years later.[121] When 'Barney' Barnett came to town in 1976, the district seemed to be sports mad!

> You would not believe how important it was back in the '70s and '80s. The football club had a bar and was the heart and soul of a town. There had been six football teams that over the years had got smaller and smaller. Margaret River joined the South West league and there was now one football team. A lot of the footballers played hockey on Saturday. The bar of the football club was busier than the hotel. Basketball was played on Monday, Tuesday, Wednesday nights, and it had to be ten o'clock before it finished. Badminton was also very strong.[122]

Increasingly, too, cultural activities were important and appreciated by the local population. The Augusta-Margaret River Arts Council was active in bringing theatre and music to the district.[123] When the Margaret River Cultural Centre was built in the 1980s, Barney was the first manager:

> The main purpose of the cultural centre was, of course, cabarets. We're talking about the 1980s. So there was pretty well a cabaret or

wedding or some function involving a band every week. The arts, not so much, but it was the home of the arts, and it enabled the symphony orchestra, for example, to play here. The theatre group in those days was extremely active, and you'd get in the vicinity of 400 people to a two-nights performance, all paying, so that was quite a thing.[124]

Sue Juniper and husband Geoff were stalwarts of the Margaret River Theatre Group:

> When the time came for building a new community facility, the shire president at the time, Alan Hillier, invited the committees of the Theatre Group and Arts Council to a meeting. A representative of the Playhouse in Perth was there as well. The configuration of the new building for use as a theatre was the top item on the agenda.[125]

When they were not treading the boards, local families could be found at the beach, fishing, swimming or diving. Elwyn Franklin enjoyed outings to a small beach between Gnarabup and Gracetown.

> We went fishing. We went to our favourite spot at Herring Bay on the back of a truck. It is still one of my favourite places. Only a tiny little bay near Kilcarnup. There would be a walk down to the beach carrying everything because it was always a full day out. We'd have lunch, Dad would catch fish and sometimes he'd catch a carpet shark on the hook. We kids would fish, swim and fossick around in the caves at either end of the beach. At the end of the day, there would be a long, tired walk back up the hill carrying everything, including hopefully, lots of fish.[126]

Many farming families, especially those living north of Margaret River, had always spent their holidays at Cowaramup Bay. In contrast to Kilcarnup, where vehicle access was eventually prohibited, the State Government decided in the early 1960s to gazette Cowaramup Bay as a townsite and to bitumenise the road. Stewart Bovell, who was Minister for Lands at the time, suggested the name Gracetown, which was adopted.

People living locally were given the opportunity to purchase blocks at a reasonable cost. The Leiper family, farming in nearby Cowaramup, had always holidayed at 'the Bay' and considered buying a block at the asking price of £350. But Robert Leiper eventually decided to invest in a television instead![127] Other farmers, like Cedar Armstrong, who retired to the coast after years of hard work on his dairy farm, took the opportunity to build homes for themselves and others at Gracetown.

> So my son took over the farm. I went on playing around building houses at the Bay, plus fishing, owning caravans and boats and travelling all over and around and backwards through Australia. I had a glorious time for eighteen years. Better than farming![128]

Other families, including the Teasdales, would camp at Gnarabup and for many years they had the place to themselves until one year when George Teasdale saw surfers at his family's favourite fishing spot. When they walked to the edge of the reef, jumped in and paddled their boards towards the distant breakers, he knew they had to be crazy.[129]

When surfers who had previously congregated at Yallingup to the north discovered the Margaret River main break, it quickly became a hub. In 1965 the North End Surf Club purchased a block in Geoff Edwards' Prevelly subdivision.

> The block in Prevelly became our base in Margaret River. We started building the shack on weekends and holidays and within twelve months we had a three-room shack with a toilet and shower – luxury! The shack only had louvre windows which were pretty drafty in winter but it sure beat hammocks.[130]

Surfing brought many more visitors as well as both fame and notoriety to Margaret River. Hassa Mann had grown up in Rosa Glen in the days when you could drive up the street on a Sunday and only see one other car.[131] But in the early 1970s he saw a big change.

> It got to a stage where you couldn't even leave your money on the bar anymore. You'd come in on a Saturday afternoon, then they'd all come in and you couldn't put your money on the bar in case it got pinched.[132]

Perhaps not surprisingly, surfer Gary Greirson found:

> the farming community here to be very conservative, following football and hating surfers. They called us Crusties because we were anti-establishment types, a bit wild, and we attracted their daughters, which didn't help a lot. They were afraid we were bringing change and marijuana, but we were straight church boys. It was the other kids coming down here and picking magic mushrooms, not us.[133]

Several of the newcomers were far from 'dropouts' and set up businesses making and selling surfboards. Rob Conneeley, who had owned a surf shop in New South Wales, came to Western Australia for the surf, after his Bondi shop was robbed twenty times in three years.[134]

> In 1973 we were renting a four-bedroom, one-bathroom farmhouse at Forest Grove and I was able to go to Witchliffe Mill and buy a mill workers' cottage for $60 to break into two and reassemble as my surfboard factory.[135]

Other surfing devotees who lacked the capital to buy a cottage, worked in timber mills or dug potatoes to earn money.

At the same time, new buildings including the Settlers Tavern, which then became the headquarters for surfing competitions, were constructed in Margaret River's main street.[136] Businessman Lloyd Shepherdson saw the building of the tavern and of Captain Freycinet Motel on the corner of Bussell Highway and Tunbridge Street as the beginning of the town's expansion – an expansion which was partly the result of the surfing boom.[137]

Initially surfing was something for the boys. Girls did not figure largely in the picture, as Di Conneeley, Rob's wife, recalled:

> All the guys would go off surfing and if you didn't want to hang out at the beach all day, you were probably left at home on your own. That was why we opened the Country Kitchen. It was meant to be a meeting place as much as a restaurant. The girls would all come in to have a cuppa and a chat and we would all get together and support each other in the things we were doing.[138]

The new restaurant did provide good and different food. This was very much appreciated by at least some longer established residents, including Sue Juniper.

> Munch into one of their sesame burgers, with its exquisite secret sauce, and you were forever a devotee. Their lovely shop at the northern end of the main street became a hub in town, the first to have outside dining and the first decent coffee in town. Only cappuccino in those days, the flat white, long black and turmeric latte were yet to arrive.[139]

While some long-term residents saw the newcomers as louts and troublemakers, the McLeod family, like the Junipers, saw the incursion differently. Keith McLeod's grandfather had established a dairy in the area in the early 1900s.

> I think Margaret River has always been eager to welcome any newcomers. We ran a dairy farm that my grandfather had established in the early 1900s, and in the very early days, survival as a dairy and timber community almost depended on them. I remember in the 1950s…celebrating the arrival of any new kid at the school…
>
> The arrival of the first surfers was a powerful moment, and measured against this welcoming backdrop, was seen by many as a fresh and exciting new chapter. The very first surfers in the late 50s would not have encountered any antagonism. They would have been seen, especially by myself as an eleven-year-old, as a brave new breed of pioneers.[140]

Keith's sister Leonie says that their father, Dudley McLeod, foresaw a future in which Margaret River would become a surfing destination known the world over.

A SMALL, RATHER SLOW, HOSPITAL AND A ROSY FUTURE

Dad was also a visionary. He said, 'One day people will come from all over the world to surf here.' Along with Geoff Edwards, with whom he had been in Crete during the war, he became heavily involved in getting the land cleared and the road put in to the Point.[141]

McLeod's prophecy was accurate. By the end of the twentieth century, Margaret River would be hosting annual surfing championships that attracted the world's best surfers. Hazel Brennan, farming at Rosa Brook, found that for the first time, the name Margaret River meant something to people living beyond the South West.

Once the surfers started to come to Margaret River, and I really think the surfers were the first people to put the Margaret River on the map. You could go to Perth and say you came from Margaret River and people would say, where's that? And I reckon it was well into the '70s when someone actually recognised it when I said I had come from Margaret River. 'Oh, that's where the surf is.' That's what we were recognised for, for a long time.[142]

At the hospital, surfing accidents were now commonly dealt with by Carolyn Scott and the other nurses: 'Back in the 1970s, in the early days, most of our emergency accidents were surfing, mainly fractures, partial drownings'.[143] The hospital admissions register for 1980 shows a number of surf-related entries such as 'concussion and abrasions'. Accidents such as 'chopped finger' were now rare while 'tooth extraction' was mainly left to the dentist. In addition to surfing injuries, causes of hospitalisation now commonly listed included abdominal pain, vomiting and nausea, urinary and viral infections,[144] ailments that the group settlers would probably not have seen as reasons for going to the doctor or to the hospital. Moreover, while in the 1920s every patient had listed a religion, the relevant column in the hospital admissions register was now left blank in most instances.[145]

Surfers were not the only people discovering Margaret River in the 1970s. Long-term residents were surprised to find their district becoming a mecca for people known as 'alternative lifestylers'. Rex Dyer, himself a migrant from England, saw:

> different types of people moving into the shire. I mean you had the orange people. They were here for a while. It used to look funny to have this person in orange riding around on a motorbike delivering mail.[146]

Barney Barnett recalls that there was a wide variety of different groups.

> We had the Potter's House, we had the Rajneeshees (orange people). We had everyone. We had hippies that weren't necessarily aligned to anything. And then you saw the emergence of the alternative schools. There was a real counterculture down here that didn't generate from the local community. Basically, the people came down here to surf or live in the bush. They often had some sort of wealth so that they could do that and there's lots of stories that I've heard about people on the dole, of course.[147]

While there was some disapproval about newcomers to Margaret River who were living off the dole, Shire President, Alan Hillier, saw an opportunity to increase the wealth of the district. According to Lloyd Shepherdson:

> Alan said, 'The government's giving out this dole money. That means that they are going to have money to spend. Why don't we have it? So we'll encourage the dole people into Margaret River so we can get their money.' He was quite open about that and it probably worked. They've got to eat and buy fuel and so they are putting a bit of money into the economy and that was the whole idea.[148]

As a nurse at the hospital, Margaret Chadwick dealt with some of these 'alternative lifestylers' and surfers:

> I remember the orange people and they didn't do any harm. They were fine. They were characters, and some of the surfers were absolute delights. We dealt with them a lot in the hospital, coming

in with surfing injuries and bits and pieces like that. They were never rude. They weren't offensive. They were covered in sand, and they had hair down to here or whatever; but they were just people doing their own thing. When the surf was 'up', they would down-tools and take advantage of it.[149]

Many new arrivals were simply in search of a different way of living, but they were all seen as surfers or 'hippies', as Lyn Serventy found when she arrived in the district with her family in the mid-1970s:

> We came down at a time when people were dropping out to Margaret River and I remember that a farmer asked us when we first arrived whether we were surfies or hippies. Since I hadn't managed to stand up on a surfboard and I had a long Indian skirt on, I said, 'Well, we must be hippies', which he accepted quite happily. But at that stage, there was a movement for people to come down and live in the country.[150]

And with their ideas about setting up alternative schools and lobbying for environmental causes, newcomers like Lyn and husband Peter were often regarded with some suspicion.

> I suppose what had been a very isolated dairy farming community had lived here and battled to stay here and now there were people coming down who didn't necessarily believe in a work ethic and who were perhaps quite content to live on the dole, do some surfing and an occasional bit of work. This was totally different to the original settlers' ethos and what had enabled them to survive in this country. And people were saying to them things like 'you shouldn't be chopping down all these trees'. And you could see that this was a total affront to them.[151]

For newcomers like the Serventy family, this was a chance to try out a different lifestyle and make a living through sustainable farming and building alternative schools for their children.

> To me it was the big romantic period of our century and people were coming down with the idea of 'let's get back, let's see if we can live differently and raise our children differently and see if we can have a

different relationship to the land'. And this spot was ideal because it was beautiful and because it was undervalued at that stage. It was part of the 'dark and dismal south-west'.[152]

The 'dark and dismal south-west' would soon become the centre of an internationally celebrated wine industry. Grape vines had first been established in the south-west by nineteenth-century European settlers, with plantings by the Bussells at Cattle Chosen, their home on the banks of the Vasse river, and on the Dawson property south of Busselton.[153] In the early twentieth century some Italians had included grape growing and winemaking among their other agricultural pursuits. In 1960 these migrants, including the Meleri and Palandri families, were still the only locals making wine. The situation began to change after visiting Californian viticulturist Harold Olmo suggested that Western Australia's best wine-growing areas might well be in the south-west. Initially it seemed that Mount Barker, north of Albany, would become the centre of such a venture. An experimental plot of vines was planted in that area in 1966 and an article in Perth's *Sunday Times* suggested the district might come to resemble Bordeaux in France.[154]

For Margaret River, the breakthrough came in 1965 when Dr John Gladstones, an agronomist whose previous research had been into lupins and clover pastures, published papers which identified Margaret River as having the best potential for producing premium wines. In particular, he pinpointed country where marri (redgum) trees grew as being particularly suitable for grape vines.[155] Gladstones' research was welcome news to Dr Tom Cullity, who had bought a property west of Cowaramup. Another doctor, Kevin Cullen, practising in Busselton, was also interested. Stan Dilkes, then an employee of the WA Department of Agriculture, was there at the beginning:

> And I always say, erroneously, that the viticulture industry started in my kitchen as I was an officer in the Department of Agriculture. And one night after work, along came two doctors, Doctor Cullen and

> Doctor Cullity, with a bottle of plonk and what they wanted from me was a bit of advice as to whether they should rent a piece of land down here or whether to go the whole hog and buy land, because these professional people at that stage of the game, far and above the ordinary dairy farmer, had capital that they could invest. So that is really how it started. Cullen and Cullity started up the vine growing around the Cowaramup area.[156]

In the 1960s and early 1970s, because dairying was barely profitable, farmers were always looking for alternative ways to make money. So when Kevin Cullen organised a meeting in Busselton on 21 July 1966 to discuss the potential for a wine industry, it was attended by over one hundred local residents. Interest increased when the *Countryman* newspaper published an article on that same day headed 'South West is tipped for top-quality wines'.[157]

The following year Tom Cullity planted 2.8 acres of vines on the property he named Vasse Felix. Another medical practitioner, Bill Pannell, bought land further north, named his vineyard Moss Wood and planted vines in 1969.[158] The Cullens' first successful planting was in 1971, although as Kevin's wife Diana recalled:

> The first one we planted in 1966, that was the year before Vasse Felix, but that was pulled out. We haven't really looked back very much. We've had lots of setbacks. First of all ridicule. All the farmers and dairy and beef farmers thought it was quite absurd to be digging holes all over the place to plant grapes. Then when they got to the tying up stage, we tied the vines up and they all collapsed and we thought, 'Oh dear someone is spraying with 2,4-D Ester'. So we got that banned by the Agriculture Department. It was a constant black hole that you poured money into. It took about 25 years to come into profit.[159]

Most of these first vineyards were north of the Margaret River townsite, west of Bussell Highway and in the Wilyabrup locality. However, the decision in the mid-1970s to market this wine region as 'Margaret River' proved to be important for the future of the district.[160] In the 1980s, books and journal articles were being written about the wineries that had sprung up in the area between Cape Naturaliste and Cape Leeuwin and by 1982, there were over 20 cellar doors in the Margaret River wine district.

While his wife was away back in Ireland, Dr John Lagan had bought some land south-west of the town. He took his wife, Dr Eithne Sheridan, out to see his new purchase.

> There was nothing on it. But then we met Dr Tom Cullity at Vasse Felix vineyard. He was running up and down to Perth every weekend, too, and sometimes he would come and stay with us. And he said, 'You've got the land, you'll have to do something with it. You don't know anything about cattle. You drink wine, so perhaps you should grow some grapes.' And that's what we did.[161]

Their new vineyard was given a romantic name:

> John was very keen on poetry and long before we came to Australia, Xanadu was in his mind. I had a brother-in-law, John Richmond, who was a classical scholar and not long before we left Omagh, we had built this new house, and my sister and her husband came up to stay and John Richmond thought that it was a very splendid sort of place and he quoted Xanadu and then my John always had that in his mind, and when we came here, he called it Xanadu.

By the 1980s, in addition to those started by medical practitioners as an interesting hobby, there were small vineyards run by cattle farmers (Gralyn), schoolteachers (Willespie and Happs), professional people in various fields (Ribbonvale, Woodlands, Clairault, Cape Mentelle, Redgate) and businessmen (Leeuwin Estate).[162]

It was not only doctors and other newcomers who benefitted from the establishment of the wine industry. Don Miller sold his farm and market milk quota in 1980 but then found easier work in this new industry.

> I retired when I was forty. I sold out. It was just too hard and I'd made enough money to retire. Anyway, I was sitting at home one day and my son-in-law rang up and said, 'Do you want a job for a couple of

weeks? We haven't got enough people down at the vineyard and we're pruning.' I said, 'All right, when do you want me?' He said, 'Now.' So I went down and seventeen and a half years later I was still there. I enjoyed it. I used to do most of the tractor work.¹⁶³

Tourism and the wine industry began to complement each other. But in the late 1970s, the local caves remained the main drawcard. Barney Barnett was working for the shire:

> The tourist bureau, of course, always ran the caves. And that was the big tourist attraction in terms of paying, and that virtually ran the rest of it. They would go out every year, every Christmas, to the Nullarbor and sit on the border, and hand out tickets for strawberries and cream at Wallcliffe House. They were volunteers, of course, trying to attract tourists to the area as they came across for Christmas. And Jonathan Terry told me that 90 per cent of those tickets would get redeemed.¹⁶⁴

Visitor accommodation was limited so people camped anywhere they could.

> I can remember the shire president flying over the shire at Easter one year, about 1978, and reporting that they counted over 5000 camping sites in the bush, none of whom were paying rent, very few of whom were coming into town and buying things. So that was the nature of tourism down here.¹⁶⁵

Farmer John Yates was also the caves guide from 1970 to 1988. His daughter Thelma (now Thelma Burnett) remembers that he would drive out to Lake and Mammoth caves after dinner, particularly at holiday time, to check where people were camped and to ensure they did not leave rubbish or damage the environment.¹⁶⁶

Some landowners soon realised that money could be made from tourism, especially by building chalets in their paddocks.¹⁶⁷ Greg Bussell saw that constructing cottages for rental on his land would provide a better lifestyle and was a better money-spinner than working in the vineyards.

> I was working at Cape Mentelle in the vineyard and discovered that working in July pruning vines wasn't fun in the wet and cold, day after day. And I came home one night and said to my wife, Mary, 'I think we should build some chalets.' There were only two lots in and around town at that time. I said, 'There's room for us to get in there.' So we built Bussells Bushland Cottages, which served us well. We were probably seen in those days as being a bit of a breakaway because we were putting land to a use other than agriculture. We were one of the early pioneers in that field.[168]

Other long-time residents, including Bob and Judy Dunbar, also saw an opportunity to profit from tourism, opening their home as bed and breakfast accommodation.

> Well, it has been great for us. We have got a foot in both camps. We are part of the old guard, the farming community, that I think in some ways resents the tourism development but for us it has been survival because without tourism we probably wouldn't be able to stay here, being a small location. But because of tourism, we have got into the bed and breakfast industry, we can survive and I think it is absolutely fabulous and I am sure that there are lots of others like us that are able to be here because of the changes.[169]

'Bed and breakfast' catered for one segment of the tourism market, but with the expansion of the wine industry and, in particular, the establishment of the annual Leeuwin concerts, short-stay accommodation of all kinds took off.

These concerts began in 1985, when businessman and owner of Leeuwin Estate vineyard Denis Horgan was asked to underwrite a visit by the London Philharmonic Orchestra to Western Australia. He agreed on the proviso that the orchestra played in Margaret River at Leeuwin Estate.[170] Local journalist Kim Murray saw the State Government suddenly willing to pour money into the district:

> Margaret River had the roads paved. They hadn't bitumenised a road in Margaret River for decades, especially not cockies' roads. But for the first Leeuwin concert, the Burke Government bitumenised the

roads around the estate. You know this kind of stuff was happening at the time in the background to the campaign for a new hospital.[171]

The Leeuwin concerts and, with them Margaret River, soon became world renowned.[172]

By 1986, the district was being promoted to visitors in glossy travel publications, including *Destinations* magazine.

> Margaret River has always been popular with families during holidays because of the beaches, the river and the bush. But in the last few years tourism has become a year-round thing because of the wineries...The shire's population swells from 4500 to 20,000 in summer and Easter but we still don't have enough facilities for them.[173]
>
> When you get tired of surfing, swimming and sunning you can spend your afternoons tasting some of the finest wines in the world. Margaret River is booming.[174]

The restaurant scene was also changing, as the same magazine article reported, 'Denis Horgan has spared nothing in creating the wine-taster's utopia, with its restaurant overlooking the estate, barbeque facilities and picnic areas'.[175]

Destinations also drew attention to the district's increasing reputation as a 'sea or tree change' for city dwellers who wanted to enjoy both forest and sea. Rammed-earth architecture was becoming popular among locals and newcomers alike. A new Catholic church, possibly the most imposing new edifice constructed in town since Bernie McKeown built the Margaret River Hotel in 1936, showcased this new building technique when it opened in 1983.[176] And in 1986 Margaret River could still be marketed as a good real estate investment.[177]

When Carolyn Scott, originally a Cowaramup girl, came back to nurse at the hospital in 1979, she found the district much changed.

> Tourism was coming to the forefront and a lot more people were coming in. The vineyards, of course. Dairying – the farming community

was taking a step back. There were more diverse interests and culture. The town was expanding.¹⁷⁸

The town, and indeed the whole district, might have been growing and changing. But the old 1924 hospital continued to serve the district. As a medical facility, it was very much beyond its 'use-by' date. When Margaret Chadwick returned to nursing in 1980, she found the hospital geography very confusing.

> I'd never worked in an old country hospital. And I remember I started on the eighth of the eighth 1980 on a Friday with an orientation. I had the weekend off and went back on the Monday and I didn't know where I was because I couldn't remember. It was like a rabbit warren.¹⁷⁹

Although Margaret soon found her way around, this was still a difficult work environment.

> It was just so scattered. We had a children's ward away around down the corridor and then past that, we had two back isolation sort of wards. You did a lot of walking; you spent all your time going from one to the other.

And to reach the permanent care wing:

> When you were on duty, you kept going up and back there out in the dark, in the rain and with only a covered way to go up to see how the patients were doing. But when you left they were on their own.

The children's ward had been built in the 1950s and, while infectious diseases such as diphtheria were no longer prevalent in the late 1970s and early 1980s,

> Everyone had their tonsils out. That was fairly mandatory. And every little boy had to have a circumcision. Dr Sheridan used to do a lot and that was accepted for all little boys to be circumcised in those days. It was just protocol. Now it's not done.¹⁸⁰

Inconveniences aside, from Carolyn Scott's perspective this small hospital remained a good place to work:

> Nursing-wise, the atmosphere was much better than in the city hospitals. All the nurses were great. A lot of us were married women with kids. It was a little bit of a shock coming from a big city hospital back to a country hospital. You had to blend in with the other nurses. But I did enjoy it here and it was more homely, more friendly. We all got along well, and there was no social stigma, no big harassment. We did everything; cleaning and giving out meals. At that stage we were moving the big oxygen cylinders. Even in the labour ward, they had the big oxygen cylinders. Yes, it was heavy work.[181]

Shelley Challis, whose mother had been the first enrolled nurse employed at the Margaret River Hospital, became a nurse herself. After training in Manjimup and then working in Perth hospitals, Shelley came to Margaret River in the 1980s: 'It was great because of the people I worked with. It was very social. I loved the old hospital, it had good vibes. Yes, it had creaky floors. But the place had a good feeling.'[182] Working there was also enjoyable for Margaret Chadwick:

> We had so much fun. We had an airing shed out the back with blankets, blue blankets, so when people were discharged the blankets would go out there. Because I used to smoke and many others did also, we'd be out there smoking amongst the blankets that were supposed to be airing. The laundry was also out there, where the ladies did the laundry for the hospital. And it was fun. When we went to morning tea, we had to go down a verandah past the kitchen to go into our own nurses' place to have our morning tea. We had lots of laughs. The cheese scones were the best.[183]

When John Crimp was working as an orderly at the hospital, his son Tim would sometimes visit him there:

> It was a good atmosphere because the staff were bush people like us. Mostly they came from farms. They had grown up in the town. So they understood how things went. Meals were always good. It was a happy place.[184]

Carolyn Scott recognised the value of workers who wore different uniforms but who all worked as part of a team.

> The assistants, the yellow uniforms, had no training at all. They were often wives from farms. But they could do everything. They looked after patients. They were wonderful. The pink girls were nursing aides. Once again, they were wonderful, often married with children. There was no stigma at all. We all got along well together.[185]

Anne Shepherdson worked as a dietitian and sometimes visited clients in the hospital.

> We would meet at morning tea, lunch. There was quite a strict seating arrangement. Dr Sheridan sat there. Dr Lagan, if he came in, he just sat anywhere. And then the people in the white coats – we still wore white coats in those days – were allowed to sit with the sisters. The others had to sit in another waiting room or eating room.[186]

Despite the morning tea arrangements,

> I don't think there was a real hierarchy. The yellow, pink and white all seemed to work well together. Steve Blakeney took a wonderful snapshot of the staff at one time and I know it is fondly looked at. Because they are all so young, the staff that were there at that time.

Hospital orderly Ralph Hofstee also recalls a good atmosphere and excellent morning teas.

> The staff were great. We had these big scones every morning, too; scones with cream and jam. I will still remember my first day I walked into the dining room and looked at all this food. It was very friendly, lovely atmosphere. It was wonderful.[187]

Food and warmth at the hospital were also attractions for the children of Matron Mary Arthur:

> We went to school from the hospital and came to the hospital after school. And at the back of the hospital where the kitchen was, there was a dining room for the staff and a dining room at the back, which

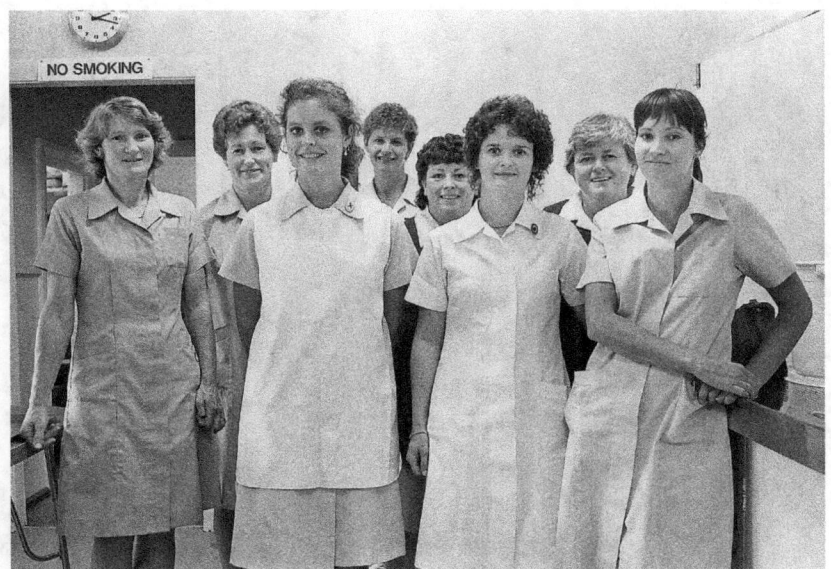

'The staff all look so young'. Stephen Blakeney

seemed to be for all of us kids. We used to get in there with our school bags and we would sit round there with the oven open and our feet in the oven and we would get treated to milk and afternoon tea with cake and biscuits. It was lovely! Nurses used to wear the winged caps and they would come in with cardboard boxes and we would make the caps up for them.[188]

For Fran Temby, after training and working for many years in city hospitals, nursing in Margaret River was something of a culture shock:

I found it a stark contrast between the Perth tertiary hospitals of Royal Perth, Sir Charles Gairdner, King Edward and Margaret River. Very old weatherboard buildings at Margaret River. The wards had sloping floors and our medicine and dressing trolleys would roll away from you. We had a walkway outside to get to the permanent care ward, which was in a separate building, the old Margaret Cecil Rest House.[189]

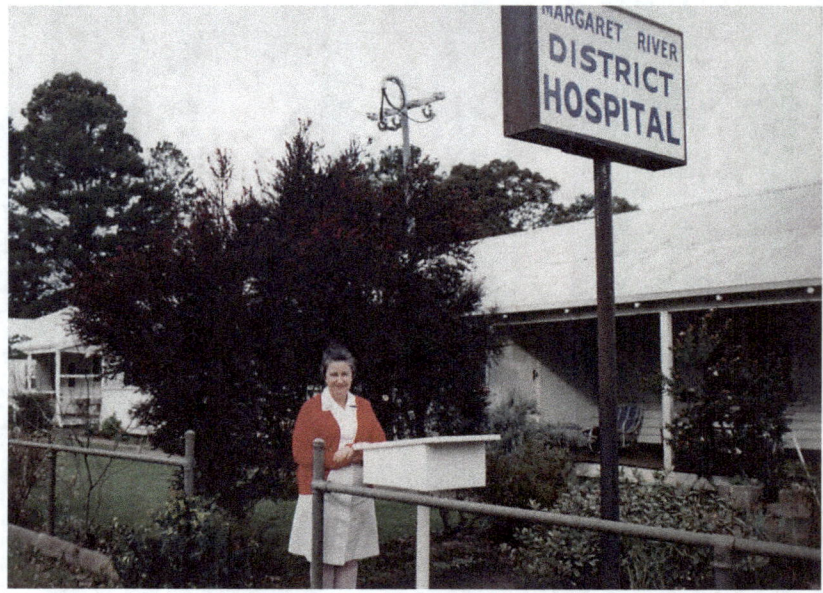

Matron Mary Arthur outside the old hospital. Courtesy Don Arthur

Fran Temby, Mary Arthur and Margaret Chadwick all worked at the old hospital.
Courtesy Judy Wake

A SMALL, RATHER SLOW, HOSPITAL AND A ROSY FUTURE

Judy Wake also found that when newcomers came to work at the Margaret River Hospital:

> It took them a little while to realise how to go with it. We knew the domestic staff. They were our friends. You didn't treat them as domestics. They were just as important as the matron, really. And they used to help if you were busy. They would come and make some beds for you, which wasn't their job. And we would go and get trays out for them. We just worked together. And if it wasn't for them, that hospital would have looked horrible by the time we left. They kept it clean and nice and put little vases of flowers in the loo, and things like that, just to give it a lift.

But keeping it clean and nice could not disguise the fact that the hospital buildings were in poor shape.

> You'd be walking up and down with a trolley, bumping up and down the passage like that, and at night time you would crawl down the edges of the thing when you were doing your night rounds because if you walked down the middle, you'd creak the boards and the patients would wake up.[190]

The domestic staff kept the hospital clean and nice. Courtesy Judy Wake

The wooden buildings also presented a serious fire risk and the nurses' dining room had an open fire. One night Fran Temby was:

> working with Betty Garstone and we were having supper. Suddenly there was a loud roaring noise and bright flames. The chimney had caught on fire. I was frightened thinking of the hospital catching on fire, and I wanted to call the fire brigade but Betty was so calm. She said, 'It's all right Fran. I'll just get a blanket.' She came back with a blue woollen blanket and held it up in front of the fire and slowly the fire went out through lack of oxygen.[191]

Occasionally the easy access to the hospital could lead to animal incursions. Judy Wake was on evening shift when she

> suddenly saw a kangaroo jumping up and down the passage. We were chasing this damn thing – it wasn't a very big one – and we chased him up and down, and he ended up in casualty. It didn't do much for the trolleys in there, but we slammed the door on him because we thought, well, you know, we can't keep chasing him round, and he's going to poo all up the passage, and I wasn't quite sure what to do. In the end somebody did come and take it away. But I thought, only in Australia, only in Margaret River could you get a kangaroo in a hospital![192]

Fran Temby found other differences between working in a city hospital and nursing in Margaret River:

> It was a huge responsibility for a registered nurse to be on duty without a doctor on site. So different from a Perth hospital. In Margaret River there were three staff on at night and one of those was in the permanent care ward which was a separate building. If a maternity patient presented, we had to call in midwives if they were not rostered. And we had to call a doctor for all serious accidents and emergencies.[193]

Yet Fran soon found that the nurses and the ambulance drivers were exceptionally skilled.

> Yes, often we had to wait for the doctor to come in and so we had to start urgent treatment. And the staff were amazing. They were

A SMALL, RATHER SLOW, HOSPITAL AND A ROSY FUTURE

Dr Clarke with midwives. Courtesy Dr Ray Clarke.

very competent, well trained. And I learned a lot from the staff that were there. There was a near drowning, there were road accidents and heart attacks. Dr Sheridan was wonderful. She would come in without hesitation in her dressing gown, court shoes and pearls. Later, Dr Clarke and Dr O'Rourke were equally responsive in giving us much reassurance.

As the population increased in the 1980s, the town needed more medical practitioners. Carolyn Scott was working at the hospital at the time.

> Dr Clarke came down from Busselton in November 1985 and Dr Shaun O'Rourke followed him two weeks later. They were very nice, approachable doctors and the public started going to them more and more. And they were needed, too, because everything was expanding. A busy town was getting busier.[194]

Ray Clarke had returned from working in the United Kingdom in 1984 and came to the South West to work in Dr Kevin Cullen's Busselton surgery. Ray soon realised that people living further south were coming to Busselton because there was only one medical practice in Margaret River:

> So, I thought, there's probably room for another doctor there. And this is the only chance I'll ever get to be my own principal in a practice. So I thought, OK, here we go. I went and bought the premises in Margaret River, at 33 Bussell Highway, the old Tin House, and started up there. A huge learning curve, learning about Medicare and all of that stuff that no one teaches you. And that's what happened. That was in November '85.[195]

The Tin House, so called because it is clad with pressed metal sheeting, dated from group settlement times and was later used for many other purposes.[196] When Ray bought the property in 1985, he was purchasing a piece of Margaret River's history. He found his new surgery:

> pretty warm in summer, cold in winter. We had a wood fire in the waiting room. And before work, I'd have to get down there quickly and light the fire and try and get the fire going to warm up the patients.[197]

Shaun O'Rourke also wanted to be a general practitioner in a country area and had relatives in the district.[198] He, too, opened a new surgery. This was initially in Town View Terrace near the post office. Later he moved his practice to the top end of the main street, near to where Dr Rigby and his immediate successors had lived and worked.[199]

Ray Clarke found that he and Shaun O'Rourke were immediately able to practise at the hospital.

> Back in those days, you didn't have to jump through a lot of hoops to get accreditation to work at a certain hospital. I just turned up and got admitting rights. We were called VMPs: visiting medical

practitioner. Nowadays you can't just walk into a town and have immediate admitting rights. You have to go through a committee and get approved. It was much simpler back then.[200]

So from one there were three.

> There was some healthy competition in the medical business. We all worked at the hospital and eventually we shared 'on call'. We developed a bit of a roster. It built up to become quite busy. I must say that back then in the late 1980s there were lots of young families and many more babies were born in Margaret River Hospital than there are now.[201]

Yet Dr Clarke soon found that although he had obstetric qualifications, as did Dr Sheridan, there were limitations to the procedures he could undertake in a small country hospital.

> I came, having not long been in the UK doing obstetrics, so I thought we will get caesarean sections happening again. But you quickly realised that in addition to your experienced nursing staff, you also needed a fully equipped operating theatre. And that's what we didn't have. So it didn't happen.

Nevertheless, Dr Clarke found the nurses at the hospital amazing: 'Judy Wake, Mary Beck, Judy Buckenara and all the others were excellent to work with. Hilary Stephens was the only one who could bandage the stump of a man with one leg.'

Fran Temby, coming from Perth in 1985, found that although medical resources were limited, not only was the nursing excellent but that this was also a community where people knew and cared for each other.

> And the farmers' wives would help out, and if somebody had to go to hospital for a while the neighbour would bring over food and when the patients arrived at the hospital, the staff there knew most of them. It was very friendly and the staff had an amazing rapport with patients. There was laughter, banter, smiles, all the while giving wonderful personal care. It was different for me coming from a

Perth Hospital where I knew no one. And I found that really special, these relationships.[202]

A caring community, more doctors, an increasing population, a surfing mecca, a popular tourism destination and a flourishing wine industry. A 1986 headline in the local newspaper said it all: 'Study Predicts A Rosy Future For The Region'.[203]

However, it was apparent to most Margaret River residents, and certainly to hospital staff, that the old 1924 group settlement hospital was no longer fit for purpose or able to meet the needs of the district. The challenge for this community was to persuade the State Government that a brand-new hospital was an essential component of that 'rosy future'.

Chapter Seven

A Perennial Source of Discontent

The final major upgrade of the old hospital was undertaken in 1978. After a visit to Margaret River that year, the department's inspector of planning wrote:

> I visited this hospital on 17 July 1978 to inspect progress on the repair and renovations programme. During this present programme, reasonably extensive upgrading is being done. For a small hospital the quantity of work being done is small for a price in excess of $100,000.
>
> The current work is bringing the buildings back to a reasonable standard but due to their age, which causes rapid deterioration, the next R&R could also be in a high-cost range. This raises the question of the economic life of the buildings. Certainly, the next R&R could easily be in the range of $50,000 to $80,000 which is an excessive amount on such a small area of buildings.
>
> Request that consideration be given to the future of the hospital so that interim maintenance by local staff can be rationalised and future R&R programmes can be more effective.[1]

Old Hospital front before closure in 1990. Courtesy Judy Wake.

The inspector did not receive a direct reply to this request, but the file copy of his report contains a handwritten note.

> I would hope that this major R&R will ensure that the buildings remain in good order for another eight years. I would agree that we should plan for a long-term replacement and at a later date research should be undertaken.[2]

Barry Blaikie, now a member of the Legislative Assembly for the Vasse electorate, was already convinced that the hospital had passed its 'use-by' date. His speech during the Assembly's 1978 budget debate was reported by the local newspaper under the heading 'New hospital long overdue':

> **Margaret River should have a new hospital...Mr Blaikie said that the time was long overdue for an immediate start on the planning of a new hospital for Margaret River because of the continuing growth of the district. He pointed out that it was the centre for the milk industry and a growing wine industry**

and in addition the tourist industry was starting to assume major proportions.

Mr Blaikie was born at the Margaret River Hospital but despite its significance for him he wants it demolished to make way for a new structure which should be given top priority.[3]

But 'top priority' for a new hospital was still more than a decade away. When Blaikie's office sent this newspaper article to Minister for Health Ray Young, the response was not encouraging: 'I regret that I can see no prospect of a new hospital for Margaret River for many years but, in the meantime, you may be assured that the present hospital will be maintained'.[4]

By 1981, the Hospital Visiting and Advisory Committee, which included the matron, doctors and nurses, was reporting that the 1978 renovations, expected to prolong the life of the hospital for six to eight years, were not satisfactory in many respects. Committee Secretary Judy Wake set out the situation in a letter sent to local organisations:

> The matron assures us that the hospital will, in a few years, become unmanageable; the task that faces us is to convince Perth-bound bureaucrats, who have never worked in these conditions, yet who guide our destiny, of the veracity of our assertions.[5]

The committee was also seeking support from local organisations in lobbying the State Government for additional permanent care beds. The existing facility (the former Margaret Cecil Rest House) could not cater for all the elderly residents requiring long-term nursing support and:

> the 'overflow' of permanent care patients has to be housed in the general section of the hospital which, in turn, causes a shortage of beds for patients in need of general, acute care. The problems sometimes become very severe and result in patients being relegated to beds in maternity/children's ward or even the corridor.[6]

Even the hallway was used to capacity. Courtesy Judy Wake.

The real issue remained the need for a new, more modern hospital building. In October 1980, the shire called a public meeting which was reported by the *Busselton-Margaret Times* under the heading: 'Growing pressure for new hospital'.[7] As Bill Hales, the department's representative at the public meeting, explained allocation of funds for new hospitals was based on population and bed usage, and Margaret River did not rate highly against these criteria compared with other south-west towns such as Mandurah and Pemberton.[8] On the other hand, staff working in the building every day could see the condition of the buildings was deteriorating year by year, as Judy Wake later reflected: 'The hospital itself was just going downhill all the time. There were rabbits burrowing underneath and some of the patients swore they could hear white ants in the walls!'[9]

When making decisions about the need for a new facility, the department looked only at the level of occupation, so doctors and nurses did their best to maximise bed numbers. When surfers and their followers presented at outpatients with minor injuries, Dr Sheridan found they would often be happy to stay overnight, which would augment the hospital's bed usage:

> We used to encourage people to come into hospital even if they were only feeling a little bit sick. Surfies were great people because they always had something wrong and they were half starved, cold and wet, and they used to love to come in. The most miserable creatures I ever saw were the girlfriends in the back of the vans and they'd have a sore throat or something and they would be shivering and miserable. And you would say, 'Well, I think maybe you should stay for the night.' And they would say, 'Oh, yes.' We would try and get people into the hospital to try and show that a new hospital was viable.[10]

Local organisations, including the Country Women's Association, joined the clamour for a new building.

> We, the CWA of Margaret River would like to add our pressure for the need for a New Hospital. Over the last ten years Margaret River has doubled its size and population. We need the accommodation for our permanent care patients…and more facilities for out-patients and everyone.
>
> It would be a fitting memorial to the early Pioneers who worked so hard to carve a home out of the bush.[11]

Ray Young, still Minister for Health, replied in non-committal language that there were no plans yet – but the idea of a memorial to early pioneers was a good idea.[12] Yet the minister did then ask the commissioner of hospital and allied services where Margaret River stood in the forward planning priorities, noting that:

> I think, in retrospect, it probably would have been better to have accepted the inevitable fate of this hospital some years ago. Of course, the upgrading is in line with my recent statements on continuing maintenance, but I think the hospital had probably been let go too far for any maintenance to improve matters very much.[13]

The minister's reflections cut no ice with departmental staff. The short answer was that Margaret River Hospital had 'no priority' and the departmental head was advised that:

> If costs are to be contained throughout this State, a heavy-handed policy of eliminating hospitals may have to be adopted though they will undoubtedly be strenuously resisted by the local population. I am convinced, however, that every proposal for major renovation or replacement buildings must be reviewed against the possibility of the hospital concerned being de-classified or completely eliminated as a hospital in the future.[14]

Expectations in Margaret River were very different. The Hospital Visiting and Advisory Committee was not thinking about 'de-classification' and certainly was not contemplating 'elimination'. The committee had already set out the problems with the current hospital, including the ineffectiveness of isolation facilities and the inadequacy of the one and only private ward:

> **Isolation.** The sole purpose of isolation nursing is to prevent the spread of infectious conditions, yet the hospital has *no* separate toilet or shower facilities for use by isolation patients; neither is there a separate sluice for the disposal of waste and care of soiled linen and utensils etc...
>
> **Private Ward.** The one and only private ward permits patients, at a cost of $75 a day, to inhabit what can be the noisiest and least private area in the hospital. The room is bounded by the intensive care room, where a lot of activity often takes place; the patients' day room with the television set right outside the private ward door because the set will not work at the other end of the room, and the linen cupboard which naturally attracts a lot of traffic. These patients have no private toilet facilities, nor a shower and there is no way to reorganise and improve these situations.[15]

The government remained unmoved and the situation was complicated by the fact that there were now two public hospitals within the Shire of Augusta–Margaret River. A small hospital had been opened at Augusta in 1965. Fran Temby's mother, Beryl Watterson, had been one of the campaigners for that facility: 'It was a long, slow drive into Margaret River along a gravel road. Augusta's population was growing at that time and more people were retiring there. There was an urgent need.'[16]

While both Augusta and Margaret River were within the same local government area, each community functioned differently and a new hospital for one would not alleviate problems in the other locality. There was already pressure from Augusta residents for additions to their facility. In May 1981, the *Busselton-Margaret Times* reported, under the heading 'Hospital bursting at the seams', that the Augusta Hospital was overcrowded.[17]

The Augusta Ratepayers Association suggested that the Margaret River Hospital should be downgraded to a C-class facility (catering only for senior citizens) in order to pave the way for expansion at Augusta. Predictably, this proposal met with a cool reception in Margaret River, with the *Busselton-Margaret Times* reporting that:

> The downgrading suggestion was sharply criticised by Margaret River Hospital Matron, Gay Peirce, who said the Margaret River Facility was centrally located and in the best position to service the shire's hospital needs.[18]

The problem of trying to meet the public hospital needs of these two different communities, forty kilometres apart, would continue for the next decade.

Meanwhile, in July 1981, the Margaret River lobby tried another approach. Advisory Committee Secretary Judy Wake wrote to Barry Blaikie, asking whether the community could establish a fund to assist with the cost of building the new hospital.[19] Blaikie forwarded this letter to Minister Young and received a response, prepared for the minister's signature, that carefully answered the question without committing the government to a new hospital at Margaret River.[20]

> It is feasible for Mrs Wake to be advised that a campaign to raise funds could go ahead. I hope you would not hold me to any figure in this day and age, but I should advise you that a hospital with the facilities envisaged by your community would probably run out to around $1.4 million.
>
> I could not envisage the community raising all of the money for such a project, even in conjunction with the Local Authority and any other interested bodies who may show concern for the necessity for the hospital.
>
> The extent of the fund raising by the community would of course determine to a great extent the priority the Government could afford to the project. I have to say, however, that it is not reasonable to ask the community to subscribe funds to a project unless there is some certainty that it will come to fruition within a reasonable period and I am not in a position to give that assurance.[21]

Minister Young stated it was his personal belief that there should be some form of new facility at Margaret River but that the funds were not currently available.[22]

The minister's announcement the following year, in June 1982, that the Augusta Hospital would be expanded to include permanent care facilities and that Margaret River would eventually be rebuilt, was welcomed by the Augusta Ratepayers Association but did little to reassure the Margaret River community.[23] The shire, which represented both populations, was concerned that priority was being given to the Augusta Hospital, and noted that the minister's statement with regard to Margaret River was vague and could lead to the phasing out of that facility. Shire President Alan Hillier commented that the hospital was the oldest public building in the district and that the community 'had been fobbed off for too many years about the Margaret River Hospital'.[24] Council then resolved:

> To urge the State Government to give high priority to the total needs of the district by replacing the Margaret River Hospital

with a modern and adequate facility that suited the needs of the community.[25]

The previous month, Peter Southgate, Director of Clinical Services in the Department of Hospital and Allied Services, had visited both Margaret River and Augusta. He, too, recommended that medical services for the two towns should be addressed separately. In relation to Margaret River, he stated that:

> This is a collection of old buildings all of which are timber-framed and weatherboard with the exception of the laundry which is of solid construction and the theatre which is asbestos sheet construction.
>
> The theatre birth suite complex is of more recent construction but constructed without any evidence of incorporation into an overall development plan…The birth suite is a completely enclosed building with no outside views and nursing staff report that after eight hours attending to a mid. patient, they go bananas! It gives one the feeling of considerable claustrophobia…
>
> I suggest that it may need to be considered that the best thing to do with Margaret River Hospital is to start from scratch again and build a purpose-built hospital on the site…The buildings are well beyond significant modification.[26]

The next year brought a Labor Government to power. Brian Burke was sworn in as the state's twenty-third premier on 25 February 1983, while Barry Hodge replaced Ray Young as Minister for Health. The Labor Party's promises before coming into power had been largely focused on transport priorities, such as reopening the Fremantle to Perth railway, closed by the Court Liberal government in an unpopular move some years earlier. Nevertheless, the Hospital Visiting and Advisory Committee lost no time in writing to the new minister for health. In his response, Barry Hodge stated that he was aware of the hospital's condition and added:

> Margaret River is one of several hospitals which will be the subject of a comprehensive study during this year. This study will result in

> a Development Brief which will provide sufficient detail to enable meaningful estimates to be listed in the 1984/85 Capital Works Programme. Funds for detailed planning will be given high priority in the allocation of funds for 1983/84.

Then came the caveat:

> There are very many hospital projects with an urgent priority and a decision as to which projects can proceed depends on the extent of availability of funds. However, every effort will be made to have the Margaret River project proceed as early as possible in 1984/85.[27]

The following year, local district hospital administrator Bill Hales was still upbeat about the likelihood of a new hospital being constructed in Margaret River, telling the *Busselton-Margaret Times*:

> It was hoped that an allocation would be made in the 1984–85 State budget to allow detailed planning to go ahead. Mr Hales said it was also hoped that planning would be completed in time for funds for the building to be allocated for the 1985–86 budget.[28]

The local newspaper went on to provide more details about the proposed new hospital, the cost of which was expected to be $1.25 million.

> The new Margaret River Hospital will be built immediately behind the present structure and it will front Farrelly Street. It will be a 24-bed hospital of which 10 beds will be for permanent care patients.[29]

Finally, planning was occurring behind the scenes. Yet when Dr Southgate asked Dr Sheridan her views about the provision of anaesthesia facilities, he – possibly deliberately – misinterpreted one of her comments. When the draft planning report was prepared, Dr Sheridan was recorded as saying that she did not give anaesthetics and thus Dr Southgate had concluded that, as she was the town's main medical practitioner, it would be unnecessary for the new hospital to include anaesthesia facilities. As one of the most highly qualified obstetricians and gynaecologists in the south-west of the state, Dr Sheridan responded to what was termed 'The Development Control Brief for the Augusta and Margaret River Hospitals':[30]

> When Dr Southgate visited Margaret River, I said that I did not like giving anaesthetics, not that I did not give them. This is usually no problem as Dr Lagan, who does like giving anaesthetics, usually gives them and I undertake whatever procedures are required to be done. Having worked for the Northern Ireland Hospital Authority as a locum Consultant Obstetrician and Gynaecologist from 1955 to 1962 I think that I am suitably qualified to deal with minor Obstetric and Gynaecological problems as they arise in my practice. Until ten days ago I thought that I could give the anaesthetic and perform a D&C or cautery without endangering the patient's life.[31]

Dr Sheridan also pointed out that:

> the provision of adequate facilities for anaesthetics would seem to be an essential part of a new hospital; non provision of anaesthetic facilities would reduce the ability to provide a full service to patients who expect to be looked after locally.

A copy of the draft planning document was provided to the Shire of Augusta-Margaret River. Shire Clerk Ken Preston was concerned that the plans did not include provision for a laundry, an omission which, he stated, would reduce local employment opportunities.[32] Local administrator Bill Hales submitted a long list of suggested changes to the plans and pointed out that if a laundry was not built, not only would jobs be lost, but also no local carrier was in a position to transport the linen on a daily basis.[33]

Liberal Member of Parliament Barry Blaikie also asked to see the plans[34] but Minister Hodge advised that the proposals were still being evaluated and that it would be premature to provide the (Liberal) Member for Vasse with this documentation.[35] Clearly, the government and the department in Perth wished to remain in control of the planning process.

At the same time, the difference of opinion about provision of anaesthetic facilities remained, with Dr Peter Southgate still asserting that such facilities would remain unused because nursing staff would not have the qualifications required to assist in surgical operations, and thus would be put 'into the awkward position of having to refuse assistance'.[36] Dr Sheridan then wrote again to Dr Southgate, refuting his recollection of his conversation with her 'on the path between the hospital and the surgery' and emphasising the importance of providing anaesthetic facilities.

> I consider that to build a new hospital costing one to $1.2 million without short anaesthetic facilities would be extraordinary and it will certainly mean that when other doctors move into the area, either when we retire, or as expected, the area grows, there will be agitation to provide such facilities.[37]

The requirement for an on-site laundry was also still under discussion, with Relieving Administrator J.C. Kerr advising that it was not feasible to *not* provide a laundry.[38] These opinions were ignored and the final hospital plans did not include a laundry.

Despite evidence that the department was now planning for a new hospital and an indication that funding would be included in the upcoming capital works budget for 1984/85, no monies were allocated for Margaret River. As the *Busselton-Margaret Times* reported: 'This news has not pleased many of the district's residents who consider that the time for the replacement of the 60-year-old building is long past'.[39]

The failure to fund a new Margaret River Hospital was particularly unpalatable to local residents, because some money ($60,000) had been allocated for the redevelopment of the Augusta Hospital. As Barry Blaikie told the *Times*, the community's view was that,

'These projects needed to be considered separately but should have proceeded together for the benefit of the two communities'.[40]

Lack of action by the Burke Labor Government spurred the Liberal Opposition – which had also failed to provide funding for the new hospital while in power – to capitalise on the current administration's lack of commitment.

> **Busselton will get a new boat harbour/marina and an improved railway jetty and Margaret River will get a new hospital if the Liberal Party is returned to power at the next State election. This was said by Opposition Leader Bill Hassell when he visited Busselton last Friday and spoke to a public meeting attended by about 50 people.**[41]

Predictably, the Hospital Visiting and Advisory Committee was focused on the lack of activity by the current State Government. The committee stepped up its campaign and 1985 became a year of unprecedented letter-writing for Secretary Judy Wake. She fired her first salvo on 11 January 1985, her prime target being Minister for Health Barry Hodge.

> The above committee wishes to voice its great disappointment that funds were not made available in the recent budget for the construction of the new hospital facility at Margaret River…it seems quite incredible that this project has been shelved yet again. One can only conclude that this is a political decision in which case it would be quite pointless to begin arguing our case further.[42]

This letter expressed particular concern about the lack of permanent care beds. Judy made her point with a literary allusion:

> If there is to be any degree of dignity and humanity maintained in the care of the aged, proper provision must be made for that care. As Aldous Huxley writes: 'Facts do not cease to exist because they are ignored'. We ask you to translate your recognition of our need into action without further delay.

The letter was copied to Premier Brian Burke and to Liberal Leader of the Opposition, Bill Hassell, as well as to local members of Parliament Barry Blaikie and Vic Ferry. Responses were predictable. Liberals Ferry and Blaikie repeated Hassell's commitment that a Liberal administration would build the new hospital. The premier passed the correspondence on to the minister for health for reply while he, in turn, asked his department to respond directly. No one in government wanted to deal with this unpopular topic! The Margaret River committee finally received a response to their letter – from a departmental official. This letter also pre-empted a question posed in the following later correspondence from the Margaret River committee to the minister:

> In your recent letter to the Augusta-Margaret River Shire Council, you give no hope that funds will be made available in the near future for this project, and the committee fiercely resents the continued neglect of the Margaret River Hospital. With a history of trying for nearly two decades to get a new facility here, we claim the right to enquire precisely what criteria were used to make this decision. An early reply would be appreciated.[43]

The department's response gave no comfort to the recipients, relying as it did on bed number statistics as seemingly the one and only yardstick for government budgetary decision-making.

> Although there is pressure on the permanent care facility, causing some overflow into the acute ward, there is no overall shortage of beds at the hospital. As at December 1984 there were only 4.4 acute beds and 7.9 permanent beds occupied on average out of a total of 26 available beds. The utilisation of the hospital has not changed significantly since the redevelopment report was completed.[44]

But for Margaret River doctors and nurses, the issue was not about bed numbers, as Judy Wake's response to the minister succinctly stated.

> The basis of the argument against the new hospital is based entirely on bed numbers. This is not an argument that we have ever laid emphasis

on. It is the inadequacy of the accommodation provided. One could, after all, put 24 beds in a barn, and say there was no bed shortage. But it would not make for suitable care.[45]

For the local committee the quality of the accommodation was the concern, while the focus in Perth was entirely, it seemed, on patient numbers. In March, the local committee produced a submission which drew on a recent (February 1985) Health Department document that had stated:

> This hospital is in a poor state of repair. Maintenance expenditure has been limited in recent years due to the possibility of building replacement. Extensive maintenance will have to be carried out shortly to preserve the building in a usable state.[46]
>
> This submission was circulated to federal and state politicians. All responses were either supportive or evasive. The responsible minister's reply was non-committal.[47]

The committee also received letters of support from prominent local businessmen, including Mark Hohnen of Oceanic Equity and Denis Horgan at Leeuwin Estate, whose company that year sponsored the first of the famed Leeuwin Concerts.[48] Horgan recommended leaving any further lobbying until the budget strategy for 1985/86 was known. Hohnen's interest in the matter was perhaps related to the government's later (1987) proposal for the hospital to be built in partnership with the private sector and, in particular, with a land developer.[49]

Perhaps unsurprisingly, when the 1985/86 capital works program was released, there was again no money for a new Margaret River Hospital. The *Times* reported that:

> **Augusta-Margaret River Shire President has again slammed the state government for not committing itself to building a new hospital at Margaret River. Cr Hillier's comments came after announcing that two new doctors Dr Ray Clarke and Dr Shaun O'Rourke had set up practices in Margaret River...**

> These two young doctors demonstrate a pioneering spirit which is refreshing to see and which they will need as they tackle the scandalous conditions of the Margaret River Hospital, a building constructed prior to the great depression for the original group settlers and which is dangerously lacking in modern facilities.[50]

The arrival of these 'two new young doctors' was evidence, if any was needed, of the growth, and growing importance, of Margaret River as a tourism destination and as a desirable place to live. The district was no longer the 'dark and dismal south-west'! In 1981 the shire population was 3,680. By 1986 this had increased by almost 2,000 to 5,333. There was more work for medical practitioners and a greater demand for hospital facilities.

In early 1986, Western Australians went to the polls and returned the Burke Labor government to power with an increased majority. Following that election there was a ministerial reshuffle. In his final letter to the secretary of the Hospital Visiting and Advisory Committee, Minister for Health Barry Hodge did not directly mention the question of a new hospital but complained about misinformation.

> There have been a number of mischievous and politically motivated statements made recently about the Margaret River Hospital by various people and I can understand that these may well have confused many people.
>
> Some statements made recently have implied that the South West Region generally is poorly served by hospitals and health care services, that the Busselton/ Margaret River/ Augusta area was particularly badly off. I have replied on several occasions to this incorrect assertion, providing details of expenditure and services available in the areas mentioned.[51]

Nurses and doctors dealing with sloping floors, white ants and a windowless birth suite would not have been impressed by this letter.

Expectations of action were raised when, following the 1986 election, Premier Brian Burke visited Margaret River on 27 March. His visit had been anticipated by Kim Murray, editor of a new local newspaper, the *Augusta-Margaret River Mail*.

In about late 1985 when I got a notion to start a newspaper in Margaret River, I was close friends with the political writer at the Daily News. We both worked on the Daily News together and he mentioned what I was doing to Brian Burke and at the time the Labor Party were facing an election and they were very keen to win the south-west. And so, Brian offered me the chance of some sort of 'keep-able' story and he asked my friend to enquire of me what the issues were in Margaret River. It was very obvious then that the need for a new hospital was paramount for the town so I relayed that through John to Brian Burke, who was an ex-journalist as well.

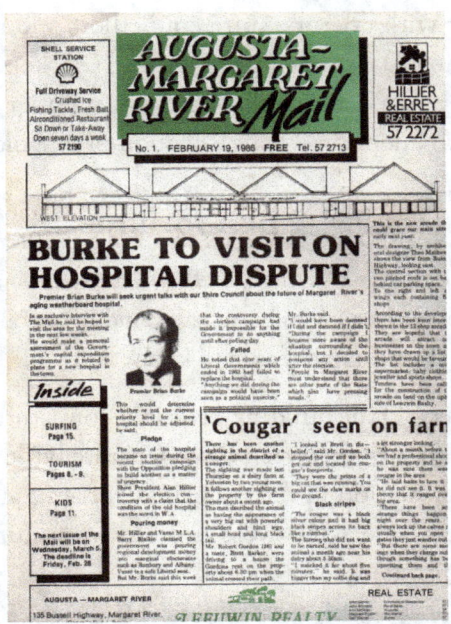

Kim Murray's headline in first edition of *Augusta-Margaret River Mail*. Augusta-Margaret River Mail February 19th 1986.

> Brian said that he would come and visit Margaret River and see for himself what this debate was about. So, he put the lid on that and then, of course, they were facing an election that year, which he won. And only about two weeks, I think, before the first edition of the *Mail* came out. So that was a story that I'd sat on and it was the first headline in the paper: 'Burke to visit on hospital dispute'. I don't know whether I played a part in that or whether it would probably have happened anyway.[52]

The *Busselton-Margaret Times* reported on the premier's visit in its next edition with the heading, 'Need for hospital recognised: Burke'. The premier was quoted as saying:

> I recognise the need; it's as pressing as any I have seen and although I cannot make any firm commitment at this stage I am quietly confident that we will be able to solve the problem during the framing of the Budget.[53]

Burke also met with doctors, shire councillors and local parliamentarians, including Barry Blaikie. Dr Ray Clarke was one of the medical practitioners accompanying the premier and the local member of Parliament on a walk-through of the old buildings.

> I remember trailing along. Barry Blaikie was there. Brian Burke, the premier, he was there, and Mary Arthur, the matron at the time, was there. And Barry was saying, 'Well, we badly need a new hospital. I love this whole place. I was born here.' And Brian Burke was heard to mutter, 'That's one good reason to knock it down!'[54]

The premier was told the building probably constituted a fire hazard; that nurses had to walk between three separate buildings; that there was a lack of ventilation in the maternity section; and that patients in the permanent care wing were isolated from nursing staff. The *Times* report continued:

> And though Mr Burke promised to consider the Hospital's future in the Budget, he pulled no punches when he said it had become something of a political football in recent months.

> 'All I seemed to have been hearing was screaming and yelling about the Margaret River Hospital,' he said. 'With me a co-operative approach or an intelligent argument always gets more results.' The Premier reiterated the need for a quiet and reasoned approach when he had an informal meeting with the shire council.⁵⁵

In correspondence addressed to Judy Wake after his visit, Brian Burke again raised hope that action would be taken.

> I appreciated the frank and informal discussion and considered it extremely fruitful in understanding the problems faced by the Margaret River Hospital.
>
> Whilst I am unable to give any firm direct commitments, I recognise the obvious needs and I am quite confident that the Government will be able to resolve the situation during the next round of Budget negotiations.
>
> In the meantime, I have also asked the Hon. Minister for Health, Mr Ian Taylor, to make arrangements to visit the Hospital in the near future.⁵⁶

The local committee would have been even more convinced that a new hospital would be included in the next budget round, had they been aware of the telex sent to the commissioner for health:

> 24 MARCH 1986 TO COMMISSIONER DR ROBERTS
>
> PREMIERS VISIT JUST CONCLUDED. RECOGNISES THE NEED AND EVERY CONSIDERATION WILL BE MADE IN THE NEXT BUDGET
>
> A.R. TEBBIT
>
> ADMINISTRATOR
>
> BUSSELTON DISTRICT HOSPITAL⁵⁷

The Health Department did continue planning for the new hospital throughout 1986 but there was no decision on funding. In June, in

State Parliament, Barry Blaikie duly asked the Minister for Health, Ian Taylor, the key question:

> Will the Government commit funds in the 1986/87 budget to build a new hospital at Margaret River?
>
> ANSWER
>
> Consideration will be given to the inclusion in the preliminary 1986/87 Capital Works Programme for the construction of a new hospital at Margaret River. The ability to proceed with the project will be dependent on the level of funds available when the budget is framed, with due consideration for the State's total health facility needs.[58]

Given this non-committal answer, the local community was probably not surprised when the 1986/87 capital works program once more failed to include any funding for a new hospital. The local committee's response to the new Minister for Health was also predictable:

> Dear Mr Taylor,
>
> I write on behalf of the committee, our annual letter expressing our bitter disappointment that the State Government has, yet again, refused to appropriate funds to provide a new hospital facility at Margaret River...
>
> If, after seeing the hospital at first hand, Mr Burke and yourself cannot make a decision regarding its future, as Mr Wenn reports, there seems to be very little point in presenting any material for consideration.
>
> Mr Burke has pointedly said that he will not listen if the committee makes 'a song and dance' over the issue, and our many years of making 'the quiet reasoned approach' have got us precisely nowhere; it is no wonder then that the committee feels that it is 'damned if it does and damned if it doesn't'. We also feel that the rights and wrongs of the situation have been buried by the political considerations and that committee submissions receive little if any attention.

> We shall continue to work to provide such comforts and equipment needed for the hospital, especially those in Permanent Care.[59]

One member of the community, Dorothy Shepherdson, was particularly unimpressed by a statement made by Labor parliamentarian Doug Wenn, MLC, that if Margaret River could not have a full hospital, then he would be pressing for at least a nursing station. Mrs Shepherdson did not mince her words:

> A nursing station would be unthinkable and out of the question for a town the size of Margaret River which is continually growing. Perhaps you don't realise the amount of building that is going on here at present. There are three doctors practising here and a fourth when required. Two timber mills operate in and near the town. Should a serious accident occur, a nursing station would be totally inadequate. It is a puerile statement, which I believe came from a politician, to say that Margaret River people can go to Busselton or Augusta. I can see the doctors who have recently moved into the town packing up and leaving should this situation occur.[60]

She went on to point out that money had been provided for hospitals in the north of the state, concluding with a pointed reference to the fact that government funds had been allocated for the 1987 defence of the America's Cup which Australia had wrested from the Americans in 1983.

> Then we have the classics, twenty-nine and a half million dollars from the Commonwealth Government and twenty million from the State Government poured into Fremantle for the America's Cup, which incidentally, I like many other others, hope finds a home elsewhere...
>
> It would seem that all these giveaways are no more than gimmicks for vote catching and because Margaret River is generally a Liberal voting community, money has been denied them out of spite.

This was obviously one of many complaints Wenn fielded at the time as, before receiving Shepherdson's letter, he had written to Minister Taylor:

Hospital Front entry. Courtesy Judy Wake.

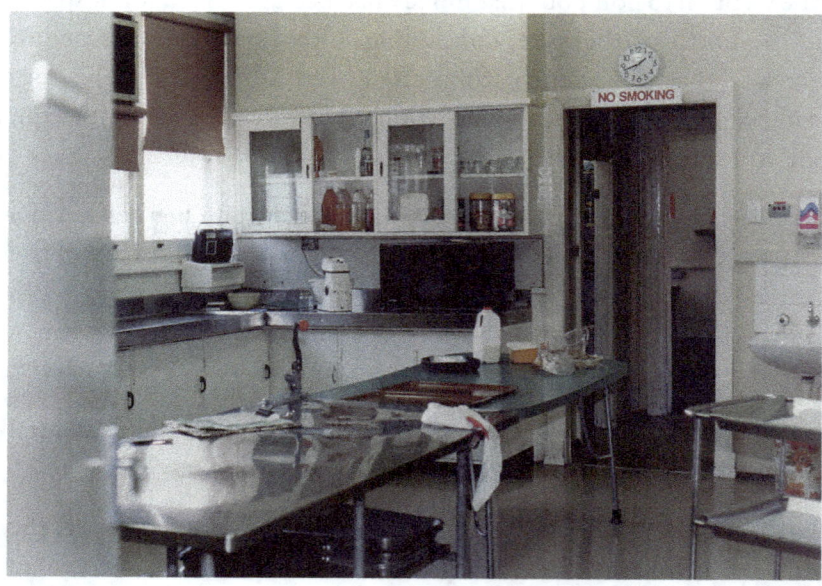

Hospital Kitchen in the 1980s. Courtesy Judy Wake.

> The saga of the Margaret River hospital is still continuing as you would be aware by the amount of mail both you and I are receiving...I would ask if you have made any decision as of yet, as to what direction you are to take on this issue.[61]

Ian Taylor's answer indicated that all available options for service provision were being investigated but made no specific commitment regarding a new hospital. His assertions would have brought little comfort to Mrs Shepherdson and other members of the Margaret River community.[62]

The hospital advisory committee stayed quiet for much of 1987, perhaps influenced by the premier's statement that he would not listen to noisy campaigning.

In August, the *Augusta-Margaret River Mail* reported that the Minister for Health had indicated that planning for the new hospital was progressing and that he was hopeful funds would be contained in the forthcoming budget. On the other hand, Barry McKinnon, leader of the Liberal Party, had stated that his party would build the new hospital if returned to power and that it would contain a theatre for minor operations.[63]

The following month the *Mail* reported that the 1987/88 budget, which was to be released shortly, would contain money to complete the planning for the new hospital. The State Government was negotiating with business interests in the town and it was expected that a major announcement would be made in the next few weeks.[64] A later report confirmed that the 'business interest' was local developer Mark Hohnen and his company, Oceanic Equity. The *Mail* article confirmed that the new hospital would be built on the current site but that the deal would result in some of the reserve being 'released for land development'.[65] The clear inference was that part of the land which had been allocated for hospital purposes since 1923 would be handed to Oceanic Equity for housing or commercial development.

The *Mail* continued to take a keen interest in the state of the existing Margaret River Hospital and the local demands for a new building. An article published late in 1987 was headed: 'Health risk in hospital plagued by white ants and sewerage problems'. While the article did not provide details of the sewerage problems, it explained graphically the white ant infestation.

> Several patients who were waiting for operations the next day said later that they were disgusted by the sight of white ants crawling up the walls of their rooms. The *Mail* was taken on an inspection by acting administrator Ern Hulbert last week.[66]

The article also quoted a statement by Barry House, now a Liberal member of Parliament for the South-West Province, that the old wooden hospital was a serious fire risk and that 'Everybody is sick and tired of this issue being used as a political football and action is urgently needed to avoid a tragedy'.[67]

The new year brought a definite 'wind change' and by February 1988 the *Mail* was able to report that:

> The State Government is aiming to have the new Margaret River Hospital completed within eighteen months. It will be a 20-bed hospital and it will be built between the aged people's complex (Mirrambeena) and the existing hospital in Farrelly Street.

The newspaper also confirmed that this facility would be built entirely by the government and that no outside developer would be involved. Oceanic Equity was no longer on the horizon.[68]

A month later, there had been a change of ministerial responsibilities. Keith Wilson, MLA, had taken over the health portfolio. On 13 April, the *Mail* reported that the new minister would fly to Margaret River 'tomorrow' to release the plans for the new hospital and that these would be most likely displayed at the council offices.[69]

Now, a new issue came into focus: what to do with the old hospital? In its 13 April edition, the *Mail* also reported that 'debate about the future of the old hospital is hotting up' and that some people were keen for the old building to become an arts and crafts centre. Hospital staff would possibly have preferred to see it bulldozed or even burned to the ground, as Judy Wake had suggested:

> I can remember when we finally left, we emptied the last of the things out, after we had moved up to the new hospital, and we were standing out the back there, and I can remember Carolyn Scott and I had discussed dropping a match as we came out because we reckoned it was a complete wreck. But we decided that we had better not because we had said it before and people would know who had dropped the match.[70]

Others, including Anne Shepherdson, could see the potential for these buildings to continue to be used for a purpose which benefitted the community.

> Well, yes, and while I think the hospital people, and I had been one of the hospital people, too, thought, 'Well, if we made a big hoo-ha about saving it then we won't get a new hospital.' But what we wanted to use it for was not for a hospital. It was more for a community-based thing. So it wasn't to do anything medical. So the pristine-ness didn't have to be quite there.[71]

Just two weeks later, there were two separate but related headlines in the *Mail*: 'Hospital plans released' and 'Group formed to save the hospital site'.[72] The Health Department had stated that it would have no further use for the old buildings and members of the local community were concerned that the site might be sold and the structures demolished. They were partly reassured when the South West Development Authority, also an arm of the State Government, made it clear that the site had not been sold to developers.[73]

When Keith Wilson, now Minister for Health, released the final design drawings for the new hospital in April 1988, he stated that the building should be ready for occupation in May the following year. The first tree was duly felled on the proposed site, on the hill above the old hospital, on 15 July 1988.[74] But there were many delays and the successful tenderer was not announced until

November that year. After that it was anticipated that construction would be completed in thirty-eight weeks – by September 1989.[75] But there were more delays and it was not until February 1990 that the move took place. In December 1989, Liberal member of the Legislative Council for the south-west Barry House spoke during the second reading of the Appropriation (General Loan and Capital Works Fund) Bill.

> The Margaret River Hospital has been a perennial source of discontent for many years, so I am pleased to see the final allocation towards that hospital. I believe work will be completed in the relatively near future, and that this will be welcomed by Margaret River residents.[76]

Local health professionals, including the doctors, had little involvement in the design and build process.

> We did go to meetings, and we did attend a 'walk through' when the hospital was half built. And we thought 'the way they've done that maybe we could have done it a bit better'. But the Health Department, it was their building and they were supplying the money so we didn't get much of a say. They had Health Department architects that design hospitals, so they knew better.[77]

For Dr O'Rourke, 'When they started to build the hospital it was a complete surprise to me really. I didn't know much of anything was going on at all'.[78]

Fran Temby was not involved on the final moving day:

> The move was delayed several times. On the day in February that they finally moved to the new hospital, I was on annual leave. Judy Wake was in charge as then matron, Mary Arthur, was also on leave.[79]

This meant that for a few weeks, Judy had responsibility for both the old and new building:

> Well, there were these two blokes from Busselton who were virtually in charge of all this business, and I had been in charge for a little while and I used to have to go up to the new hospital from the old hospital

every evening. I used to have to walk around and make sure every door and window was closed and I used to have to walk out the back door and set the alarm as I went out, and I hate things like that, hate gadgets, so I used to go back down to the old hospital and I used to phone Perth and say, 'Is my hospital safe?' And they used to laugh and say, 'Yes, you can go home now.'[80]

New hospital under construction. Courtesy Judy Wake.

Moving Day at the old hospital. Courtesy Judy Wake.

Carolyn Scott was one of many staff who moved equipment to the new hospital.

> For many weeks beforehand, a lot of us, in our spare time, gradually moved stuff from the old hospital to the new hospital on our days off; it was Lyn Jakovich, a lot of the domestic staff, what have you.[81]

Final moving day was Monday 26 February 1990 and the transfer of patients began at 9 in the morning. Judy Wake was grateful to everyone who came in to help.

> A lot of staff came in and they didn't get paid for it. They came in voluntarily and we moved the patients up and then we had to keep two casualties open and so the casualty in the old hospital was the last thing that went.[82]

The previous day, Sunday 25 February at 5.10 in the afternoon, the last baby, Morgan Hofstee, was born in the old hospital. His mother, Fiona, remembers the day well:

> because I was in labour and they were shifting. My husband Ralph was an orderly at the hospital. And he was on duty that day. So, when he went to work at seven o'clock, I didn't really want to stay home by myself. So I just went to work with him. I spent the day on the verandah. All the doors to the wards came out onto the verandah. So they just said, 'well just stay out of our way, you are not ready yet'. So I was on the verandah most of the day.[83]

But it was hot on the verandah and Morgan was still not quite ready to be born, so Fiona was sent to sit on a beanbag in the labour ward, which had an air conditioner. The move was now on in earnest:

> And I remember the maintenance guys from Busselton coming in and starting to remove all the equipment from the labour ward. So I called out, 'Stop, you can't do that.' And they went, 'Oh, what are you doing there?' So I said, 'Well, you can't take that equipment. I'm in labour.'

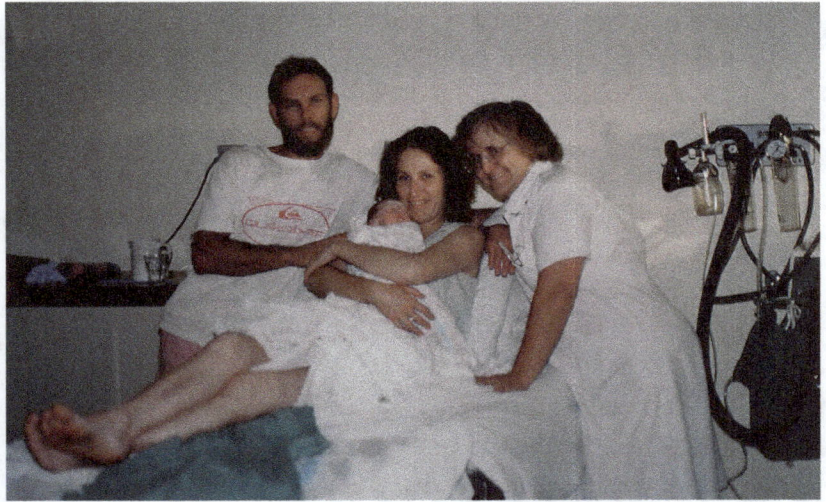

Fiona and Ralph Hofstee with Morgan, the last baby born in the old hospital. Midwife: Milly Preedy. Courtesy Fiona Hofstee.

> They said, 'Oh, but we must. We are moving it to the new hospital.' So I looked around and saw a heater, and it was pretty hot. So I said, 'Well, you can have that. But you can't have anything else.' So they had to go and find out what they were supposed to do because they couldn't move it. So that was kind of funny.

Fiona then became one of the first patients in the new hospital.

> It was really exciting. Ralph had already seen the inside of it because he was a staff member. They all had a look. But the next morning, there was one other mother who'd had the baby the day before me. So, the next morning at about quarter to nine, they took us one at a time. She went first. They put her in the car with her baby and drove around the corner. And then they came back and they picked me up and they drove me around the corner. It was all very shiny and new.

Carolyn Scott was on duty that day:

> My role was to move the resuscitation gear from the old hospital to the new hospital. So I loaded all the equipment into the boot of my

Kingswood Holden and I arrived at the new hospital five minutes later, and my first patient was Dr Sheridan – with chest pain. And I said to her, 'Doctor, don't die yet, because all the resus gear is in the boot of my car.' True story!

And next day Dr O'Rourke and I set up the theatre in our days off because Dr White wanted to do a procedure. And my first patient, my first official patient in the emergency department, via ambulance, was my mother with a pulmonary embolism and I saved her. So there you go.[84]

Dr O'Rourke found a use for some of the old hospital beds:

My only involvement was getting some stuff from the old hospital that they were just chucking out, making sure that it went to the right place – like, to me, as in I'm quite fond of junk. So when we moved to the new hospital, we got a couple of old hospital beds, which are made out of, like, solid iron, and they stood about three foot off the ground. And my kids slept with those for years because they could climb up over the end like a ladder. And my wife liked it because it's the perfect height for her back to make the beds.[85]

Betty Dyer gives a final mop to casualty. Courtesy Judy Wake.

A PERENNIAL SOURCE OF DISCONTENT

For Acting Matron Judy Wake, it had been a long day, and the move to the new hospital a long time coming: 'When I locked the front door and put this notice up that said, "Please go round the corner", I nearly cried.' The permanent care patients were moved from their 'home' in the Margaret Cecil Rest House.

The old hospital is now closed. Courtesy Judy Wake.

The new hospital is now open. Courtesy Judy Wake.

> The ones that really suffered were the oldies. I don't think that place was nearly as nice as the old one. It was a little old building that they were in but it was a 'home', not a row of wards.[86]

On the evening of 26 February 1990, it was time for Judy Wake, and everyone involved, to remember a shared life in the old hospital.

> That evening, staff held a barbeque at the old hospital and we 'laid the ghosts' of many years, remembering times of drama and sadness and some of laughter and satisfaction shared over the time. From cook to domestic to orderly to nurse to clerical staff, to sister to matrons and doctors, all take their part in a small hospital caring for its community. As they shared the care, staff shared the wake and never have ghosts been more truly laid![87]

Official opening of the new hospital: March 1990. Courtesy Judy Wake.

Chapter Eight

An Extension of Life

Initially it was not clear whether these wooden buildings would survive once the old hospital closed. As it turned out, the buildings found a new life as a home for the Margaret River Community Centre and, over thirty years later, they are still being used for this purpose, and cared for, as centre manager Lydell Huntly relates:

> We have a five-year building scope of works that will be quite extensive. And when you look at restumping, roofing sections and upgrading your insulation, repairing your old doors and windows. We are going to be doing that in stages for the next five years. That will be intrusive for tenants. It will also be amazing to see a beautiful old building revived and given an extension of life.[1]

For heritage architect Kris Keen, who has advised on maintenance and restoration, there was nothing unusual about using an existing building for a different purpose.

> I was brought up in a seventeenth-century farmhouse in Oxfordshire, so 'old' to me is 150 years. But before I had done this building, I had

done various other buildings where you say, 'How can I use this building because it was used for that before?' And if you have been brought up in England, you have been using a building for a different thing at a different time. So this is no different from doing that sort of jigsaw.[2]

In the lead-up to the old hospital's closure, several organisations had expressed an interest in acquiring the site and possibly retaining the buildings. The existing Margaret River Community Centre, which had been set up by local women in 1985 and had outgrown its current premises, was one interested party. Jennifer Gherardi was an early member of that group:

> There were a few community centres sprinkled around WA and some people brought the idea to us and said, 'Look, this is really great for community building and resilience.' There was a real need for it to create a greater connection. The wine industry had got on its feet. The town was growing and it was obvious that we needed to make the town feel as if they had services. We were still a small town but we had lots of people with energy and motivation who came along and we had a motivated group who were running it.[3]

The local newspaper reported on the establishment of the community centre under the heading, 'Packed hall for new centre':

> **Visitors from Perth, Busselton, Cowaramup and Augusta as well as district residents heard speakers on topics ranging from the social needs of rural communities to the beneficial effects of the community centre. These will come through an increased range of services such a centre can put into action to improve the quality of individual community life.**[4]

Almost immediately, the new organisation leased an old cottage in town on the corner of Wallcliffe and Station roads. Previously this had been the local headquarters of the government's Forests Department. Jennifer Gherardi sought the help of the shire clerk in organising the lease:

Ken Preston was then the shire clerk. I was only a young mother and I will never forget going into his office with one of the other committee members, I think it might have been Anne Shepherdson. I hadn't done that type of thing before. I was really asking for something that was quite substantial. His response was wonderful. He said, 'Of course, you are doing something for the community. Of course, I'll get behind you.' And he was really positive and instrumental in helping us get through the governance issues, in terms of getting hold of a whole house. It was in a great location. It had a huge yard and we paid a peppercorn lease.[5]

The new community centre initially focused on learning through the provision of short educational courses. A summer school was organised for January 1986 and this provided the impetus for an official opening by local land developer Mark Hohnen on 19 January.[6] Hohnen said that the group had been formed because certain needs were not being met by the formal educational system and that this was a place for people of all ages to come together.[7]

The community centre immediately offered a wide range of courses and while the initial focus tended to be on crafts, such as making potpourri and an introduction to spinning, there was one on car maintenance. Ros Blakeney took that course:

The first Margaret River Community Centre in Station Road. Margaret River Community Centre (MRCC).

> I remember the basic car maintenance was one side of it. And the car that we worked on was jacked up. We learned how to look at spark plugs and change the oil. I quickly decided that that was a job for a mechanic and not a woman. I was happy for a man to fix my car for me! But it was interesting and it was good fun. They did a lot of courses like that at that time, on that property.[8]

While the focus on running courses remained, the Margaret River Community Centre began to move into broader fields, as Anne Shepherdson, initially the vice-president, recalled.

> Yes, I was involved right from the word go. I can't quite remember quite how we all started. But we came together whether it was BPW (Business and Professional Women) or different groups that came together. So we started the adult day care. The Silver Chain person at the time came and talked to us. We organised a bus. We had luncheons. People came in from the farms and different places. So we started what is now the bigger day care. We had community events; we had workshops; just lots of things going on.[9]

The organisation placed an emphasis on services for families. In September 1986 twenty children were able to participate in a creative children's art workshop and, at a time when there were few places a parent could leave their child in occasional care, the centre operated a creche for mothers attending courses. There were also holiday activities for school-age children.[10]

Social events organised by the centre included Melbourne Club lunches at Leeuwin Estate ($30 a head) and, as Ros Blakeney remembers, funds were raised through an annual fun run.

> I think they did the first fun run in Margaret River and there are some pictures of that where it started out opposite what was Archie Martins on the hill and Cape Mentelle.[11]

But the Community Centre's major focus remained providing opportunities for life-long learning. Its March 1988 newsletter

The first fun run in support of the Community Centre. MRCC.

published a list of upcoming courses that ranged from meditation to paper making; from knitting to sacred dances.[12]

Increasingly, the major barrier to offering more courses and other activities was the limited space at the Station Road cottage. Sally (now Tess) Minett became involved with the centre in the late 1980s.

> Around the time I got involved there, the town of Margaret River was growing quite rapidly and the need for a larger centre was very evident because the three or four rooms available at the house were over-utilised.[13]

While the community centre committee began to realise that they needed larger premises, the potential for the old hospital to become a community facility was also coming to the fore.

In the same edition that it reported on the release of the new hospital plans (see Chapter 7), the *Augusta-Margaret River Mail* ran an article on the same page with the heading, 'Group formed to save hospital site'. The local newspaper reported that this group was initially known as the Save the Heart of the Town Committee.

While this committee was not initially closely connected to the community centre in Station Road, its formation did lead the organisers to consider a possible future in this much larger building complex, right in the heart of town.

Retaining the old hospital for the community became a cause that attracted the interest of artist Clifton Pugh, who donated a painting valued at $3,500, more than the £1,100 it had cost to build the original 1924 hospital! Pugh was particularly attracted by the bushland site, saying 'What a wonderful opportunity you have to preserve this area for the community'.[14] While many groups, including those wanting the building dedicated to arts and crafts, were initially interested in acquiring the old hospital, the community centre soon became the strongest contender, as Anne Shepherdson recalls:

> I think it was always an idea. I don't even know who started the idea to use the hospital, but we were very pro; it was always there for me. It was something we were always going to do, or try to do.
>
> Well, Joyce Bennett was a leading light, I think. Joyce Bennett and Sally Minett. These were people from the old Station Road. I mean Ros Blakeney and myself and others I suppose. We were all there as well. But Joyce was the spokesperson.[15]

Ros Blakeney recognises Joyce's important role in obtaining the old hospital for the community centre.

> Everybody talks about Joyce, she was amazing. She would get a vision of something in her head. And she had the energy and enthusiasm and she could pull together a group of people around her that were buoyed by her vision and would just help out. She just seemed to be one of those people; in our modern words, we would say charismatic. She was just a person that got up, got out of bed and did stuff; made it happen.[16]

Yet there were many hurdles to overcome before the old hospital could become a community facility.

AN EXTENSION OF LIFE

Ros Blakeney and Joyce Bennett at the new community centre (the old hospital). MRCC.

In December 1988, Kim Murray, editor of the *Augusta-Margaret River Mail*, broke the news that Margaret River might become the site for an annexe of the then proposed Notre Dame University. While Margaret River was one of several country towns being considered, the article was headed 'University for hospital site' and the first paragraph suggested that the location could well be the old hospital grounds.[17] This proposal alarmed the Station Road committee. Chairman L.A. Barber immediately wrote to the then Minister for the South West, the Hon. Julian Grill, MLA, putting the case for the old hospital to become the community centre's home. The letter was copied widely to other state and local government politicians, with the writer reminding Minister Grill that the recently released South West Development Authority's strategy plan included a commitment to develop the hospital site for community purposes.[18]

For now, the shire council continued to support the concept of the old hospital being vested in the local authority and becoming a facility for community organisations. This proposal was contained in a recreation study commissioned by the council, and suggested an emphasis on arts and crafts facilities. The report stated that:

> The old hospital site has many existing attributes which would be of immense benefit to the arts community and the satisfaction of their demands...The number of usable workspaces available make it an attractive proposition to market those areas on a lease basis to some of the professional artisans who reside within the shire. It may also attract others, from outside the area.[19]

However, proponents of the proposal for the old hospital to become a community facility would have been alarmed to read:

> The old hospital site is a suitable venue for an arts centre but long-term development of the town centre could see the site being needed for commercial purposes in accordance with planning objectives, currently being formulated.[20]

The conflict between commercial and not-for-profit interests continued to be a major feature of the fight to retain these buildings for the community. At the same time, other community organisations, including the local playgroup, joined the queue to use the old hospital.

> A permanent centre which is solely ours would mean that we would be able to hold more sessions, or longer sessions. We could also leave equipment set up for children's activities without worrying about interference by other groups and damage.
>
> Our children and their parents have a need in our community.[21]

Inevitably, there was a question mark over the condition of the buildings. Hospital staff fighting to get a new hospital for the district had publicised the sloping floors and the white ant problem. The aim had been to build a case for a new hospital at least partially on the grounds that the current building was ready for demolition.[22] In fact a report by the government's Building Management Authority released in March 1989 indicated that the buildings were in a generally sound condition and suggested that they could be renovated at a cost of less than $35,000. It described the buildings, including their juxtaposition on the site, as having 'little architectural merit or aesthetic appeal and are typical of country hospital buildings of the period'. On the other hand, the report acknowledged that the site location in relation to the town centre and mature bush setting presented 'a comfortable appearance'.[23]

The same edition of the *Mail* reported on a community meeting held to establish a group which would advise the shire on the community's aims for the buildings. Joyce Bennett, president of the Margaret River Community Centre, was a key member of the Old Hospital Advisory Committee. This body now replaced the Save the Heart of the Town Committee, which was formally dissolved.[24] The new committee immediately set to work and organised a workshop to plan a submission to council. Architect Linton Hodsdon was present:

> The Old Hospital Community Planning Day was quite an event. We've had lots of these group events where you get together and you come up with ideas, and then you put Post-Its on the board and then you cut it down to the top four. This was an early version of that but it didn't get cut down. There was all this information to form the brief to the transition. There was this coming together of minds; it was quite wonderful.[25]

It was becoming apparent that there was now a serious proposal for the old hospital to become the agricultural wing of Notre Dame University, which was about to be established in Western Australia.

FIGHT LOOMS OVER HOSPITAL

> The group calling itself the Old Hospital Advisory Committee wants to use the eight timber buildings for a human resource centre. But it is worried that proponents of the university which include prominent business man Denis Horgan, are interested in buying the buildings. A group spokesman, Dr Frances Heussenstamm, said there was speculation that Mr Horgan would make an offer for the buildings that the Government could not refuse.[26]

The West Australian reported that Horgan was acting on behalf of the proposed university and that Margaret River, as well as other locations, were still under consideration.

When Notre Dame's submission went to the shire council in late April 1989, councillors called a public meeting to discuss all proposals. The *Mail* reported that 'their decision to hold the meeting followed pressure from a big lobby group that is working towards the retention of the old hospital for the community'.[27] Pressure was increasing on all sides. Notre Dame had advised the shire council that the State Government was prepared to sell the property to them, while Denis Horgan insisted that he did not wish to be in conflict with the local community over this issue.[28] Not surprisingly, the meeting held on 15 May 1989 was a lively affair. Architect Theo Mathews, a member of the Old Hospital Advisory Committee, recalls that:

> it was high theatre. It was high drama. You have got all these combatants coming together, eye-balling each other. And the stakes were high. We said Father Glover was bussing in dead Catholics. It was getting to that stage. It was really a very tense atmosphere there.[29]

Ros Blakeney was an observer:

> One enduring vision I have is of looking down and seeing lots of grey-haired people that nobody in town knew, that had been bussed in as meeting stackers. People were very passionate about keeping it

for the community. People were passionate about using it for another purpose. So it was a very interesting meeting but I, personally, felt it was stacked in favour of Notre Dame. At the time we all knew each other in town. It was a whole different ball game. I mean you see a whole load of people streaming in off a bus that you don't know, you go, 'Yeah, what's going on here?'[30]

There were clearly valid arguments on both sides. Dr Peter Tannock, representing the university, made it clear that he, personally, was opposed to establishing the facility in the town if the community did not want it. Yet when Member of Parliament Barry Blaikie asked the meeting whether it wanted a university in the district, the answer was a resounding 'yes'.[31] The *Busselton-Margaret Times* summed up the views of the meeting:

VOTE CALLS FOR DIFFERENT SITE

Though the establishment of an agricultural wing of the proposed Notre Dame University would be welcomed in the town, it should not be located at the old hospital.[32]

The *Mail*'s report focused on the evidence of diverse views:

HOSPITAL MEETING REVEALS SPLIT IN THE COMMUNITY

A well-attended meeting in Margaret River on Monday night voted for the shire council to support the community's fight for the old hospital.[33]

The same issue of the *Mail* covered a very different concern – an issue from the past – in an article headed 'Former matron says part of old hospital not for sale'. Agnes Thomas, formerly Matron Dunbar and now a senior citizen resident at Mirrambeena (accommodation for senior citizens to which the remaining funds held by Margaret Cecil Rest House committee had been donated in 1977), pointed out that the rest house wing of the hospital had been built specifically for the women of the district, that it was not part of the hospital and should not be sold off to anyone.[34]

Agnes Thomas, the former Matron Dunbar, says the Margaret Cecil Rest House is not for sale.
Augusta-Margaret River Mail 17 May 1989.

The plea to honour this history made no impact on events that played out in 1989. The original status of the Margaret Cecil Rest House was conveniently forgotten. The issue now was the future of all the old wooden buildings on the site and these were deemed to be, in their entirety, government property.

While the shire council, the State Government and many people in the district supported the Notre Dame proposal, the council, faced with the strong community opposition, delayed making a decision on the old hospital's future. This dilemma was largely resolved when, in September 1989, the university dropped its plan to establish an agricultural annexe in Margaret River.[35]

In reporting that Notre Dame would not be seeking to use the old hospital buildings, the *Busselton-Margaret Times* also announced that the council would ask the State Government to give it the hospital premises free of charge, although there was no immediate commitment to make the buildings and the site available for community use.[36] These were still the property of the Western Australian Government which, because of budgetary difficulties, had established an Assets Management Taskforce to identify land and buildings which were surplus to government requirements. The intent was to sell off unwanted land assets to private entities or to local government with the proceeds going to augment the treasury funds. In March 1990 the *Mail* reported that the

> future of the old hospital may be known soon. The Assets Management Taskforce that advises the state government on the disposal of properties was expected to consider the property earlier this week. The Premier, Carmen Lawrence, chairs the Taskforce. Dr Lawrence would not be drawn on the issue during her visit last week.[37]

On this visit, the premier had formally opened the new hospital, but two months later no decision had been made about the old buildings.

> The old hospital was pledged to the council in November 1988 when the State Government released its much-quoted South West Strategy known as the People's Plan. One of the initiatives listed in the People's Plan is: Support will be provided to the Shire of Margaret River to plan and develop the present Margaret River Hospital site for community and other uses.[38]

But two years is a long time in politics and it appeared that the government had now put a price tag, estimated to be around $300,000, on the title to the old hospital.[39] Eventually, in July 1990, the sale price for the whole of the remaining hospital reserve was set at $270,000. But the shire could not afford to pay such a sum.

Anne Shepherdson's husband, Lloyd, was a member of the shire council at the time and spearheaded efforts to have the land and buildings vested in the shire without any monetary payment. Lloyd was a supporter of the proposal for the community centre to take over the buildings and he was able to persuade the premier that if the site was vested in the shire, the council would in return hand over to the State Government two other plots of land in the town.

> To get the community centre, I had a meeting with Premier Carmen Lawrence and our CEO and a planning officer. We sat down with her and showed her the benefits to her of being able to get back what was the community centre at the corner of Station Road and Wallcliffe Road and which was the old Forests Department manager's house. We also said that we would raise no objection to the State Government using the Stewart Street block behind what was the police station house. I think this was the sewerage or effluent overflow from the old hospital so it was land that a developer might have had quite a bit of problems in getting through the council's planning approvals etc. But we did say we won't raise objections if you can develop that land in a sensible fashion for housing. And then we, the community, can retain the hospital. I know that the shire president came away saying well, 'You've told them they can use their land and we'll keep some of it. You are trading their land for the hospital land', sort of thing.[40]

Lloyd's ruse worked. The government agreed to vest the old hospital buildings and grounds in the Augusta-Margaret River Shire Council for no monetary cost. It was indeed a sleight of hand as both the old house and the land which had been the hospital's sewerage outflow (and which had caused many problems in previous years) were already state owned!

Lloyd was satisfied that he had been able to secure the future of the hospital buildings: 'It is heritage. It is weatherboard, which is what the whole district is really. It is good to see some of these buildings kept.' Lloyd's wife, Anne, shares his sentiment:

> There are not a lot of wooden buildings left in the South West, so it is great that historically they have been able to have been saved. I think that is a vital part of keeping the old hospital going.[41]

Ros Blakeney is particularly delighted that the Margaret Cecil building was saved:

> I am thrilled that the old hospital became the community centre. I particularly have a very warm feeling for the Margaret Cecil building, which was the original maternity wing. I think that is a very precious

thing to think that so many of our original people living in the town were born there. And they would still be alive now, I am sure.[42]

No doubt the former Matron Dunbar would also have been pleased that the community retained ownership of the former Margaret Cecil Rest House.

The decision to hand over the old hospital to the shire was agreed in September 1990, with the *Mail* announcing, 'Old Hospital: It's ours. Government goes for land swap'.[43] But it was not until March 1991 that this newspaper was also able to tell its readers that the old hospital site had been vested in the Augusta-Margaret River Shire for use as a community centre.[44] Council was not happy with the wording of the vesting order, however, and asked that 'community centre' be changed to 'community purposes'.[45]

By this time, the community centre, now the Margaret River Community Resource Centre, was well entrenched in its new premises. While the manoeuvres about ownership were taking place between the two levels of government, Joyce Bennett and her volunteers had secured a lease over the site and buildings. Peter Dowding was the premier when the initial deal for the community centre to occupy the old hospital was struck. Tess Minett was involved in securing at least a temporary hold on the now vacated buildings:

> Ostensibly it was empty but I realised, walking past there one day, that in fact there was a doctors surgery on the site and that it had been there for yonks. I learned that the party responsible for the site as a whole was the South West Development Authority. So I got in touch with a lady there. And I asked her about the doctors surgery and, apparently, they had a lease that was continuing for some time after the rest of the hospital was vacated. So I realised obviously then that it was possible to lease other areas of the grounds, not just the grounds, but the buildings. And she said, 'Yes, of course it is!'
>
> And around about the same time, there was a conference in Perth, and it just so happened that the premier was there, Peter Dowding. And I snaffelled him after the Saturday night dinner and told him

all about the community centre, the potential for the enlarged community centre at the old hospital; that it was in fact in good condition, that it was not riddled with white ants. And after about half an hour, he said, 'Look you'd make a great politician. I wish you were on my side. It's yours.'[46]

The lease was signed on 27 July 1990 on behalf of the Margaret River Community Resource Centre. A successful open day was held on 1 September 1990. The community centre vacated its Station Road premises and moved into its new home in October.[47] Jennifer Gherardi had been a member of the Station Road committee.

> We joined the two committees together and I stayed on the committee for a while. And we were able to bring all the furnishings, the programs from the community centre over to the community resource centre, and started running the programs there. And, of course, there was such a great amenity and there was so much space that we were immediately able to start letting it out to other groups, community groups. That was fabulous.[48]

Joyce Bennett, centre, pictured with Alison Brown (South West Development Authority), left and Tess (Sally) Minett, right, signs the agreement to lease the old hospital for the Margaret River Community Resource Centre. Augusta-Margaret River Mail/MRCC.

Anne Shepherdson helped with the practicalities of the move:

> Yes, I was moving stuff from A to B. It was just clearing out and setting up again. You just had some computers in those days. It is not quite the same as what it is now. I think the hospital had been left very tidy. And it was a matter of just moving in.[49]

There was still that one other lease in place within the grounds: the doctors surgery. This building was the original 1924 staff quarters, hastily built for the first matron, Matron Ward, a few months after the hospital opened. Later used as the domestic staff quarters, this free-standing group settlement-type cottage had been leased for many years by doctors Lagan and Sheridan. Now, however, the shire council wanted to use the cottage to house a youth worker and wished to terminate the lease. The doctors were very unhappy with this proposal. Dr Sheridan wrote an open letter which was published in the *Mail* recalling the circumstances of their 1968 arrival:

> Far from having a practice as promised we came to a run down town whose population was diminishing yearly because of the general economic down-turn and because there had been no resident doctor for three years.

She asked that, as she and her husband were in the final years of their careers, they be spared the difficulty of finding alternative premises.[50] The council remained unmoved and the doctors finally left their surgery of over twenty years. The building was then relocated, as Ros Blakeney explained.

> We decided that we would open up the grounds, so originally the building that was the doctors surgery and is now the soup kitchen was at the front of the complex. And we moved that around so that it started to create a sort of courtyard because we wanted that feeling of an English country green.[51]

The community centre committee was also concerned about the potential for vandalism now that no one was living on the premises.

Back of the doctors surgery before it was moved. Stephen Blakeney.

A decision was made to install caretakers. Margot Edwards and partner Gerry Riley took on that role:

> And yeah, the opportunity came up to be caretakers in the old nurses quarters. This is in 1990. I had my first baby while we were there, in February '91. Very convenient – got to walk across the trees to the hospital.[52]

But it seemed to Margot that the building was not quite 'empty'.

> It got to the point where I wouldn't lock up at night. I was pregnant and it just gave me the heebie-jeebies being in the main hospital building. And I was sure there were ghosts, wandering souls. I suppose the operating theatre saw so many lives come through and some lives lost; and I think they leave an imprint on a building. I can walk in there now and there are absolutely no imprints there at all. It was only ever the imprint from the past that I sensed. This was very early on. And it had been vacated and we were there right from that very beginning. And there weren't actually many tenants.

AN EXTENSION OF LIFE

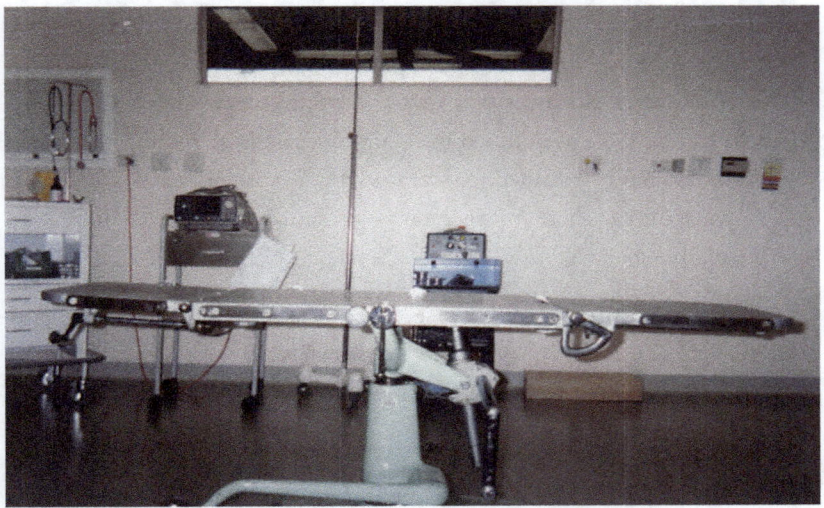

Operating theatre in the old hospital. Courtesy Judy Wake.

Once the euphoria of obtaining the old hospital for the community had dissipated, serious financial issues emerged. The shire provided an initial $30,000 but much of this was swallowed up in the cost of connecting the buildings to the deep sewerage.[53] After this, as Ros Blakeney recalled, the community centre was very much on its own.

> Well, I think it went back to the very first point when people wanted it for a different use. So, when it was vested in the shire, they just didn't want to know about spending any money on it. They just saw it as a ruin that would be a pit for money to be shovelled into.

Hiring out of spaces on long-term and short-term bases was seen as a major income source. But tenants were initially hard to come by. The Margaret River Business Enterprise Centre run by Barbara Maidment was one of the first occupants.

> So it was a little bit lonely initially. And even to get a cup of tea we had to wander down a dark, dismal hallway to what used to be the

hospital kitchen and it was a little bit awkward at first. A lot of the rooms were still as they had been left when the hospital moved to its new premises. So there was frayed carpeting and one of my rooms still had an old hospital bed in it, and one of those old metal bedside tables, which I purloined for storage. But it was really a bit humorous to walk in, to where my secretary was supposed to sit, to discover a hospital bed.[54]

One of the committee's busiest roles was writing funding submissions.[55] John Alferink was the treasurer when initial grants were received from the Lotteries Commission.

The first grant was to set up, because they had all these rooms available and they wanted to get them all done up. And then the biggest group we wanted to get in there was TAFE. And we had enough money coming in from them to employ a full-time person on site. And that was Donna Dornan. We signed Donna on.[56]

Donna's appointment as administrator proved to be a master stroke, as the centre's second treasurer, Noel Conway, recalled:

Margaret Cecil Rest House – as TAFE. MRCC.

> Donna was brilliant. People considered her bossy, I think. But if she hadn't been bossy, things wouldn't have got done. It was only her vision for the centre. Getting that church relocated to the community centre was her doing. Getting the childcare centre up and running was her doing. I think the soup kitchen was already there and Dave Seegar had a lot to do with that. But really, without Donna I don't think that the centre would have developed the way that it did or grown. It became very self-sufficient, independent of council. It supported itself. I don't see that it would have had the same history without Donna being there during those early years. And it wasn't just the early years. About fifteen years, I think, she was manager there.[57]

Money was always required and Donna seemed to be good at finding what was needed.

> And to tell the truth, I think the style of management at that time would have to be called 'a wing and a prayer'. We had a grant which didn't cover very much at all, and things happened organically. We would get a little bit of money and we would do this, and we would get a little bit more money and we would do that, or sometimes we had no money. We would just do it anyway and rely on local tradesmen to be our saviours.[58]

Donna came on board as the centre's part-time administrator in early 1992. In March that year, the shire council rejected an application from the community centre committee for a grant of $100,000 over two years to support a restoration and building program estimated to cost $436,000.[59] As one councillor stated: 'I see no point or purpose into putting money into a building that has had its day'.[60] When financial support from the local council was not forthcoming, the Lotteries Commission (Lotterywest) came to the rescue with a $250,000 grant to fund the much-needed building renovations. Linton Hodsdon, who had recently joined the centre's committee, was then appointed architect to oversee this work.

> The biggest problem was the fact that the buildings were very low set, so any rain would drain under the buildings which meant it would

Donna Dornan was successful in getting grants from the Lotteries Commission. MRCC.

damage the stumps. So, the first thing was to stabilise the structure. There was no point in building new stuff on dodgy floors. So it was trying to level the floors up, re-stumping. Only the outside stumps needed to be done but we had to dig out from there to get to them and, number two, to keep the water from flowing into there. Things like taking the plasterboard off the wall frames and finding out how the walls were built in 1924.[61]

In December 1993 the *Mail* reported on the results of the renovations.

> The heart of the Margaret River community is beating strongly at the Community Resource Centre in Tunbridge Street. Renovations to the old hospital buildings have created a bright new face for the New Year and the hundreds of people who use the centre are celebrating.

> Things have come a long way since a small and dedicated committee started working to retain the old hospital as a community centre several years ago.[62]

Once this work was completed, there was an official opening and, with Donna Dornan at the helm, the centre was able to offer new services.

> But after that, after we renovated and we had the opening, then we could really get stuck in to projects, and that is when we started doing things; and they came to us. I mean I'd like to say that I single-handedly set up the Centrelink office and the Kids Club and this, that and the other thing. A lot of these fell into our lap. The local government and social services were waiting in this area for a community group to take the initiative.[63]

Many services provided by the centre in the 1990s, such as out-of-school care, youth services and employment services, were later taken on by other agencies or moved to new locations, as former committee chair Sally Hays explained:

> We've always prided ourselves on, as being a bit of an incubator. So we've quite often brought in services, and subsidised them, even on the very low subsidy rents we charge already. We've supported and enabled various groups until they get on their feet and can move on elsewhere. There was the Wine Association and the Margaret River and Districts Historical Society. Various people have come in and trialled ideas for catering businesses, for example, and used the kitchen for six months and then either said 'No that doesn't work' or gone on to their own strength. I think that is probably a big part of the value as well.[64]

This eventually became the case with the Margaret River Farmers Market, which grew too big for the available space. Initially it seemed like a great idea. Donna Dornan was in her office one day when:

> Don Hancy, Ian Parmenter and Niomi O'Hara walked in and said, 'We'd like to hire the centre for a market and I said to my committee, 'They want to hire it for a market.' 'Yes, let them do it,' and then we embraced it and it was a fantastic event for quite a while until Don and Ian got busy in other areas, and it slumped a bit. But the centre still supported it and then it became big again, and then of course it became one of those things that, even though the market was only for four hours a week, it was dominating the whole centre, and I think we go back to that thing about the centre being a seeder. Let's grow this idea until it's profitable and then let's find another spot for it and wish it well, and wish it good luck. And we did.

The successful weekly market eventually moved to Margaret River's new education campus. TAFE had also moved to the same site and the community centre lost a lucrative permanent tenant. Sally Hays and Ros Blakeney were both on the committee at that time.

> When TAFE was leaving to go to the education campus, we were at a real hiatus in terms of what are we going to do when we lose that funding? Because that was the strongest rent base that we had and that was when we made the decision to take the eight-place occasional child care and turn it into a 26-place long day care.[65]

Ros remembers when they first had this good idea.

> We were out the back and wandering around and Donna said, 'Look, one of the ideas I've had is the need for child care in Margaret River.' And we all stopped and said, 'Yes, that's it!' And then we started dancing under the pine trees. It was just crazy because we never do that kind of thing. We are going to be able to care for people and care for families, fathers, mothers, children in that place. That was what the Margaret Cecil Rest House was built for: a place for mothers to give birth and for families to start. So we felt it was absolutely the right fit for that building.

Opening the Childcare Centre was a very big undertaking. Donna Dornan was in charge.

I rang up the Children's Services; we already had an occasional day care, which was great, so we knew people in the industry etc. We had a building, even though it was quite old. And the thing about being fiercely independent and not involving the shire is we didn't actually tell them what we were doing until the health inspector got wind of it and came round about two days before we were going to be opening. I said, 'You will have to give us permission because if we don't open, you will be lynched because we are already full.'

Lynda Green, previously in charge of the centre's occasional care, was responsible for transforming the former Margaret Cecil Rest House into the day care centre.

> They hired me in the childcare centre in the July. And we didn't open until, I think it was October or November. So I had several months where I worked with the tradespeople. We opened up the laundry to the outside and put a little toilet there so the children could access the toilet when outside. A lot of the glass had to be replaced with child-safe glass; fencing had to be a certain height and with pool fencing around. All those sorts of things, and once you've got all that, the regulatory body comes down and makes sure that it is fine before you are allowed to open.[66]

The wheel had come full circle. This building, which had originally provided shelter for women awaiting the birth of their babies, would now house babies and young children.

The Margaret Cecil building has also been home to children's theatre. Margot Edwards was the producer and creator of many of these events. Before the childcare centre was established, they often used the Margaret Cecil building and the old laundry drying shed, which they named the Trellis Theatre.

> We were in the Margaret Cecil building for quite some time. That was our home. As the community centre grew, the youth theatre moved around when different parts of the community centre started to be needed for different things. And we were really only using it on Saturdays and sometimes at weekends. School holidays, mind you,

The Community Centre for Children. Stephen Blakeney.

Children's theatre included the Kids' Circus. MRCC.

> I would run longer workshops and we would use the grounds, we would use the Trellis Theatre, but the Margaret Cecil building was wonderful because it had a big central area. So we did media club shows in there.[67]

There is little doubt Margaret Cecil would have approved of these uses of the building that bears her name, while her mother, Lady Cecil, a keen gardener, would have appreciated the community centre garden, with its roses and memorial to the pioneer women of the district.

Lady Cecil was also a painter, so it is also fitting that, as Donna Dornan noted, the centre has always patronised the visual arts and artists.[68] Lyn Moorfoot worked at the centre for 25 years from 1995 and remembers when the first artworks were purchased.

> I was there when the first artworks were bought, which were a couple of photos that are in the foyer, black and white photos, that were from the high school exhibition. And that's become a regular thing now where committee members go to the high school exhibition every year. We usually buy two, plus for a while we had the artist-in-residence program. The artists had to run community workshops and when they left, they were to donate a piece of their art to the centre.[69]

The old laundry, the only brick building on the site and another link with the past, has been repurposed as an art studio. The old hospital heritage precinct also retains links with the broader history of Margaret River, originally a settlement built within a forest of tall trees.

In 2002 the community centre committee arranged for two other local buildings to be moved to the centre. One was in danger of demolition, while the other was no longer required for its original purpose. Both buildings were gifted to the centre with the proviso that they be moved to the precinct. First to arrive was the Isaacs' Cottage, home to Fred Isaacs, a descendant of the original Wadandi inhabitants of Wooditjup (Margaret River). Sally Hays was there when the cottage was installed:

Opening of art exhibition in Isaacs Cottage. MRCC.

The Brick Laundry became an art studio. MRCC.

> It cost us $11,000 to bring it 100 metres down the road. We had three police cars. We were lifting power poles. We had to take out a portion of the front fence and a couple of bushes to get the truck into the central courtyard and then we had an amazing character called Percy Putt who was a house removalist. And we reviewed the site and said where we wanted it. We wanted it to sit in parallel with the soup kitchen building, the old doctors surgery, and so we could eventually link the verandahs when we got a bit more money. And Percy backed this massive truck with this house on it, through the courtyard. And he reversed it in, and there was a point at which the front corner of the truck was about three millimetres away from the chimney of the Margaret Cecil building as you came around the corner.

Barbara Maidment watched the second 'new' building, the former Uniting Church, arrive.

> I was in my office when I knew that that building was going to be moved. So I had my camera with me. And I went out, stood in the middle of Tunbridge Street, which is kind of a dangerous thing to do…and I took photographs of that old church being pulled up Tunbridge Street by Percy Putt and his moving crew and the Western Power guys were out there with big poles to hold up the cross-street wiring so that this building could get underneath! I mean if one thing went wrong, the whole thing might collapse. But that was an interesting day in the history of the centre.

When the old hospital was established in 1924, the people of the district, many of them group settlers, had little money to spare. While the Margaret River district is now seen as prosperous and relatively wealthy, there are still many people with few resources who make use of the community centre's emergency relief and facilities such as hot showers. In 1995 another service, now associated strongly with the centre, was born, as the local newspaper reported:

The Old Uniting Church arrives at the Margaret River Community Centre, 2002. MRCC.

The doctors surgery was moved and is now the soup kitchen. MRCC.

> Soup kitchen for the needy
>
> A soup kitchen for those in need will start this Saturday evening at the Youth Centre in Tunbridge Street behind the Community Resource Centre.
>
> Organiser Dave Seegar said the idea of starting a free service came primarily from the frontpage story in *The Mail* several weeks ago on young homeless people in Margaret River.[70]

The youth centre, formerly the doctors surgery and before that living quarters for the hospital matron and domestic staff, became the soup kitchen. It was founded by Dave Seegar, and continues to operate as such.

> When I came along, I am pretty sure it was Donna Dornan who was the matriarch back then. She was a wonderful matriarch. When I offered them the idea, they said it was something they had thought about casually for some time. So when I came in and proposed to do it, they just embraced it. It was wonderful they just gave me the run of the kitchen, the run of the centre, and helped me with everything that we needed. They were just brilliant.[71]

For over a quarter of a century, Dave operated the very popular and successful soup kitchen. While this institution provides nutritious vegetarian food for people in financial need, as Lyn Moorfoot, long term administrative assistant at the centre, explains, it has also become a meeting place that welcomes everyone.

> The soup kitchen at Margaret River is a quite different thing to what people imagine a soup kitchen is. It performs a lot of functions other than feeding people who are hard up for food. It is a wonderful place where people on limited incomes and families can go and socialise and network in an alcohol-free environment. I see that rather than the food side of it; I've always seen that as its most useful function for the community.[72]

SETTLEMENT, STRUGGLE AND SUCCESS

Dave Seegar started the Soup Kitchen in 1995. Stephen Blakeney.

In 2016, when the centre celebrated a quarter of a century of service to the community, Dave was marking twenty-one years of running the soup kitchen in partnership with the centre, which he commented was 'probably the best thing about Margaret River: having somewhere central with a committed bunch of people who are here solely to provide for the wellbeing of the town'.[73]

Two years earlier, in May 2014, the old hospital celebrated its ninetieth anniversary. This was an opportunity for the building's current occupants, the Margaret River Community Centre, to pay tribute to the hospital's role in servicing the community between 1924 and 1990. It also showcased the important role that the centre now plays in that same community.

> 'It was a great day of sharing years of memories,' CRC (Community Resource Centre) co-ordinator Niomi O'Hara said. 'It was a whole community gathering from children discovering their first egg and spoon race to old hospital

staff reminiscing about working here and ex-patients with tales of having tonsils removed as children.'[74]

If walls could talk! And as committee member Sally Hays acknowledges, the link between hospital and community centre remains:

> Hospitals are such a crux for community care and community support, particularly this one. Just the very nature of how the hospital evolved, how the town evolved, and how much they are cross-linked. And also really interesting, linking with social support.
>
> The community centre has also played an important role when there has been an emergency of some kind on several occasions, with the bushfires in 2011 and with the Miles family tragedy, the council and the police have come to the community centre and said, 'We need this to be a place where people can come to get support'. It was a very important base after the Gracetown cliff collapse.[75]

So what do these old wooden buildings mean to architect Linton Hodsdon?

> We can't appreciate it unless we'd lost it. Let's hope we don't because it is a really special place. We take it a little bit for granted. It's a safe place for people and activities that don't fit anywhere else. Not coping with things? Go there. Because there's various counselling services there as well. It's a safe zone, shall we say.[76]

For playwright and former caretaker Margot Edwards, the ghosts are long gone but the continuity with the past is still important.

> Oh, I am so grateful to the committee of people who saved those buildings for the community, because a community centre is only what people are in it and what those people make it to be. So, if you've got these lovely rambling buildings that do have this echo of the past, that do hold souls, that do speak to you and you've got a layout that has this safe centre and you've got the potential for artists, children's groups, play groups and now a small gallery and a soup kitchen.
>
> All sorts of people walk in there. It's adjacent to the library. It's adjacent to town. It's safe, it's a soulful place with a lovely vibe and

those old souls that we met in those first dark nights closing up, I sense they are long gone. They happily left. They went, 'OK, our time's done,' dissolved into the walls and became a really lovely sense of place there that holds history. I don't think that they left anything but an imprint of life and death. And life goes on and the hospital became a community centre.[77]

For bookseller Keith McLeod, whose family has lived in the district since well before the old hospital was built, the continuing existence of these old wooden buildings also demonstrates continuity:

You know, people say to me, 'Oh, you must have seen so many changes! Do you even recognise the place?' I tell them the river's still at the bottom of the hill, the main street's still in the same place and, just up there, (from the bookshop I can point) is the community centre, the old hospital, the place where I was born.[78]

The Old Hospital – now the Community Centre today. Stephen Blakeney.

The Old Margaret River Hospital, 1924–2024

The following is taken from the Heritage Council of WA's assessment documentation for the Old Hospital Complex, comprising the hospital building (1924), the Doctors Surgery (1925), Margaret Cecil Rest House (1929) and the Nurses Quarters (1929) — all timber-framed buildings clad with jarrah weatherboard and roofed with corrugated iron — other ancillary buildings and bushland setting. It has cultural heritage significance for the following reasons:

- The place forms a historical precinct which facilitates an understanding of the development of the region.

- The place is representative of buildings constructed during the period of the group settlement era.

- The place reinforces the image of Margaret River and represents a link with the original character of 'a town in a forest'.

- Margaret Cecil Rest House is of historical importance for its close association with the provision of services to women who pioneered the development of the South West in the 1920s.[79]

Site 3314. Listed on WA Register of Heritage Places in 1996

NOTES

Chapter One: Wooditjup Bilya–Margaret River

1. Undalup Association, no date, https://www.undalup.com/home, viewed 5 March 2023.
2. Iszaac Webb in interview with Bill Bunbury, 6 June 2019.
3. George Webb in interview with Ramona Johnson, November 1989, Busselton Oral History Group (SLWA OH 2522).
4. Nature Conservation Margaret River Region and Margaret River Collaborative Management Group, Wooditjup Bilya Protection Strategy, 2019, https://natureconservation.org.au/wp-content/uploads/2020/02/Wooditjup-Bilya-Protection-Strategy-2019-v5-3.pdf, viewed 26 February 2023.
5. Marion Aveling in interview with Bill Bunbury, *Talking History*, ABC Radio National, 1992.
6. J. Matthews, 'The naming of Margaret River', in G. Jennings (ed.), *Margaret River Stories 1913–2013*, Margaret River and Districts Historical Society, Margaret River, 2013, pp. 11–13.
7. ibid.
8. G. Lilleyman, *Purpose Built: The Making of Caves Road*, Gillian Lilleyman, Claremont, WA, 2022, pp. 49–51.
9. ibid.
10. G. Lilleyman (ed and annoted.), *Pioneer Daughter: The Diary of Frances Louisa (Fanny) Brockman (nee Bussell)*, Gillan Lilleyman, Claremont, WA, 2018, p. 9.
11. I.D. Heppingstone, 'The story of Alfred and Ellen Bussell: pioneers of the Margaret River', *Early Days, Journal of the Royal WA Historical Society*, vol. 6, part 3, pp. 33–45.
12. G. Cresswell, *The Light of Leeuwin*, Augusta-Margaret River Shire History Group, Margaret River, 1990, p. 71.
13. G. Lilleyman, *A Garden on the Margaret: The Path to Old Bridge House*, Gillian Lilleyman, Claremont, WA, 2011, p. 17.
14. Heppingstone, *Early Days*.

NOTES

15 Greg Bussell, in interview with Bill Bunbury, 22 November 1922.
16 Iszaac Webb, in interview with Bill Bunbury, 29 April 2023.
17 F. Terry, *They Came to the Margaret*, South West Publishing and Printing Company, Margaret River, 1978, p. 57.
18 ibid., p. 40.
19 Lilleyman, *Pioneer Daughter*, p. 30.
20 Terry, *They Came to the Margaret*, p. 174.
21 I. Webb interviews, 2019 and 2023.
22 V.G. Fall, *Giants in the South: A History of Western Australia's Land of the Leeuwin*, SLWA, Print material: 994.12 SOU, 1974, p. 23.
23 I. Webb, interview, 2019.
24 I. Webb, interview, 2023.
25 G. Bolton, *Spoils and Spoilers: A History of Australians Shaping their Environment, 1788–1980*, George Allen & Unwin, Sydney, pp. 3–4.
26 Terry, *They Came to the Margaret*, p. 173.
27 Robert Breeden, in interview with Margaret Tickle, May 2010, Busselton Oral History Group (Inc,), SLWA, OH. 4170.
28 The *West Australian*, Saturday 9 April, 1938, p. 5.
29 Deborah Buller-Murphy papers, 'South west Aboriginal language or dialect', SLWA, ACC 1648AD/5C <https://purl.slwa.wa.gov.au/slwa_b1694477_189>; 'Notebook volume 1, concerning the South-West Aborigines and their dialect', SLWA, ACC 1648AD/5A <http://purl.slwa.wa.gov.au/slwa_b1694477_186>.
30 I. Webb, interview, 2023.
31 G. Webb interview, 1989, SLWA, OH 2522.
32 ibid.
33 G .Bussell, interview, 2022.
34 Cresswell, *The Light of Leeuwin*, p. 72.
35 I. Webb, interview, 2019.
36 Maurice Coleman Davies, Australian Dictionary of Biography, Viewed online 2 May 2023. https://adb.anu.edu.au/biography/davies-maurice-coleman-295.
37 Lilleyman, *Pioneer Daughter*, p. 96.
38 Quoted in Terry, *They Came to the Margaret*, p. 174.
39 Terry, *They Came to the Margaret*, p. 175.
40 I. Webb interview, 2019.
41 Viewed online 7 April 2023, https://www.monumentaustralia.org.au/themes/people/indigenous/display/60221-samuel-isaacs
42 Terry, *They Came to the Margaret*, p. 39.
43 Keith McLeod, personal communication to the authors, 7 June 2023.
44 B.F Hamling, Maurice Coleman Davies, *Early Days, Journal of the Royal WA Historical Society*, vol. 6, 1969, pp,38-56.
45 *Norseman Times*, 6 October 1908, p. 3.
46 *South-Western News*, 30 July 1909, p. 3.
47 ibid.

NOTES

48 *South-Western News* 13 August 1909, p. 3.
49 *South-Western News*, 4 October 1912, p. 3.
50 Cresswell, *The Light of Leeuwin*, p. 117.
51 Roger Underwood, 'Memories of the 1961 bushfires', in *Landscape*, vol. 26, no. 3, Autumn 2011, Department of Conservation and the Environment, p. 27.
52 Lilleyman, *A Garden on the Margaret*, pp. 51 and 58.
53 Lilleyman, *Purpose Built* p. 24.
54 Cresswell, *The Light of Leeuwin*, p. 145.
55 Lilleyman, *A Garden on the Margaret*, p. 25.
56 ibid., p. 37.
57 ibid., p. 39.
58 ibid.
59 ibid., p. 40.
60 Lilleyman, *Purpose Built*, p. 11.
61 Advertisement in the *West Australian*, 20 February 1893. Vasse was the still the postal address for Margaret River settlers.
62 Lilleyman, *Purpose Built*, p. 14.
63 ibid., p. 13.
64 ibid.
65 Terry, *They Came to the Margaret*, p. 185.
66 Obituaries Australia, *Alfred John (Jack) Bussell (1865–1940)*, National Centre of Biography, Australian National University, <https://oa.anu.edu.au/obituary/bussell-alfred-john-jack-13742/text24549>, viewed 25 October 2023.
67 Lilleyman, *Purpose Built*, p. 13.
68 *Northam Advertiser*, 7 March 1900, p. 4.
69 *WA Record,* Perth 15 February 1902, p. 13.
70 Heritage Council, Convict Hospital site, place no. 05322, 2017, <http://inherit.stateheritage.wa.gov.au/Public/Inventory/Details/9d5b87df-b78a-4ad0-8888-2dcb36cbbe77> viewed 22 January 2022.
71 Lilleyman, *A Garden on the Margaret,* p. 51.
72 ibid., pp. 56–58.
73 John Alferink, personal communication, 20 January 2022.
74 *South-Western News,* December 25, 1908, p. 3.
75 *South-Western News*, 16 August 1918.
76 *South-Western News*, 14 November 1913.
77 *South-Western News*, 16 August, 1918.
78 *South-Western News*, 15 October 1920, p. 3.
79 A. Green, C. Given and Stephen Carrick Architects, *Shire of Augusta-Margaret River Heritage Inventory*, 2012, p. 28.
80 M.L. Wise, *A Research Source on Margaret River Town, 1894–1984*, Book One, Margaret River Library, 994.12 WIS, pp. 1–3.
81 *South-Western News*, 14 February 1913, p. 3.
82 Green et al., Shire of Augusta-Margaret River Heritage Inventory, p. 28.

83 *South-Western News*, 18 August 1916, p. 3.
84 I. Webb, interview, 2023.
85 Anna Haebich, in interview with Bill Bunbury, *Talking History*, 86, Australian Broadcasting Corporation, 1993.
86 Bill and Jenny Bunbury, *Many Maps: Charting Two Cultures: Australians and Europeans in Western Australia*, UWA Publishing, Perth, 2020, p. 209.
87 M. Allbrook, *Henry Prinsep's Empire: Framing a Distant Colony*, ANU Press, Canberra, 2014 p. 243.
88 *Aborigines Act (WA) 1897*, long title.
89 *Aborigines Act (WA) 1905*, s. 3.
90 ibid.
91 H.C. Prinsep to Daisy Bates, Daisy Bates papers, folio 7/473-5, SLWA, Acc. 6193/A, quoted in M. Allbrook, *Henry Prinsep's Empire: Framing a Distant Colony*, ANU Press, Canberra, 2014, p. 244.
92 L. Tilbrook, *Nyungar Tradition, Glimpses of Aborigines of South-western Australia, 1929–1914*, University of Western Australian Press, Perth, 1983, p. 5.
93 Jack Davis, in interview with Bill Bunbury, ABC Radio National, *Out of Sight, Out of Mind*, 1986.
94 I. Webb, interview, 2023.
95 Thomas William Doyle in interview with Michael Adams, December 1977 to May 1980, State Library of WA, OH 297.
96 I. Webb, interview, 2019.
97 Doyle, interview, 1977-1980, OH 297.
98 Information on the Isaacs family, historical information compiled by Mae Wise held at the Augusta Margaret River Library, folder no. 16.
99 A. Stewart, *This Green Corner*, Battye Library, MN 1646, Papers of Athol Ferguson Stewart, SLWA, Acc. 5068A, pp. 254–5.
100 Deborah Buller-Murphy, *'An attempt to eat the moon: and other stories recounted from the Aborigines'*, Georgian House, Melbourne, 1958.

Chapter Two: Endeavor Expedite!
1 1911 Commonwealth of Australia Census data (April 1921) for the Augusta Road Board (which covered what is now the Shire of Augusta-Margaret River). Wikipedia, *Shire of Augusta-Margaret River*, 2023, <https://en.wikipedia.org/wiki/Shire_of_Augusta%E2%80%93Margaret_River>, viewed 25 October 2023.
2 T. Rowse, 'Notes on the history of the Aboriginal population of Australia', in A. Dirk Moses, *Genocide and Settler Society: Frontier Violence and Stolen Indigenous Children in Australian History*, Berghahn Books, New York, 2004, p. 315.
3 Letter to the Premier, Sir James Mitchell, from Secretary of the Margaret River Progress Association, 14 September 1922, SROWA series 268, cons. 1003, 1922/4509.

NOTES

4 B. Bunbury, *Reading Labels on Jam Tins*, Fremantle Arts Centre Press, Fremantle, 1991, p. 76.
5 G. Bolton, in interview with Bill Bunbury, *They said you'd own your own farm*, ABC Radio, 1983.
6 ibid.
7 G. Jennings (ed) *Margaret River Stories*, 1913–2013 Margaret River and Districts Historical Society, Margaret River , 2013, p. 85.
8 ibid.
9 Thomas William (Tom) Doyle, in interview with Michael Adams, December 1977–May 1980, SLWA, OH 297.
10 Thomas Cleave in interview with Jean Teasdale 1976, SLWA, OH 102, transcript pp. 110–111.
11 Agda Wyatt, *My Recollections of Early CWA Days at Margaret River*, Margaret River CWA, 1931–56, Margaret River and Districts Historical Society, 1986, p. 3.
12 Bill Bunbury, 'They said you'd own your own farm', in *Reading Labels on Jam Tins*, Fremantle Arts Centre Press, South Fremantle, 1993, p. 4.
13 G. Cresswell, *The Light of Leeuwin*, Augusta-Margaret River History Group, Margaret River, 1990, pp. 207–214.
14 L.C. Burton, *Barefoot in the Creek: A Group Settlement Childhood in Margaret River*, University of Western Australia Press, Nedlands, 1997, p. 4.
15 K. Cain (ed.), *Rich Beyond Measure: A Collection of Family Memories of Edward and Phyllis Blain (nee Hosking) as Remembered by their Children*, unpublished, no date (no page numbers).
16 'Margaret River District Progress Association', *South-Western News*, 9 November 1923, p. 5.
17 Stan Dilkes, in interview with Bill Bunbury, *Margaret River: A Changing Landscape*, ABC Radio National, 1996.
18 P.E.M. Blond, *A Tribute to the Group Settlers*, University of Western Australia Press, Nedlands, 1987, p. 6.
19 ibid., p. 19.
20 Thomas William Doyle in interview with Michael Adams, OH 297 (verbatim transcript pp. 119–120).
21 MR Progress Assn to Premier, Sir James Mitchell, 4 September 1922, SROWA AU WA series 5268, cons. 1003, 1922/4509.
22 Memorandum from Principal Medical Officer to Under Secretary for Health, 22 November 1922, SROWA AU WA 5268, cons. 1003, 1922/4509.
23 Colonial Secretary to Margaret River Progress Association, 1 December 1922, SROWA series 5268, cons. 1003, 1922/4509.
24 'Margaret River Progress Association', *South-Western News,* Friday 15 December 1922, p. 4.
25 ibid.
26 Burton, *Barefoot in the Creek*, p. 84.

NOTES

27 H. Crofts, Secretary, Margaret River Progress Association, to Colonial Secretary, 14 December 1922, SROWA series 268, cons. 1003, 1922/4509.
28 H.C. Trethowan, Colonial Secretary, to the secretary Margaret River Progress Association, 21 December 1922, SROWA series 268, cons. 1003, 1922/4509.
29 L. Hugall, Secretary, Margaret River and Districts Progress Association to Colonial Secretary, Perth, 5 April 1923, SROWA series 268, cons. 1003, 1922/4509.
30 Dr Everitt Atkinson, Principal Medical Officer, to Under Secretary, 11 April 1923, SROWA series 268, cons. 1003, 1922/4509.
31 Principal Medical Officer to Secretary, Margaret River and Districts Progress Association, 19 April 1923, SROWA series 268, cons. 1003, 1922/4509.
32 R.S. Sampson, Colonial Secretary, to W.G. Pickering, MLA, 15 May 1923, SROWA series 268, cons. 1003, 1922/4509.
33 ibid.
34 'Margaret River District Progress Association', *South-Western News*, 10 August 1923, p. 4.
35 L. Hugall, Secretary, Margaret and Districts Progress Association to the Hon Colonial Secretary, SROWA series 268, cons. 1003, 1922/4509.
36 'Departure of Dr and Mrs Rigby', *Collie Mail*, 8 October 1920; 'Medical officer and Miners' Union: interview with Dr Rigby', *Collie Mail*, 18 October 1919, p. 4.
37 Jennings, *Margaret River Stories*, p. 122.
38 *Southern Times*, Bunbury, 8 January 1916, p. 4.
39 'Big cricket', *South-Western News*, 23 March 1928, p. 6.
40 At that time, this section of Wallcliffe Road was known as Mitchell Street
41 Don McKenzie, in interview with Mae Wise, papers held by the Augusta Margaret River Library, 1985.
42 Doyle, interview, p. 257.
43 Myra Willmott, in interview with Mae Wise, Margaret River and Districts Historical Society, 1985.
44 Enid Garstone, in interview with Mae Wise, Margaret River and Districts Historical Society, 1983.
45 Doyle, interview, p. 255.
46 V. Everett, *Light in the Distance*, Valerie Everett, Mount Hawthorn, 2006, pp. 201–202.
47 Doyle, interview, p. 145.
48 'Margaret River District Progress Association', *South-Western News*, 12 October 1923, p. 6.
49 Dr Everitt Atkinson, Principal Medical Officer to Hon Minister for Public Health, SROWA series 268, cons. 1003, 1922/4509.
50 Dr Atkinson to Dr Rigby, 8 November 1923, SROWA series 268, cons. 1003, 1922/4509.
51 Dr Rigby, handwritten telegram to Atkinson, Principal Medical Officer, Perth, 9 November 1923, SROWA series 268, cons. 1003, 1922/4509.

NOTES

52 Surveyor-General to Under Secretary for Lands, 4 September 1923, SROWA cons. 541, 1923/0792; Margaret River Progress Association. Reserve for Hospital Site, SROWA series 268, cons. 541, 1923/0792.
53 Memorandum from the Surveyor General to Under Secretary for Lands, 29 November 2023, SROWA series 268, cons. 541, 1923/0792.
54 Copy of Executive Council Minute, 29 May 1923, SROWA series 268, cons. 541, 1923/0792.
55 R.S. Sampson, Colonial Secretary to Hon Minister for Health, 21 November 1923, SROWA series 268, cons. 1003, 1922/4509.
56 Memorandum, (F.J. Huelin) Secretary to Acting Under Secretary, Medical, 26 November 1923, SROWA series 268, cons. 1003, 1922/4509.
57 *South-Western News*, Friday 21 December 1923, p. 5.
58 Memorandum: Author F.J. Huelin, Secretary, Medical, 4 January 1924, SROWA series 268, cons. 1003, 1922/4509.
59 ibid.
60 ibid.
61 Secretary, Medical, to Mr L. Hugall, Secretary, Medical Scheme Committee, Margaret River, 16 January 1924, SROWA series 268, cons. 1003, 1922/4509.
62 L. Hugall to F.J. Huelin, Secretary Medical, 22 January 1923, SROWA series 268, cons. 1003, 1922/4509. Emphasis added.
63 Secretary, Medical to Principal Architect, Dept of Works and Labour, 21 May 1929, series 268, cons. 1003, 1924/1499.
64 Judy Wake in interview with Bill Bunbury, 12 January 2022.
65 M.A. Ward, Matron, Govt Hospital, Margaret River to Mr (Secretary) Huelin, 24 May 1924, SROWA series 268, cons. 1003, 1924/1499.
66 Hospital Admissions Register 1924 – onwards, located at new Margaret River Hospital.
67 ibid.
68 W. Angwin, Minister for Lands, to Hon W. Munsie, 14 June 1924, SROWA series 28, cons. 1003, 1924/1499.
69 Matron Ward to F.J. Huelin, 13 June 1924, SROWA series 28, cons. 1003, 1924/1499.
70 Hospital Admissions Register 1924 – onwards.
71 Dr Rigby to Principal Medical Officer, 14 July 1924, SROWA series 28, cons. 1003, 1924/1499.
72 Dr Rigby to Principal Medical officer, 16 August 1924, SROWA series 28, cons. 1003, 1924/1499.
73 Secretary to Dr Rigby, 18 August 1924, SROWA series 28, cons. 1003, 1924/1499.
74 David Black, *Collier, Philip, 1873–1948*, Australian Dictionary of Biography, 1981, <https://adb.anu.edu.au/biography/collier-philip-5732>, viewed 10 February 2022.
75 Extract from letter sent by Dr Rigby to the Premier, Hon Philip Collier and dated 18 August 1923, SROWA series 28, cons. 1003, 1924/1499.

NOTES

76 Dr Rigby to Principal Medical Officer, 25 August 1924, SROWA series 28, cons. 1003, 1924/1499.
77 F.J. Huelin, Secretary Medical to Under Secretary (Colonial Secretary's office), 6 September 1924, SROWA series 28, cons. 1003, 1924/1499.
78 F.J. Huelin, Secretary Medical, to Dr Rigby, 18 September 1924, SROWA series 28, cons. 1003, 1924/1499.
79 F.J. Huelin, Secretary Medical, to Under Secretary, 13 December 1924, SROWA series 28, cons. 1003, 1924/1499.
80 F.J. Huelin, Secretary, Medical, file note, 1 March 1924, SROWA cons. 1003, 1922/4509.

Chapter Three: A Primitive Wooden Structure

1 Matron Ward, Margaret River District Hospital to (F.J. Huelin), Secretary Medical, Perth, 20 October 1924. SROWA series 268, cons. 1003, 1924/1499.
2 Myra Willmott in interview with Mae Wise, 1985. Papers held by the Margaret River and Districts Historical Society.
3 Ted Ashton, in interview with Danielle Haigh, *Augusta-Margaret River Mail*, 29 August 1990.
4 Willmott, interview, 1985.
5 Ashton, interview, 1990.
6 Willmott, interview, 1985.
7 ibid.
8 F.J. Huelin, Secretary, Medical to Under Secretary, 13 December 1924, SROWA series 268, cons. 1003, 1924/1499.
9 Under Secretary for Works and Labour to Under Secretary, Colonial Secretary's Department, 30 January 1925, SROWA series 268, cons. 1003, 1924/1499.
10 Matron Ward to Secretary Medical, 15 May 1925, and following correspondence, SROWA series 268, cons. 1003, 1924/1499.
11 Secretary Medical to Matron, Government Hospital Margaret River, 30 July 1925, SROWA series 268, cons. 1003, 1924/1499.
12 *South-Western News*, 18 July 1924, p. 5.
13 *Group Settlement Chronicle and Margaret-Augusta Mail*, 5 August 1924, p. 3.
14 *South-Western News*, 24 October 1924, p. 4.
15 J.P. Gabbedy, *Group Settlement Part 1: Its Origins, Politics and Administration*, University of Western Australia Press, Nedlands, 1988, p. 211.
16 K. Cain (ed.), *Rich Beyond Measure: A Collection of Family Memories of Edward and Phyllis Blain (nee Hosking) as Remembered by their Children*, unpublished, no date.
17 Gabbedy, *Group Settlement Part 1*, p. 211.
18 G. Cresswell, *The Light of Leeuwin*, Augusta-Margaret River Shire History Group, Margaret River, 1990, p. 201, quoting interview with Mrs Allie Clark.
19 Gabbedy, *Group Settlement Part 1*, p. 213.
20 ibid.

NOTES

21 ibid., p. 214.
22 John Tonkin, personal communication to Bill Bunbury, 1983.
23 Gabbedy, *Group Settlement Part 1*, p. 218.
24 *South-Western News*, 11 June 1909, p. 2
25 P.E.M. Blond, *A Tribute to the Group Settlers*, University of Western Australia Press, Nedlands, 1987, p. 19.
26 Willmott, interview, 1985.
27 ibid.
28 *Group Settlement Chronicle and Margaret-Augusta Mail*, 11 November 1924, p. 3.
29 ibid.
30 Stan Dilkes in interview with Bill Bunbury for *Margaret River: A Changing Landscape*, ABC Radio National, *Hindsight*, 1996.
31 Jean Bussell in interview with Mae Wise, 1985. Papers held by the Margaret River and Districts Historical Society.
32 Keith McLeod, personal communication to the authors, 7 June 2023.
33 Thomas William Doyle in interview with Michael Adams, December 1977–May 1980, State Library of WA, OH 297.
34 ibid.
35 Cresswell, *The Light of Leeuwin*, p. 220.
36 Margaret River Hospital Admissions Register 1924-onwards, located at new Margaret River Hospital.
37 ibid.
38 Dr W.H. Rigby to Premier Collier, 19 August 1924, SROWA series 268, cons. 1003, 1924/1409.
39 G. Jennings (ed.), *Margaret River Stories 1913–2013*, Margaret River and Districts Historical Society, Margaret River, 2013, p. 198.
40 Thelma Burnett, personal communication to the authors, 7 July 2023.
41 Doyle, interview, 1977–1980, OH 297.
42 Shire of Augusta-Margaret River, *Local History*, <https://www.amrshire.wa.gov.au/region/local-history/>, viewed 11 January 2022. See also *Augusta-Margaret River Mail*, '100 years of Margaret River: timeline', <https://www.margaretrivermail.com.au/story/1286597/100-years-of-margaret-river-timeline/>, viewed 5 October 2023.
43 Notes from interview with Enid Garstone, probably by Mae Wise, 1983. Papers held by the Margaret River and Districts Historical Society.
44 *Western Mail*, 24 June 1926, p. 15.
45 *South-Western Times*, 29 November 1927, p. 3.
46 Garstone, interview, 1983.
47 Elwyn Franklin in interview with Bill Bunbury, 31 October 2022.
48 Franklin, interview, 2022.
49 Garstone, interview, 1983.
50 J.D. Payne, *Over the Bridge: An Authentic Account of Group Settlement*, J.D. Payne, Margaret River, 1987, p. 31.

NOTES

51 ibid., pp. 27–28.
52 ibid., p. 28.
53 Letter from A.W. Wilson, Chairman Karridale Medical Association, to Minister for Public Health, 26 November 1923, SROWA series 268, cons. 1003, 1923/3018.
54 Letter from Secretary (Medical) to Mr A.W. Wilson, Chairman, Karridale Medical Association, 29 December 1923, SROWA series 268, cons. 1003, 1923/3018.
55 *Daily News,* 27 December 1923, p. 1.
56 *Group Settlement Chronicle and Margaret-Augusta Mail,* 12 February 1924, p. 3.
57 File Note 29 December 1923, SROWA series 268, cons. 1003, 1923/3018.
58 *Group Settlement Chronicle and Margaret-Augusta Mail,* 12 February 1924, p.3.
59 Letter from F.J. Huelin, Secretary, to Health to Revd. Foley-Whaling, 4 January 1924, SROWA series 268, cons. 1003, 1923/3018.
60 File note, 1 March 1924, Karridale Hospital, SROWA series 268, cons. 1003, 1923/3018.
61 Doyle, interview, 1977–1980, SLWA OH 297.
62 Willmott, interview, 1985.
63 *Sunday Times,* Perth, 23 August 1925, p. 1.
64 B. Biddulph, *Riding the Bumps: Football in Augusta Margaret River, 1904–1965,* B. & J. Biddulph, 2013, p. 6.
65 Cresswell, *The Light of Leeuwin,* p. 308; B. Biddulph, *Riding the Bumps,* p. 71.
66 Herbert (Smiler) Gale, in interview with Bill Bunbury, 9 July 2020.
67 *South-Western News,* 2 September 1932.
68 Under Secretary (Health) to Under Secretary for Works and Labour, 7 June 1927, SROWA series 268, cons. 1003, 541, 1924/1499.
69 Acting Matron Rae to Secretary, Medical, Perth, 6 December 1927, SROWA series 268, cons. 1003, 541, 1924/1499.
70 Secretary Medical. to Acting Matron, Government Hospital, Margaret River 12 December 1927, SROWA series 268, cons. 1003, 541, 1924/1499.
71 Margaret River Hospital Admissions Register.
72 Garstone, interview, 1983.
73 Letter from Kittie Bussell to Filomena Terry, 21 July 1927, Mae Wise papers, folder no. 2 held at Augusta Margaret River Library.
74 Acting Matron, Government Hospital, Margaret River to the Secretary, Medical, 21 February 1928, SROWA series 268, cons. 1003, 541, 1924/1499.
75 Huelin, Secretary Medical to Principal Architect, 24 February 1928, SROWA series 268, cons. 1003, 541, 1924/1499.
76 Matron McWhinney to Huelin, 13 August 1926, SROWA series 268, cons. 1003, 1924/1499.
77 ibid.
78 ibid.
79 Secretary, Medical, to Secretary Bush Nursing Trust, 22 April 1927, SROWA series 268, cons. 1003, 1499/1924.

NOTES

80 Under Secretary to Hon Minister (for Health), 1 September 1927, SROWA series 268, cons. 1003, 1499/1924.
81 Commonwealth Parliamentary Association, *History of the Commonwealth Parliamentary Conference (CPC)*, <https://www.cpahq.org/media/hownq4eb/cpa-history-cpc-annual-conference-updated-april-2019.pdf>, viewed 5 October 2023.
82 *Weekly Times* (Melbourne), 16 October 1926, p. 12.
83 *The Mercury* (Hobart), 22 November 1926, p. 8.
84 *Group Settlement Chronicle and Margaret-Augusta Mail*, 26 October 1926, p. 3.
85 *The Daily Mail* (Brisbane), 7 October 1926, p.14.
86 ibid.
87 *Group Settlement Chronicle and Margaret-Augusta Mail*, 26 October 1926, p. 3.
88 S. Minter, *The Well-connected Gardener: A Biography of Alicia Amherst, Founder of Garden History*, Book Guild, Brighton, UK, 2010, pp. 91–92, quoting Alicia Amherst, (Lady Cecil) *Wild Flowers of the Great Dominions of the British Empire*, 1935.
89 Biographical Register of members of the Parliament of Western Australia, *Mr William Charles Angwin*, <https://www.parliament.wa.gov.au/parliament/library/MPHistoricalData.nsf/(Lookup)/1B00F353F145E336482577E50028A504?OpenDocument> viewed 5 October 2023.
90 Secretary Huelin to Hon. Minister (for Health), 4 June 1927, SROWA series 268, cons. 1003, File 1499/1924.
91 *The Daily News* (Perth), 22 November 1927, p. 11.
92 Memorandum from Under Secretary Public Works and Labour to Under Secretary, Chief Secretary's Department, 15 December 1928, SROWA series 268, cons. 1003, File 1499/1924.
93 The marriage of the Hon. Margaret Cecil and Captain Herbert Lane took place on 7 February 1929. https://www.thepeerage.com/p3715.htm, Viewed online 31 October 2023.
94 Letter from Mrs Margaret Lane to Mr G.W. Barnard, MLC, 1 April 1929, Margaret Cecil Rest House Association Trustees Minute Book, Margaret Cecil Cabinet Showcase (MCCS), new Margaret River Hospital.
95 Book listing the names of all the Margarets contributing to the building of the Margaret Cecil Rest House, MCCS.
96 Receipt December 1929, in Margaret Cecil Rest House Association Trustees Minute Book.
97 *South-Western News*, 31 May 1929, p. 2.
98 ibid.
99 *Western Mail* (Perth), 6 June 1929, p. 62.
100 *South-Western News*, 31 May 1929, p. 2. The *South-Western News* of 7 June 1929, p. 2, carried a letter of thanks from the Margaret Cecil Rest House Committee.
101 Secretary – File Note, Memorandum Margaret River Hospital – Premises 1 July 1929, SROWA series 268, cons. 1003, 1929/1163.

NOTES

102 Secretary, Medical, to Principal Architect, Department of Works and Labour, 7 September 1929, SROWA series 268, cons. 1003, 1929/1163.
103 Principal Architect, Department of Works and Labour to Secretary Medical, 27 September 1929, SROWA series 268, cons. 1003, 1929/1163.
104 F.J. Huelin for Under Secretary to the Under Secretary for Works and Labour, 1 October 1929, SROWA series 268, cons. 1003, 1929/1163.

Chapter Four: Very Little Money

1   Jean Bussell in interview with Mae Wise, *Stories of the Margaret River Hospital*, Margaret River and Districts Historical Society, 1985.
2   Greg Bussell, in interview with Bill Bunbury, 22 November 2022.
3   J. Bussell, interview, 1985.
4   ibid.
5   Under Secretary (Huelin) to Matron Margaret River District Hospital, 9 December 1932, SROWA series 268, cons. 1003, 1929/1163.
6   Thomas William Doyle, in interview with Michael Adams, December 1977 to May 1980, SLWA, J.S. Battye Oral History Program, OH 297.
7   Biographical Register of Members of the Parliament of Western Australia, *William Joseph Mann*, <https://www.parliament.wa.gov.au/parliament/library/MPHistoricalData.nsf/(Lookup)/8534F2ACAD66BEB8482577E50028A6DC?OpenDocument> viewed 5 October 2023.
8   W.J. Mann inaugural speech to the Legislative Council of the WA Parliament, Hansard, 26 August 1926, p. 524.
9   L.G. Burton, *Barefoot in the Creek: A Group Settlement Childhood in Margaret River*, University of Western Australia Press, Nedlands, 1997, p. 109.
10 ibid., pp. 109–10.
11 ibid., pp. 120–21.
12 ibid. p. 112.
13 J.D. Payne, *Over the Bridge: An Authentic Account of Group Settlement*, J.D. Payne, Margaret River, 1987, p. 161.
14 ibid., p. 158.
15 ibid., p. 172.
16 *South-Western News*, 12 August 1932, p. 3.
17 *South-Western News*, 17 December 1942, p. 2.
18 Augusta Margaret River Road Board Minute Books 2 July 1932, in People folder compiled by Mae Wise, Augusta Margaret River library.
19 Mae Wise, People folder (Wallcliffe), Augusta Margaret River library.
20 Dr Taylor Thomas to Under Secretary Department of Public Health, 15 June 1932, SROWA series 268, cons. 1003, 1929/1163.
21 Under Secretary to Dr Taylor Thomas, 21 June 1932, SROWA series 268, cons. 1003, 1929/1163.

NOTES

22 Hospital Operations Register 1924 – onwards, located at new Margaret River Hospital.
23 Under Secretary, Memorandum, 28 June 1932, SROWA series 268, cons. 1003, 1929/1163.
24 Dr Taylor Thomas to Under Secretary for Public Health, 12 July 1932, SROWA series 268, cons. 1003, 1929/1163.
25 Dr Taylor Thomas to Under Secretary for Public Health, Perth 1 August 1932, SROWA series 268, cons. 1003, 1929/1163. Emphasis added.
26 Under Secretary (Huelin) to Matron, Margaret River District Hospital, 9 December 1932, SROWA series 268, cons. 1003, 1929/1163.
27 Dr Taylor Thomas to Under Secretary Huelin, 19 February 1933, SROWA series 268, cons. 1003, 1929/1163.
28 Under Secretary to Dr Taylor Thomas, 20 June 1933, SROWA series 268, cons. 1003, 1929/1163.
29 Principal Architect to Under Secretary Department of Public Health, 17 June 1933, SROWA series 268, cons. 1003, 1929/1163.
30 Under Secretary to the Matron District Hospital, Margaret River, 12 July 1933, SROWA series 268, cons. 1003, 1929/1163.
31 Constable Wyatt, Police Department, Margaret River Police Station, 21 January 1931, SROWA series 268, cons. 1003, 1929/1163.
32 Under Secretary to Matron, Government Hospital Margaret River, 20 August 1931, SROWA series 268, cons. 1003, 1929/1163.
33 Fred Collins, Forester in charge, Busselton to Mr Copping (Medical), 19 September 1931, SROWA series 268, cons. 1003, 1929/1163.
34 A.E. Ashton to Public Health Department, 14 September 1932, SROWA series 268, cons. 1003, 1929/1163.
35 Under Secretary, Public Health Department to Matron Murray, Government Hospital Karridale, 30 June 1930, SROWA series 268, cons. 1003, 1930/0791.
36 Under Secretary, Public Health Department, to Manager Agricultural Bank, 22 March 1933, SROWA series 268, cons. 1003, 1930/0791.
37 Under Secretary to Manager Agricultural Bank, 22 March 1933, SROWA series 268, cons. 1003, 1930/0791.
38 W. Vickery, Manager Agricultural Bank, to Under Secretary Department of Public Health, 18 March 1933. SROWA series 268, cons. 1003, 1930/0791.
39 *South-Western News*, 1 March 1935, p. 3.
40 Under Secretary to the Matron, District Hospital Karridale, 17 November 1936, SROWA series 268, cons. 1003, 1934/0782.
41 S. Rowe in I. Howie-Willis, *St John, Ambulances and Western Australia: A Centenary Anthology, 1892–1992*, St John Ambulance Australia, Perth, 1992, pp. 310–11.
42 *South-Western News*, 30 October 1931, p. 4.
43 *South-Western News*, 18 November 1932, p. 5.
44 *South-Western News*, 23 October 1936, p. 6.
45 *South-Western News*, 17 March 1933, p. 3.

NOTES

46 *South-Western News*, 6 September 1935, p. 4.
47 '70 years of dedicated ambulance service', *Augusta-Margaret River Mail*, 7 September 2005, p. 10.
48 *South-Western News*, 27 September 1935, p. 3.
49 *South-Western News*, 15 November 1935, p. 5.
50 *South-Western News*, 17 January 1936, p. 5.
51 *South-Western News*, 24 July 1936, p. 3.
52 *South-Western News*, 22 January 1937, p. 2.
53 *Augusta-Margaret River Mail*, 7 September 2005, p. 10.
54 Under Secretary to the Matron, District Hospital, Margaret River, 4 February 1937, SROWA series 268, cons. 1003, 1934/0782.
55 Under Secretary to the Principal Architect, 16 December 1936, SROWA series 268, cons. 1003, 1934/0782.
56 Burton, *Barefoot in the Creek*, p. 79.
57 Bert McLean in interview with Mae Wise, 'McLean William, Katherine and family' in People folder, compiled Mae Wise, Augusta Margaret River Library, no date.
58 *Manjimup and Warren Times*, 11 December 1930, p. 4.
59 *The Workers Star*, 11 March 1938, p. 5.
60 Cedar (George) Armstrong, *A story of the Armstrong Family by Cedar Snr and Jnr Armstrong*, Arthur Thomas (Cedar) and Cedar (George) Armstrong, Margaret River and Districts Historical Society, no date.
61 M. Bignell, *Little Grey Sparrows of the Anglican Diocese of Bunbury, Western Australia*, University of Western Australia Press, Nedlands, 1992, p. 12.
62 J. Bartlett, *Journey: A History of the Anglican Diocese of Bunbury, 1904–2004*, Anglican Diocese of Bunbury, 2004, p. 107.
63 ibid., p. 108.
64 Bignell, *Little Grey Sparrows*, p. 27.
65 Rev. Mother's diary notes, 1927, pp. 47–51, quoted in Bignell, *Little Grey Sparrows*, p. 28.
66 Bartlett, *Journey*, p. 118.
67 Rev. Mother Elizbeth in Confraternity of Divine Love (CDL) newsletter, St Stephen, 1930, quoted in Bignell, *Little Grey Sparrows*, p. 54.
68 Bignell, *Little Grey Sparrows*, p. 45.
69 Agda Wyatt, 'My recollections of early CWA Days at Margaret River', *Margaret River CWA, 1931–56*, Margaret River and Districts Historical Society, 1986.
70 Rev. Mother Elizabeth (written from Convent of St Elizabeth, South Bunbury) to the Minister of Public Health, February 24 1931, SROWA series 268, cons 1003, 1929/1163.
71 Rev. Mother Elizabeth Diary notes, Friday 23 January 1931, p. 9, quoted in M. Bignell, *Little Grey Sparrows*, p. 58.
72 Minister for Health to Rev. Mother Elizabeth, 27 February 1931, SROWA series 268, cons. 1003, 1929/1163.

NOTES

73 Minister for Health to Rev. Mother Elizabeth, 15 July 1932, SROWA series 268, cons. 1003, 1929/1163.
74 Ellie Metcalfe, in interview with Bill Bunbury, 14 July 2021.
75 ibid., 2021.
76 Ellie Metcalfe, memoir recorded by Lyn Moorfoot at the Margaret River Community Centre, 2014.
77 Bignell, *Little Grey Sparrows*, p. 14.
78 Unknown author (probably Father Clissold, Parish Priest at Margaret River, 1932–1939) quoted in V. Cain, *Group 85 Osmington Church*, Dynamic Print. Bunbury, n.d., p. 42.
79 ibid., p.42.
80 Bignell, *Little Grey Sparrows*, p. 106.
81 Mother Elizabeth in CDL (Confraternity of Divine Love) Newsletter, 1936, quoted in Bignell, *Little Grey Sparrows*, p. 101.
82 M.H.R. Southcombe, *To Call Our Own: Pioneering the Group Settlements*, Hesperian Press, Victoria Park, 1988, p. 45.
83 Kim McKeown, talk to Community Care, 13 September 2006, recorded by Mae Wise, folder no. 17, Augusta Margaret River Library.
84 Wyatt, 'Recollections', *Margaret River CWA 1931–1956*.
85 *South-Western News*, 17 April 1936, p. 2.
86 Keith McLeod, personal communication to the authors, 7 June 2023.
87 Tom Doyle, interview, OH 297.
88 Kim McKeown, talk to Community Care, 13 September 2006.
89 Metcalfe, interview, July 2021.
90 Bernice McLeod (formerly McKeown), 'Life and personalities of the early days of the Margaret River Hotel', *Margaret River Hotel Characters*, Margaret River and Districts Historical Society, 1984.
91 Don McKenzie, in interview with Mae Wise, People folder, Augusta Margaret River Library.
92 *Margaret River Hotel Characters*, Bernice McLeod (nee McKeown), Margaret River and Districts Historical Society, 1984.
93 Kim McKeown, talk to Community Care, 2006.
94 S. Supski, *A Proper Foundation: A History of the Lotteries Commission of Western Australia*, Black Swan Press, Perth, 2009, p. 29.
95 ibid., p. 31.
96 Supski, *A Proper Foundation*, p. 31.
97 May Wilson, Matron District Hospital Margaret River to Under Secretary Medical, Perth, 15 May 1934, SROWA. series 268, cons. 1003, 1933/0946. Emphasis added.
98 Acting Under Secretary to the Matron, District Hospital, Margaret River, 18 May 1934, SROWA series 268, cons. 1003, 1933/0946.

NOTES

99 Memorandum from the Principal Architect, Department of Works and Labour, to Under Secretary Department of Public Health, 5 March 1935, SROWA series 268, cons. 1003, 1933/0946.
100 *South-Western News*, 2 August 1935, p. 2.
101 Principal Architect, Department of Works and Labour, to Under Secretary, Department of Public Health, 5 March 1935, SROWA series 268, cons. 1003, 1933/0946.
102 Dr Mandelstam to Under Secretary, Medical, Perth, 6 September 1935, SROWA series 268, cons. 1003, 1933/0946.
103 Under Secretary to Dr Mandelstam, 2 August 1935, SROWA series 268, cons. 1003, 1933/0946.
104 Enid Garstone in *Margaret River CWA, 1931–56*, Margaret River and Districts Historical Society, January 1986.
105 *Daily News* (Perth), 1 October 1935, p. 5.
106 Hospital Admissions Register 1924 – onwards, located at new Margaret River Hospital.
107 *South-Western News*, 11 October 1935, p. 3.
108 *South-Western News*, 31 July 1936, p. 3.
109 Herbert (Smiler) Gale, in interview with Bill Bunbury, 9 July 2020.
110 *South-Western News*, 31 July 1936, p. 3.
111 Hospital Admissions Register 1924 – onwards.
112 Matron, Margaret River District Hospital, to Under Secretary (Medical), 1 August 1935, SROWA series 268, cons. 1003, 1933/0946.
113 *South-Western News*, 4 February 1938, p. 5.
114 Augusta-Margaret River Road Board minutes, 4 July 1936.
115 Dr Mandelstam, District Medical Officer, to the Under Secretary Medical, 7 May 1935, SROWA series 268, cons. 1003, 1933/0946.
116 Secretary Lotteries Commission to F.J. Huelin, Under Secretary, Department of Public Health, Murray St, Perth, 16 August 1935, SROWA series 268, cons. 1003, 1933/0946.
117 Secretary Medical to Under Secretary for Lands, 24 August 1938, SROWA series 268, cons. 1003, 1933/0946.
118 Margaret River Hospital Admissions Register 1924 – onwards.
119 ibid.
120 ibid.
121 *Margaret River CWA, 1931–56*.
122 ibid.
123 Wyatt, 'Recollections', *Margaret River CWA, 1931–56*.
124 Mrs K.F.M. Bussell to Hon. Minister for Health, 31 July 1934, SROWA series 268, cons. 1003, 1933/0946.
125 Norman Terry, Secretary, Augusta-Margaret River Road Board to Hon. Minister for Health, 10 July 1934, SROWA series 268, cons. 1003, 1933/0946.

126 May Wilson, Matron, to Under Secretary (Medical), 31 July 1934, SROWA series 268, cons. 1003, 1933/0946.
127 Under Secretary to the Matron, District Hospital, Margaret River, 28 August 1934, SROWA series 268, cons. 1003, 1933/0946; Under Secretary to Mrs K.F.M. Bussell, 28 August 1934, SROWA series 268, cons. 1003, 1933/0946.
128 Mrs K.F.M. Bussell, to Secretary Medical, 23 May 1935 SROWA series 268, cons. 1003, 1933/0946.
129 Acting Under Secretary to Mrs K.F.M. Bussell, Secretary CWA Margaret River, 29 May 1935, SROWA series 268, cons. 1003, 1933/0946.
130 *South-Western News*, 20 May 1938, p. 6.
131 *South-Western News*, 17 June 1938, p. 2.
132 *South-Western News*, 15 January 1937, p. 1.
133 ibid.
134 Robert Saunders, in interview with Bill Bunbury, 18 July 2022.
135 Doctors in Margaret River 1925 to 1986, Mae Wise, folder no. 18, People A-K, Augusta Margaret River Library.
136 Metcalfe, interview, 2021.
137 ibid.
138 *South-Western News*, 25 November 1938, p. 5.
139 ibid.
140 Hon. W.H.F. Willmott, MLA, to the Hon Minister for Health, 30 November 1939, SROWA series 268, cons. 1003, 1933/0946.
141 Under Secretary (Huelin) to the Hon. Minister for Health, 5 December 1939, SROWA series 268, cons. 1003, 1933/0946.
142 *South-Western News*, 16 June 1939, p. 2.
143 *South-Western News*, 21 July 1939, p.5.
144 Copy of cable from Agent General in London, Margaret Cecil Rest House Association Minute books located in the Margaret Cecil Cabinet Showcase (MCCS) at the Margaret River Hospital.
145 *West Australian*, 16 July 1940, p. 9.
146 ibid.
147 *South-Western News*, 19 July 1940, p. 3.
148 ibid.
149 ibid.
150 Stan Dilkes, in interview with Bill Bunbury, *Hindsight – Margaret River: A Changing Landscape*, ABC Radio National, 1996.
151 John Brennan, in interview with Bill Bunbury, *Hindsight – Margaret River: A Changing Landscape*, ABC Radio National, 1996.
152 Betty Earl, in interview with Bill Bunbury, 13 November 2020.
153 John Brennan, *The Australian Brennans of Rosa Brook,* no date, copy held by Margaret River Library (Mae Wise folders).
154 Jessie Sharp (nee Campbell), unknown interviewer, Margaret River and Districts Historical Society, recorded November 1986.

NOTES

155 Smiler Gale, interview, 9 July 2020.
156 Mrs E.J. Halton, Bramley, letter to the Education Department, 24 June 1922. MR&DHS, courtesy Greg Halton.
157 F.B. McLeod, Matron, District Hospital, Margaret River to the Under Secretary Medical, 1 December 1937, SROWA series 268, cons. 1003, 1933/0946.
158 Under Secretary to Chairman, Lotteries Commission, Perth, 14 April 1938, SROWA series 268, cons. 1003, 1933/0946.
159 Secretary, Augusta-Margaret River Road Board to the Secretary, Medical Section, Public Health Department, 8 November 1938, SROWA series 268, cons. 1003, 1933/0946.
160 District Architect to Principal Architect, Department of Public Works, 18 January 1939, SROWA series 268, cons. 1003, 1933/0946.

Chapter Five: A Proper Standard

1 *South-Western News*, 19 July 1940, p. 3.
2 *South-Western News*, 9 October 1947, p. 4.
3 Notes on the Margaret River Rest House, 8 March 1975, Margaret River and Districts Historical Society.
4 *Margaret River News*, 31 July 1941, p. 3.
5 ibid.
6 Thomas William (Tom) Doyle, *An interview with Thomas William Doyle*, conducted by Michael Adams, December 1977 to May 1980, State Library of WA, J.S. Battye Oral History Program, OH 297.
7 C. Salmaggi and A. Pallavisini, *2194 Days of War: An Illustrated Chronology of the Second World War*, Windward, W.H. Smith and Son, London, 1977, pp. 137, 141.
8 *South-Western News*, 12 February 1942, p. 3.
9 *South-Western News*, 13 April 1934, p. 1.
10 Mae Wise Papers, folder no. 16, Augusta Margaret River Library.
11 Robert (Bob) Dunbar, in interview with Bill Bunbury, 13 May 2020.
12 ibid.
13 ibid.
14 Matron Dunbar to Under Secretary, Medical, 21 January 1940, SROWA series 268, cons. 1003, 1940/0334.
15 File memorandum from Clerk in Charge Medical, 2 February 1940, SROWA series 268, cons. 1003, 1940/0334.
16 Salmaggi & Pallavisini, *2194 Days of War*.
17 *South-Western News*, 12 February 1942, p. 3.
18 J. Shervington, *The Early Life and Times of Jane Shervington (nee McKeon)*, John Shervington, n.d., p. 75.
19 Bill Darnell, in interview with Vendla Tinley, 1996–97, Margaret River and Districts Historical Society.
20 T. Doyle, interview, OH 297.

NOTES

21 Cedar (George) Armstrong, in interview with Mae Wise, 1985, Margaret River and Districts Historical Society.
22 *South-Western News*, 2 August 1945, p. 1.
23 Kevin Coate, in interview with Bill Bunbury, 22 August 2022.
24 C. Armstrong, interview.
25 Email from Terry Reidy, Margaret River RSL to Heather Anderson, RSLWA Branch, 7 February 2006. Copy provided, to the authors by Terry Reidy, 22 November 2022.
26 *South-Western News*, 25 January 1945, p. 3.
27 *South-Western News*, 18 January 1945, p. 3.
28 *South-Western News*, 13 December 1945, p. 3.
29 K. Coate, interview, 2022.
30 Senate Select Committee on Health, *Hospital Funding Cuts: The Perfect Storm. The Demolition of Federal–State Health Relations 2014–2016. Final* Report, Commonwealth of Australia, Canberra, 2016, Chapter 2, <https://www.aph.gov.au/Parliamentary_Business/Committees/Senate/Health/Health/Final%20Report/c02> viewed 6 October 2023.
31 ibid.
32 Under Secretary to Acting Matron Wright, Margaret River Hospital, 8 January 1946, SROWA series 268, cons. 1003, 1945/0436.
33 SROWA series 268, cons. 1003, 1945/0436.
34 Commonwealth Bureau of Census and Statistics, *Census of the Commonwealth of Australia, 30 June 1954, Vol. V, Western Australia*, Canberra, 1954, p. 4, <www.ausstats.abs.gov.au/ausstats/free.nsf/0/CF2B5277672E74BACA257872001F139E/$File/1954%20Census%20-%20Volume%20V%20-%20Part%20I%20WESTERN%20AUSTRALIA%20Analysis%20of%20Population%20in%20LGA.pdf> viewed 6 October 2023. The census excludes some Aboriginal people and contains racist terminology in use at the time.
35 *The West Australian*, 8 May 1946, p. 11.
36 Francine (Fran) Temby, in interview with Bill Bunbury, 17 November 2022.
37 *The West Australian*, 8 May 1946, p. 11.
38 K. Coate, interview, 2022.
39 P. Cook, *Tobacco Growing in the South-West of Western Australia*, with particular reference to the Karridale-Warner Glen area, 1986, p. 7.
40 ibid., p. 12.
41 ibid., pp. 8–9.
42 ibid., p. 8.
43 Matron, Margaret River District Hospital to Under Secretary, 1 February 1944, SROWA series 268, cons. 1003, 1944/0272.
44 *South-Western News*, 19 April 1945, p. 1.
45 ibid.
46 *South-Western News*, 20 September 1945, p. 1.

NOTES

47 Sister Wright Acting Matron to Under Secretary Medical, 14 February 1946, SROWA series 268, cons. 1003, 1940/0334.
48 *South-Western News*, 7 February 1946, p. 1.
49 Sister Wright, Acting Matron to Under Secretary Medical, February 14 February 1946, SROWA series 268, cons. 1003, 1940/0334.
50 Hon. John Tonkin, MLA, Minister for Education, to Hon. Emil Nulsen, MLA, Minister for Justice and Health, 18 March 1946, SROWA series 268, cons. 1003, 1940/0334.
51 H. Stifold, Under Secretary, Medical, to Hon. Minister for Public Health, 2 April 1946, SROWA series 268, cons. 1003, 1940/0334.
52 Charles Hall, District Architect to Principal Architect, 5 October 1943, SROWA series 28, cons. 1003, 1940/0334.
53 J. Thurkle, Clerk in Charge Medical, Memorandum following visit to Margaret River Hospital, 16 March 1944, SROWA series 28, cons. 1003, 1940/0334.
54 *South-Western News*, 26 July 1945, p. 3.
55 Acting Matron Wright Margaret River Hospital, to Under Secretary, Medical, 30 November 1945, SROWA series 268, cons. 1003, 1940/0334.
56 *The West Australian,* 7 August 1946, p. 8.
57 Acting Matron Wright, Margaret River Hospital, to Under Secretary, Medical, Perth, 1 January 1946, SROWA series 268, cons. 1003, 1940/0334.
58 Acting Matron Wright, Margaret River Hospital to Under Secretary, Medical, Perth, 17 January 1946, SROWA series 268, cons. 1003, 1940/0334.
59 Acting Matron Wright to Under Secretary Medical, May 1946, SROWA series 268, cons. 1003, 1940/0334.
60 Acting Matron Wright to Under Secretary Medical, 23 July 1946 SROWA series 268, cons. 1003, 1940/0334.
61 *South-Western News*, 11 September 1947 p. 1.
62 ibid.
63 *South-Western News*, 9 October 1947, p. 4. The committee had been established under section 25 of the legislation (*Hospitals and Health Services Act 1927*) with the following terms of reference: (a) visit and inspect the hospital premises; (b) solicit and receive donations and subscriptions and expend the same on the welfare and comfort of the patients and staff and any other object of benefit to the Hospital; (c) submit reports and recommendations to the (Health) department. See also *South-Western News*, 24 July 1947, p. 7.
64 *South-Western News*, 9 October 1947, p. 4.
65 *Margaret River News*, 20 February 1941, p. 3.
66 *South-Western News*, 19 December 1946, p. 1.
67 ibid.
68 *South-Western News*, 9 October 1947, p. 4.
69 'In this connection the committee wishes to acknowledge the generosity of the following organisers, societies etc, who subscribed to the funds handed over by the trustees, viz-Mr A. Abbott (collections) £ 2/15/-: Mr C. West

NOTES

(collections) £4/2/-: P&C Association East Witchcliffe £17/15/6: P&C Rosa Glen £2/14/-, Returned Servicemen's League, Karridale £1/1/-: Returned Servicemen's League, Margaret River, £2/2/-; Gymnasium Club Margaret River £13/-: Augusta-Margaret River Football Association £10/14/6: Forest Grove Football Club £2: Forest Grove Hockey Club £1: Independent Order of Odd Fellows, Margaret River £1/8/6: Masonic Lodge £2: Ancient Orders of Foresters, Cowaramup £2/2/-: CWA Rosa Brook 10/6: CWA Cowaramup £1/1/-: CWA Margaret River £2/13/-. Total £57/12/2. On New Year's Eve the Committee conducted a successful ball which augmented the above fund by a further £40/10/3.' *South-Western News*, 5 February 1948, p. 6.

70   Smiler Gale, in interview with Bill Bunbury, 9 July 2020.
71   K. Coate, *Forestry through the Fifties: A Young Forestry Officer's Journey with the Western Australian Forests Department*, Hesperian Press, Victoria Park, WA, 2021 p. 25.
72   *South-Western News*, 25 March 1948, p. 6.
73   *South-Western News*, 11 November 1948, p. 7.
74   *South-Western News*, 6 January 1949, p. 2.
75   C.D. Shepherdson to Under Secretary Public Health, 22 March 1948, SROWA series 268, cons. 1003, 1947/0009.
76   C.D. Shepherdson, Secretary Margaret River Hospital Visiting and Advisory Committee, to Minister for Health, 2 August 1948, SROWA series 268, cons. 1003, 1947/0009.
77   K.G. Shepherdson, Secretary, Augusta-Margaret River Road Board, 9 September 1948, SROWA series 268, cons. 1003, 1947/0009.
78   Under Secretary to Secretary, Augusta-Margaret River Road Board, 14 September 1948, SROWA series 268, cons. 1003, 1947/0009.
79   Under Secretary Medical, to Mr H.H. Stuchbury, Secretary SW Council, Australian Labour Party, 19 August 1949, SROWA series 268, cons. 1003, 1944/0272.
80   Principal Architect, Public Works Department, to Under Secretary Medical, 25 July 1949, and Under Secretary to The Chairman, Lotteries Commission, 2 August 1949, SROWA series 268, cons. 1003, 1947/0009.
81   Under Secretary to Principal Architect, Public Works Department, 24 February 1950, SROWA series 268, cons. 1003, 1947/0009.
82   Under Secretary to Principal Architect, 8 December 1950, following memorandum from Assistant Under Secretary Medical, 30 November 1950, SROWA series 268, cons. 1003, 1947/0009.
83   Margaret River Hospital notifiable diseases forms, viewed at the new Margaret River Hospital 29 March 2023.
84   T. Jupp, L. Lord and S. Steele, *Poliomyelitis in Western Australia: A History*, Post Polio Network of WA, Floreat, 2013, p. 87.
85   ibid., p. 101.
86   ibid., p. 134.

87 Margaret River Hospital notifiable diseases forms, viewed at the new Margaret River Hospital 29 March 2023.
88 C.D. Shepherdson, Secretary Hospital Visiting and Advisory Committee, to Hon. Minister for Health, Department of Public Health, 22 December 1950, SROWA series 268, cons. 1003, 1947/0009.
89 E.J. Bragg, District Supervisor, Department of Public Works, to the Principal Architect, PWD, 8 April 1951, SROWA series 82, cons. 689, 1939/0729.
90 District Supervisor, PWD, to Principal Architect, PWD, 18 October 1954, SROWA series 82, cons. 689, 1939/0279.
91 Principal Architect to Under Secretary, Public Health Department, 22 July 1952, and Augusta Margaret River Road Board to Commissioner of Public Health, 5 December 1952, SROWA series 268 cons. 1003, 1944/0272.
92 Under Secretary to Principal Architect, PWD, 30 July 1952, SROWA series 268 cons. 1003, 1944/0272.
93 Dr Barrett to the Augusta Margaret River Board, 4 March 1953, SROWA series 268 cons. 1003, 1944/0272.
94 Assistant Under Secretary, Medical, to Commissioner of Public Health, 16 June 1953, SROWA series 268 cons. 1003, 1944/0272.
95 Deputy Chief Inspector of Public Works to Commissioner of Public Health, 6 August 1953, SROWA series 268 cons. 1003, 1944/0272.
96 C. Harland, Secretary Augusta Margaret River Road Board to the Commissioner, Department of Public Health, 16 March 1954, SROWA series 268 cons. 1003, 1944/0272.
97 Margaret River Hospital Admissions Register 1924 onwards, viewed on site 23 April 2023.
98 Deputy Commissioner for Public Health to the Secretary, Augusta Margaret River Road Board, 5 April 1954, SROWA series 268 cons. 1003, 1944/02722; Under Secretary, Public Works, to Under Secretary, Medical, 18 May 1954, SROWA series 268 cons. 1003, 1952/5335.
99 Principal Architect to Under Secretary, Medical, 30 March 1957, SROWA series 268 cons. 3, 1952/5335.
100 Lloyd Shepherdson, in interview with Bill Bunbury, 28 November 2022.
101 John Alferink, personal communication to authors, 27 August 2022.
102 City of Gosnells, *Thornlie Child Health Centre: place no. 20072*, Heritage Council, 2020, <http://inherit.stateheritage.wa.gov.au/Public/Inventory/Details/09e20b6a-549c-4204-a798-a74c51da11df> viewed 6 October 2023.
103 *The West Australian*, 25 January 1946, p. 10.
104 ibid.
105 'Rosa Glen recently held an evening which returned £4 1/5 and Margaret River has donated the return from their Paddy's market of £2/5/-. Witchcliffe branch is conducting an evening this week and a dance in the Margaret River Hall on Saturday. Cowaramup is very active and is running dances and other functions.' *South-Western News*, 9 May 1946, p. 5.

NOTES

106 *South-Western News*, 18 September 1947, p. 4.
107 Anon. local resident (probably Mae Wise). Unsigned and undated notes. Margaret River and Districts Historical Society.
108 *South-Western News*, 7 October 1954, p. 1.
109 K. Coate, *Growing up in Margaret River*, unpublished memoir, 2021, p. 15. Copy at Margaret River and Districts Historical Society.
110 Marion Lilly, in interview with Bill Bunbury, 17 May 2022.
111 Elwyn Franklin, in interview with Bill Bunbury, 31 October 2022.
112 Temby, interview, 17 November 2022.
113 Lloyd Shepherdson *A Mill Kid's Perspective*, unpublished memoir, n.d. Copy provided to the authors by Lloyd Shepherdson.
114 ibid.
115 'Fifty years of post-war migration', *Making Multicultural Australia,* Fact Sheet 30, Department of Immigration and Ethnic Affairs, Canberra, 1995, <www.multiculturalaustralia.edu.au/doc/immdept_3.pdf>, viewed 25 October 2023
116 '"The last million": Eastern European displaced persons in postwar Germany', *The National WWII Museum of New Orleans*, 4 April 2022, <www.nationalww2museum.org/war/articles/last-million-eastern-european-displaced-persons-postwar-germany>, viewed 25 October 2023.
117 Coate, *Growing up in Margaret River*, 2021, p. 7.
118 Ellie Metcalfe, in interview with Bill Bunbury, 14 July 2021.
119 ibid.
120 Letter from Alan Hillier to Jan Matthews, 6 June 2016, describing his role in disposing of Bolis Kasparis' effects in the 1970s. Copy of letter held by Margaret River and Districts Historical Society.
121 Coate, *Growing up in Margaret River*, p. 6.
122 Metcalfe, interview 2021.
123 Western Australian Museum, *Welcome Walls: Kovalevs, Nikolajs*, Fremantle, panel 283, <https://museum.wa.gov.au/welcomewalls/names/kovalevs-nikolajs> viewed 6 October 2023.
124 L. Shepherdson, *A Mill Kid's Perspective*.
125 ibid.
126 L. Shepherdson in interview with Bill Bunbury. 28 November 2022.
127 Coate, *Forestry through the Fifties*, pp. 46–47.
128 ibid.
129 ibid.
130 Joyce Challis, in interview with Bill Bunbury, 19 December 2022.
131 J. Challis, interview.
132 Metcalfe, interview.
133 Greg Bussell, in interview with Bill Bunbury, 22 November 2022.
134 L. Shepherdson, interview.
135 Franklin, interview.
136 L. Shepherdson, interview.

137 Plan attached to correspondence from the Under Secretary for Lands to the Conservator of Forests, 12 September 1958, SROWA series 1984, cons. 5927, 010185F2730, 1958-01-01.
138 Under Secretary, Medical, to Assistant Under Secretary, 26 November 1958, SROWA series 268, cons. 1003, 1957/5600.
139 Under Secretary for Lands to Margaret Feilman, 20 June 1958, SROWA series 211, cons. 541, 1923/0792.
140 Under Secretary, Department of Land Administration, to Conservator of Forests, 12 February 1959, SROWA series 1984, cons. 5927, 010185F2730, 1958-01-01.
141 Report of meeting between Minister for Lands and Forests and the Hon. W.S. Bovell, and a deputation from the Augusta-Margaret River Road Board, 20 April 1959, SROWA series 211, cons. 541, 1923/0792, 010185F2730, 1958-01-01.
142 D.R.M. Stewart, District Superintendent of Forests to Conservator of Forests, SROWA series 1984, cons. 5927, 010185F2730, 1958-01-01.
143 ibid.
144 *South-Western News*, 6 January 1949, p. 2.
145 *South-Western News*, 25 October 1951 p. 1.
146 *South-Western News*, 18 October 1951, p. 4.
147 Principal Architect, Department of Public Works, to Under Secretary, Public Health Department, 30 August 1950, SROWA series 268, cons. 1003, 1947/0009.
148 Under Secretary to Under Treasurer, 18 September 1950, SROWA series 268, cons. 1003, 1947/0009.
149 *South-Western News*, 4 June 1953, p. 1.
150 Bill Darnell in interview with Vendla Tinley, 1996, Margaret River and Districts Historical Society, and Battye Library, OH 3894.
151 *South-Western News,* 4 June 1953, p. 1.
152 Darnell, interview, 1996.
153 Extract from booklet issued at opening of new post office, 19 March 1956, Margaret River and Districts Historical Society.
154 ibid.
155 J. Challis, interview.
156 Lynda Williams and Don Arthur, in interview with Bill Bunbury, 16 June 2023.
157 A. Green, C. Given and Stephen Carrick Architects, *Shire of Augusta-Margaret River Heritage Inventory,* prepared for the Shire of Augusta-Margaret River, 2012, p. 30, <https://mrdhs.com.au/documents/AMR_Heritage_Inventory.pdf>.
158 Coate, *Growing up in Margaret River*, p. 21.
159 G. Edwards, *The Road to Prevelly*, E.G. Edwards, Armadale, 1989, p. 65.
160 ibid., p. 65.
161 ibid., p. 118.
162 Landgate, *Town names*, Government of Western Australia, 2021, <https://web.archive.org/web/20220314101618/http://wwwo.landgate.wa.gov.au/maps-and-imagery/wa-geographic-names/name-history/historical-town-names#M>, viewed 25 October 2023.

163 Mae Wise, 'Margaret River schools', in *A Research Source of the Margaret River town, 1894–1954, Book 2. West of the Bussell Highway*, 1994, copy at Augusta Margaret River Library.
164 Coate *Growing up in Margaret River*, p. 24.
165 Cedar (George) Armstrong in interview with Delys Forrest, 23 March 2004, Margaret River and Districts Historical Society.
166 Judy Dunbar, in interview with Bill Bunbury, *Hindsight – Margaret River: A Changing Landscape,* ABC Radio National, 1996.
167 Carolyn Scott, in interview with Bill Bunbury, 24 August 2022.
168 J.N. Smith, A *History of One Teacher Schools in WA, 1930–1962*, Teachers Higher Education Certificate thesis, 1962.
169 Darnell, interview, 1996-97.
170 Coate, *Growing Up in Margaret River*, p. 29.
171 Don Miller, in interview with Bill Bunbury, 3 June 2020.
172 Temby, interview.
173 *South-Western News*, 3 November 1949, p. 11.
174 Norm Scott, *Bramley Research Station*, Margaret River and Districts Historical Society, August 1986.
175 C. Scott, interview.
176 Scott, *Bramley Research Station*.
177 Lilly, interview.
178 D. Miller, interview.
179 Y. Coate, in interview with Bill Bunbury, 22 August 2022.
180 ibid.
181 K. Coate, interview.
182 Coate, *Growing up in Margaret River*, p. 9.
183 Robert Saunders, in interview with Bill Bunbury, 18 July 2022.
184 Gale, interview.
185 Coate, *Growing up in Margaret River*, p. 23.
186 John Alferink, pers. comm., 28 August 2022.
187 *Beverley Times*, 9 May 1957, p. 3.
188 *The Messenger*, Church of England, Bunbury, March 1957 (Bishop's Letter), in M. Bignell, *Little Grey Sparrows of the Anglican Diocese of Bunbury, Western Australia*, University of Western Australia Press, Nedlands, 1992.
189 Under Secretary to the Diocesan Secretary, Bunbury, 18 March 1957, SROWA series 268, cons. 1003, 1957/5335.
190 Bignell, *Little Grey Sparrows*, p. 183.
191 Rest House Minutes, 17th AGM, 10 August 1946, Margaret Cecil Rest House Association Minute books located in the Margaret Cecil Cabinet Showcase (MCCS) at the Margaret River Hospital.
192 Rest House Minutes, 28 November 1949.
193 Rest House Minutes, 13 March 1950.
194 *South-Western News*, 25 May 1950, p. 1.

NOTES

195 ibid.
196 Letter from Mrs Young to Secretary, Rest House Association, 23 May 1950, in Rest Association Minute Book, MCCS at the Margaret River Hospital, viewed 23 June 2023.
197 Metcalfe, interview.
198 Ellie Metcalfe, memoir recorded by Lyn Moorfoot, Margaret River Community Centre, 2014.

Chapter Six: A Small, Rather Slow, Hospital and a Rosy Future

1 Under Secretary, Medical Department, to Principal Architect, 12 June 1957, SROWA series 268, cons. 1003, 1957/5600
2 Matron Flynn to Under Secretary, Medical Department, 16 March 1959, SROWA series 268, cons. 1003, 1957/5600.
3 John McGrath Acting Chief Clerk Building and Supplies, Memorandum after visit to Margaret River Hospital, 15 May 1959, SROWA series 268, cons. 1003, 1957/5600.
4 Administrative Officer, Medical Department, to Clerk in Charge, Building and Supplies, after visit to Margaret River, 18 December 1961, SROWA series 268, cons. 1003, 1957/5600.
5 Letters from Augusta-Margaret River Board and from Dr Wilson to Under Secretary, Medical, both dated 28 November 1960, SROWA series 268, cons. 1003, 1957/5600.
6 Fran Temby, notes on 'Early Days', provided to the authors, November 2022.
7 Secretary, Hospital Visiting and Advisory Committee, to Under Secretary, Medical, 20 June 1961 and 22 September 1961, SROWA series 268, cons. 1003, 1957/5600.
8 Under Secretary, Medical Department, to Matron Flynn, Margaret River District Hospital, 25 September 1961, SROWA series 268, cons. 1003, 1957/5600
9 Matron Flynn to Under Secretary, 6 August 1962, SROWA series 455, cons. 1541, 1963/5596.
10 ibid.
11 Under Secretary to Matron Flynn, 17 August 1962, SROWA series 455, cons. 1541, 1963/5596.
12 Secretary, Hospital Visiting and Advisory Committee, to the Under Secretary, Medical Department, 22 August 1962, SROWA series 455, cons. 1540, 1962/6643.
13 Secretary, Hospital Visiting and Advisory Committee, to Under Secretary, Medical Department, December 1962, SROWA series 455, cons. 1540, 1962/6643.
14 Under Secretary to Secretary, Hospital Visiting and Advisory Committee, 7 August 1969 and August (n.d., received 25 August) 1970, SROWA series 455, cons. 1540, 1962/6643.
15 Carolyn Scott, in interview with Bill Bunbury, 24 August 2022.
16 Fran Temby, in interview with Bill Bunbury, 17 November 2022.

NOTES

17 Keith McLeod, personal communication to the authors, 20 June 2023.
18 File Note: Under Secretary, Medical Department, to Assistant Under Secretary, Medical, 16 January 1961, SROWA series 268, cons. 1003, 1960/5479.
19 Report by Principal Matron to Commissioner of Public Health on visit to Margaret River District Hospital, 13 May 1958, SROWA series 268, cons. 1003, 1957/5600.
20 Report by Principal Matron to the Commissioner of Public Health on visit to Margaret River District Hospital, 11 June 1959, SROWA series 268, cons. 1003, 1957/5600.
21 Memorandum from the Principal Matron to Under Secretary, 29 May 1963, SROWA series 455, cons. 1541, 1963/5596.
22 Clerk in Charge, Building and Supplies, Medical Department, to Assistant Under Secretary, 23 May 1963, SROWA series 455, cons. 1541, 1963/5596.
23 Elwyn Franklin, in interview with Bill Bunbury, 31 October 2022.
24 Under Secretary to Matron, Margaret River District Hospital, 30 July 1963, SROWA series 455, cons. 1541, 1963/5596.
25 Clerk, Works and Supplies, memorandum 29 November 1963 following visit to Margaret River 2 November 1963, SROWA series 455, cons. 1541, 1963/5596.
26 Assistant Under Secretary to Under Secretary (Medical Department), 13 May 1965, SROWA series 455, cons. 1541, 1963/5596.
27 Judy Wake, in interview with Ann Basili, 28 March 2017, recording held by Margaret River and Districts Historical Society.
28 Judy Wake, in interview with Bill Bunbury, 12 January 2022 (SLWA OH 4652).
29 Mae Wise, Notes on doctors in Margaret River 1925-1986, folders held at the Augusta Margaret River Library.
30 Matron Peirce to Under Secretary, Medical, 22 December 1965, SROWA series 455, cons. 1541, 1963/5596.
31 File note, Medical Department, 12 April 1967, SROWA series 455, cons. 1847, 1966/6038.
32 Matron Peirce to Under Secretary, Medical, 22 December 1965, SROWA series 455, cons. 1541, 1963/5596.
33 Extract from P&C Minutes, Margaret River Junior High School, Mae Wise, in *A Research Source on the Margaret River Town, 1894 to 1984. Book 2 and appendix*, lodged with Augusta Margaret River Library, 12 May 1984.
34 Wake, interview, 2022.
35 Dr Clark Stephenson to the Secretary, Hospital Amenities Committee, 12 July 1966, SROWA series 2523, cons. 6704, 05/01, 1985-03-39- 1986-10-01 (folios 1-2).
36 Stewart Bovell to Hon. Minister for Health, 25 July 1966, SROWA series 2523, cons. 6704, 05/01, 1985-03-39- 1986-10-01 (folio 4).
37 *Busselton-Margaret Times*, 18 August 1966, p. 7.
38 *Busselton-Margaret Times*, 4 August 1966, p. 1.
39 File note to Under Secretary (Medical Department), n.d., SROWA Planning, series 2523, cons. 6704, 05/01, 1985-03-39- 1986-10-01.

NOTES

40 Administrative Officer, JMH, to Assistant Under Secretary after visit to Margaret River Hospital, 4 October 1966, SROWA series 455, cons. 1847, 1966/6038.
41 ibid.
42 Minutes of meeting held in Perth in the Medical Department's conference room on 10 April 1967, SROWA series 2523, cons. 6704, 05/01, 1985-03-39- 1986-10-01.
43 Judy Wake, personal communication to the authors, December 2022.
44 Margaret River Hospital Theatre Register 1963-1970, viewed on site 29 March 2023.
45 Shire of Augusta-Margaret River, *Council History and Honour Roll: Augusta-Margaret River Shire Council from 1961*, <www.amrshire.wa.gov.au/shire-and-council/council/council-history-and-honour-roll#AugustaMargaretRiverShireCouncilFrom1961> viewed 6 October 2023.
46 Barry Blaikie, MLA, at opening of new hospital, quoted in G. Jennings (ed.), *Margaret River Stories 1913–2013*, Margaret River and Districts Historical Society, 2013, p. 261.
47 Dr Eithne Sheridan, in interview with Bill Bunbury, 9 February 2022.
48 ibid.
49 Wake, interview, 2022.
50 Rex Dyer, in interview with Ann Basili, 1 June 2017, Margaret River and Districts Historical Society.
51 Scott, interview.
52 Sheridan, interview.
53 Wake, interview, 2017.
54 Tim Crimp, in interview with Bill Bunbury, 19 June 2023.
55 ibid.
56 Ellie Metcalfe, in interview with Bill Bunbury, 14 July 2021.
57 Judy Dunbar, in interview with Bill Bunbury, 13 May 2020.
58 Don Miller in interview with Bill Bunbury, 3 June 2020.
59 Franklin, interview.
60 ibid.
61 Temby, interview.
62 Pat Gray, in interview with Bill Bunbury, 30 November 2021.
63 Sheridan, interview.
64 John Alferink, written memories, unpublished, copy viewed in Mae Wise Papers, folder no. 16, at Augusta Margaret River Library.
65 G. Cresswell, *The Light of Leeuwin*, Augusta-Margaret River Shire History Group, Margaret River, 1990, p. 273.
66 Miller, interview.
67 Greg Bussell, in interview with Bill Bunbury, 22 November 2022.
68 Crimp interview, (quoting Bill Darnell).
69 G. Bussell, interview.
70 ibid.

NOTES

71 Margaret Chadwick, in interview with Bill Bunbury, 25 November 2022.
72 Smiler (Herbert) Gale, in interview with Bill Bunbury, 9 July 2020.
73 ibid.
74 Crimp, interview.
75 Miller, interview.
76 Crimp, interview.
77 Cresswell, *The Light of Leeuwin*, p. 320.
78 Arts Margaret River website, <https://artsmargaretriver.com/>, viewed 18 June 2023.
79 J. Chetovich and D. Gare, *A Chain of Care: A History of the Silver Chain Nursing Association, 1905–2005*, University of Notre Dame Australia Press, Fremantle, for the Silver Chain Nursing Association, 2005, p. 179.
80 Sheridan, interview.
81 Dorothy Wickham, *A History of the Margaret River Branch of the Silver Chain Nursing Association from 1972 to 1985*, unpublished notes, n.d., viewed 15 February 1992 and now located at MR&DHS (courtesy Heidi Hutchings, Margaret River Silver Chain).
82 Obituary for Dot Wickham, Margaret River and Districts Historical Society, 2005.
83 Wickham, *A History of the Margaret River branch of the Silver Chain Nursing Association*.
84 Gray, interview.
85 Lynda Williams, in interview with Bill Bunbury, 16 June 2023.
86 Temby, interview.
87 Minutes of Hospital Visiting and Advisory Committee, 13 June 1972, MR&DHS.
88 Notes on Meals on Wheels, Margaret River and Districts Historical Society.
89 Form letter signed by secretary Pat Rose setting out the operational arrangements of Margaret River Meals on Wheels, n.d. (c. 1974/5), Margaret River and Districts Historical Society.
90 Hospital Visiting and Advisory Committee to Mr Noonan, Managing Secretary, Busselton District Hospital, 10 June 1970, SROWA series 2523, cons. 6704, 05/01, 1985-03-39- 1986-10-01.
91 Principal Matron, Extract from report after inspection visit, 17 November 1971, SROWA series 2523, cons. 6704, 05/01, 1985-03-39- 1986-10-01.
92 Mrs H.M. West to the Hon. Minister for Health, 17 March 1971, SROWA series 2523, cons. 6704, 05/01, 1985-03-39- 1986-10-01 (folio 22).
93 Ron Davies, MLA, Minister for Health, to Mrs H.M. West Secretary, Margaret Cecil Rest House Association, 8 April 1971, SROWA series 2523, cons. 6704, 05/01, 1985-03-39- 1986-10-01 (folio 23).
94 Judy Wake, pers. comm. to the authors, 12 January 2022.
95 Parry and Rosenthal to Hon. Minister for Works, 28 September 1976, SROWA series 82, cons. 6781, 1975/1119.

96 Final Certificate of Contract for contract let to H.C. and M/L Cooke, issued by Chief Administrative Officer, Architectural Division, Public Works Department, 20 May 1977, SROWA series 82, cons. 6781, 1975/1119.
97 List of Margaret River Hospital Additions and Alterations, Job no. B22/75 Brief Schedule of Works, August 1975, SROWA series 82, cons. 6781, 1975/1119.
98 T.W. Noonan, Managing Secretary, Margaret River Hospital, to Under Secretary, Medical Department, 19 April 1969, SROWA series 455, cons. 1847, 1966/6038.
99 List of Margaret River Hospital Additions and Alterations, Brief Schedule of Works, August 1975, p. 3, SROWA series 82, cons. 6781, 1975/1119.
100 Medical Department file note, 12 April 1967, SROWA series 455, cons. 1847, 1966/6038.
101 T.W. Noonan, Managing Secretary, Busselton and Margaret River Hospitals to Under Secretary, Medical Department, 9 September 1969, SROWA series 455, cons. 1847 1966/6038.
102 Wake, interview, 2017.
103 Temby, interview.
104 Minutes of the Margaret River Rest House Association, June 1977, Minute books located in the Margaret Cecil Cabinet Showcase (MCCS) at the Margaret River Hospital.
105 Mrs Hilda West to Alan Hillier, Margaret River Homes for Senior Citizens, 18 July 1977, Papers held by the Margaret River and Districts Historical Society.
106 J.D. Reidy-Crofts to Hilda West, 9 August 1977, Mirrambeena papers held by the Margaret River and Districts Historical Society.
107 Final Minutes Rest House Association. Minute books located in the MCCS at the Margaret River Hospital.
108 ibid.
109 A.P. Hillier President, Margaret River Homes for Senior Citizens Inc. to the Honorable Minister for Health and Community Welfare, 6 June 1974, SROWA series 2523, cons. 6704, 05/01, 1985-03-39- 1986-10-01.
110 Chairman's Annual Report for 1975–76, Margaret River Homes for Senior Citizens inc. Mirrambeena papers held by the Margaret River and Districts Association.
111 Scott, interview.
112 Wake, interview, 2022.
113 Dyer, interview.
114 ibid.
115 *Augusta-Margaret River Mail*, 7 September 2000, p. 10.
116 Wake, interview, 2022.
117 Scott, interview.
118 Crimp, interview.
119 ibid.
120 Wake, interview, 2022

NOTES

121 Cresswell, *The Light of Leeuwin*, p. 313.
122 Robert (Barney) Barnett, in interview with Bill Bunbury, 24 August 2022.
123 Arts Margaret River, *History*, <artsmargaretriver.com/history>, viewed 18 June 2023.
124 Barnett, interview.
125 S. Juniper, *Our Little Life: A Memoir*, Sue Juniper, Margaret River, 2019, p. 134.
126 Franklin, interview.
127 Judy Dunbar, pers. comm. to the authors, November 2022.
128 Cedar (George) Armstrong, in interview with Delys Forrest, March 2004, Margaret River and Districts Historical Society.
129 Jennings, *Margaret River Stories*, p. 236 (first published as 'Crank up the Vee-Dubb and off to Margs' by Neale Carpenter in the *Augusta-Margaret River Mail*, December 1999).
130 Geoff Culmsee, in S.-L. Aldrian-Moyle, *Surfing Down South: Discovering Yallingup & Margaret River*, Margaret River Press, Witchcliffe, 2014, pp. 66–69.
131 Hassa Mann in Aldrian-Moyle, *Surfing Down South*, p. 75.
132 ibid.
133 Gary Greirson in Aldrian-Moyle, *Surfing Down South*, p. 128.
134 Robert Conneeley in Aldrian-Moyle, *Surfing Down South*, p. 170.
135 ibid.
136 Settlers Tavern, in Aldrian-Moyle, *Surfing Down South*, p. 150.
137 Lloyd Shepherdson, in interview with Bill Bunbury, 28 November 2022.
138 Jennings, *Margaret River Stories*, p. 239.
139 Juniper, *Our Little Life*, p. 115.
140 Keith McLeod in Aldrian-Moyle, *Surfing Down South*, p. 91.
141 Leonie McCleod in Aldrian-Moyle, *Surfing Down South*, p. 92.
142 Hazel Brennan, in interview with Bill Bunbury, *Hindsight – Margaret River: A Changing Landscape*, ABC Radio National, 1996.
143 Scott, interview.
144 Hospital Admissions Register 1924 – onwards, located at new Margaret River Hospital.
145 ibid.
146 Dyer, interview.
147 Barnett, interview.
148 L. Shepherdson, interview.
149 Chadwick, interview.
150 Lyn Serventy, in interview with Bill Bunbury, *Hindsight – Margaret River: A Changing Landscape*, 1996.
151 ibid.
152 ibid.
153 P. Forrestal and R. Jordan, *The Way It Was: A History of the Early Days of the Margaret River Wine Industry*, Margaret River Press, Witchcliffe, 2017, p. 7.
154 ibid., p. 44.

NOTES

155 Jan O'Connell, *1966 Margaret River wine region identified*, Australian Food Timeline, <https://australianfoodtimeline.com.au/1966-margaret-river-wine-region-identified/> viewed 6 October 2023.
156 Stan Dilkes, in interview with Bill Bunbury, *Hindsight – Margaret River: A Changing Landscape*.
157 Forrestal and Jordan, *The Way It Was*, pp. 64–65.
158 ibid., p. 113.
159 Diana Cullen, in interview with Bill Bunbury, *Hindsight – Margaret River: A Changing Landscape*.
160 Forrestal and Jordan, *The Way It Was*, p. 129.
161 Sheridan, interview.
162 ibid.
163 Miller, interview.
164 Barnett, interview.
165 ibid.
166 Thelma Burnett, pers. comm. to the authors, 7 July 2023.
167 Mark Exeter, in interview with Margaret Tickle, Busselton Oral History Group, 2005, State Library of WA, OH 2856.
168 G. Bussell, interview.
169 Judy Dunbar, in interview with Bill Bunbury, *Hindsight – Margaret River: A Changing Landscape*.
170 W. Caccetta, 'The original and the best: 30 years of Leeuwin concerts, *Perth Now*, 17 February 2014, <www.perthnow.com.au/news/australia/the-original-and-the-best-30-years-of-leeuwin-estate-concerts-ng-5bab0d2e6ddf38ece3a3b59ea7eb017b> viewed 6 October 2023.
171 Kim Murray, in interview with Bill Bunbury, August 2020.
172 Jennings, *Margaret River Stories*, p. 257.
173 Ken Preston, Shire Clerk, in *Destinations* Magazine, summer 1986, pp. 18–23.
174 ibid.
175 ibid.
176 M. Hutton, *A History of the Catholic Community of the Margaret River District*, produced for the official blessing and opening of the parish church dedicated to St Thomas More at Margaret River on Monday, 31 January 1983.
177 *Destinations*, p. 18.
178 Scott, interview.
179 Chadwick, interview.
180 Scott, interview.
181 ibid.
182 Shelley Challis, in interview with Bill Bunbury, 19 December 2022.
183 Chadwick, interview.
184 Crimp, interview.
185 Scott, interview.
186 Anne Shepherdson, in interview with Bill Bunbury, July 2020.

NOTES

187 Ralph Hofstee, in interview with Bill Bunbury, 11 October 2022.
188 Williams, interview.
189 Temby, interview.
190 Wake, interview, 2022.
191 Temby, interview.
192 Wake, interview, 2022.
193 Temby, interview.
194 Scott, interview.
195 Dr Ray Clarke, in interview with Bill Bunbury, 1 December 2022.
196 A. Green, C. Given and Stephen Carrick Architects, 'The Tin House', *Shire of Augusta-Margaret River Heritage Inventory,* prepared for the Shire of Augusta-Margaret River, 2012, pp. 446–48.
197 Clarke, interview.
198 Dr Shaun O'Rourke, in interview with Bill Bunbury, 12 December 2022.
199 ibid.
200 Clarke, interview.
201 ibid.
202 Temby, interview.
203 *Augusta-Margaret River Mail*, 26 August 1987, p. 1.

Chapter Seven: A Perennial Source of Discontent

1 D. Carmond, memorandum to A/C.C, Planning and Maintenance, 24 July 1978, SROWA series 2523, cons. 6704, MR05 05/01, 1985-3-29-1986-10-01.
2 Annotation on memorandum from D. Carmond, 1 August 1978, SROWA series 2523 cons. 6704, MR05 05/01, 1985-3-29-1986-10-01.
3 *Busselton-Margaret Times*, 23 November 1978, p. 1.
4 Ray Young MLA, Minister for Health, reply to Barry Blaikie, MLA, for Vasse, 22 December 1978, SROWA series 2523 cons. 6704, MR05 05/01, 1985-3-29-1986-10-01.
5 Judy Wake extract (p. 4) from letter to local organisations, 8 February 1981, papers held by the Margaret River and Districts Historical Society (MR&DHS)
6 Judy Wake letter to organisations and associations in Margaret River from the Hospital Visiting and Advisory Committee, 8 February 1981, papers held by MR&DHS.
7 *Busselton-Margaret Times*, 30 October 1980, p. 1.
8 ibid.
9 Judy Wake, in interview with Ann Basili, 22 March 2017, MR&DHS.
10 Dr Eithne Sheridan, in interview with Bill Bunbury, 22 February 2022.
11 Mrs G. Goldstone, Hon. Sec. CWA, Margaret River Branch, to the Honorable Minister for Health, Mr Ray Young, received 23 March 1981, SROWA series 2523 cons. 704, MR05 05/01, 1985-3-29-1986-10-01.

NOTES

12   Ray Young, Minister for Health to CWA of WA, Margaret River Branch, 5 May 1981, SROWA series 2523 cons. 704, MR05 05/01, 1985-3-29-1986-10-01.
13   Minister Young to Commissioner, Hospital and Allied Services, 9 June 1981, SROWA series 2523 cons. 704, MR05 05/01, 1985-3-29-1986-10-01.
14   H.H. McGrath, Acting Director Administration, to Commissioner, Hospital and Allied Services, 25 June 1981, SROWA series 2523 cons. 704, MR05 05/01, 1985-3-29-1986-10-01.
15   Judy Wake, Secretary, Hospital Visiting and Advisory Committee, letter sent to local organisations, 8 February 1981. Copy held by MR&DHS.
16   Fran Temby, in interview with Bill Bunbury, 17 November 2022.
17   *Busselton-Margaret Times*, 21 May 1981, p. 1.
18   ibid.
19   Judy Wake to Barry Blaikie, MLA, 2 July 1981, SROWA series 2523 cons. 704, MR05 05/01, 1985-3-29-1986-10-01.
20   H.H. McGrath, for Commissioner, Hospital and Allied Services, to Hon Minister for Health, 3 August 1981, SROWA series 2523 cons. 704, MR05 05/01, 1985-3-29-1986-10-01.
21   Hon Ray Young, MLA, Minister for Health, to Barry Blaikie, MLA for Vasse, 26 August 1981, SROWA series 2523 cons. 704, MR05 05/01, 1985-3-29-1986-10-01.
22   ibid.
23   *Busselton-Margaret Times*, 10 June 1982, p. 1, and 17 June 1982, p. 5.
24   *Busselton-Margaret Times*, 17 June 1982, p. 5.
25   ibid.
26   Dr Peter Southgate to Commissioner, Hospital and Allied Services, 24 May 1982, SROWA series 2523 cons. 704, MR05 05/01, 1985-3-29-1986-10-01.
27   Barry Hodge, Minister for Health, to Mrs J. Wake, Secretary, Margaret River Hospital Visiting and Advisory Committee, 28 March 1983. Papers held by MR&DHS.
28   *Busselton-Margaret Times,* 29 March 1984, p. 1.
29   ibid.
30   R.J. Brown for Commissioner Hospital and Allied Services to W.G. Hales, Regional Administrator, District Hospital, Busselton, 6 January 1984, SROWA series 2523 cons. 704, MR05 05/01, 1985-3-29-1986-10-01.
31   Dr Sheridan to the Commissioner, Hospital and Allied Services, received 2 February 1984, SROWA series 2523 cons. 704, MR05 05/01, 1985-3-29-1986-10-01.
32   Ken Preston Shire Clerk, Shire of Augusta Margaret River, to Commissioner Hospital and Allied Services, 3 February 1984, SROWA series 2523 cons. 704, MR05 05/01, 1985-3-29-1986-10-01.
33   W.G. (Bill) Hales, Administrator, District Hospital, Busselton to Commissioner Hospital and Allied Services, 7 February 1984, SROWA series 2523, cons. 6704, MR 05 05/01, 1985-3-29-1986-10-01.
34   Barry Blaikie, MLA, to Minister Hodge, 17 February 1984, SROWA series 2523 cons. 704, MR 05 05/01, 1985-3-29-1986-10-01.

NOTES

35 Barry Hodge, Minister for Health to Barry Blaikie, MLA for Vasse, 19 April 1984, SROWA series 2523 cons. 704, MR05 05/01, 1985-3-29-1986-10-01.
36 Dr Peter Southgate to Dr E. Sheridan, 23 February 1984, SROWA series 2523 cons. 704, MR05 05/01, 1985-3-29-1986-10-01.
37 Dr Sheridan to Dr Southgate, Department of Hospital and Allied Services, 8 March 1984, SROWA series 2523 cons. 704, MR05 05/01, 1985-3-29-1986-10-01.
38 Relieving administrator, J.C. Kerr to Department of Hospital and Allied Services. attn. Mr R.J. Brown, 6 June 1984, SROWA series 2523 cons. 704, MR05 05/01, 1985-3-29-1986-10-01.
39 *Busselton-Margaret Times*, 18 October 1984, p. 3.
40 ibid.
41 *Busselton-Margaret Times*, 1 November 1984, p. 1.
42 Judy Wake, Secretary, Hospital Visiting and Advisory Committee, to Barry Hodge, Minister for Health, 11 January 1985, SROWA series 2523, cons. 704, MR05 05/01, 1985-3-29-1986-10-01.
43 Judy Wake, Secretary, Hospital Visiting and Advisory Committee to Barry Hodge, Minister for Health, 27 February 1985, SROWA series 2523 cons. 704, MR05 05/01, 1985-3-29-1986-10-01.
44 A.R. Keating, Executive Director, Health Department of Western Australia, to Mrs J. Wake, Secretary, Margaret River District Hospital Visiting and Advisory Committee, 14 March 1985, SROWA series 2523 cons. 704, MR05 05/01, 1985-3-29-1986-10-01.
45 Judy Wake, Secretary, Hospital Visiting and Advisory Committee to Barry Hodge, Minister for Health, 25 March 1985, SROWA series 2523 cons. 704, MR05 05/01, 1985-3-29-1986-10-01.
46 Submission with regard to the need for a new hospital facility at Margaret River, prepared on behalf of the Margaret River District Hospital Visiting and Advisory Committee, 28 March 1985, papers held by MR&DHS.
47 Barry Hodge, Minister for Health, to Mrs J. Wake, Secretary, Margaret River District Hospital Visiting and Advisory Committee, 18 April 1985, copy held by MR&DHS.
48 Mark Hohnen, Oceanic Equity, to Mrs Judy Wake, Secretary, Margaret River District Hospital Visiting and Advisory Committee, 10 May 1985 and Denis Horgan to Secretary, Margaret District Hospital Advisory Committee, 5 June 1985, copies held by MR&DHS.
49 *Augusta-Margaret River Mail*, 23 September 1987, p. 2.
50 *Busselton-Margaret Times*, 8 November 1985, p. 3.
51 Barry Hodge, Minister for Health to Judy Wake, Secretary, Margaret River District Hospital Committee, 11 February 1986, copy held by MR&DHS.
52 Kim Murray, in interview with Bill Bunbury, August 2020.
53 *Busselton-Margaret Times*, 3 April 1986, p. 1.
54 Dr Ray Clarke, in interview with Bill Bunbury, 1 December 2022.
55 *Busselton-Margaret Times*, 3 April 1986, p. 1.

NOTES

56 Brian Burke, WA Premier, to Judy Wake, c/o Margaret River Hospital, 3 April 1986, copy held by MR&DHS.
57 Telex copy Premier's Office from A.R. Tebbit, Administrator Busselton District Hospital to Dr Roberts, SROWA series 2523, cons. 704, MR05 05/01, 1985-3-29-1986-10-01.
58 Parliamentary Question, No 213, Legislative Assembly, Mr Blaikie to the Minister for Health, Thursday 12 June 1986.
59 Judy Wake, Hon. Sec. Margaret River District Hospital Visiting and Advisory Committee, to Minister for Health, Mr I.F. Taylor, 25 October 1986. See also Ian Taylor to Mrs J. Wake, Hon. Secretary, Margaret River District Hospital Visiting and Amenities Committee, 17 February 1987. Copy held by MR&DHS.
60 Mrs Dorothy Shepherdson, to Mr Doug Wenn, 13 November 1986, SROWA series 2523 cons. 704, MR05 05/01, 1985-3-29-1986-10-01.
61 Hon. Doug Wenn, MLC, to Ian Taylor Minister for Health, 7 November 1986, SROWA series 2523 cons. 704, MR05 05/01, 1985-3-29-1986-10-01.
62 Ian Taylor, Minister for Health and Lands, to Hon. Doug Wenn, J.P. MLC, Member for South West Province. 12 November 1986, SROWA series 2523 cons. 704, MR05 05/01, 1985-3-29-1986-10-01.
63 *Augusta-Margaret River Mail*, 26 August 1987, p. 2.
64 *Augusta-Margaret River Mail*, 9 September 1987, p. 3.
65 ibid.
66 *Augusta-Margaret River Mail*, 18 December 1987, p. 2.
67 *Augusta-Margaret River Mail*, 18 December 1987, p. 7.
68 *Augusta-Margaret River Mail*, 17 February 1988, p. 3.
69 *Augusta-Margaret River Mail*, 13 April 1988, p. 5.
70 Wake, interview, 2017.
71 Anne Shepherdson, in interview with Bill Bunbury, 2 July 2020.
72 *Augusta-Margaret River Mail*, 27 April 1988, p. 3.
73 *Augusta-Margaret River Mail*, 4 May 1988, p. 3.
74 Judy Wake, speech on 90th anniversary of the old hospital opening, 2014.
75 Information provided by Matron Mary Arthur to the Hospital Visiting and Advisory Committee. Minutes of meeting on 11 October 1988 held by MR&DHS.
76 Hon. Barry House MLC speech during second reading debate in the Legislative Council on the 1989 Appropriation (General Loan and Capital Works Fund) Bill, *Hansard*, 20 December 1989.
77 Clarke, interview.
78 Dr Shaun O'Rourke, in interview with Bill Bunbury, 12 December 2022.
79 Temby, interview.
80 Judy Wake, in interview with Bill Bunbury, 2022.
81 Carolyn Scott, in interview with Bill Bunbury, 14 August 2022.
82 Wake, interview, 2022.
83 Fiona Hofstee, in interview with Bill Bunbury, 11 October 2022.

84 Scott, interview.
85 O'Rourke, interview.
86 Wake, interview, 2022.
87 ibid.

Chapter Eight: An Extension of Life
1   Lydell Huntly, in interview with Bill Bunbury, 6 August 2020.
2   Kris Keen, in interview with Bill Bunbury, 7 August 2020.
3   Jennifer Gherardi, in interview with Bill Bunbury, 11 August 2020.
4   *Busselton-Margaret Times*, 18 April 1986.
5   Gherardi, interview.
6   *Busselton-Margaret Times*, 23 January 1986, p. 8.
7   ibid.
8   Ros Blakeney in interview with Bill Bunbury, 25 July 2020.
9   Anne Shepherdson in interview with Bill Bunbury, 2 July 2020.
10 *Augusta-Margaret River Mail*, 30 March 1988, p. 7.
11 Blakeney, interview.
12 Community Centre newsletter, March 1988. Copy in records held at the Margaret River Community Centre.
13 Tess (Sally) Minett, in interview with Bill Bunbury, 30 July 2020.
14 ibid.
15 A. Shepherdson, interview.
16 Blakeney, interview.
17 *Augusta-Margaret River Mail*, 5 December 1988, p. 1.
18 Draft of letter from L.A. Barber, chairman, Margaret River Community Centre, to Mr Julian Grill, 15 December 1988, copy in Margaret River Community Centre files.
19 *Busselton-Margaret Times*, 5 January 1989, p. 10.
20 ibid.
21 *Busselton-Margaret Times*, 9 February 1989, p. 9.
22 Theo Mathews in interview with Bill Bunbury, 14 July 2020.
23 *Augusta-Margaret River Mail*, 22 March 1989, p. 18.
24 ibid.
25 Linton Hodsdon, in interview with Bill Bunbury, 19 August 2020.
26 *The West Australian*, 6 April 1989, p. 30.
27 *Augusta-Margaret River Mail*, 26 April 1989, p. 3.
28 *Augusta-Margaret River Mail*, 3 May 1989, p. 1.
29 Mathews, interview.
30 Blakeney, interview.
31 *Busselton-Margaret Times*, 18 May 1989, p. 10.
32 ibid.
33 *Augusta-Margaret River Mail*, 17 May 1989, p. 1.

34 ibid., p. 3.
35 *Busselton-Margaret Times*, 21 September 1989, p. 11.
36 ibid.
37 *Augusta-Margaret River Mail*, 14 March 1990, p. 1.
38 *Augusta-Margaret River Mail*, 23 May 1990, p. 5.
39 *Augusta-Margaret River Mail*, 16 May 1990, p. 1.
40 Lloyd Shepherdson, in interview with Bill Bunbury, 28 November 2022.
41 A. Shepherdson, interview.
42 Blakeney, interview.
43 *Augusta-Margaret River Mail*, 19 September 1990, p. 1.
44 *Augusta-Margaret River Mail*, 6 March 1991, p. 8.
45 ibid.
46 Minett, interview.
47 *Augusta-Margaret River Mail*, 10 October 1990, p. 8.
48 Gherardi, interview.
49 A. Shepherdson, interview.
50 *Augusta-Margaret River Mail*, 17 July 1991, p. 2.
51 Blakeney, interview.
52 Margot Edwards, in interview with Bill Bunbury, 13 August 2020.
53 Len Calneggia, Shire Clerk, *Augusta-Margaret River Mail*, 11 April 1990, p. 5.
54 Barbara Maidment, in interview with Bill Bunbury, 27 July 2020.
55 Gherardi, interview.
56 John Alferink, interview with Bill Bunbury, 21 July 2020.
57 Noel Conway, in interview with Bill Bunbury, 2 August 2020.
58 Donna Dornan, in interview with Bill Bunbury, 23 July 2020.
59 *Augusta-Margaret River Mail*, 6 March 1992, p. 3.
60 ibid.
61 Hodsdon, interview.
62 Danielle Haigh, 'A new heart beats in the old hospital', *Augusta-Margaret River Mail*, 22 December 1993, p. 3.
63 Dornan, interview.
64 Sally Hays, in interview with Bill Bunbury, 4 August 2020.
65 ibid.
66 Lynda Green, in interview with Bill Bunbury, 14 August 2020.
67 Edwards, interview.
68 Dornan, interview.
69 Lyn Moorfoot, in interview with Bill Bunbury, 11 August 2020.
70 *Augusta-Margaret River Mail*, 26 July 1995, p. 1.
71 Dave Seegar, interview with Bill Bunbury, 25 August 2020.
72 Moorfoot, interview.
73 *Augusta-Margaret River Times*, 28 October 2016, p. 7.
74 *Augusta-Margaret River Times*, 16 May 2014, p. 10.
75 Hays, interview.

76 Hodsdon, interview.
77 Edwards, interview.
78 Keith McLeod, pers. comm. to the authors, 21 June 2023.
79 Heritage Council, *Old Hospital Complex, place no. 03314*, 2021, <http://inherit.stateheritage.wa.gov.au/Public/Inventory/Details/7110963d-efc4-4909-8d5f-3935b76d7d8a> viewed 29 December 2022.

BIBLIOGRAPHY

INTERVIEWS

By Bill Bunbury
John Alferink 2020
Marion Aveling #
Don Arthur 2023
Robert (Barney) Barnett 2022
Ros Blakeney 2020
Geoffrey Bolton #
John and Hazel Brennan #
Greg Bussell 2022
Margaret Chadwick 2022
Joyce Challis 2022
Shelley Challis 2022
Kevin Coate 2022
Yvonne Coate 2022.
Dr Ray Clarke 2022
Noel Conway 2020
Tim Crimp 2023
Diana Cullen #
Jack Davis #
Stan Dilkes #
Donna Dornan 2020
Judy and Bob Dunbar # and 2020
Betty Earl 2020
Margot Edwards 2020
Elwyn Franklin 2022
Herbert (Smiler) Gale 2020
Jennifer Gherardi 2020

BIBLIOGRAPHY

Pat Gray 2021
Lynda Green 2020
Anna Haebich #
Sally Hays 2020
Linton Hodsdon 2020
Fiona Hofstee 2022
Ralph Hofstee 2022
Lydell Huntly 2020
Kris Keen 2020
Marion Lilly 2022
Barbara Maidment 2020
Theo Mathews 2020
Ellie Metcalfe 2021
Tess (Sally) Minett 2020
Don Miller 2020
Lyn Moorfoot 2020
Kim Murray 2020
Dr Shaun O'Rourke 2022
Robert Saunders 2022
Carolyn Scott 2022
Dave Seegar 2020
Lyn Serventy #
Anne Shepherdson 2020
Lloyd Shepherdson 2022
Dr Eithne Sheridan 2022
Fran Temby 2022
Judy Wake 2022
Iszaac Webb June 2019 and 2023
Lynda Williams 2023

Interviews for ABC Radio National, 1983–1996

By Other Interviewers

Cedar Armstrong (senior), interview with Mae Wise, Margaret River and Districts Historical Society (MR&DHS), 1985.

Cedar Armstrong (Armstrong Family), interview with Delys Forrest, MR&DHS, 2004.

Albert Ashton, MR&DHS (unknown interviewer), 1985.

Ted Ashton, interview with Danielle Haigh, *Augusta–Margaret River Mail*, 29 August 1990.

Robert Breeden, interview with Margaret Tickle, Busselton Oral History Group, SLWA, OH 4170, 2010.

Jean Bussell, interview with Mae Wise, MR&DHS, 1985.

BIBLIOGRAPHY

Thomas Cleave, interview with Jean Teasdale, SLWA, OH 102, 1976.
Bill Darnell, interview with Vendla Tinley, MR& DHS, 1996–97.
Thomas William (Tom) Doyle, interview with Michael Adams, December 1977 – May 1980, SLWA, OH 297.
Rex Dyer, interview with Ann Basili, MR& DHS, 2017.
Mark Exeter, interview with Margaret Tickle, Busselton Oral History Group, SLWA, OH 2856, 2005.
Enid Garstone, interview with Mae Wise, MR&DHS, 1983.
Don McKenzie, interview with Mae Wise, Augusta Margaret River Library, 1985.
Bert Mclean, interview with Mae Wise, Augusta Margaret River Library, n.d.
Ellie Metcalfe, memoir recorded by Lyn Moorfoot, Margaret River Community Centre, 2014.
Jessie Sharp (nee Campbell), unknown interviewer, MR&DHS, 1986.
George Webb, interview with Ramona Johnson, Busselton Oral History Group, SLWA, OH 2522, 1989.
Myra Willmott, interview with Mae Wise, MR&DHS, 1985.

STATE RECORDS

State Library of Western Australia

Robert Breeden, interview with Margaret Tickle, Busselton Oral History Group, OH 4170.
Deborah Buller-Murphy papers, Acc. 1648AD/5C.
Thomas Cleave, interview with Jean Teasdale, OH 102.
Thomas William (Tom) Doyle, interview with Michael Adams, OH 297.
Mark Exeter, interview with Margaret Tickle, Busselton Oral History Group, OH 2856.
George Webb, interview with Ramona Johnson, Busselton Oral History Group, OH 2522.

State Records Office of Western Australia

Forests Department – Land and Tenure – Application for Sussex – Proposed Hospital Reserve at Margaret River Sussex Locns 3636 3618 3621 3623 3631 [FD 19580929]
Karridale Hospital – Application to register hospital for reception of maternity cases
Karridale Hospital – Medical and nursing facilities
Karridale Hospital – Report of inspection
Karridale Hospital – Sir James Lee Steere
Margaret River – hospital, medical and nursing facilities for
Margaret River District Hospital – Planning
Margaret River Hospital – additions
Margaret River Hospital. Alterations & Additions – Commission to Parry & Rosenthal (Bunbury)

Margaret River Hospital. Board of Management – Proposal re appointment of
Margaret River Hospital. Buildings
Margaret River Hospital – buildings and grounds
Margaret River Hospital – Hospital and Medical Fund
Margaret River Hospital. Visiting and Advisory Committee
Margaret River Progress Association. Reserve for Hospital Site Reserve 41625 Margaret River Lot 2020 Community Centre
Medical – Margaret River Hospital – Water Supply and Drainage

PRIMARY SOURCES HELD ELSEWHERE
Margaret River Community Centre (MRCC)
Margaret River and Districts Historical Society (MR&DHS)
Augusta Margaret River Library
Margaret River Hospital

BOOKS, ARTICLES & UNPUBLISHED MANUSCRIPTS
'100 years of Margaret River: timeline', *Augusta-Margaret River Mail*, <www.margaretrivermail.com.au/story/1286597/100-years-of-margaret-river-timeline/> viewed 26 October 2023.

Aldrian-Moyle, S.-L., *Surfing Down South: Discovering Yallingup & Margaret River*, Margaret River Press, Witchcliffe, 2014.

Allbrook, M., *Henry Prinsep's Empire: Framing a Distant Colony*, ANU Press, Canberra, 2014.

Bartlett, J., *Journey: A History of the Anglican Diocese of Bunbury 1904–2004*, Anglican Diocese of Bunbury, Bunbury, 2004.

Bayley Jones, C., *Augusta Tourism: A Study of the Growth of Tourism, Its Present State and Likely Trends*, Murdoch University, 1976.

Bignell, M., *Little Grey Sparrows of the Anglican Diocese of Bunbury, Western Australia*, University of Western Australia Press, Perth, 1992.

Biddulph, B., *Riding the Bumps: Football and Life in Augusta Margaret River 1904–1965*, B. & J. Biddulph, 2013.

Blond, P.E.M., *A Tribute to the Group Settlers*, University of Western Australia Press, Perth, 1987.

Bolton, G., *Spoils and Spoilers: A History of Australians Shaping their Environment, 1788–1980*, George Allen & Unwin, Sydney, 1981.

Bradshaw, J., *Jinkers and Whims: A Pictorial History of Timber-Getting*, Vivid Publishing, Fremantle, 2012.

Brady, B., *Wines, Winemakers and Vignerons of the South-West and Great Southern*, Apollo Press, Perth, 1982.

Brennan, J. *The Australian Brennans of Rosa Brook*, n.d. and unpublished, copy held by Augusta Margaret River Library.

BIBLIOGRAPHY

Buller-Murphy, D., *An attempt to eat the moon: and other stories recounted from the Aborigines*, Georgian House, Melbourne, 1958.

Bunbury, B., *Reading Labels on Jam Tins*, Fremantle Arts Centre Press, Fremantle, 1991.

Bunbury, B and J, *Many Maps: Charting Two Cultures: Australians and Europeans in Western Australia*, UWA Publishing, Perth, 2020.

Burton, L.C., *Barefoot in the Creek: A Group Settlement Childhood in Margaret River*, University of Western Australia Press, Perth, 1997.

Caccetta, W., 'The original and the best: 30 years of Leeuwin concerts, *PerthNow*, 17 February 2014, <www.perthnow.com.au/news/australia/the-original-and-the-best-30-years-of-leeuwin-estate-concerts-ng-5bab0d2e6ddf38ece3a3b59ea7eb017b> viewed 6 October 2023.

Cain, K. (ed.), *Rich beyond Measure: A Collection of Family Memories of Edward and Phyllis Blain (nee Hosking) as Remembered by their Children*, unpublished, n.d.

Cain, V., *Group 85 Osmington Church*, printed by Dynamic Print, Bunbury, n.d.

Chetkovich, J. & Gare, D., *A Chain of Care: A History of the Silver Chain Nursing Association, 1905–2005*, University of Notre Dame Australia Press, Fremantle, for the Silver Chain Nursing Association, 2005.

Coate, K., *Growing up in Margaret River*, unpublished memoir, 2021, copy at Margaret River and Districts Historical Society.

Coate, K., *Forestry through the Fifties: A Young Forestry Officer's Journey with the Western Australian Forests Department*, Hesperian Press, Perth, 2021.

Commonwealth Bureau of Census and Statistics, *Census of the Commonwealth of Australia, 30 June 1954, Vol. V, Western Australia*, Canberra, 1954, <www.ausstats.abs.gov.au/ausstats/free.nsf/0/CF2B5277672E74BACA257872001F139E/$File/1954%20Census%20-%20Volume%20V%20-%20Part%20I%20WESTERN%20AUSTRALIA%20Analysis%20of%20Population%20in%20LGA.pdf> viewed 6 October 2023.

Commonwealth Parliamentary Association, *History of the Commonwealth Parliamentary Conference (CPC)*, <https://www.cpahq.org/media/hownq4eb/cpa-history-cpc-annual-conference-updated-april-2019.pdf> viewed 5 October 2023.

Cook, P. *Tobacco Growing in the South-West of Western Australia with particular reference to the Karridale-Warner Glen area*, 1986, SLWA Q338.17371 COO.

Cresswell, G., *The Light of Leeuwin*, Augusta-Margaret River History Group, Margaret River, 1990.

Doyle, T., *Doyles on Group 12*, Margaret River and Districts Historical Society, Margaret River, 1969 (retyped and rebound 2017). Also available Battye Library Acc. 8380A.

Doyle, T., *An Interview with Thomas William Doyle*, conducted by Michael Adams, December 1977 to May 1980, State Library of Western Australia, J.S. Battye Oral History Program, OH 297.

Dyer, R.W., *Cats only have Nine Lives: The Autobiography of Rex Warner Dyer*, unpublished, June 2011. Copy available at MR&DHS.

Edwards, G., *The Road to Prevelly*, E.G. Edwards, Armadale, 1989.

BIBLIOGRAPHY

Everett, V., *Light in the Distance*, Valerie Everett, Mt Hawthorn, WA, 2006.

Fall, V.G., *Giants in the South: A History of Western Australia: Land of the Leeuwin*, SLWA, print material: 994.12 SOU, 1974.

'Fifty years of post-war migration', *Making Multicultural Australia*, Fact Sheet 30, Department of Immigration and Ethnic Affairs, Canberra, 1995, www.multiculturalaustralia.edu.au/doc/immdept_3.pdf, viewed 25 October 2023

Forrestal, P and Jordan R., *The Way It Was: A History of the Early Days of the Margaret River Wine Industry*, Margaret River Press, Witchcliffe, 2017.

Gabbedy, J.P., *Group Settlement Part 1: Its Origins, Politics and Administration*, University of Western Australia Press, Perth, 1988.

Gabbedy, J.P., *Group Settlement Part 2: Its People, their Life and Times: An Inside View*, University of Western Australia Press, Perth, 1988.

Green, A., C. Given and Stephen Carrick Architects, *Shire of Augusta-Margaret River Heritage Inventory*, prepared for the Shire of Augusta-Margaret River, 2012, <https://mrdhs.com.au/documents/AMR_Heritage_Inventory.pdf>.

Hunt, I.L., *A History of Group Settlement in the South-West of W.A.*, MA thesis, 1957, Battye Library, Q.333.7.

Haigh, Danielle, 'Ted recalls the old days at the hospital', *Augusta-Margaret River Mail*, 29 August 1990.

Haigh, Danielle, 'A new heart beats in the old hospital', *Augusta-Margaret River Mail*, 22 December 1993.

Hamling, B.F. Maurice Coleman Davies, *Early Days, Journal of the Royal WA Historical Society*, vol. 6, 1969, pp. 38–56.

Heppingstone, I.D., 'The story of Alfred and Ellen Bussell: pioneers of the Margaret River', *Early Days, Journal of the Royal WA Historical Society*, vol. 6, part 3, 1964, pp. 33–45.

Howie-Willis, *St John, Ambulances and Western Australia: A Centenary Anthology, 1892–1992*, St John Ambulance Australia, Perth, 1992.

Hutton, M., *A History of the Catholic Community of the Margaret River District*, produced for the official blessing and opening of the parish church dedicated to St Thomas More at Margaret River on Monday, 31 January 1983.

Jamieson, R., *Charles Court, I Love this Place*, St George Books, Osborne Park, 2011.

Jennings, G. (ed.), *Margaret River Stories 1913–2013*, Margaret River and Districts Historical Society, 2013.

Juniper, S., *Our Little Life: A Memoir*, Sue Juniper, Margaret River, 2019.

Jupp, T, L. Lord and S. Steele, *Poliomyelitis in Western Australia: A History*, Post Polio Network of WA, Floreat, 2013.

Landgate, *Town names*, Government of Western Australia, 2021, <https://web.archive.org/web/20220314101618/http://wwwo.landgate.wa.gov.au/maps-and-imagery/wa-geographic-names/name-history/historical-town-names#M>, viewed 25 October 2023

Lane, M. *Book listing names of contributions to the building of the Margaret Cecil Rest House*, unpublished, Margaret Cecil Memorial Cabinet, Margaret River Hospital.

Lilleyman, G., *A Garden on the Margaret: The Path to Old Bridge House*, Gillian Lilleyman, Claremont, WA, 2011.

Lilleyman, G. (ed.), *Pioneer Daughter: The Diary of Frances Louisa (Fanny) Brockman (nee Bussell)*, Gillian Lilleyman, Claremont, WA, 2018.

Lilleyman, G., *Purpose Built: The Making of Caves Road*, Gillian Lilleyman, Claremont, WA, 2022.

Margaret River CWA, 1931–56, Margaret River and Districts Historical Society, 1986.

Margaret River Hospital Admissions and Surgery Registers, 1924 onwards, viewed at Margaret River Hospital.

McKeown, Bernice, 'Life and personalities of the early days of the Margaret River Hotel', *Margaret River Hotel Characters*, Margaret River and Districts Historical Society, 1984.

Minter, S., *The Well-connected Gardener: A Biography of Alicia Amherst, Founder of Garden History*, Book Guild, Brighton, UK, 2010.

Moses, A. Dirk, *Genocide and Settler Society: Frontier Violence and Stolen Indigenous Children in Australian History*, Berghahn Books, New York, 2004.

Nature Conservation Margaret River Region and Margaret River Collaborative Management Group, *Wooditjup Bilya Protection Strategy*, 2019, <https://natureconservation.org.au/wp-content/uploads/2020/02/Wooditjup-Bilya-Protection-Strategy-2019-v5-3.pdf>.

O'Connell, Jan, *1966 Margaret River wine region identified*, Australian Food Timeline, <https://australianfoodtimeline.com.au/1966-margaret-river-wine-region-identified/> viewed 6 October 2023.

Payne, J.D., *Over the Bridge: An Authentic Account of Group Settlement*, J.D. Payne, Margaret River, 1987.

Rowe, S. in Howie-Willis, I, *St John, Ambulances and Western Australia: A Centenary Anthology, 1892–1992*, St John Ambulance Australia, Perth, 1992.

Rowse, T., 'Notes on the history of the Aboriginal population of Australia', in A. Dirk Moses, *Genocide and Settler Society: Frontier Violence and Stolen Indigenous Children in Australian History*, Berghahn Books, New York, 2004, pp. 312–325.

Salmaggi, C. and A. Pallavisini, *2194 Days of War: An Illustrated Chronology of the Second World War*, Windward, W.H. Smith and Son, London, 1977.

Scott, N. *Bramley Research Station*, Margaret River and Districts Historical Society, 1986.

Senate Select Committee on Health, *Hospital Funding Cuts: The Perfect Storm. The Demolition of Federal–State Health Relations 2014–2016*. Final Report, Commonwealth of Australia, Canberra, 2016, Chapter 2, <https://www.aph.gov.au/Parliamentary_Business/Committees/Senate/Health/Health/Final%20Report/c02> viewed 6 October 2023.

Shepherdson, Lloyd, *A Mill Kid's Perspective*, unpublished memoir, n.d., copy provided by Lloyd Shepherdson to the authors.

Smith, J.N., *A History of One Teacher Schools in WA, 1930–1962*, Teachers Higher Education Certificate thesis, 1982?

BIBLIOGRAPHY

Shervington, J. *The Early Life and Times of Jane Shervington (nee McKeon)*, John Shervington, n.d.

Southcombe, M.H.R., *To Call Our Own: Pioneering the Group Settlements*, Hesperian Press, Perth, 1988.

Stewart, A., *This Green Corner*, Battye Library, MN 1646, Papers of Athol Fergusson Stewart, SLWA, Acc. 5068A, n.d.

Supski, S., *A Proper Foundation: A History of the Lotteries Commission of Western Australia*, Black Swan Press, Perth, 2009.

Terry, F., *They Came to the Margaret*, South West Publishing and Printing Company, Margaret River, 1978.

'"The last million": Eastern European displaced persons in postwar Germany', *The National WWII Museum of New Orleans*, 4 April 2022, <www.nationalww2 museum.org/war/articles/last-million-eastern-european-displaced-persons -postwar-germany>, viewed 25 October 2023.

Tilbrook, L., *Nyungar Tradition, Glimpses of Aborigines of South-western Australia, 1929–1914*, University of Western Australian Press, Perth, 1983.

Wake, J., History of the Margaret River Hospital 1924-1990, unpublished, n.d. Copy held by the Margaret River and Districts Historical Society.

Wake J., The Building of the New Hospital Facility Margaret River 1988-1990, unpublished, n.d. Copy held by the Margaret River and Districts Historical Society.

Western Australian Museum, *Welcome Walls: Kovalevs, Nikolajs*, Fremantle, panel 283, <https://museum.wa.gov.au/welcomewalls/names/kovalevs-nikolajs> viewed 26 October 2023.

Wickham, Dorothy, *A History of the Margaret River Branch of the Silver Chain Nursing Association from 1972 to 1985*, unpublished notes, n.d.

Wise, M.L., *A Research Source on the Margaret River Town, 1894–1984, Book 1, chapters 1, 2 and 3*, unpublished, 2004. Copy held at Augusta Margaret River Library.

Wise, M.L., *A Research Source on the Margaret River Town, 1894–1984, Book 2: West side of Bussell Highway*, unpublished, 2004. Copy held at Augusta Margaret River Library.

Zekulich, M., *Wines and Wineries of the West*, St George Books, Perth, 1990.

NEWSPAPERS, MAGAZINES & JOURNALS

Augusta-Margaret River Mail
Augusta-Margaret River Times
Beverley Times
Busselton-Margaret Times
Collie Mail
Daily Mail (Brisbane)
Daily News
Destinations Magazine

BIBLIOGRAPHY

Group Settlement Chronicle and Margaret–Augusta Mail
Inquirer and Commercial News
Manjimup and Warren Times
Margaret River News
The Mercury (Hobart)
Norseman Times
Northam Advertiser
Southern Times
South-Western News
South-Western Times
The Messenger (Bunbury Anglican diocese)
The Sunday Times
WA Record
Weekly Times (Melbourne)
The West Australian
The Workers Star

WEBSITES

Arts Margaret River <https://artsmargaretriver.com/>
Australian Dictionary of Biography <https://adb.anu.edu.au/>
Biographical Register of Members of the Parliament of Western Australia <https://www.parliament.wa.gov.au/parliament/library/MPHistoricalData.nsf/Search?openform>
Heritage Council <http://inherit.stateheritage.wa.gov.au/Public/>
Obituaries Australia <https://oa.anu.edu.au>
Shire of Augusta-Margaret River <www.amrshire.wa.gov.au>
Undalup Association <https://www.undalup.com/home>

PHOTOGRAPHIC CREDITS

3   Wadandi Cultural Custodian, Iszaac (Zac) Webb. Courtesy Nature Conservation Margaret River.
5   Ellensbrook, the Bussell family's first home *circa* 1920. Courtesy David Jenkins.
11 Alfred John Bussell known as John or Jack. Courtesy Vernon Bussell.
19 Timber mill at Karridale 1912. Courtesy State Library of Western Australia 229171PD.
19 Herbert Davies (son of M.C Davies) house at Karridale. MR&DHS.
22 Bridge over the Margaret River near Burnside, November 1901. Courtesy State Library of Western Australia 025902PD.
25 Wallcliffe House surrounded by bush 1901. Courtesy State Library of Western Australia 02542PD & RWAHS BA 819.
27 First car to visit the Margaret River caves and Cape Leeuwin 1907. Courtesy State Library of Western Australia 21350PD RWAHS BA110.
34 Edith Bussell at Ellensbrook. Courtesy David Jenkins.
37 Sam Isaacs and son Fred 1917. Margaret River and Districts Historical Society (MR&DHS).
38 Margaret River: the Rivermouth. Courtesy Scott Baxter, Gralyn winery.
42 The Doyle family (young Tom at left of picture) at Bassendean just prior to going on Group 12. Courtesy State Library of Western Australia 3847B/2.
43 A group settlers tin hut. Courtesy State Library of Western Australia 005130D.
44 Gelignite was used to blast timber. MR&DHS.
46 Settlers home near Karridale 1924. Courtesy State Library of Western Australia 005145D.
53 Dr William Rigby – first doctor in Margaret River. Courtesy Coalfields Museum Collie.
58 Sir James Mitchell and settlers, 1925. Courtesy State Library of WA SLWA 005129D.
60 Hospital morgue built 1924, before restoration. MRCC.

PHOTOGRAPHIC CREDITS

60   Original Hospital Admissions Book and record of surgeries performed. Courtesy Margaret River Hospital. Stephen Blakeney.
63   Margaret River District Hospital *circa* 1924. MR&DHS.
66   The hospital in the 1920s. MR&DHS.
67   First matron and nurses quarters – a group-type house, built 1924. MR&DHS.
70   North Jindong group school. Courtesy Ros Craig.
71   Group 6 school at Nuralingup (Forest Grove) with John Tonkin Teacher. Courtesy State Library of Western Australia 000884D.
74   Harold and Tom Doyle cultivating in market garden. Courtesy State Library of Western Australia 3847B16.
76   Colonel Ernest Le Souef at his home in Glen Ellie. Courtesy State Library of Western Australia BA1101/1/10/382.
81   Group settlement houses were often surrounded by ring-barked and dead trees. MR& DHS.
90   Empire Delegation 1926 meeting with Group Settlers. Courtesy State Library of Western Australia 005132D.
93   Margaret Cecil raised funds from the Margarets of England and Scotland for a rest house for pregnant women. Margaret Cecil Rest House Memorial Cabinet, courtesy Margaret River Hospital.
97   Opening of the Margaret Cecil Rest House, May 1929. Courtesy MR&DHS.
100 The hospital still had only basic facilities. Courtesy MR&DHS.
103 Group house at Warner Glen 1930s. Courtesy Ros Craig.
111 Tom Doyle. Commander of the Order of St John (for services to St John Ambulance). MR&DHS
113 St John's Ambulance in Margaret River 1937. MR& DHS.
115 Butter factory, Opening Day, 1930. Courtesy Kevin Coate.
120 The Anglican nuns: Sister Marion second from left back & Ellie Metcalfe (Carpenter) girl at front. Courtesy Ellie Metcalfe.
122 Osmington Church: one of the 'hundred pound' churches' paid for by English benefactors. Stephen Blakeney.
124 Margaret River Hotel opened in 1936. MR&DHS.
126 Sleepers were sent by rail to Busselton and Bunbury ports. MR&DHS.
136 Nurses 1936. Sister Cross at front with magpie. Courtesy Judy Wake (provided by Sister Cross for 60th anniversary 1984).
137 Nurses with Dr Salvi one of A several of 'locum' doctors in the 1930s. Courtesy Judy Wake (provided by Sister Cross for 60th anniversary 1984).
138 Cowaramup main street. MR&DHS.
140 Margaret Cecil Rest House 1936 before conversion to Maternity Ward. Courtesy Judy Wake (provided by Sister Cross).
147 Wheatbelt farmers were shocked at the state of the farms. Courtesy Thelma Burnett.
152 Sister Agnes Livingstone marries Alec Dunbar, Sept 1934. Courtesy Bob and Judy Dunbar.

PHOTOGRAPHIC CREDITS

153 The hospital before renovations MR&DHS.
156 Some farmers took over abandoned group settlement blocks. Courtesy Thelma Burnett.
159 Bulldozers at work. Courtesy Ros Craig.
161 Some war service farmers were given old group houses. MR&DHS.
163 The Butter factory's tank provided water for the hospital. Courtesy Kevin Coate.
163 Acting Matron Wright with Nurse Belcher 1947. Courtesy Judy Oxenbould.
165 Hospital front 1950s. MR&DHS.
167 Covered way between the main hospital and the maternity wing in the Margaret Cecil Rest House built 1946–1947. Stephen Blakeney.
180 European refugees living in Margaret River in the 1950s. Courtesy Kevin Coate.
183 Dr Paddy Barrett, Margaret River's doctor in the 1950s. Courtesy Ellie Metcalfe.
185 Jarrah remained the most important timber. Courtesy Thelma Burnett.
188 Hospital coronation float – Medical Queen. Courtesy Ellie Metcalfe.
190 Margaret River post office, 1956. Courtesy State Library of Western Australia BA1289/99.
190 Opening of the Augusta-Margaret River District Library 1959. Courtesy State Library of Western Australia 231763PD.
200 Margaret Lane in later life, Margaret Cecil Rest House Memorial Cabinet. Courtesy Margaret River Hospital.
202 Matron Catherine Flynn – longest serving matron at Margaret River Hospital. MR&DHS.
202 Margaret River Hospital nurses with Matron Flynn (back centre) 1950s. Courtesy Judy Wake Photo originally provided by Pat Acheson.
203 Margaret River main street 1950s. Stephen Blakeney.
209 Carolyn Scott with incubator. Stephen Blakeney.
212 The Brick Laundry built in 1960s and trellis drying shed. Stephen Blakeney.
213 Judy Wake at work. Stephen Blakeney.
214 Matron Gay Peirce. MR&DHS.
220 Dr Eithne Sheridan. Courtesy Patricia Lagan.
233 Old Domestic Quarters and Doctors Surgery, 1970s to 1990s. Stephen Blakeney.
235 Verandah enclosed as Day Room. Courtesy Judy Wake.
236 Dr Shaun O'Rourke at hospital barbeque. Courtesy Judy Wake.
236 Permanent care: Mrs Busetti with nurse Jenny Slapp. Stephen Blakeney.
239 Margaret Cecil Rest House memorial plaque. Courtesy Judy Wake.
259 'The staff all look so young'. Stephen Blakeney.
260 Matron Mary Arthur outside the old hospital. Courtesy Don Arthur.
260 Fran Temby, Mary Arthur and Margaret Chadwick all worked at the old hospital. Courtesy Judy Wake.
261 The domestic staff kept the hospital clean and nice. Courtesy Judy Wake.

PHOTOGRAPHIC CREDITS

263 Dr Clarke with midwives. Courtesy Dr Ray Clarke.
268 Old Hospital front before closure in 1990. Courtesy Judy Wake.
270 Even the hallway was used to capacity. Courtesy Judy Wake.
283 Kim Murray's headline in first edition of *Augusta-Margaret River Mail*. Augusta-Margart River Mail February 19th 1986.
288 Hospital Front entry. Courtesy Judy Wake.
288 Hospital Kitchen in the 1980s. Courtesy Judy Wake.
293 New hospital under construction. Courtesy Judy Wake.
293 Moving Day at the old hospital. Courtesy Judy Wake.
295 Fiona and Ralph Hofstee with Morgan, the last baby born in the old hospital. Midwife: Milly Preedy. Courtesy Fiona Hofstee.
296 Betty Dyer gives a final mop to casualty. Courtesy Judy Wake.
297 The old hospital is now closed. Courtesy Judy Wake.
297 The new hospital is now open. Courtesy Judy Wake.
298 Official opening of the new hospital: March 1990. Courtesy Judy Wake.
301 The first Margaret River Community Centre in Station Road. Margaret River Community Centre. MRCC.
303 The first fun run in support of the Community Centre. MRCC.
305 Ros Blakeney and Joyce Bennett at the new Community Centre (the old hospital). MRCC.
310 Agnes Thomas, the former Matron Dunbar, says the Margaret Cecil Rest House is not for sale. Augusta-Margaret River Mail 17 May 1989.
314 Joyce Bennett, centre, pictured with Alison Brown (South West Development Authority), left and Tess (Sally) Minett, right, signs the agreement to lease the old hospital for the Margaret River Community Resource Centre. Augusta Margaret River Mail/MRCC.
316 Back of the Doctors Surgery before it was moved. Stephen Blakeney.
317 Operating theatre in the old hospital. Courtesy Judy Wake.
318 Margaret Cecil Rest House – as TAFE. MRCC.
320 Donna Dornan was successful in getting grants from the Lotteries Commission. MRCC.
324 The Community Centre for Children. Stephen Blakeney.
324 Children's theatre included the Kids' Circus. MRCC.
326 Opening of art exhibition in Isaacs Cottage. MRCC.
326 The Brick Laundry became an art studio. MRCC.
328 The Old Uniting Church arrives at the Margaret River Community Centre, 2002. MRCC.
328 The Doctors surgery – was moved and is now the Soup kitchen. MRCC.
330 Dave Seegar started the Soup Kitchen in 1995. Stephen Blakeney.
332 The Old Hospital – now the Community Centre today. Stephen Blakeney.

INDEX

Images are in italics.

Aboriginal
  stockmen 6–7, 18
  see Wadandi
Aborigines Act 1905 (WA) 32–35
accidents 21, 75–81, 85–7, 113, 129–31, 133, 139, 182, 241–2, 247, 249
Adelaide Timber Company 184
Alferink, John xiii, 198, 225, 318
Agricultural Bank (of Western Australia) 104, 109, 145
agricultural shows 113–14
Agriculture Department 73, 160, 250–1
Airdale 184
Airey, Captain, J.J. 112
Alexandra Bridge xv, 82, 109–10
ambulance xii, 110–13, *111*, 113, 130, 137, 188, 206–8, 223, 240–1, 262, 296
Anglican
  church 21, 116–18, 121, 133, 198
  convent 116, 117–20, 198–9
Angwin, W.C. 60–1, 71, 91–3
Apex Club 229
Armstrong (Sr), Alfred Thomas (Cedar) 115, 155
Armstrong (Jr), George (Cedar) 115–16, 155, 193–4, 244
Arthur, Don 192, 260
Arthur, Mary (nee Coulter) 192, 230, 258–9, *260*, 284, 292
Arts Margaret River *see* Augusta-Margaret River Arts Council
Assets Management Taskforce 311

Atkinson, Dr Everitt 48, 50, 55, 94
Ashton, A.E. 108–9
Ashton, Ted (son of A.E. Ashton) 66–7
Atkins family 79
Augusta (Talanup) 2, 26, 77, 84–6, 114, 142, 182, 191, 216, 223, 230, 242, 300
  doctor/hospital 87, 218, 221, 229, 272–8, 282–3,
  Ratepayers Association 273–4
  Busselton–Augusta road 23, 30, 273
  see also Group Settlement Scheme; timber industry
Augusta-Margaret River Arts Council 229, 242–3
Augusta-Margaret River Mail xi, xiii, *283*, 289–91, 303, 305, 307–11, *310*, 313, *314*, 315, 320–1, 329
Augusta-Margaret River Road Board 37, 39, 44, 52, 88, 95, 140, 158, 174, 185–6, 237
  see also Shire of Augusta-Margaret River
Augusta-Margaret River Tourist Bureau Association 192

Baltic migrants 179–80, *180*
Barber, L.A. 305
Barnard, G.W. 92–4
Barnett, Robert (Barney) 242, 248, 253
Barrett, Dr Paddy 125, 170–3, 177, 182–4, *183*, 206, 214
Beck, Mary 265
Bennett, Joyce 304, *305*, 307, 313, *314*
Blain, Bill 45, 69
Blain, Edward 69
Blaikie, Barry, MLA 217, 268–9, 273, 277–8, 280, 284–6, 309

INDEX

Blakeney, Ros vii, xii, 301–4, *305*, 308–9, 312–17, 322
Blakeney, Stephen vii, xi, *60, 93*, 122, *167, 203, 209, 212–13, 233, 236*, 258, *259*, 316, *324, 330, 332*
Blond, Philip 46, 72
blood donation 139
Bolton, Geoffrey 9–10, 40
Boulter, Mabel 237, 239
Bovell, W.S. (Sir Stewart) 186, 189, 215, 237, 239, 243
BPW (Business and Professional Women's Club) 229, 302
Bramley 49, 70, 146, 184, 223
Bramley Research Station 194–5
Brand, David, MLA 187
Breeden, Robert 10
Brennan, Hazel 247
Brennan, John 144–5
Bridge House 23
Brockman, E.V., MLA 112, 123, 127
Brockman, Fanny 7, 17, 22–5, 28
Buckenara, Judy 265
Building Management Authority 307
Buller-Murphy, Deborah 38, 379
Bunbury (Goomburrup) 2, 24, 110, 116–18, 125–6, 161, 178, 182, 184, 194, 196, 232
  diocese 116, 198–9
  doctor/hospital 14, 80, 119, 130, 177
Burke, Brian 254–5, 275, 279–86
Burnett, Thelma (nee Yates) xii, *147, 156*, 253
Burton, Leonard 102–4, 113
Bush Brotherhood of St Boniface 116, 133
  see also Anglican
Bush Nursing Trust 89
bush, getting lost in 82
Bussell, Alfred John (Jack) 7–8, 10–14, *11*, 16, 24–6, 38
Bussell, Alfred Pickmore 3–10, 17–18, 24, 26, 37–8
Bussell, Edith 33–4, *34*, 36
Bussell, Ellen 4–8, 16, 37–8
Bussell, Desmond 73–4, 99
Bussell family xiii, *5*, 16, 18, 21, 28, 33, 38, 73, 250
  Athole Stewart 37–8
  Deborah Buller-Murphy 38
  Filomena Terry 38
Bussell, Fanny *see* Brockman, Fanny
Bussell, Frederick Aloysius Weld 26, 29, 73–4, 99

Bussell, Grace 18, 38
Bussell, Gregory 6, 16, 99–100, 183–4, 226, 253–4
Bussell Highway 52, 123, 129, 160, 188, 195, 245, 251, 264
Bussell, Jasper 7
Bussell, Jean (nee McDonald) 73–4, 99–101, 229, 237, 239
Bussell, John Garrett 3–4, 7, 33
  Charlotte (wife) 4, 26
  Josephine (daughter) (later Prinsep) 33
  William (father) 4
Bussell Kittie 74, 87, 92, 134
Bussell, Marion (nee Reynolds) 24–5
Busselton 3, 7, 18, 24, 26, 28, 39, 41, 50, 72, 75, 92, 108, 125, 154, 188, 251, 279, 292, 294, 300
  doctor/hospital 20–1, 25, 39, 51, 54–5, 87, 89, 99–100, 119, 171, 175–6, 210, 216, 229, 250, 263–4, 282, 285, 287
  rail line 28, 45, 72, 83, 91, 139, 184, 196–8
  see also Cattle Chosen; Ellensbrook; Group Settlement Scheme; Vasse-Karridale Road
Busselton and Districts Oral History Group xiii
Busselton-Margaret Times 215–16, 270, 273, 276, 278–9, 281–2, 284, 310
butter factory *xvi*, 114–15, *115*, 124, 145, 147, 161–2, *163*, 187

Callaghan, Tam xi
Calwell, Arthur 179
Campion, Lady 94–5
Cape Leeuwin xv, 26, *27*, 112, 252
Cape Mentelle 252, 254, 302
Cape Naturaliste xv, 27, 252
Cardell-Oliver, Mrs Florence 171
Carpenter, Normellie *see* Metcalfe, Ellie
Captain Freycinet Motel 245
cars 72, 87, 109, 116, 128–30, 157, 176, 182–4, 201, 209, 244
Castle, F.V. 158
caves 24–30, 112, 126, 241, 243, 253
Caves Road 22, 155, 209
Cecil, Alicia, Lady 90–2, 238, 325
Cecil, Lord Evelyn 89–90, *90*
Cecil, Margaret *see* Lane, Margaret
cemetery 152
Chadwick, John 226–7
Chadwick, Margaret 227, 248–9, 256–7, *260*

INDEX

Challis, Joyce 182–3, 191–2
Challis, Shelley 257
Chapman, Arthur 47, 76–7
cheese factory *see* butter factory
Clarke, Dr Ray 235, 263–5, *263*, 281, 284
Cleave, Thomas (Tom) 42–4
Coate, Yvonne (nee Smith) 196
Coate, Kevin 115, 155, 157, 160, *163*, 169, 177, 179, *180*, 182, 193–4, 197
Colebatch, Sir Hal 40
Collins, Fred 108
Collier, Philip, MLA 62, 75, 134
Confraternity of Divine Love 121
Conneeley, Di 245–6
Conneeley, Robert 245–6
Colonial Secretary 20, 29, 48–51, 68, 84
Conway, Noel 318–19
Coronation celebrations, Margaret River (1953) 188
Country Kitchen (café) 246
Countryman 251
Country Women's Association (CWA) 21, 128, 133–4, 137, 175, 181, 271
Court, Sir Charles 225–6, 275
Cowaramup xv, 46, 114, 121, 133, 135, 138, *138*, 144, 146, 156, 175–6, 184, 188, 194–5, 222–3, 229, 242–3, 250–1, 255, 300
Cowaramup Bay *see* Gracetown
Crete 150, 154, 192, 247
Crimp, John 221–2, 241, 257
Crimp, Tim 221, 228
Crofts, Harold 39, 45, 88
Cullen, Diana 251
Cullen, Dr Kevin 216, 250–1, 264
Cullity, Dr Tom 250–2

dairying 40, 73–4, 102, 114, 145, 155, 159–60, 179, 182, 195–6, 221–6, 228, 246, 249, 251, 255–6
  Bussells 8, 17
  market 23, 221
  milk quotas 225–6, 252
  see also butter factory; Group Settlement Scheme
dances 21, 69–70, 112, 114, 168–70, 182, 199, 223–4
Darnell, Bill 154, 189, 194, 224, 226, 229
Darnell's stores 114, 181–2
Davies, Maurice Coleman 17–23, 86
Davies, Ron, MLA 232
Davis, Jack 35

Denmark (WA) viii, 44, 75, 89, 105, 221
dentistry 14, 177–8, 247
  performed by GPs 53, 85, 138
Department of Hospital and Allied Services *see* Health Department
Department of Works and Trading Concerns *see* Public Works Department
Destinations magazine 255
Dilkes, Stan 46, 73, 143–4, 250–1
diphtheria 133–6, 139, 171, 256
diseases 47, 75, 133–5, 171, 173–4, 256
  infectious 133–5, 171, 256
doctors surgery 52–3, 62, 85, 125, 160, 177, 214, 233–4, *233*, 264, 313–16, *316*, 327–9, *328*, 333
Dornan, Donna 318–25, *320*, 329
Dowding, Peter 313–14
Doyle, Helen 106–7, 133
Doyle, Thomas (Tom) 36, 41–2, *42*, 47, 52, 54–5, 74–7, *74*, 101, 111, 124, 150, 154–5
drugs *see* medicine
Dunbar, Agnes *see* Thomas, Agnes
Dunbar, Alec 88, 151, *152*
Dunbar, Robert (Bob) 151–2, 254
Dunbar, Judy (nee Leiper) 150–1, 194, 222, 254
Dyer, Betty 240, *296*
Dyer, Rex 219, 240–1, 248

Earl, Betty (nee Clews) 144–5
Earl, R.H. 158
Education Department 36, 69–70
Edwards, Geoffrey 192, 244, 247
Edwards, Margot 316, 323–5, 331–2
electricity
  at hospital 66–8, 77–8, 101, 126–8, 131–2, 146, 187, 196
  in Margaret River and District 123, 126, 146, 196
Ellensbrook 5–6, 16, *34*
Elmers, Mr 108
Empire parliamentary delegation 89–92, *90*
environmental causes 249

Fairbrass, Amber xi
farming 8, 17–18, 26, 29, 34, 76–7, 144–5, 154–6, 193, 195–6, 198, 224–7, 244, 249
  Aboriginal practices 9
  community 99–100, 104, 143, 188, 223, 228–31, 241–5, 251–8, 265, 302
  potato 8–9, 35–6, 77, 159, 245
  sheep 4, 155

INDEX

tobacco 160
see also dairying; Group Settlement Scheme; war service blocks
Feilman, Margaret 185–6
Ferry, Vic, MLC 280
fire brigade 188–9
fires 21, 88, 107–8, 132, 331
    Aboriginal practices 2
    risk of 43, 132, 187, 196–7, 262, 284, 290
Flynn, Catherine 139, 167–70, 201, *202*, 205–7, 209–13
Foley-Whaling, Rev. J.W. 84
Forests Department 108, 182, 185–6, 300, 312
forestry *see* timber industry
Forest Grove (Nuralingup) 49, 70, *71*, 78–9, 145, 193, 245
Franklin, Elwyn (nee Streatfield) 81, 178, 184, 223, 243

Gale, Herbert (Smiler) 86, 131, 145–6, 169, 197, 227–8
Gale, Pat 227
Garstone, Betty 262
Garstone, Enid 54, 77–8, 80–2, 87–8, 128–9
Garstone, Tom 77
Gherardi, Jennifer 300–1, 314
Gillespie, Jimmy 35
Gillespie, Vilma 35
Gladstones, John 250
Gloucester Park (Margaret River Sportsground) xvi, 37, 114, 188
Glover, Father 308
Gnarabup 192, 243–4
Gracetown *xv*, 243–4, 331
Gray, Pat 224, 230
Great Depression 96, 99, 101–4, 108–10, 115–16, 127
Green, Lynda 323
Greirson, Gary 245
Grill, Julian, MLA 305
Group Settlement Chronicle 72–3
Group Settlement Scheme vii–viii, 1, 31, 39–63, *43*, 68, 72–6, 79, *81*, 82–6, 89–92, *90*, 101–5, *103*, 109–10, 113, 115–16, 121, 127, 133, 143–6, 158, 184, 198–9, 230
    abandoned blocks 101, 102, 109, 144–5, *147*, 155, *156*, 195
    buildings 144, *161*, 233, 264, 315, 333
    foreman, role of 44–5, 76–7
    hardships 43, 90, 101
    lack of farming experience 43–5, 101–2

medical fund 48–51, 58–9, 68–9
sustenance pay 45, 49, 55, 68
use of gelignite 44, 78–80

Haebich, Anna 32
Haigh, Danielle xi
Hall, Charles 153, 161
Hales, Bill 270, 276–7
Halsall, Viv xii
Hancy, Don 322
Harris, Joan 192
Hassell, Bill, MLA 279–80
Hawke, Albert, Minister for Works and Water Resources, WA 161
Hays, Sally xi, 321–2, 325–7, 331
Health Department 231, 267–72, 281, 285–6, 291–2
    Department of Hospital and Allied Services 275–80
    Medical Department 205–10, 216, 234, 239
    Public Health Department 50–1, 55–62, 65, 68, 84–5, 89, 94, 101, 105–10, 127, 132, 134–6, 141, 149, 151, 158, 164, 169–75, 186, 216
Heppingstone, Ellen *see* Bussell, Ellen
Heppingstone, Ian 4–5
Herring Bay 243
Heussenstamm, Frances 308
Hicks, Stuart xiii
Higgins family 23, 30
Hillier, Alan 237, 243, 248, 274, 281
Hodge, Barry, MLA 275–82
Hodge, Mabel *see* Mother Elizabeth
Hodsdon, Linton 307, 319–20, 331
Hofstee, Fiona 294, *295*
Hofstee, Morgan 294, *295*
Hofstee, Ralph 258, *295*
Hohnen, Mark 281, 289–90, 301
Horgan, Denis 254–5, 281, 308
Hospital Amenities Committee *see* Hospital Visiting and Advisory Committee
Hospital Benefits Act 1945 157–8
Hospital Visiting and Advisory Committee 84, 149, 168–72, 205–9, 215, 231, 269, 272–6, 279–82, 285–6, 289
hotel 74, 122–6, *124*, 145, 157, 191–2, 218, 242, 255
Hoult family 78–9
House, Barry, MLC 290, 292
Huelin, F.J. 58, 60, 62, 68, 86–8, 91–2, 94–6, 101, 106–7, 110, 127, 141–2

INDEX

Hugall, M.L. (Les) 49–51, 59, 69
Hugall, Mrs Les 133
Huntly, Lydell xi, 299
Hulbert, Ern 290

Infant Health Association of Western Australia 175
Infant Health Centre, Margaret River 175–7
Isaacs family 39, *326*
Isaacs, Fred 36–7, *37*, 67, 325
Isaacs, Sam 18, 36–7, *37*

Jackson, Emily xii
Jakovich, Lyn 294
Jarrahdene mill 18, 21
Jemmy 7
Jolie, Mrs Tawse 90
Juniper, Geoff 243
Juniper, Sue 243, 246

Karridale 18–23, *19*, 28, 39, *46*, 53–5, 83, 86, 113–14, 142, 155, 160, 195, 223
  hospital 20–1, 83–7, 109–10, 112–13
Kasparis, Bolis 180–1, 357n
Keen, Kris 299–300
Keenan, Stewart 23
Kelly's Farewell 5
Kenny, Sister Rosina 110, 113
Kerr, J.C. 278
Kilcarnup 126, 243
Kniveton, (Cr) 215
Kovalevs, Nick 181
Kudardup *xv*, 54, 110, 130, 146, 159, 195, 197, 209, 230

Labor Party 71, 134, 275–6, 279, 282–3, 287
  see also Burke, Brian; Tonkin, John
Laffer, Nurse 109
Lagan, Dr John xii, 217–19, 229, 233–4, 252, 258, 277, 315
Lane, Margaret 91–4, *93*, 141–2, 150, 199, *200*, 237–8, 325
Lawrence, Carmen 311–12
Le Souef, Colonel Ernest 76, 111
Leiper, Judy *see* Dunbar, Judy
Leiper, Robert 244
Leeuwin Estate 252, 254–5, 281, 302
Liberal Party 275, 277–80, 287, 289–90, 292
library xiii, *190*, 191
Lilly, Marion 177
Lloyd George, David 40

Loaring, A.C.R. 22, 28–9
Long, Jimmy 7
Lotteries Commission 112, 127–8, 141, 143, 146, 168–9, 171, 177, 318–19
Lotterywest *see* Lotteries Commission
Lower Margaret 22–4, 28

Maidment, Barbara 317–18, 327
Mandelstam, Dr M. 112, 128–30, 132–3, 136–7
Manjimup 41, 114, 257
Manjimup and Warren Times 114
Mann, A.E. 107, 117
Mann, Hassa 244–5
Mann, W.J., MLC 93–5, 101–2, 142–3
Margaret Cecil Rest House viii, 59, 88–9, 92–5, *97*, 128, *140*, 150, 154, 186–7, 201, 237–8, *239*, 310, 312–13, 327, 333
  Child Care Centre 322–3
  maternity wing 140–3, 152, 166, *167*, 206
  permanent care wing 201, 231–2, 235–7, 259, 269, 297
  TAFE centre *318*
  Trellis Theatre 323–5, *324*
  see also Margaret River Homes for Senior Citizens
Margaret Cecil Rest House Association 92, 142–3, 149, 150–4, 199, 232
  21st birthday ball 199–200
  winding up 237–9, 309
Margaret River Community Centre vii, ix–xii, 1, 59, 127, 290, 299–332, *305, 314, 324, 326, 328, 332*
  at Station Road 300–5, *301*, 312–14
Margaret River Cultural Centre 242–3
Margaret River Farmers Market 321–2
Margaret River Homes for Senior Citizens 237–40
  see also Mirrambeena
Margaret River and Districts Historical Society xii–xiii, 321
Margaret River and Districts Progress Association *see* Margaret River Progress Association
Margaret River Community Resource Centre *see* Margaret River Community Centre
Margaret River News 149–50
Margaret River Progress Association 28–31, 39, 45, 47–51, 59, 68–9, 104, 133
Margaret River Theatre Group 243

393

INDEX

Margaret River Wine Association 321
Marybrook xv, 35
matrons 61–2, 66, 89, 94, 101, 108, 119, 135, 137, 160–1, 165, 176, 184, 209, 241, 269
    Dawson 100
    Elphick (Karridale) 84–5
    McLeod 146
    Murray (Karridale) 109
    Unbehaun, Lena (1929) 94
    Wright (acting) 158, 162, *163*, 165–7
    see also Arthur, Mary; Doyle, Helen; Flynn, Catherine; Peirce, Agatha (Gay); Rae, Haidee; Dunbar (later Thomas), Agnes; McWhinney, May; Wake, Judy; Ward, Margaret; Wilson, May
Mathews, Theo 308
May, C.E. 26–7
McCallum, Alexander 72–3
McDonald, Jean *see* Bussell, Jean
McKenzie, Alison xi
McKenzie, Don 125
McKeown, Bernard 122–4, 255
McKeown, Bernice *see* McLeod, Bernice
McKeown, Kim 124–6
McLean, Bert 114
McLeod, Bernice (nee McKeown) 123, 125–6, 381
McLeod, Dudley 18, 74, 123, 192, 246–7
McLeod, Duncan 150
McLeod, Keith xii, 18, 37, 209, 246, 332
McLeod, Leonie 246–7
McLeod, Neil 22
McLeod, Pauline xii
McWhinney, May 87–8
Meals on Wheels 231
meat 23–4, 34, 44, 60, 73–4, 76–7, 104, 115–16, 133
Medical Department *see* Health Department
medicine
    Aboriginal 12–16, 31
    Western 14–16, 46–8, 52–3, 72, 113, 128, 130, 136–7, 146, 156–7, 171, 183, 276–7
Meleri family 250
mental health 80–2, 88, 121, 219, 242, 331
Metcalfe, Ellie (nee Normellie Carpenter) 119–20, *120*, 125, 139, 180–1, 183, *188*, 201, 222
Metcalfe, Ron 222
Metricup *xv*, 5, 112, 196
milk quotas 225–6, 252

Millars Karri and Jarrah Company 20, 83–4
Millars Trading Store 21
Miller, Don 194–6, 223, 225, 228, 252–3
Miller, W.A. 158
Milyean 2–3
Minett Tess (formerly Sally) 303–4, 313–14
Mirrambeena 57, 240, 290, 309
Mitchell, Sir James 39–41, 48, 57, *58*, 62, 114
Mokidup, *see* Ellensbrook
Moondyne Arts and Crafts Group 229
Moore, Jim 116
    see also Bush Brotherhood of St Boniface
Moore River (institution) 35–6
Moorfoot, Lyn xi, 325, 329
Mother Elizabeth 116–22
    see also Sisters of the Order of St Elizabeth of Hungary
Munsie, Selby 96, 134
Murphy, Pam xi
Murray, Kim 254–5, 283–4, 305
Murray (Matron Karridale) 109

Nandinong, Granny 7–8
Nelligan, Jack 47
Ngarut 2–3
Ngilgee, Granny 7–8
Nichol, B.E. 207
Nilsson, Jack 53
Northcliffe 41
Notre Dame University 305–10
Nulsen, Emil MLA 164, 177

Oceanic Equity Ltd *see* Hohnen, Mark
O'Hara, Niomi 322, 330
Old Bridge House *see* Bridge House
old hospital 63, 65–68, 72, 74, 77–80, 85–6, 105, 110, 117–20, 235
    atmosphere 213, 257–9, 265
    building works and renovations viii, 59–62, 107, 127–8, 132, 140–3, 164, 166–7, 171–4, 211, 232–4, 267–9
    complaints about 60–2, 106, 135, 164–5, 172, 174, 205–8, 210–11, 215, 269, 272
    drying shed 107, 166–7, *212*, 323
    electricity supply 66–8, 77–8, 101, 126–8, 131–2, 146, 187, 196
    grounds 68, 88, 95–6, 107–8, 132, 185–6
    laundry 201, 211, *212*, 257, 275, 277–8, 323, 325, *326*

INDEX

maternity patients 75, 77–8, 88, 94, 100, 119, 140–3, 149–50, 165, 176, 200, 216–17, 231–2, 294–5
matrons and nurses quarters 65, 67, 100–1, 127, 152–3, 168, 170, 191, 199, 233, 329
morgue 59, *60*
patient numbers 65–6, 75, 87, 150, 157–8, 171, 216, 218, 270–1, 280–1
planning for initial hospital 49–51, 55–8, 62
planning for new hospital 57, 167–8, 185–7, 215–16, 255–6, 266–298
sewerage 146–7, 162, 164, 167–75, 290
staff xiii, 65–6, 99–100, 139, 145, 151, 166, 174, 180–1, 201, 209–14, 221–2, 257–8, 261–3, 265
wards 100–1, 106, 133–5, 140, 171–2, 256
water supply 61, 67–8, 101, 146–7, 160–2, 170, 187, 201
see also ambulance; doctors surgery; fires: risk of; Hospital Visiting and Advisory Committee; Karridale: hospital; Margaret Cecil Rest House; matrons; medicines; surgical procedures
Old Hospital Advisory Committee 307–8
Olmo, Harold 250
operating theatre *see* surgical procedures
orange people *see* Rajneeshees
O'Rourke, Dr Shaun 235, *236*, 263–5, 281–2, 292, 296
Osmington 49, 102, 113, 121–2
mill 184
Palandri family 250
Pannell, Bill 251
Panton, A.H., MLA 143, 149, 203
Parmenter, Ian 322
Payne, Joyce 82–3, 104
Pearce, Ronald 85
Peel Estate 41
Peirce, Agatha (Gay) 139, 208–9, *214*, 220, 234, 239, 241, 273
Peirce, Barbara 209
Perth 9, 24–5, 42, 51, 68, 76, 82, 84, 86, 103, 118, 121, 130, 166, 181, 184–5, 197, 199, 206, 211, 225, 230, 240–1, 243, 247, 250, 252, 257, 259, 262, 265, 275, 300, 313
see also Health Department
Pickering, W.G., MLA 50, 55, 57
picture shows 114, 182
Pilgrim's Mill 75

Pilgrim, J.T. 75
police 6, 44, 95, 107–8, 112, 117, 137, 173–4, 189, 312, 327, 331
poliomyelitis 171, 174
population 39–41, 48, 61, 102, 109, 155, 158, 179–80, 193, 198, 217, 228, 231, 246–8, 256, 263, 270
Port Moresby 154
postal service *xvi*, 21, 30, 146, 181, 189–91, *190*, 248, 264
Preston, Ken 277, 301
Prevelly 192–3, 244
property prices 227–8, 255
Public Health Department *see* Health Department
Public Works Department 56–7, 187, 205–7, 211, 232
  Department of Works and Labour 86, 105–6, 127, 132
  Department of Works and Trading Concerns 68
Pugh, Clifton 304
Putt, Percy 327

Quindalup 16–17
mill 16
quokkas 8, 77

radio 132, 157, 168–70, 240–1
Rae, Haidee 87–8
railway *xv*, 18, 26–8, 31, 45, 57, 61, 72–3, 75, 83, 124–6, 147, 179–81, 196–8, 225, 275, 279
Rajneeshees (orange people) 248–9
Red Cross 89, 181
Redman, Jenny xii
refugees 179–81
Reidy-Crofts, J.D. 238
Reynolds, Marion *see* Bussell, Marion
Rifle Butts 192
Rigby, Dr William 51–62, *53*, 72, 75, 79–80, 85–7, 105–6, 110, 119, 133, 264
Rockingham 41
Roelands Mission 35
Rosa Brook vii, *xv*, 41, 45, 49, 133, 135, 142, 145–6, 154, 156, 177, 189, 194, 224, 247
Rosa Glen *xv*, 133, 142, 156, 221, 228, 241, 244
Rotary Club of Margaret River 208, 229

St John's Ambulance *see* ambulance
Salvi, Dr 130, 137

395

INDEX

Samworth family 88, 133, 151–2
Saunders, Dr John, 138
Saunders, Robert 197
scarlet fever 133–6, 171, 174
schools vii, 20, 28, 34, 36, 49, 69–72, *70, 71,*
144–6, 160, 191–5, 198, 209, 223, 252
alternative 248–50
Scott, Carolyn 194–5, 208, *209*, 219, 240–1,
247, 255–8, 263, 291, 294–6
Seegar, Dave 319, 329, *330*
Serventy, Lyn 249–50
Settlers Tavern 235, 245
sewerage, hospital 146, 162, 167–8, 170–75,
312, 317
Sharp, Jessie (nee Campbell) 145
Shepherdson, Anne xi, 258, 291, 301–2, 304,
311–12, 315
Shepherdson C.D. (Doug) 168, 170
Shepherdson, Dorothy 287, 289
Shepherdson, Lloyd 178–9, 181, 184, 245, 248,
311–12
Shepherdson, Ray 228
Sheridan, Dr Eithne xii, 217–20, *220*, 224–5,
229, 231, 233, 239, 252, 256, 258, 263,
265, 271, 276–8, 296, 315
Shervington, George 154, 181, 186, 229
Shire of Augusta-Margaret River 185–6, 193,
215, 217, 272–4, 277, 280–1, 312–13
Silver Chain Nursing Association 57, 89,
229–31, 302
Sisters of the Order of St Elizabeth of
Hungary 116–21, *120*, 198–9
see also Anglican
Sister Barbara 117
Sister Marion 117, *120*, 121
sleeper cutters 75, 125, 133
Smith, Charles 116
see also Bush Brotherhood of St Boniface
Smith, Eva 237, 239
Smith family (Alexandra Bridge) 83, 104
see also Payne, Joyce
Smith family (Margaret River) 196
Smith, James 104
Smith, Stewart 229
soup kitchen 315, 319, 327–31
see also Seegar, Dave
Southgate, Dr Peter 275–8
South West Development Authority 291, 305,
313–14
South-West Strategy (People's Plan) 311

South-Western News 20, 29–30, 45, 57, 69,
72–3, 80, 86, 94–5, 101, 105, 123, 128,
131, 135, 142, 155, 157, 161–2, 165,
167–9, 186–7, 199
sport 20, 37, 52, 86, 114, 128–9, 154, 169, 179,
212, 219–20, 242, 245, 355n
see also surfing
Stang, Dr Eleanor (Rita) 175–6
State Records Office xiii, 377–8
Stephenson, Dr Clark 214–16
Stephens, Hilary 265
Stewart, George 110–11
Streatfield, Beatrice 82
Streatfield, Cecil 81–2
Streatfield, Eric 82
Stuchbury, Myra *see* Willmott, Myra
Sunday Times, The 250
surfing viii, 244–50, 255, 270–1
surgical procedures 21, 55, 62, 75, 85, 100–1,
106–7, 132–3, 178, 182, 216–19, 256,
265Sussex electoral district 50, 112, 127
see also Vasse electoral district
Sutton, Leanne xi

Tannock, Peter 309
Taylor Thomas, Dr F.S. 105–7, 110–12, 119,
132–3
Taylor-Thomas, Mabel 177
Taylor, Ian, MLA 285–9
Teasdale, George 244
Tebbit, A.R. 285
Temby, Fran (nee Watterson) xii, 159, 178, 195,
206, 208, 223–4, 230–1, 235–6, 259, *260*,
262, 265, 273, 292
Terry, Brian 192
Terry, Filomena (Mena) 38, 105
Terry, Frances 7–8, 10
Terry, Jonathan 253
Terry, Owen 114, 123
Thomas, Agnes (Matron Dunbar) 150–4, *152*,
165, 309, *310*, 313
timber industry 2, 16–24, *19*, 31, 39–41, 61–2,
75–6, 83–6, 111, 116, 125, 133, 145,
178–88, 195, 222, 245–6, 287
Todhunter, Mary 237, 239
Tonkin, John 70–2, 164
tourism viii, 22–9, 122, 125–6, 192–3, 199,
244–5, 253–56, 268–9, 282
Tunbridge, Dr Ewen 136–43, 150, 168, 170,
177, 186–7

INDEX

Unbehaun, Lena 94
United Friendly Societies 111–12
Upper Margaret 23, 28, 30

Vasse *see* Busselton
Vasse electoral district 50
Vasse Felix 251–2
Vasse-Karridale Road 22–3, 27, 30
Volunteer Defence Force 154, 192

Wadandi ix, 1–18, 21, 26, 31–39, 325
    drugs, medicines and magic 12–14
    language xiii, 7
see also Isaacs, Fred; Webb, Iszaac
Wake, Judy xii, 136–7, 140, 202, 212–16, 213, 219–21, 232, 235–6, 239, 240–2, 260, 261–2, 265, 268, 269, 270, 273, 279–81, 285, 288, 291–8, 317
Wallcliffe House 5–6, 17–18, 24–9, 25, 38
war service blocks 156, 158–61, 161
War Service Land Settlement Scheme 158–9
Ward, Margaret 60–1, 65, 68, 315
Warner Glen 103, 142, 160
water supply and water tanks, hospital 37, 61, 67, 146, 160, 162
water supply, town 67, 146–7, 160–1, 187, 196
Watterson, Beryl 159, 237, 239, 273
Watterson, Francine *see* Temby, Fran
Watterson, Frank 159
Webb, George 2, 14–16, 35–6
Webb, Iszaac (Zac) xiii, 1–3, *3*, 6–9, 14, 18, 31, 36
Wenn, Doug, MLC 286–9
Weld Frederick, Aloysius 99
'Welfare' Department 35–6
West Australian, The 10–11, 24, 158–60, 308
West, Charles 229
West, Hilda 232, 237
Wheatbelt 89, 99, 144
Whicher, James 4
Whicher, Margaret 4

Wholley, Jack 85
Wickham, Dorothy (Dot) 229–31
Wilkinson, Arthur 129–30
Williams, Dr John (Augusta) 216, 229
Williams, John 7
Williams, Lynda 192, 230
Willmott, Myra (nee Stuchbury) 54, 65–6, 72–3, 85, 100, 237
Willmott, Edward 94
Willmott, W.H.F 141–2, 168
Wilson, A.W. (Scotty) 209
Wilson, Dr John 214, 216
Wilson, Keith, MLA 290–1
Wilson, May 127, 131, 134
Witchcliffe 27, 45, 69, 72, 114, 130, 133, 135, 146, 154, 156, 168, 176, 181–2
Witchcliffe, East 75–6, 111, 178–9, 181, 184
Wilyabrup 230, 251
wine industry viii, 250–55, 268
Wise, Mae xiii
Wooditj 2–3
Wooditjup Bilya 2–3
Workers Star (newspaper) 115
World War I 40, 46, 81, 115, 156
World War II 138, 144, 147, 150, 154, 156, 165, 179–81, 192, 196
Worrall, Jessica xi
Wright, Sister/Acting Matron 158, 162–3, 165–6
Wyatt, Agda 44, 117, 133–4
Wyatt, Constable 44, 107

Xanadu vineyard 252

Yallingup 29, 244
Yates, Brian 228
Yates, John 253
Yates, Captain Robert 4
Young, Mrs D. 199–200
Young, Ray, MLA 269–75
youth centre 329

www.ingramcontent.com/pod-product-compliance
Lightning Source LLC
Chambersburg PA
CBHW060937230426
43665CB00015B/1976